LAND BEHIND BAGHDAD

Aerial view of ancient Nahrawān canal and radiating branches, looking southeast from Quantara weir

LAND BEHIND BAGHDAD

A HISTORY OF
SETTLEMENT ON THE DIYALA PLAINS

ROBERT McC. ADAMS

CHICAGO AND LONDON
THE UNIVERSITY OF CHICAGO PRESS

Library of Congress Catalog Card Number: 65-17279

THE UNIVERSITY OF CHICAGO PRESS, CHICAGO & LONDON
The University of Toronto Press, Toronto 5, Canada

To the Memory of
JAMES FELIX JONES
ERNST HERZFELD
Who first saw on the Old Khurâsân Road
a Path for Scholarship

PREFACE

Geography without History seemeth a carkasse without motion, so History without Geography wandreth a Vagrant without certaine habitation.

John Smith, *General Historie of Virginia*, 1624

THE STUDY of changing patterns of land-use, both in the present and ancient past, has been given new relevance by ambitious programs of agricultural development in many lands. Particularly in arid and semi-arid regions where irrigation is a prerequisite, significant enlargement of zones already in cultivation usually depends on heavy investments in dams, headworks, drainage canals, and similar facilities. Planners charged with the responsibility for directing these investments understandably have begun to ask about the periodic development and decline of similar, large-scale enterprises in the historic record.

We do not imply, of course, that modern agricultural programs are directly comparable to those of antiquity. Immense technical changes in all aspects of contemporary agriculture have been coupled with the rapid growth of an organized and comprehensive body of scientific insight into its physical and biological processes. Together these factors differentiate, to a degree, present approaches to agricultural development from their antecedents and provide means for the implementation of modern programs without recourse to the lessons of earlier failures and successes. But the rapidity of technological and scientific advance in this field is also its limitation: agricultural-development studies lack a perspective on massive, long-range problems of human interaction with the environment because as yet there has not been sufficient opportunity to study them. Here the social historian and archaeologist may play at least a limited role, seeking to supplement the processual understanding of the agronomist or pedologist with records of change and continuity that extend through far longer spans of time than can be approximated in the laboratory.

The present study is part of such an attempt. The full program of the Diyala Basin Archaeological Project embraced both textual investigations of a wide spectrum of problems concerning ancient Mesopotamian agricultural history and archaeological field investigations of the remains of early settlement and irrigation in a particular area.[1] These findings, based primarily on archaeological field reconnaissance conducted in 1957–58, seek to identify in that area some of the converging natural and human forces which shaped its successive phases of advance and decline over a total period of perhaps six millenniums. While necessarily touching at times on particular historical events, its central focus is not the sharply defined ebb and flow of the historical record, but the underlying, more slowly changing relation of man to land in a relatively small (about 8,000 sq. kms.) and, historically, for a long time somewhat marginal part of the Mesopotamian alluvium.

While dealing in the main with somewhat diffuse processes that can be apprehended only through an even lengthier chain of inferences than is usual in historical research, it is hoped that this study will not be without significance for the historian as well as for the natural scientist. Undoubtedly there are unique and hence relatively unimportant local features about the Diyala plains, or any similar small region, but concentration upon such a region also permits us to glimpse the working-out of widely acknowledged general trends in Mesopotamian, or even Near Eastern, history in terms which deserve to be better understood—as patterns of human adaptation to, and exploitation of, a highly specialized natural setting. In this framework, moreover, it becomes possible to treat the entire time span of settled life without regard to the prevailing subdivision into separate prehistoric, Assyriological, classical, Islamic, and modern fields, each with its own major sources, assumptions, and emphases. Perhaps as a result, long-term developmental continuities which deserve closer scrutiny within the specialized disciplines can be brought into relief.

The problem imposed by such an objective is, of course, that it must draw from a number of widely divergent, highly specialized fields—with the attendant risk of being insufficiently well-grounded in most of them. Particularly in fields more distant from the author's own primary training in anthropology and Near Eastern archaeology, it has been necessary to rely heavily upon secondary works for an understanding of the changing historical context into which the evolving patterns of the region fit. Even greater reliance has been placed on advice freely given by many colleagues, both during the initial intensive fieldwork and in the frequently interrupted years of study since. While the responsibility for its shortcomings is obviously my own, this study could not have been undertaken without their aid.

The author is particularly indebted to Thorkild Jacobsen, who directed the Diyala Basin Archaeological Project on behalf of the Oriental Institute and the Directorate General of Antiquities of the Government of Iraq, in many ways that cannot be adequately spelled out here. The survey was, as has been indicated, a component of a larger study, and much of its stimulus and strategy was drawn from the larger design which Professor Jacobsen was in full charge of

executing. In addition to his direct participation in the earlier phases of the reconnaissance itself, his contribution to the interpretation of the findings continued in the field and at home in the form of many penetrating questions and observations which have been inextricably woven into the fabric of this study.

Professor Jacobsen also is to be credited with the initial discovery of the surface reconnaissance methods applied here, with a realization of their promise which he succeeded in communicating to the author some years before the Diyala Basin Archaeological Project became a reality, and with the successful demonstration of these methods on a smaller scale for the reconstruction of ancient waterways. As described more fully in Appendix A, observations made in the initial reconnaissance in the Diyala area conducted by Professor Jacobsen in 1937 have been included in the data of this report. If the findings of the Diyala Project have any influence on future irrigation planning, perhaps there is a lesson here which applies beyond the limits of archaeology and history: the true value of a piece of research is not to be sought in its immediate practical application—surely none was envisaged when methods of topographic reconnaissance were first worked out—but in the enhancement of basic understanding that it brings or the new analytical tools that it provides. The contributions of original research are always unexpected.

It is also a pleasure to acknowledge the substantial debt this study owes to Sayyid Fuad Safar, Inspector General of Excavations in the Department of Antiquities of the Republic of Iraq. Both during the course of fieldwork in the Diyala area and in an earlier season of reconnaissance in ancient Akkad, the author drew repeatedly upon his unsurpassed knowledge of ceramic sequences in establishing the list of dating criteria for surface collections given in Appendix B. Moreover, the great majority of surface collections from individual sites in the Diyala series were jointly examined by the author and Professor Safar. In many stimulating discussions we considered together the respective claims of unsystematized impressions at the site or of the numerous collected sherds not easily embodied in any condensed system of classification, in relation to the relatively small numbers of dating criteria that ultimately were recorded for each collection. Repeatedly, new types were proposed, considered, tested for usefulness in the field situation, and then either embodied in the regular series of dating criteria or rejected. In some cases these types could be defined from published excavation reports, in others from Professor Safar's knowledge of the unparalleled collections of the Iraq Museum, and in still others from the author's observation of common features at sites whose approximate contemporaneity was assured by other dating criteria or by their dependence on a single branch-canal network. In a word, this too was a process of continuing, friendly interchange which contributed greatly not only to the author's education but to our conjoint effort.

The possible hazards of regarding a single region like the lower Diyala plains as accurately reflecting, albeit in microcosm, the changing fortunes of Mesopotamia as a whole during Sassanian and Islamic times have been called to the author's attention by Professor Marshall G. S. Hodgson. He has suggested several lines of apparently divergent development in neighboring areas, and with his permission these possibilities have been incorporated into the text. The same problem is of course even more serious for earlier eras, before repeated conquests and widespread ethnic movements had so largely blurred the distinctive local characteristics of regions like the Diyala plains. For more than the first half of the time span with which this study deals, the dominant characteristic of the Diyala region was its marginality to the geographic and cultural core of the alluvium. And yet, save for rare intervals, the difficulties of the cuneiform sources are such that within the core itself even the basic institutional structure of society is poorly understood. In that sense, as Professor Benno Landsberger pointed out in one of many helpful comments which led to a number of revisions in the manuscript, this study seeks to describe a dialect before the paradigm of the heartland is known. Let the reader beware, therefore; this study can only represent the region of the Diyala plains, and the task of assessing its representativeness for Mesopotamia as a whole is one which remains largely for the future. In any case, what is important to the author is not the degree of deviation of this or any other region from some undefined "norm" but the encouragement of the study of general historical trends in the differing regional contexts in which they were manifest.

The tradition in regional studies of utilizing the re-sults of several scholarly disciplines to trace patterns of human occupation with a long time perspective is one from which this work has drawn heavily and to which it aspires. Two important recent contributions to this tradition deserve mentioning which, although they focus on different areas and differ widely in their methods, substantially anticipate at least the approach and outlook of this study. The first, carried on for two decades by a large team of archaeologists, historians, ethnographers, and specialists in the natural sciences under the leadership of Academician S. P. Tolstov, has transformed our understanding of a great and historically pivotal region along the lower Amu Darya and Syr Darya in Soviet Central Asia. The primary record of results of the Choresm expeditions is now embodied in an extensive series of publications in Russian, and it is a matter of regret that the author has been unable to consult them except in incomplete and abridged translations.[2] With a scale and intensity of study many times exceeding that which we undertook in the Diyala hinterlands of Baghdad, the Choresm Project provides a more richly documented and continuous sequence of changing cultural patterns from archaeological evidence than can be offered for the Diyala area. Perhaps more important still, it also illustrates strikingly the extent of architectural—and inferentially social—diversity within and between ancient sites which before excavation appeared as indistinguishable mounds. We may suspect corresponding diversity during many historical periods on the Diyala plains as well, but the evidence on which this study relies is much less adequate to substantiate it.

The second example, not otherwise cited in these pages although it played a central role in shaping the author's own viewpoint, is Gordon R. Willey's pioneering study of prehistoric settlement in north coastal Perú.[3] While procedures of surface reconnaissance and dating employed here differ substantially from those employed by Willey and his co-workers, the Virú Valley Project of the Institute for Andean Studies has brilliantly succeeded in demonstrating the usefulness of viewing the development of a complex ancient civilization through the microcosm of its effect on settlement in a particular region.

To the specialized Arabist, the Arabic names and terms included in this study may well appear a morass of inconsistencies. With the benefit of advice and aid from Professor Muhsin Mahdi, an attempt has been made to steer the difficult course between commonly accepted usage and philological accuracy. Responsibility rests with the author alone, however, and has been borne perhaps too lightly in the belief that complete precision was neither necessary nor expected in view of the reliance throughout this work on Arabic sources only as they are available in translation. It should be noted that the names for sites in the Diyala area given in Appendix C are an exception to this generalization; the great majority of them are given as they were recorded and transliterated by Sayyid Fuad Safar after interrogating local informants.

The reference map of the Diyala area was prepared by Janis Indans, from an original map drawn by Myron Rosenberg which was checked and revised during the course of fieldwork. Ceramic types regarded as diagnostic for dating purposes (Figs. 11–16) were drawn by Nancy Engle, who also prepared final drawings of the ancient irrigation works and other structures excavated by the Diyala Basin Archaeological Project (Figs. 17–22). Original field drawings were made by Sayyid Mohammed Ali Mustafa, who also supervised the excavation program. It is anticipated that a full report on the excavations will be published at a later date.

On many occasions, both during the conduct of the survey and in the interpretation of its preliminary results, material aid and helpful advice were furnished by members of the investigative or engineering staffs of firms responsible for irrigation planning in the area. Thanks are due in particular to Ian S. G. Matthews, of Sir Murdoch MacDonald and Partners, Ltd., and to Stuart A. Harris, then of Hunting Technical Services, Ltd., respectively, for a practical introduction to the problems of canal construction and maintenance and for generously shared insights into some of the interrelated problems of soils and topography. The description of the contemporary scene contained in

Part I of this study, and especially the discussion of agricultural practices contained in Chapter 2, draws heavily upon two reports to the Iraq Development Board[4] with whose preparation Ian Matthews and Stuart Harris were associated. In addition, Mr. Harris undertook to prepare a map of ancient waterways in the lower Diyala area that might be inferred from the distribution of coarse textured sediments as plotted from soil surveys made by Hunting Technical Services.

A further basic source of agricultural information utilized in this study consists of an unpublished report prepared for the Diyala Basin Archaeological Project by Dr. Adnan Hardan, then a student at the Iraq Agricultural College in Abū Ghraib. On the basis of interviews with landowners' agents and ordinary farmers in a number of towns and villages throughout the area, Hardan was able to prepare glossaries of variant Arabic terminology for crops and weeds as well as brief descriptions of basic agricultural practices. Incidental points are contained in notes where these observations expand upon or differ from the more comprehensive Development Board studies. They also have contributed substantially to the general understanding of the traditional agricultural system that is set forth in Chapter 2.

Other scholars to whom the author is particularly indebted for encouragement in the pursuit of this study, and for critical comments which have been incorporated into the manuscript, include Professor Hans Bobek of the Geographical Institute of the University of Vienna and Academician I. M. Diakonoff of the Institut Nazodov Azii in Leningrad. Finally, Meryush Jaʿata, a resident of the district near our base camp at Khafājah, served as a guide during much of the reconnaissance. To him is owed a special debt of gratitude for his rich knowledge of the region and its problems, and for unflagging assistance in occasionally difficult circumstances.

CONTENTS

ILLUSTRATIONS

TABLES

TABLES

PART 1

THE CONTEMPORARY SETTING

1

MAJOR NATURAL VARIABLES:
CLIMATE, FLORA AND FAUNA, LAND AND WATER

THE PLAINS adjoining the lower Diyala River form an ill-defined geographical entity which comprises much of the northern end of the Mesopotamian lowlands. It may be described briefly as an irregular, fan-shaped alluvium that falls very gently toward the south and was laid down for the most part by the waters of the Diyala on their way to join the Tigris River. From its apex at a point where the river breaks through the arid low folds of the Jebel Hamrīn, the last low outlier of the rugged Zagros chain that guards the approaches to the Iranian plateau, the alluvial fan extends a minimum of perhaps 50 kms. to the west-southwest and upward of 130 kms. to the south and southeast. On its southern and western extremities its deposits blend imperceptibly with those of the far larger and more destructive Tigris. On the east it disappears in a band of salt marsh and seasonal swamp that is annually replenished by the Diyala winter flood as well as by a score of ephemeral mountain torrents from the east. All of these geographic boundaries, as will be seen presently, have shifted from time to time over the six millenniums or more that man has practiced agriculture within them, as a result both of human intervention and of a convergence of natural agencies.

In still another—more important—respect, the lower Diyala basin is difficult to define satisfactorily.

Save for the division between mountaineers and plainsmen, currently between Kurds and Arabs, which crosses the Diyala River not far above the Jebel Hamrīn, we find little or no congruence of geographic with enduring cultural or political boundaries. The region, to be sure, has served as chief granary or tax-farm to several passing empires and has seen two great capitals grow up along the margin of the Tigris River. But no empire was native here; all were originally imposed by outside forces. Repeatedly, it has been a battleground caught between other power centers, with its wealth and economic life destroyed or drained away in the ensuing contention. Repeatedly, its ethnic composition has been altered drastically, both by incursions of nomads on the heels of decaying central authority and as a consequence of outright invasion. Its administrative divisions, in consequence, form a changing, arbitrary patchwork of little chronological depth or cultural significance. Only in a few relatively brief periods of peace in its historic past have its problems been approached as an integral unit, with a degree of comprehensive planning. One such episode led to the initial construction of the gigantic Nahrawān canal, designed to supplement Diyala waters (which prosperity and burgeoning population had made inadequate) with an assured irrigation supply from the Tigris. Having now

3

been abandoned over much of its length for a period of some eight centuries, the remains of this great trench still provide the region's most impressive landmark and symbolize its potential unity and richness.

If much of the terrain today still remains empty and desolate, its forbidding climate provides no ready explanation of past greatness. There are only two pronounced seasons, a summer of intense heat that extends from May until early October, and a winter lasting from November through March. During the summer, the soil is effectively dried to a depth of about one meter and all vegetation shrivels under a burning sun and generally cloudless sky; strong

TABLE 1

TEMPERATURE, PRECIPITATION, AND RELATIVE HUMIDITY AT BAGHDAD, 1937–56

MONTH	TEMPERATURE IN ° C.			MEAN RAINFALL IN MM.	MEAN RELATIVE HUMIDITY
	Mean Max.	Mean Min.	Mean		
Jan.	15.7	4.1	9.4	23.4	69
Feb.	18.4	7.4	11.7	29.0	62
March	21.9	8.9	15.5	28.8	55
April	28.8	14.3	21.5	13.6	46
May	35.8	19.6	27.4	3.3	31
June	40.8	22.9	31.9	tr.*	23
July	43.3	25.0	34.2	tr.	23
Aug.	43.3	24.7	33.6	tr.	24
Sept.	39.7	20.9	30.1	0.1	28
Oct.	29.4	17.5	24.0	3.1	36
Nov.	24.7	10.5	16.6	19.0	56
Dec.	17.4	5.3	10.6	28.0	73

* tr. = trace.

Source: Government of Iraq, Development Board, 1958, Sect. 2, pp. 4–5. Lower Diyala Development: soils, agriculture, irrigation, and drainage. Diyala and Middle Tigris projects, Report no. 2. London: Sir M. MacDonald and Partners, Ltd.

northwest winds, rising by day, bring dust that helps to drive the population to shelter. Drawing air toward a low pressure area over the Persian Gulf, these dry winds (the *shimāl*) blow on nine days out of ten and mitigate the intensity of the heat for the human population while greatly increasing moisture losses through evaporation and transpiration. Water is everywhere a scarce commodity, and all life shrinks back toward the rivers and major canals.

A different pattern of atmospheric circulation obtains in winter. The high-pressure system of central Asia, extending into Iran, guides a flow of air from the northeast toward the Arabian peninsula. This flow is drawn down the Mesopotamian trough as cold northwesterly winds, and during their presence relatively clear days still occur. However, there are frequent interruptions marked by the passage of atmospheric

depressions from the Mediterranean, and the accompanying southeasterly winds (the *sharqī*) bring colder weather, cloudy skies, and rain.[1] Frosts are common, and even snow may linger briefly. The laboriously accumulated supply of brushwood that screens each peasant household dwindles rapidly as it is consumed for firewood, and the heavy work of cultivation is punctuated with anxieties over the timeliness of rain or the imminence of floods. Periodic, heavy rains turn the featureless plain into a morass which can be traversed only along the slightly raised levees of present or former watercourses. After a few brief weeks of pleasant weather in the spring, the rains disappear and the temperature once again begins its inexorable rise. By the time of the harvest in May the weight of summer is felt.

As recorded at Baghdad, which sprawls across great tracts on the western margin of the Diyala plains, this harsh, seasonal rhythm, is summarized in Table 1. Whatever the changing political fortunes and cultural heritage of the inhabitants, there can be little doubt that since its most ancient past this sharp division of the seasons has strongly affected human life in the region.

In two important respects the figures given in Table 1 are misleading when applied to the Diyala plains as a whole. Marked annual fluctuations occur, in the first place, and they have an effect not only upon the natural vegetation but upon the agricultural output of what is misleadingly regarded as an irrigation regime independent of rainfall. Thus while the mean annual precipitation at Baghdad for the twenty-year period of 1937–56 was 139.3 mm., in fact it varied from 72.3 mm. to 315.7 mm. during this period.[2] Second, precipitation increases gradually as one moves northeast toward the Jebel Hamrīn. Table 2, comparing rainfall at Baghdad with that at Al-Mansūrīya (Delli ʿAbbās), almost at the foot of the Jebel, clearly establishes this difference and in addition suggests the pattern of variations in monthly precipitation in both localities.

Setting aside for the present the plants introduced by man, the natural vegetation of the region obviously responds not only to the seasonal rhythm of climate but to the increasing amount of rainfall toward the northeast and to the wide annual variation. Yet even in good years and in the vicinity of the Jebel Hamrīn the vegetation is generally sparse. Classifiable as that

4

of a semi-arid steppe, it is limited both in numbers of species and in extent of coverage not merely by the rainfall but also by a very high incidence of soil salinity in uncultivated areas. Only in the spring is the aspect of both climate and open countryside an appealing and harmonious one. The steppe is then briefly tinged with green and splashed with the color of low flowering annuals wherever sufficient moisture gathers, and some of the sedentary cultivators leave their winter quarters behind to range widely with their flocks.

It must be understood, however, that the natural vegetation is not merely a passive reflection of climatic and edaphic conditions outside the control of man; in fact, over the greater part of the area natural vegetation survives only as weeds of cultivation, and hence intimately interacts with the prevailing agricultural regime. Perhaps this is most evident, or at any rate currently best understood, in the case of shauk (Prosopis farcta or stephaniosa). Described in a recent study as "perhaps the most typical weed of the irrigated land," the predominance of shauk is related less to its fortunately beneficial effects upon agricultural productivity than to its own highly effective adaptation to the ecological niche created by the prevailing fallow system. As the foregoing study notes, it "matures very late and, therefore, competes hardly at all with wintersown crops. Even in summer crops, it is probable that, with its extremely deep root system, it does not actively compete with comparatively shallow-rooted crop plants, and such competition as may occur is likely to be more than offset by the value of its root system to the internal drainage of the soil and its importance as a source of fuel and as a forage weed. As a legume, it may also contribute to nitrogen fixation; well-developed nodules have been observed on shauk roots."[3] Since it is a deep-rooted perennial, shauk easily survives semiannual cultivation with the traditional Iraqi shovel-pointed plow, an implement capable only of a parting action at shallow depth in contrast to the deep turning action of the mold board plow prevalent in the West.[4] Agul or "camel-thorn" (Alhagi maurorum) is another perennial legume sharing many of these characteristics.

Few other currently important weeds are as helpful as shauk and agul in any of their functions—as improvers of soil structure and drainage, as legumes,

fodder, firewood—and many of them constitute a serious deterrent to agricultural productivity. A number of annual grasses, including shūfan or wild oats (Avena sp.) and ruwaita (Lolium temulentum), are difficult to eradicate and, growing strongly during periods when maximum growth of crop plants should be expected, are serious competitors for nutrients and space. The annual khuzaima (Scorpiurus sulcata) is reported to be the commonest weed in the area, while another harmful legume, wild licorice (Glycyrrhiza glabra) occurs in such quantities as to smother crops under local conditions of canal seepage. Thistles, including several Centaurea spp., not infrequently in-

TABLE 2

MONTHLY RAINFALL AT BAGHDAD AND AL-MANSŪRĪYA
(DELLI ʿABBĀS) IN MM.

	1954		1955		1956		1957	
	Bagh-dad	Man-sūrīya	Bagh-dad	Man-sūrīya	Bagh-dad	Man-sūrīya	Bagh-dad	Man-sūrīya
Jan.....	13.8	25.0	54.1	62.2	7.5	24.4	12.1	18.0
Feb.....	44.4	50.0	11.3	67.1	8.5	......	51.5	46.0
March..	69.5	99.0	15.1	4.8	26.1	67.1	58.9	75.0
April...	21.6	45.0	31.7	57.9	44.8	......	72.9	96.0
May...	tr.*	......	13.0	39.6	......	......	28.5	76.0
June...	......	......	2.5	......	......	......	tr.	......
July....	......	......	......	......	......	......	......	......
Aug....	......	......	tr.	......	tr.	......	......	......
Sept....	......	......	......	......	......	......	......	......
Oct.....	10.8	19.0	10.8	......	......	......	2.8	2.2
Nov....	27.0	33.0	12.5	13.7	tr.	......	......	......
Dec.....	90.1	40.0	27.5	125.0	4.6	27.0	......	......
Total.	143.4	311.0	167.6	370.0	91.5	118.5	246.7	313.2

* tr. = trace.
    Source: Government of Iraq, Development Board, 1958, Sect. 3, p. 87. Lower Diyala Development: soils, agriculture, irrigation, and drainage. Diyala and Middle Tigris projects, Report no. 2. London: Sir M. MacDonald and Partners, Ltd.

fest fields so densely as to impede harvesting or even prohibit it entirely.[5]

Similarly, in areas not under cultivation, the natural flora are deeply affected by human activity. The widespread "gilgai" formations (poorly drained depressions with leached soils of very low porosity, and radial patterns of cracks and shallow gullies), for example, cannot be cultivated themselves but frequently are maintained in flooded condition through being used as runoffs for excess irrigation water. Their plant communities, dominated by the perennial grass ʾachrish (Aeluropus agopioides), are used extensively as summer pasturage. Other areas that are perennially flooded as a consequence of the irrigation regime, notably around the modern towns of Khālis and Kanʿan, support a vegetation which also includes a

5

number of aquatic grasses, sedges, and rushes (*Phragmites*, *Typha*, *Scirpus*, and *Juncus* spp.), as well as a white-flowered water crowfoot (*Ranunculus cf. heterophylla*).[6] Although ranging widely and destructively, it is in such surroundings that the wild pig finds a home—protected alike by difficulty of access, by heavy vegetation, and by deeply rooted patterns of religious avoidance.

Even in the empty land of the Nahrawān district in the south central part of the region, the absence of human influence is more apparent that real. Given the relatively low precipitation in normal years, the brief but intensive exploitation of its grazing potential in the spring seriously reduces its vegetation cover and undoubtedly has a determinative effect on the observed patterns of dominance among plant species.[7] In still another sense, the heavy reduction of wild fauna through hunting must have had important secondary effects on the flora as well. Only foxes, porcupines, jackals, and the Iraqi hare continue to flourish, while gazelles have entirely disappeared and the larger predators, hyenas and reputedly wolves, have withdrawn to the most remote portions of the region and there face imminent extinction. Finally, it may be noted that the vegetation of the empty lands is a response to topographic and soil conditions created by past human activities, in the form of the levees and depressions left behind by the historic Nahrawān canal system.

On the recent alluvial soils of the levees, normally the least saline, is to be found the most varied vegetation in the area. The species are predominantly annuals, dominated by the yellow-flowered *Adonis dentata* and the grass *samaᶜa* (*Stipa tortilis*), but *shauk*, the spiny shrub *ᶜausaj* (*Lycium barbatum*), and *zifra* (*Haplophyllum propinquum*) are among the perennials that also occur. In the much larger areas of formerly irrigated plain surface characterized by solonchak soils, the typical vegetation is dominated by the annual *Aizoon hispanicum;* but the prevailingly high salinity of such soils is reflected in numerous large patches that are completely barren. Along the slopes of the depressions created by intersecting levees, the moderately leached solonetz soils support a community dominated by the yellow composite *baibūn* (*Matricaria aurea*) and the grass *Aeluropus lagopioides*, and including the annual grasses *Koeleria phleoides*, *Alopecurus myosuroides*, and *Ere-*

mopyrum buonopartis, the small blue or purple *ᶜunsalan* (*Iris sisyrinchium*), the annual chenopod *Halocharis sulphurea*, and the ubiquitous *shauk* and *agul*.[8]

Turning to consider the processes by which these generally barren and yet historically important plains were established, our attention is directed first to the most active and primary agent, the river itself. The Diyala rises in the mountains of western Iran, with a catchment area of approximately 30,000 sq. kms.[9] With minor exceptions, this area is entirely under 2,000 m. in altitude. Hence the discharge of the river is largely a consequence of the runoff of winter rainfall, with melting snow in the late spring playing a relatively modest part in its over-all pattern of flow. In this respect the Diyala contrasts with the Tigris and all of the other Tigris tributaries, a difference that is clearly reflected in the timing and character of the spring floods. That of the Diyala takes place in February, March, and April, with a maximum occurring at the Jebel Hamrīn generally rather suddenly, between mid-March and mid-April. The Tigris flood at Baghdad, on the other hand, is comparatively low in February and rises gradually to a maximum in May.[10] In both cases, it may be noted, the plentiful supplies of irrigation water that are always associated with a flood danger make their appearance only in the latter half of the winter growing-season for the major crops.

Records covering several decades are available for the Diyala discharge just above its outlet at the foot of the Jebel Hamrīn. At its highest flood during this interval a flow of 3,420 cubic meters per second (cumecs) was recorded,[11] but the mean annual flood maximum is only 850 cumecs.[12] Moreover, the flow during the remainder of the year is very much less than either of these figures. The mean annual discharge is approximately 161 cumecs while the mean dry season discharge is only 36 cumecs.[13] Due primarily to withdrawals for irrigation above a weir at the foot of the Jebel Hamrīn, seasonal variation is even more marked if measured at the Diyala's confluence with the Tigris; in many years no flow at all occurs in the lower Diyala channel during the late summer.

The course of the Diyala through the Jebel Hamrīn is a meandering one which has become deeply entrenched with the gradual rise of the Jebel, but its course still clearly exhibits the morphology of the ma-

6

ture floodplain stream it must have been prior to that geological transformation. At this point the Jebel is about six kms. in width and exhibits a strikingly regular pattern of folding and subsequent erosion. Its name, "the red range," describes the red clays and sandstones which flank a gypsiferous core, and these deposits are overlain, particularly on the northeastern flank, by conglomerates and alluvium. "The plain to the south is lower than that to the north, and the southern slopes are steeper than the northern, so that the range is more like the rise and tread of a staircase step up to the Assyrian plains than a barrier range. But passage is not easy, because small plateaux, shelves, and terraced ridges parallel to the main ridge are deeply dissected by stony lateral ravines sometimes with brackish streams. The northern slopes are more undulating and supply some pasture, but the southern are bare, and the whole range is treeless."[14] Such is the upper boundary, and the only fixed one, of our region.[15]

The alluvial plain crossed by the Diyala below the Jebel is typical of much of lower Mesopotamia. Predominantly calcareous and consisting of medium to fine textured soils, it is derived from marine sediments of Mesozoic and Tertiary age that have been carried down and redeposited by the river. Across this surface the river follows a pronouncedly meandering course, flowing first to the southwest and then southward and dropping approximately 40 m. in a total bed distance of 171 kms. to the Tigris. The character of the bed, however, is by no means as uniform as this description may suggest. After emerging from the Jebel, the channel at first is more than one kilometer in width and exhibits a "braided" character with many bifurcating and rejoining courses. Within ten kilometers or so these courses recombine in a single narrower channel, which becomes increasingly entrenched within steeply cut banks in the alluvium that reach a maximum height of about 15 m. at Baʿqūba. So deep is this entrenchment that overtopping does not occur even at times of the highest recorded flood crests until a point 30 kms. or so above the Diyala's confluence with the Tigris (i.e., south of about 33°30′ N. Lat.).[16] The lowermost portion of the course of the Diyala is paralleled by natural levee deposits which have been surmounted with massive artificial bunds. In most seasons these bunds easily contain the maximum spring discharge. They were

last breached in 1954, when an escape channel had to be opened that conducted part of the Tigris flood east of Baghdad and into the lower Diyala.

The Tigris River, forming the western and southern boundary of the area, is known to have encroached substantially upon the northwestern part of the Diyala plain in a major change of course in the thirteenth century A.D. At the point where the Tigris turns from an easterly to a southerly course not far from the modern town of Khālis, the river flows beneath 15 m. cliffs like those at the same latitude on the Diyala, and, like those on the Diyala, these heights slope away to the south. South of Khān Banī Saʿad they are also no longer sufficient to contain the river in its characteristically savage floods,[17] and even the restraining bunds flanking the river south of that point occasionally had to be breached prior to the recent construction of the Sāmarrā barrage and Wadi Tharthar diversion channel and reservoir.

As it has been described above, a number of problems are posed by the present morphology of the lower Diyala plain and course which are pertinent to the primary concern of this study, the reconstruction of ancient patterns of irrigation and settlement. In order to consider these properly, it is perhaps advisable to begin with a brief general summary of the common characteristics of aggrading streams and their floodplains. While the changing systems of ancient rivers and canals in the region will be reconstructed largely on the basis of other evidence, it is an ancillary task of our reconstructions to delineate differences between the modern and ancient regimes and to help explain how some of these "anomalous" features may have emerged.

Perhaps the most fundamental aspect of the action of aggrading streams in their floodplains is that of levee formation. Natural levees built up of silt or sand deposited primarily by flood waters are, in fact, the dominant landforms of floodplains in general. Their growth occurs as a consequence of the tendency of streams in flood to overtop their banks at many places simultaneously, even under conditions where there have been substantial artificial alterations in bank height and form. Upon escaping from their relatively narrow channel floodwaters rapidly lose velocity, depositing their load of sediments on the backslope of the banks and thus enlarging the natural ridge upon which the stream in time comes to flow.

7

Coarse-textured sediments, of course, are laid down most quickly, while progressively finer silts and clay are found at greater distances down the backslope from the parent watercourse. It is thought that the height of natural levees above the surrounding floodplain is, in the main, a function of the stage difference between high and low water in the streams which have formed them; large watercourses that have been stable over long periods find their expression in wider levee ridges with gentler backslopes rather than necessarily in higher ones.[18] These processes, it should be understood, are typical but not entirely uniform in their application. At any one time local variation will be found from place to place as a result of such factors as the differing degrees of consolidation of the bank materials. Even the gross description of a river in its floodplain as occupying an aggradational regimen needs to take account of the active local erosion that takes place at many points along its course.[19]

A companion feature to the levee is the low-lying basin or back-swamp. Having overtopped their banks, floodwaters gradually find their way laterally to ill-defined depressions tending to parallel the course of the parent stream. In the Mesopotamian context, under conditions of insequent drainage, swamps and salt marshes are formed which shrink or even disappear during the heat and low-water of the summer. Depending on local topographic conditions, surface water in such depressions may or may not find its way back into the channel of the parent watercourse, but in any case only far downstream. While supporting and giving refuge to a rich fauna, and while providing excellent forage for large herds of sheep and goats during the spring, these depressions offer no inducement to permanent settlement and ordinarily are characterized by soils too badly leached for agriculture.[20]

In a broad sense, natural streams and artificial canals blend into one another as descriptive categories and are complementary in their distribution over a floodplain like that of the lower Diyala. Where an aggrading stream flows above the level of the surrounding plain, irrigation can be carried out directly through short breaches in the levee banks.[21] When it is desired to water fields at a greater distance, consuming a greater portion of the stream's contents for this purpose, these breaches need only be extended

gradually. It is significant that neither an ancient nor modern terminological distinction is made in Iraq between canals and natural streams. In fact, in order to make a distinction it is possible at best to suggest a heuristic but misleading polarity in their functions: canals distribute most or all of their supplies into smaller canals or fields for irrigation purposes, while natural streams discharge the bulk of their contents (except perhaps during floods) into channels connected with the ocean. As this distinction clearly implies, it is possible for a particular watercourse to make the transition from an essentially natural to an essentially artificial regime and back again over a period of time according to the use to which it is put.

In their respective contributions to the formation of the alluvial plain, canal irrigation and natural flooding also are complementary and have similar effects, although by different means. Canals, too, tend to form levees, as an examination of the reference map for the area will show. In the case of canals, however, the building-up of the levee proceeds in a different manner. Since the sediment-carrying capacity of a watercourse is proportional both to its slope and its cross-sectional area, sediment is rapidly laid down in the beds of canals as they branch radially from the larger parent stream. This process is repeated on a decreasing scale and with successively finer alluvial materials being laid down in the smaller branches of an irrigation system, until the ephemeral field-canals tend to become clogged with silt even while serving to transport sediment into the cultivation furrows. In addition to the direct but uneven aggradation along a branching series of levees that is thus brought about, rain erosion of the spoil-banks removed from the canals during annual cleaning slowly reduces topographic irregularities by spreading the bank material into surrounding fields. Wind erosion and deposition also may play a part, although there is little evidence that it has been more than a minor factor in the lower Diyala region. Dunes are found only in a small area (shown by stippling in the reference map) not far south of the river's gorge through the Jebel Hamrīn.

Since all but the major canal branches are shifted from time to time as it ceases to be profitable to maintain their courses between increasingly high banks, the ultimate effect of large-scale canal irrigation is to form a broad, irregular levee whose backslope encompasses the entire dendritic system of shifting branches. Beyond its greater width, there is one important respect in which this type of levee differs from that of a natural stream. Over a period of time the component sub-levees formed by shifting systems of branches intersect to isolate scores of minor depressions flanking the main canal, from which surface drainage in the event of floods or over-irrigation no longer is possible.[22] Conditions thereby may be created for a disastrous rise in the level of saline ground-waters, and for the deterioration of soil structure through leaching, culminating in the highly distinctive, widespread, and uncultivable "gilgai" soils, that is associated with this process.

Just as in the case of a natural watercourse, the main or trunk canal of an essentially artificial irrigation system forms its central axis; and it is maintained in this position along the levee's crest in order to provide for transport of the irrigation water at the greatest possible height relative to the field surfaces where it is to be consumed. While no direct comparison of the levees of canals and of natural streams as mutually exclusive phenomena is meaningful in the Iraqi context, it would appear from these considerations that there are two gross morphological distinctions between them which may be summarized as follows: (1) relative to the size of the parent watercourse, the artificial distribution of irrigation waters should establish a wider, more gently sloping levee for the canal than quickly dissipated flood waters could do for the natural stream; and (2) the contours of the irrigation canal levee will tend to be more distorted by active or relic radiating branches which interrupt its natural drainage and thus establish the conditions for soil salinization and waterlogging.

Levees, whether laid down by natural streams or by branch canals constructed for irrigation, offer a number of advantages for settlement and agriculture. Their backslopes provide relatively favorable conditions for surface drainage. Their soils, as has been indicated earlier, tend to be coarser, permitting easier cultivation and better subsurface drainage. Because they are higher than the surrounding plain and depressions, they offer at least a relative degree of protection against the dangers of floods. Similarly, they offer some protection against the crop-killing frosts which frequently settle into low-lying areas during the winter growing-season.[23] And to these natural ad-

vantages must be added a still more compelling and primary one: the close access which the crest of the levee offers to the canal or stream which has created it, the sole source of water both for irrigation and household purposes in a semi-arid country with intensely hot summers. For all of these reasons, it is no surprise to find that watercourses and their levees have always constituted the major axes along which human settlement in southern Mesopotamia takes place.

It is unfortunate that data are not available to provide more than a suggestion of the rate and extent of modification of the plain surfaces in the Diyala region as a result of alluviation. There is no doubt that a very heavy blanket of sediment has been laid down along the major river or canal of levees,[24] although within the Diyala region this can be confirmed at present only from archaeological soundings at Tell Asmar (244) and Tell Khafājah (421) and from a boring at Khashim Wāwi (628). At Tell Asmar, virgin soil underlying remains of the late fourth millennium B.C. lay at a depth of more than 10 m. below the present level of the plain adjoining the site. The initial occupation of Tell Khafājah, perhaps of a slightly greater age, is today more than eight m. below plain level. In the case of the unexcavated site of Khashim Wāwi, not far from the banks of the Nahrawān canal, sherds obtained at a depth of approximately seven m. below plain level appeared to belong to the late third millennium B.C.

To be sure, since these sites lay alongside watercourses which have remained in use fairly continuously, they cannot serve to indicate the thickness of recent sediment in areas more distant from ancient rivers or major canal branches. Reasoning from the fact that at present there is seldom more than a two to three meter difference between basin and levee elevations in any given area, it might be concluded that increments in the basins are only slightly less substantial than those along the levees. The flaw in this argument is that a periodically flooded alluvial plain provides a highly insecure foundation to support the weight of levees, so that some disproportionate subsidence of levee deposits must be expected to have accompanied their growth.[25] On the other hand, at least the approximate magnitude of alluviation reflected in these soundings finds confirmation in a recent estimate, based on a calculation of stream sedi-

9

ments and aeolian deposition, that the average rise in the Tigris-Euphrates plain level "is of the order of 20 cms/century."[26] At this rate, the fifty centuries since the foundation of Tell Asmar would have seen the accumulation, on the average, of the full depth of sediments that was recorded there.

Turning from the basic processes by which floodplains are formed, it is necessary to consider briefly the general morphology of floodplain streams. On a relatively flat alluvial plain, streams tend to form networks of shifting, indecisive channels, intermittently bifurcating and rejoining in their course of flow. Because of the continuous formation of levees, it is often difficult for smaller tributaries to break through directly into larger channels; instead, often they are diverted into parallel but separate courses meandering slowly downstream until a point is reached where a junction can be effected. Streams with deferred junctions of this kind generally are referred to as "Yazoo" tributaries, after a well-known example on the floodplain of the lower Mississippi River.[27]

Two fundamental aggrading stream patterns, meandering and braiding, usually are distinguished. Since braiding is a consequence of a relatively high sediment load in proportion to carrying capacity, it tends to be associated with watercourses which are heavily charged with coarse detritus like gravel and whose longitudinal slope necessarily is fairly high.[28] As mentioned earlier, this pattern occurs today in the lower Diyala basin only at the outlet of the Diyala gorge. Meandering, on the other hand, is characteristic of virtually the entire course of the lower Diyala River, as it is in most other floodplains composed primarily of clays and silts.

The complex processes by which a shifting or meander pattern comes into being are the subjects of dispute, but the effect, at least, "can be summed up in the word *oscillation*."[29] Perhaps as a consequence of the tendency for more rapidly moving waters to erode along the outside bank of a stream bend while deposition is going on along the inside bank, a meander pattern involves a relatively continuous, if not necessarily rapid, change in stream course. At the same time, the limits of the pattern are by no means random. As measured between tangents to their outer bends, it has been found that mature meanders, which are not inhibited by highly resistant bank material, tend to remain quite uniformly within a so-called meander

belt eighteen times wider than the channel forming them.[30] Although derived from observations in other areas, it may be observed that this relationship holds very closely for both the Diyala and Tigris rivers within the region of study, including not only their present courses but also those recently abandoned loops which can be discerned on air photographs. In oscillating within this belt, a stream forms, in addition to a set of natural levees appropriate to its course at a particular time, a lower but much wider and more regular meander-belt levee composed of accumulated sediments from many such natural levees covering the entire period through which the stream has followed that approximate course. To a degree, therefore, it is possible to distinguish relatively recent courses from those which have been followed by a stream for a long period by noting the completeness of development of their meander-belt levees.

There is disagreement as to the general process of meander movement. According to one view, the normal process consists of a steady and continuous migration or "sweep" downstream.[31] Abandoned oxbow bends, then, are regarded as "deformities" largely attributable to the unevenness of bank material.[32] Pertinent here is the wry comment of a prehistorian dealing with another floodplain: "If this were true of the Lower Mississippi, we might find ourselves with very little archeology to work on. Sites on the river's banks would have very little chance of survival before the inexorable sweep of the meanders, and the archeological material would have to be sought at the bottom of the Gulf of Mexico."[33] In the case, at least, of the lower Mississippi River, specialized studies have made it clear that this theory fails to describe the prevailing pattern of movement. Instead, it appears that "as a rule any single meander moves down valley only a short distance, considerably less than its width, before a cut-off takes place which leaves that particular meander as an ox-bow lake. In fact, the upper limb of the meander may move upstream. The process may best be described as a slow increase in the radius of the meander curve which proceeds until the lower curve of one meander meets the upper curve of the meander next below."[34]

In the Diyala region, the available evidence strongly suggests that the formation, lateral growth and decline, and final extinction of meander loops proceed with very little downstream movement. This is particularly clear along the deeply entrenched por-

10

tion of the course of the Diyala below the Jebel Hamrīn, where most of the old oxbows are easily traceable in air photographs. In the case of the Tigris course along the western and southern margins of the region, the same conclusion may be reached from a comparison of the present bed with that of 1837;[35] during this interval the size and shape, but not the positions, of many loops have changed appreciably. For longer ranges of time, additional evidence for the non-migration of Tigris loops is provided by the persistence of settlements or ruins like Ctesiphon (666), Deir-al-ʿĀqūl (791), and Jarjarāyā within the meander belt of the river during the seven centuries since the decline of the Abbasid caliphate, a period during which human interference with bank erosion and channel movement could not have been a serious factor. Ctesiphon is of especial interest in that the river's original course lay west and south of its wall while it now virtually bisects the ruins. Had this shift been brought about through the downstream migration of a meander loop, at least one-half of the ruins would have been destroyed in the process. In short, while the available data do not permit a detailed chronology of changing meander patterns along either the Tigris or the Diyala, it does appear that the lateral pulsation of meander loops was accompanied by little downstream movement.

In light of the account just given of the general characteristics of aggrading streams and the processes by which floodplains are formed, it seems appropriate to enumerate a number of features of the contemporary Diyala regime which are "atypical" and which consequently offer problems in accounting for the development of the lower Diyala plain.

One of the problems raised by the modern river regime that has long been recognized stems from its failure to overtop its banks for the greater part of its course below the Jebel Hamrīn. If the lower Diyala basin is an alluvial fan laid down by the Diyala itself, it is clear that this must have been done under conditions other than those which prevail at present. Moreover, the canals which irrigate the northern part of the basin only are made possible under contemporary conditions by the existence of an artificial weir at the outlet of the Jebel Hamrīn gorge; without the weir, alluviation would be brought to a virtual standstill in the areas which they serve.

A number of possible explanations may be offered as to why a regime has come into existence so manifestly different from that under which the basin must have been formed. It may be observed at once that these alternatives are by no means mutually exclusive. One, introduced by M. G. Ionides, visualizes a much longer Diyala course in ancient times than it occupies at present, with the lower Diyala following approximately the bed of the later Nahrawān canal.[36] With a longer course between the foot of the Jebel Hamrīn gorge and the river's confluence with the Tigris the slope of its bed probably would have been less. If so, instead of following its present downcutting regime in a deeply incised bed across the upper portion of the plain it might have established a raised levee and maintained the build-up of the alluvial fan through frequent flooding. But while conceivably a mere shift in the position of the Diyala's mouth could have had this effect, it is not clear why the Diyala, during the period when presumably it followed an aggradational regime and before the construction of the massive constraining bunds of modern times, should have maintained a single course rather than distributing its waters across the plain in a dendritic network of interlacing channels. We shall see that there is evidence for exactly such a dendritic network rather than a single channel in ancient times, while there were contemporary mouths of the river not only far downstream along the Tigris as envisioned by Ionides but also near the present confluence. This tends to minimize the importance of the position of the Diyala's confluence with the Tigris as a major and independent explanatory factor while underlining the broad and recent change from an aggradational to a downcutting regime which Ionides posited.

Another possibility is that the regime of the Diyala has been alternately an aggrading or degrading one depending upon a delicate balance in the volume or periodicity of its discharge. This balance could have been changed by many natural factors affecting the stream's headwaters. A slight climatic shift or erosional changes in the watershed of one of its upper tributaries, for example, might have been sufficient to account for the anomalous conditions observed at present. Cultural factors might also tend to disrupt this balance. To cite the most obvious case, the probable effect of deforestation through woodcutting or overgrazing would have been an increase in the rapidity of runoff and hence also a heightened tendency for the stream to scour its bed.[37]

11

Finally, an important study of tectonic movements elsewhere in the Mesopotamian plain[38] raises the possibility that the entrenchment of the Diyala in the upper part of the plain is a consequence of the continuing, slow upthrust of the Jebel Hamrīn and even of the plain itself. With the general instability of the plain having been conclusively demonstrated, another student of the subject has concluded more recently that vertical crustal movements of this sort are "the chief controlling factor in the physiographic evolution of the country."[39] Perhaps corroborative evidence for this process from the Diyala region can be found in the canals that radiate from the Diyala weir, for the control gates and headworks on these canals largely insulate them from climatic or topographic changes affecting the hydrology of the parent river. Yet, like the river itself, the upper reaches of these canals all are rapidly downcutting in spite of well-developed meander patterns, necessitating the installation of artificial spillways in some of them and the reliance on lifting devices for irrigation in others.[40] This argues that it may be the changed slope of the plain in this region that is primarily responsible for the end of the aggradational regime by which the plain surface originally was established, although the existence of such a change is difficult to demonstrate directly and its magnitude and rate are virtually impossible to establish.[41]

Several additional, minor, features of the present Diyala bed and course also point to the possibility of a change in the river's regime. First, it should be observed that a fully developed meander-belt levee does not occur even along the lowest portions of the course where flooding is a present hazard. Perhaps equally significant is the absence of a wide meander-belt "channel" in the incised upper portion of the river's course, where the shifting positions of meander loops cut into the soft bank material (a process that can be seen during the spring flood) in time might be expected to excavate a broad, regular depression. Instead of such a depression we find only a valley of quite irregular width and cross-sectional slope, with traces of only a few abandoned loops evident in the contours or on the air photographs. The second of these observations suggests that the incision of the upper part of the river's bed below the Jebel Hamrīn has occurred in relatively recent times and perhaps is still continuing, a possibility that may be best explained by the hypothesis of tectonic movement.[42] The absence of a meander-belt levee along the lower

reaches of the Diyala suggests that this portion of the course also may be fairly recent—a view which subsequently will be found to have strong support in the archaeological and historical evidence. Finally, it should be pointed out that the simple and direct junction of the Diyala with the Tigris exhibits none of the Yazoo-like features which might be expected of the confluence of a relatively minor tributary with a powerful, destructively flooding stream like the Tigris. As with the previous features, this too provides a hint of recent changes in the river's gradient or volume, particularly when contrasted with the rather different position and character of the junction in earlier times.

To summarize, it appears that the regime of the lower Diyala departs in a number of significant respects not only from the patterns generally to be anticipated for streams in their floodplains but also from the pattern under which most of the constituent material of its own floodplain must have been deposited. Under natural conditions one might best imagine most of the lower Diyala plains having been laid down by irregular, anastomosing networks of small river channels distributed widely over the whole land surface. The modern existence of but a single channel that does not overflow its banks for most of its length, together with the limited zone in which aggradation through irrigation now is possible even with an artificial weir, strongly implies that contemporary conditions differ from those of the past. The two primary, but not mutually exclusive, explanations that were indicated previously may be advanced again to account for the change: tectonic movement, probably consisting of a slow uplift, and an alteration in the volume or a shift in the periodicity of the Diyala discharge through possibly interacting climatic and cultural agencies. While the data of this study by themselves permit neither of these processes to be demonstrated conclusively, we shall attempt in the sequel to date and describe the gradual onset of the apparent effects of one or both of them as seen in the cumulative transformation of the pattern of watercourses that has occurred during the last six millenniums. At any rate, having demonstrated the fact of change, and having sought to suggest its complexity and magnitude, the way is clear to reconstruct the ancient geography of the region in its own terms—without the static assumption that the contemporary river course and regime must closely approximate those of the past.

2

BASIC PATTERNS OF AGRICULTURAL SUBSISTENCE

FAR-REACHING changes are under way in the traditional agricultural systems which have been followed in the lower Diyala region since times of remote antiquity. A high dam, which vastly increases supplies of summer irrigation water, was completed recently at Derbendi Khān, in the upper Diyala watershed. With this resource, a fully intensive system of crop rotation will become possible for the first time, permitting substantial increases in agricultural income and shifting the major orientation of the area from subsistence farming toward production for the market. In some cases, changes in land-leveling, drainage, canalization, and communications are under way and probably will move slowly ahead even if local initiative is unaided by government investment. Should these interrelated improvements continue to receive government encouragement, it is reasonable to predict that within the space of a few years the face of the countryside will be entirely transformed.

What lies in prospect for Iraqi agriculture, however, is not the subject of this study. Involving at many points a radical departure from the traditional farming patterns, the newly emerging patterns can provide few insights for the study of the past. Hence it is fortunate that the engineering studies leading to their institution were accompanied by the first close and systematic description of the earlier patterns still prevailing in the region. To be sure, little attention has been paid to what might be called the traditional technology of Iraqi agriculture, e.g., the implements and the manner of their use, detailed cultivation methods, prescriptions for irrigation or combating pests, and the like. But the ecological adjustments implicit in the traditional agricultural system, and their consequences for the rural economy and demography, are increasingly well understood. And it is only with respect to these broad environmental and economic relationships, in any case, that the presently available historical and archaeological data allow any possibility of useful interpretation and comparison.

Briefly to describe the traditional agricultural system of the Diyala plains, at least as it existed on the eve of the Iraq Revolution of 1958 when the fieldwork for this study was completed, it is overwhelmingly of an extensive rather than an intensive variety. Over 95 per cent of the cultivable land is devoted to field crops, including principally winter-grown barley or wheat that is alternated with a winter season under a weed fallow. Into this primitive rotation of very great antiquity[1] is fitted as much land under summer crops as the availability of summer irrigation water will permit, but the proportion of such land under summer cultivation is even smaller than the 4 per cent or so that is permanently devoted to orchards.

Except for a district along the Tigris southeast of its confluence with the Diyala, where pump irrigation has opened new tracts to commercial cotton production and where unusually large landholdings have tended to concentrate available capital, the mecha-

13

nization of agriculture is little advanced. Livestock are relatively numerous, but they are not integrated with cultivation so as to constitute an effective mixed farming system. They consist mainly of herds of sheep and goats which are allowed to subsist for most of the year on the natural weed growth of the waste and fallow land, supplemented by grazing on stubble and straw after the harvest and frequently by an early browsing on young barley shoots before the latter have produced ears of grain.[2] Larger livestock, and

TABLE 3
IRRIGATED CROP AREAS IN THE LOWER DIYALA REGION

Crops	Crop Area (1952/53 Agricultural Census) Mesharas*	Crop Area 1952/53 as Per Cent of Irrigated Area (1,138,400 Mesharas)
Perennial crops:		
Date groves and orchards.............	48,000	4
Winter crops:		
Barley.............................	375,000	
Wheat..............................	145,000	
Linseed............................	?	
Winter legumes (broad bean, lettuce, radish, cabbage, cauliflower, spinach)	?	
	520,000	44
Summer crops:		
a) Spring sown		
Cotton.......................	11,700	
Vegetables (watermelon, sweet melon, okra, eggplant, tomato, haricot bean, marrow, squash)......	8,000	
	19,700	
b) Summer sown		
Rice.........................	15,000	
Sesame.......................	1,500	
Miscellaneous (vetch, lentils, sorghum, maize, greengram).......	1,500	
	18,000	
Total summer crops...............	37,700	3

Source: Government of Iraq, Development Board, 1958, Sect. 3, p. 98.
*4 Mesharas=1 ha.

especially good draft animals, are in very short supply, and, except for orchards and vegetable plots, manuring is not practiced systematically enough to raise fertility significantly.[3]

A summary of irrigated crop lands in the lower Diyala area is given in Table 3. Although it excludes regions near the mouth of the Diyala and along the Tigris that are supplied by pumps rather than by gravity-flow canals, it describes the prevailing pattern on the major part of the irrigated lands; moreover, the proportions it suggests probably are approximately correct for the entire region.

Cultivation under these circumstances is obviously of an extensive rather than an intensive variety. As a result, average productivity per agricultural worker is very low, and there is considerable underemployment. Allowing for uncultivated and fallow lands, two hectares for each full- and part-time agricultural worker appears to represent the annually cultivated norm for the region.[4] Yet according to Iraq Development Board assessments an average family (assumed to consist of two adult males, one adult female, and four children) could cultivate 12.5 hectares without mechanization or the use of paid labor, representing an average of perhaps three or more hectares per worker.[5]

In the absence of extensive summer irrigation and a fully integrated mixed farming system, there is a predominant seasonality to agricultural employment. This is best understood not by dealing with the annual aggregate of labor requirements for agriculture but rather in terms of the monthly schedule of normal operations. Observations permitting the presentation of such a schedule, made in connection with the agricultural development program, are given in Table 4. As tabulated therein, the man-days of labor under a fallow rotation system give "a realistic idea of the degree of labour utilisation through the seasons that is normally found at the present moment in the Lower Diyala." Based on an assumed normal half-month period of $12\frac{1}{2}$ working days and a cultivated area of 12 hectares, it is evident at once that this area "is comfortably within the capacity of two men especially when their women folk are available for extra work at peak periods."[6] Table 4 also makes clear that it is harvesting and threshing time, rather than sowing time, that sets the upper limit to the area which one family can cultivate without hired assistance.

While average figures like these illuminate some basic features of the agricultural system, they may obscure others. Areas actually cultivated by individual families vary greatly, and although some differentiating factors may be distributed throughout the region in a relatively random fashion (e.g., family workforce size), others apparently have a highly selective influence upon large areas. Detailed demographic data permitting all of these variables to be recognized are not available for the Diyala region, but evidence from there and from another part of the

14

lower Mesopotamian plain makes it possible to specify two of the principal variables.

Different systems of land tenure are the first factor affecting population density. A recent, detailed study of agricultural economics in the Hilla-Diwāniya region discloses that, except in the case of intensively worked orchard holdings, the median holding of small-farm owners working their own lands is about 6 hectares, while that of tenant farmers is about 12 hectares. In data gathered just before the Iraq Revolution of 1958, land rents, service, and water fees are said to have cost the tenant farmer from one-half to three-fifths or even two-thirds of his crop, while average family size varied from 5.9 to 6.7 persons among subgroups of both tenants and small-farm owners. There are two points of interest here. The first is that population density in an area of tenant farming, because of the onerous obligations which can be met only by cultivating as large an area as possible, tends to be only about half as large as in a comparable area of freeholders. Of course, this difference will help to support a proportionately greater urban population subsisting directly and indirectly on tenants' fees, but at least the patterns of settlement in the countryside are markedly different. Second, it appears that small-farm-owning families commonly maintain at least a minimum level of subsistence with as little as one hectare of land per person. However, to the produce of this area under the traditional fallow system must be added their present income from off-season employment in the towns and from summer-cropping the relatively high average of approximately 15 per cent of their winter crop area.[7] This sharply bimodal distribution of population densities probably is not fully matched in the Diyala area, where small freeholding cultivators are much less numerous, but at least such data serve to remind us of the wide demographic variations that can be induced by social institutions not directly dependent upon the subsistence system.

The second variable affecting density has to do with the distribution of orchards. While it has been noted that the total proportion of land devoted to orchards is small, it does not occur in uniformly dispersed plots but in pronounced local clusters. The largest of these are along the banks of the Diyala in the vicinity of Baᶜqūba and around the town of Khālis, but lesser concentrations of orchard cultivation occur near many other towns where adequate

supplies of summer irrigation water are assured. Perhaps the prevailing high degree of specialization within such clusters may be suggested by figures available for Abū Saᶜda *nāhiya*, a small administrative district along the Diyala northeast of Baᶜqūba, where 22.1 sq. kms. are devoted to orchards and only 1 sq. km. to the cultivation of wheat and barley.

TABLE 4

SEASONAL LABOR REQUIREMENTS FOR TWELVE HECTARES IN FALLOW ROTATION

Month	Half-month Period	Man-days in Fallow Rotation
Jan.	1 2	2 3
Feb.	1 2	2 3
March	1 2	4 4
April	1 2	4 2
May	1 2	14 25
June	1 2	16 19
July	1 2	13 14
Aug.	1 2	13 18
Sept.	1 2	15 14
Oct.	1 2	10 11
Nov.	1 2	18 13
Dec.	1 2	8 4

Source: Government of Iraq, Development Board, 1958, Sect. 3, p. 113.

Orchards represent a highly intensive pattern of land use, although direct evidence is not available from the Diyala area on fruit crop yields in relation to cereal crops. The great fractionation of landholdings in areas devoted primarily to orchards certainly suggests that relatively small areas can sustain large populations, even if this impression is difficult to quantify in the region itself. In Baᶜqūba *nāhiya*, for example, a district famed for its fruits, the Agriculture and Livestock Census[8] indicates that out of 3,861 landholdings existing there 2,595 were of one hectare or less, 531 were of one-fourth hectare, and 706 were

15

less than one-fourth hectare in size. To be sure, although suggestive of great concentration, these figures simply do not indicate what proportion of an individual family's income could be provided by holdings of one-fourth hectare or less. Data from the Hilla-Diwāniya area, however, fully corroborate the impression of substantially greater productivity per unit area. In predominantly date-growing areas there freeholding families averaging 7.3 persons in size subsisted by cultivating an average of one-fourth hectare of winter and summer crops of their own, one hectare

as tenants, and one hectare of orchards of their own[9] —less than one-third of the average area needed by cereal cultivators in the same region. Not surprisingly, this difference is reflected directly in population distribution. Densities are many times greater in the date-growing areas,[10] although part of this may be explained by the proximity of those areas to the urban center of Hilla.

Table 5 presents the changing round of agricultural operations in terms of a calendar of primary activities associated with winter and summer cropping.[11] No

TABLE 5

CALENDAR OF AGRICULTURAL ACTIVITIES FOR PRINCIPAL ANNUAL CROPS

October
  Winter cropping
    a) Preparing land with irrigation, plowing, and cross-plowing*
    b) Sowing barley
    c) Preparing land and sowing winter vegetables (lettuce, radish, onions, cabbage, and cauliflower)
  Summer cropping
    a) Harvesting and threshing rice
    b) Picking cotton
    c) Late threshing of winter cereals

November
  Winter cropping
    a) Continuation of land preparation for barley, wheat, and linseed
    b) Sowing barley
    c) Sowing wheat in latter part of month
    d) Sowing linseed
  Summer cropping
    a) Final harvesting of late planted rice
    b) Picking cotton

December
  Winter cropping
    a) Late sowing of barley
    b) Sowing wheat and linseed
  Summer cropping
    a) Late picking of cotton and uprooting of cotton plants

January
  Winter cropping
    a) Late sowing of wheat in abnormally dry years
    b) Sowing of early planted summer vegetables (tomato and eggplants)
    c) Cropping winter vegetables

February
  Winter cropping
    a) Irrigating winter crops
    b) Tending tomato and eggplant seedlings
    c) Cropping winter vegetables

March
  Winter cropping
    a) Irrigating winter crops
    b) Transplanting tomato and eggplants
  Summer cropping
    a) Preparation of land for summer vegetables and cotton
    b) Sowing summer vegetables
    c) Planting cotton in latter half of month

April
  Winter cropping
    a) Last irrigation on winter cereals and linseed†
    b) Harvesting of any early ripened barley at end of the month
  Summer cropping
    a) Preparation of land for vegetables and cotton
    b) Sowing vegetables
    c) Planting cotton
    d) Sowing sorghum

May
  Winter cropping
    a) Harvesting barley
    b) Harvesting wheat and linseed in latter part of month
  Summer cropping
    a) Late planting cotton
    b) Weeding cotton
    c) Preparation of land for planting rice
    d) Planting rice

June
  Winter cropping
    a) Harvesting of wheat and linseed
    b) Carting winter cereals and linseed
  Summer cropping
    a) Preparation of land for planting rice and sesame
    b) Planting rice
    c) Sowing sesame
    d) Weeding cotton

July
  Winter cropping
    a) Threshing barley and wheat
  Summer cropping
    a) Planting rice

August
  Winter cropping
    a) Threshing and winnowing barley and wheat
  Summer cropping
    a) Picking cotton
    b) Harvesting sorghum

September
  Winter cropping
    a) Threshing and winnowing wheat and barley
  Summer cropping
    a) Picking cotton
    b) Harvesting sesame

Source: Government of Iraq, Development Board, 1958, Sect. 3, pp. 101–3. Lower Diyala Development: soils, agriculture, irrigation, and drainage. Diyala and Middle Tigris projects, Report no. 2. London: Sir M. MacDonald and Partners, Ltd.

* On coarser textured soils and using a horse-drawn plow, one man can plow, broadcast the seed, and cross-plow ¼ hectare in approximately seven hours. With heavier and bad-structured soils, this rate of progress may be slowed as much as 50 per cent (Government of Iraq, Development Board, 1958, Sect. 3, p. 185). Hardan's informants in Khān Banī Saʿad indicated that plowing began at 3 A.M. and continued until evening with a two-hour interruption at midday. On that basis, almost twice as large an area can be plowed daily as these figures indicate. The time of fall plowing is determined by the timing of the first rain or the availability of irrigation water. There is a strong preference for the earliest possible date, since an early maturing crop is less subject to losses from insects and disease. But sometimes first plowing must be postponed until as late as early January.

† Hardan's informants indicated that normally wheat crops would be irrigated four times between December and April, while barley would receive an additional irrigation after flocks had been allowed to graze on the young shoots. Obviously these are rules of thumb which are adjusted according to the time and amount of precipitation.

reference is made to the feeding or supervision of the livestock since to a large degree this is entrusted to children too young to participate in other economic activities. The distribution of livestock in the three *liwās* among which the Diyala plains are administratively divided is recorded in Table 6. While reflecting a substantially larger area than the Diyala plains alone—exclusive of the pump-irrigated lands along the Tigris and lower Diyala, the latter are said to provide for "some quarter of a million units,"[12] or less than one-fourth of the total in the three *liwās*—the approximate proportions indicated by that table probably are fully applicable to our region.

The harvest of the major winter cereal crops obtained in the Diyala region is reported to maintain a moderately high average level in spite of a number of adverse natural and social factors. The average yield from 77 randomly sampled fields of barley in the area served by gravity-flow canals emanating from the Diyala weir was 1,396 kgs. ± 67.5 per hectare, very little less than the average for the United States although only one half as large as the yield in the United Kingdom and an even smaller fraction of other European figures. For wheat, the average of 265 sampled fields was 1,132 kgs. ± 24.8 per hectare.[13] The seed rate used in both cases is reported to be a relatively low one, 60 to 80 kg. per hectare for barley and 48 to 72 kg. for wheat,[14] stressing that average yields are relatively favorable in spite of the prevailing primitive agricultural technology and the chronic shortages of irrigation water.

There is a substantial difference between the sample yields reported above and the official statistics for the four *qadhās* of the Diyala *liwā'* that lie south of the Jebel Hamrīn. Covering approximately the same area and time as the samples, the latter indicate yields of only 1,020 kg. per hectare for barley and 764 kg. for wheat. Part of this loss, at least in the case of barley, can be attributed to the practice of deliberately leaving 10–25 per cent of the harvest on the ground as feed for livestock. In addition, normal harvest losses in cutting or threshing were entirely eliminated in the collection of the samples. "Even so the official estimate of the yield is low," the report comments.[15] Probably at least a part of the explanation lies in the generally hostile relations that obtain between the

tenant farmers conducting the harvest and their absentee landlords.

Aside from irregularities in the availability of irrigation water, and indeed the prospective, over-all deficiency of water as the cultivated area continues to grow, the major natural deterrent to higher yields arises from soil salinity and poor soil structure. With the main canal courses following raised levees of coarser textured deposits, areas along their banks tend to be relatively well drained and non-saline. But as noted earlier, the numerous intersecting branch canals radiating away from the main canals impede the surface drainage of low-lying areas between them. And given the relatively fine-textured sediments which are deposited in these depressions, their sub-

TABLE 6

DISTRIBUTION OF LIVESTOCK IN THREE IRAQI *Liwās*

	Baghdad	Diyala	Kūt
Sheep	257,234	212,150	163,110
Goats	70,446	58,845	36,627
Cattle	69,302	53,472	34,979
Donkeys	27,799	39,738	17,707
Horses	20,581	12,271	15,593
Camels	3,780	1,300	586
Buffaloes	4,618	496	885
Mules	376	1,619	125
Proportion of landholdings employing mechanical power* (in per cent)	19.9	0.1	35.2

* This category consists principally of landholdings employing a single tractor for plowing. In Kūt Liwā', for example, there were 618 tractors and 4 harvesting combines on 539 individual holdings. (Government of Iraq, Principal Bureau of Statistics, 1954, p. 69.)

surface drainage also is poor. Hence the region as a whole consists of intersecting areas of high and low salinity whose boundaries tend to follow the surface contours. With excessive applications of irrigation water, the highly saline ground-water tends to rise toward the surface, expanding the areas in which fertility is affected by salinity for varying distances up the slopes toward the levee crests. With well-founded uncertainties over future precipitation and irrigation supplies, there is of course a tendency on the part of farmers to over-irrigate whenever water is available, thus accelerating losses from salinity and inadequate drainage. In this sense, the problems of irrigation management and soil salinity are inseparably linked.

Under the traditional agricultural system, artificial drainage channels have never been employed, and agriculture has depended upon "living with" salinity in a somewhat unstable equilibrium rather

17

than seeking to eliminate it. With the winter rains and irrigation the saline water table rises toward the surface, bringing salts up into the root zone or even to the surface by capillary action to reduce yields in large areas and to remove some areas from cultivation altogether. In spite of the salinity problem, however, over 70 per cent of the area within the present irrigated boundaries is classified as arable. Roughly equal parts of the remainder are classified as nonarable because of high salinity and because of poor drainage and soil structure, but it is conceded that almost 85 per cent of the former can be reclaimed gradually by leaching while 30 per cent of the latter is suitable for non-intensive cropping.[16] Thus losses in agricultural output through salinity and poor drainage, although very large and widespread, differ substantially from area to area and even from year to year. Their effects on average yields, while surely considerable, accordingly cannot be calculated.

With the end of the winter rains and irrigation, the level of the water table gradually falls. Partly this is a result of the direct, deep, drying of the surface with the extreme summer heat and low humidity. Deeprooted perennials like *shauk* and *agul* contribute to the reduction of moisture through transpiration from their leaves. Finally, there appears to be a slow natural drainage of subsurface water toward the south, facilitated by a lateral movement into the deep trench of the Diyala during its summer low-water phase.[17] These factors are only slightly offset by the very limited application of summer irrigation water, so that under normal conditions the level of the water table returns approximately to its starting point by the beginning of the next agricultural season in October.[18]

Aside from accepting losses in yield under the traditional agricultural system, "living with" salinity involves a periodically shifting selection of crops based in part upon their relative degree of salt tolerance. This emerges most clearly in the case of barley and wheat, for, unlike wheat, barley can grow well on moderately saline soils. For the irrigated lands served by the Diyala canals, figures on the respective preferences for barley and wheat are available, unfortunately, only for the following three growing seasons:[19]

	Barley (in hectares)	Wheat (in hectares)
1952–53	93,750	36,250
1955–56	116,500	47,500
1956–57	80,500	31,250

It is evident that the area devoted to winter wheat and barley cultivation is subject to a fairly wide annual fluctuation based on the adequacy of irrigation water. Of the total of the two types of cultivation, however, the proportion devoted to barley remains consistently in excess of 70 per cent. To be sure, neither salinity nor any other single factor is responsible alone for this high proportion. Barley flour is said to be preferred for the making of the local unleavened bread, and barley has additional advantages as a supplementary food for livestock. On the other hand, wheat normally commands more than twice as high a price in the market,[20] and more than half of the harvested barley crop is sold rather than being consumed on the farm.[21] At any rate, the conclusion can hardly be questioned that salt tolerance is *one* of the major considerations that continues to dictate the very high preference for the cultivation of barley in the Diyala region.

Orchard crops, too, are differentially responsive to salinity. Date palms, which constitute not merely the largest single category but probably also the absolute majority of all fruit trees in the area,[22] are able to bear fruit under a wide variety of conditions of soil salinity and texture. Given the intensive watering that is necessary for dates, "a hot head and wet feet," the water table often is permanently elevated to within 150 cm. or less of the surface within the date gardens.[23] Under these conditions a very high level of salinity may be maintained in the surface soils by capillary action, including even white surface encrustations of deliquescent salts. On the other hand, while deciduous and citrus fruit trees are often interspersed with date palms, these mixed gardens apparently are never located on saline soils.[24] Well-drained, coarse-textured deposits along the Diyala banks, and especially on a single high terrace within the deeply incised river channel both north and south of Baʿqūba, are particularly suitable for these highly productive, market-oriented, mixed gardens. Among the possible advantages of an intermixing of trees where soils permit it are the provision of some protection for the citrus trees in particular against winter frosts and intense summer heat, as well as providing both a summer and a winter crop from the same piece of land.[25]

Turning from the traditional agricultural regime to the irrigation system which sustains it, the contemporary layout of major canals and branches is

18

given in Figure 1. The uppermost canal-head on the lower Diyala plains is the Khālis, the largest of the region, which irrigates lands on the right bank of the Diyala southward almost to Baghdad. Taking off above the weir a short distance downstream from the Khālis are four large left-bank canal-heads: the Khurāsān-Mahrūt (which bifurcates almost immediately), the Shahrābān, the Hārūnīya, and the Rūz. These gravity-flow canals all are similar in type. They are controlled by modern regulators at their headworks, and (except for the Hārūnīya and Shahrābān, which are privately owned) the dispersal of their water into branches is determined by the government engineers through regulation of input-pipe size. Responsibility for their maintenance also rests with the central government; today it is largely discharged with the employment of excavation machinery, but formerly it was done with hand labor under the direction of government engineers and the immediate supervision of landowners' agents. Taken together, these six canals serve to irrigate an area of slightly less than 300,000 hectares, or 3,000 square kms. Data on the main Diyala canals are summarized in Table 7.

All the remaining irrigated areas in the lower Diyala region depend upon canals fed by lift machinery at their heads, which is able to draw water from reaches of rivers running substantially below plain level. One such zone of pump-fed-canal irrigation lies along both banks of the Diyala near its confluence with the Tigris, since only inadequate supplies are available for this area from the tails of the gravity-flow canals south of about 33°30′ N. Lat. Approximately 53,750 hectares, or 537.5 sq. kms., are fed from this source. In addition, a zone of 10,000 hectares, or 100 sq. kms., of lift-irrigation along the left bank of the ʿAdheim River may be mentioned; although outside of the Diyala basin from a geographical point of view, it is included within one of the census and administrative units making up the region. A much larger area is irrigated by lift-canals from the left bank of the Tigris. Unfortunately, the available census data are not arranged to correspond with the administrative boundaries previously taken to define the lower Diyala region. As a provisional estimate, however, the total irrigated area along the left bank of the Tigris from Samarra downstream to Kūt is 2,350 sq. kms. Planimetric map study indicates that of this figure not less than 1,775 sq. kms. lie within the lower Diyala region as here defined.

Combining 2,958 sq. kms. of irrigated tracts fed by the canals stemming from above the Diyala weir with 2,412 sq. kms. of pump irrigation, irrigated agriculture in the Diyala region can be seen to total about 5,370 sq. kms. The Diyala plains themselves, counting the empty lands of the Nahrawān region and the seasonal swamp of the Haur es-Subaicha to the east, comprise approximately 8,000 sq. kms. Without supplementary water beyond that normally supplied by the Diyala's winter flood—obtained either through construction of a high storage dam like that at Derbendi Khān or a feeder-conduit from the Tigris like the ancient Nahrawān or both—this represents very

TABLE 7

AREAS SERVED BY MAIN DIYALA CANALS FROM RECORDS OF WATER RIGHTS

CANALS	LENGTH (kms.)	AREAS SERVED (hectares)		
		Gardens	Arable Lands	Total
Right bank of Diyala:				
Khālis...........	60	3,850	107,500	111,350
Left bank of Diyala:				
Khurāsān........	81	5,950	37,500	43,450
Mahrūt..........	46	1,175	71,825	73,000
Shahrābān.......	23	350	8,575	8,925
Hārūnīya........	25	....	6,250	6,250
Rūz.............	63	650	52,225	52,875
Total left bank.	238	8,125	176,375	184,500
Totals........	298	11,975	283,875	295,850

Source: Government of Iraq, Development Board, 1958, Sect. 1, p. 5.

nearly the maximum extent of irrigation that is possible in the area.[26] Thus it is water, not land, which constitutes the crucial, limiting variable to the further expansion of agriculture in this environment.

It remains to consider briefly those limited agricultural activities independent of irrigation. While it is customary to generalize that the 200 mm. isohyet marks the extreme limit of dry farming without supplementary irrigation under Mesopotamian conditions, and that the alluvial plain of southern Iraq lies entirely outside that limit, both of these statements are somewhat inaccurate in their application to the Diyala region. In the first place, the decisive characteristics of rainfall in the area are not merely that it is relatively low, but that it varies widely from year to year. No rigid boundary exists, in other words, between zones of settlement based on dry and irrigation agriculture. Instead, there is a wide and amorphous "zone of uncertainty"[27] in which dry farming is successful during some but not all years.

Secondly, the data in Table 1, inadequate as they are, clearly indicate that the 200 mm. isohyet runs across the Diyala plains and not above them, probably paralleling the Jebel Hamrīn at a considerable distance to the southeast. Yet no villages practicing dry agriculture as a major source of subsistence are to be found on the plains below that geographical and cultural barrier. Instead, there are only sedentary irrigation farmers who carry on supplementary rainfall cultivation in empty steppe areas beyond the reach and capacity of their canal networks. Particularly in the empty lands of the Nahrawān region small plots of shallow cultivation are sporadically to be found by the traveler during the winter and spring, placed for the most part on the slopes of depressions where a natural concentration of runoff may increase the available moisture. Local informants report that moderate yields can be expected in the Nahrawān region in one year out of three, and that in most other years there will be at least a low stand of barley grass to serve as forage for their livestock. This return might not seem high enough to justify the expense and effort of annual speculative planting, except that it comes to the cultivator without the deduction of the landlord's very substantial customary share. With the onset of summer heat, in any case, even the free spirits who maintain this vestige of transhumance fold their tents, collect their meager harvest, and return with their flocks to mud villages along permanent watercourses. The Diyala region counts on rain to supplement the always inadequate irrigation supplies and to provide weed forage, but its essential way of life is irrigation agriculture.

3

RECENT TRENDS IN SETTLEMENT

RARELY in the modern world does one find as stark a contrast between city and countryside as exists between Baghdad and its hinterland. Its broad plazas and crowded bazaars, its imposing government buildings and modern shops, and the restless urgency of its crowds all proclaim the intense interest and participation of the capital in international affairs. On the rural scene change proceeds far more slowly, for outside influences are sharply attenuated by poverty and isolation. The school, the lorry, the bicycle, the radio, the bolt of machine-woven cloth, each brings its partisan and prophet into complex, gradually spreading patterns of interaction with the peasantry, but most of the landscape still exhibits no trace of these or similar imports.

From a political and social point of view, the emergence of this rural-urban contrast during the later nineteenth and early twentieth centuries provides some of the essential background for understanding the emergence of Iraq as a nation. For our purposes, however, Baghdad sprawls across a margin of the lower Diyala region and yet is not part of it. It draws its wealth and population from, and makes decisions for, the whole of the nation and so cannot usefully be considered merely in relation to a single rural district that happens to lie beyond the crumbling ruins of its former walls. While a comprehensive account of the Diyala region would have to deal on many levels with the ramifying effects of the city's current, quite unprecedented growth, it is only possible here to examine recent patterns of rural settlement in the area as if they were in isolation—as sys-

tems of occupance detached from the more rapidly changing forces of the city with which in reality they have been in constant interplay. But even if palpably inadequate as an explanation of the genesis of modern conditions, a brief sketch of the region outside of the metropolis may help to clarify some of the apparently different demographic patterns of the ancient past.

Of the fourteen *liwās* or provinces into which Iraq is divided, census data from parts of three are applicable to the lower Diyala region as here defined. These *liwās* each are subdivided into several districts called *qadhās*, which in turn are subdivided into *nāhiyas* or parishes. Each of the subdivisions centers on a town as its administrative headquarters, although the bulk of the agricultural population lives dispersed in villages and hamlets throughout the irrigated areas. Beyond its police post, school, officials' club, and improved communications (road, telephone) there may be little to distinguish the town centers of the smaller *nāhiyas* from surrounding villages; at any rate, the absence of a sharp difference in size renders the distinction between towns which are "urban" and villages which are "rural" (in the census reports) somewhat arbitrary. Demographic data applying to the lower Diyala region, unfortunately not all deriving from the same year, are summarized in Table 8.

If the population of Baghdad is excluded, it is apparent from Table 8 that the lower Diyala region is preponderantly rural in character. Of a total population of 409,426 outside the metropolitan area, only 47,792 or 11.7 per cent are said to have lived in towns

21

in 1957, even when one example with a population of only 506 people is included under the rubric of "towns." Moreover, since towns are characterized by the presence of resident administrative officers, it is likely that they are relatively more fully reported in the census than rural areas; hence, to the degree that the data are incomplete, they probably tend to exaggerate the proportion of the population living in towns. Rural dispersion is made even more evident

in settlements too small to be classified even as villages by modern census-takers,[1] and that less than one-eighth of the population lives in towns. Of course, it must be borne in mind that these calculations exclude the urban population of Baghdad, an unknown but presumably very small part of which is primarily concerned with the lower Diyala region or is dependent on its resources for support.

Although fully comparable data are not obtainable,

TABLE 8

POPULATION OF THE LOWER DIYALA REGION ACCORDING TO THE 1957 CENSUS

ADMINISTRATIVE Unit	AREA* (sq. kms.)	TOTAL POPULATION	"URBAN" (City-Town)	"RURAL" (Village)	NUMBER OF VILLAGES†	
					<200	>200
Baghdad Liwāʾ:	(12,752)					
Baghdad Qadhāʾ	(1,984)					
Adhamīya Nāhiya	302	171,348	110,518	60,830	14	19
Karrāda Nāhiya	171	208,408	128,364	80,044	26	13
Salmān Pāk Nāhiya	1,313	24,799	2,687	22,112	7	19
Diyala Liwāʾ:	(16,121)					
Baʿqūba Qadhāʾ						
Baʿqūba Nāhiya	685	56,693	18,547	38,146	52	29
Kanʿan Nāhiya	600	13,680	506	13,174	–‡	–‡
Khālis Qadhāʾ						
Khālis Nāhiya	875	34,876	5,512	29,364	18	30
Banī Saʿad Nāhiya	601	18,319	764	17,555	38	20
Mansūrīya Nāhiya	2,137§	25,239	1,125	24,114	30	14
Mandalī Qadhāʾ						
Balad Rūz Nāhiya	2,065	18,896	3,618	15,278	28	24
Miqdadīya Qadhāʾ						
Miqdadiya Nāhiya	—	32,960	7,626	25,384	26	18
Abū Saʿda Nāhiya	1,116	15,969	2,889	13,080	96	20
Kūt Liwāʾ:	(16,554)					
Suwaira Qadhāʾ	(5,227)					
ʿAzīzīya Nāhiya	2,628	27,121	4,518	22,603	3	15
Totals (without Baghdad)	12,493	648,308 (409,426)	286,674 (47,792)	361,684	338	221

(Source: Republic of Iraq, Ministry of Economics, Principal Bureau of Statistics, 1958.)

* Areas taken from: Sousa, Ahmed, 1953. Liwāʾ and qadhāʾ totals in parentheses include some areas not in lower Diyala region.

† Government of Iraq, Director General of Census, 1950. Census of Iraq, 1947. Baghdad.

‡ Figures for number of villages included with Miqdādīya Qadhāʾ. Based on data from 1952–53, it was estimated that there were 74 villages of varying sizes (Government of Iraq, Development Board, 1958, Sect. 1, p. 9). Lower Diyala Development: soils, agriculture, irrigation, and drainage. Diyala and Middle Tigris projects, Report no. 2. London: Sir M. MacDonald and Partners, Ltd.

§ Not more than about 200 sq. kms of this nāhiya are included within the lower Diyala basin as defined here. This includes the nāhiya town center and virtually all of the presently irrigated area, but a breakdown of settlements and population is not available.

upon examining in Table 8 the two right-hand columns that deal with village size and distribution. No data are available for calculating the average size of settlements included under the "village" rubric, but a reasonable estimate might be that those listed with a population of less than 200 persons averaged 150 persons, while villages listed as having a population in excess of 200 persons averaged 300 persons. On this basis, the total population living in villages would be only 116,400, or little more than one-third of the total rural population. In short, it appears that almost 60 per cent of the region's population may live

there is a significant contrast between the pattern of rural dispersion evident in the Diyala region and patterns with a more nucleated, urban emphasis farther to the south of the Mesopotamian alluvium. According to a recent geographical study of the middle Euphrates valley, sixteen large towns there (defined as having populations in excess of 6,000 persons) had a total population of 401,936 persons. Thirteen small towns (with between 2,000 and 6,000 inhabitants) had a total of 48,462 persons. Villages were defined as having from 100 to 2,000 inhabitants, and a total of 155,220 persons were tabulated as residing in 1,329

22

villages. By contrast, there were just 216 hamlets consisting of less than 15 houses, with a total population of only 11,928 persons. It is acknowledged that there were also isolated farmsteads that were not tabulated; they are described only as "scattered" and were apparently negligible in number.[2] Clearly, in this area all but an insignificant proportion of the population lives in nucleated villages housing more than 100 persons or in towns rather than in smaller settlements. In part, the contrast may be an outgrowth of the relatively recent resettlement of much of the Diyala region, but in part also it must reflect an enduring difference between the southern and northern parts of the plain that is at least as old as Mesopotamian civilization itself.

Further insight into the character of settlement in the region may be obtained from a consideration of one of the towns for which a wider range of information is available. Data from Baʿqūba, the capital of Diyala Liwāʾ and the largest town in the lower Diyala basin (as before, excluding Baghdad), are summarized in Table 9. If it is remembered that Baʿqūba is by several times the largest town in the area, that it is the only liwāʾ capital in the area and so has a unique concentration of governmental personnel, that it is a noted center of commercial fruit production for the Baghdad market, and that it is an important rail and highway junction, it will be clear that Baʿqūba represents an extreme of diversification and specialization rather than a norm for town life on the lower Diyala plains. Yet even in Baʿqūba, it appears from Table 9, almost half of the population (47.3 per cent) must find their sole source of support in agricultural labor. For other, smaller towns, it is only reasonable to assume that the proportion of inhabitants directly engaged in agriculture is substantially higher. Taken together, these data tend to strengthen our earlier generalization as to the preponderantly rural character of the area: if Baghdad is excluded, the bulk of even those inhabitants listed as "urban" in Table 8 are engaged in primary agricultural pursuits.

If we exclude the urban population of Baghdad as being almost wholly engaged in non-subsistence activities and supported by a national income that includes oil royalties, the gross population of the Diyala region has been shown to be 409,426. With relatively minor exceptions in towns like Baʿqūba, the conclusion has been drawn that virtually the whole of this population is directly engaged in and supported by irrigation agriculture. Further, it has been calculated that the irrigated area which supports this population is about 5,370 sq. kms. From this it would appear that about 1.4 hectares per person of cultivable area are sufficient in at least this part of the Mesopotamian plain not only for subsistence but also for a surplus drained off to the city. Of course, such a figure represents only a rough approximation; important variables like intensive orchard cultivation, conditions of land tenure, and the relation of crop yields to soil salinity already have been adumbrated in the previ-

TABLE 9

POPULATION, HOUSING, AND EMPLOYMENT IN BAʿQŪBA, 1957

Resident population	13,203
Total housing units	1,964
Average number of persons per house	6.7
Average number of rooms per house	2.9
Proportion of houses constructed of fired brick or stone (in per cent)	38
Number of private, commercial, service, and industrial establishments	463
Number of full-time employees in private establishments	774
Number of persons employed in administration and government services	620
Total non-agricultural employment	1,394
Proportion of population supported by non-agricultural employment (assuming five family members per wage earner)	6,970
	(52.7 per cent)

(Source: Government of Iraq, Principal Bureau of Statistics, 1958. Figures for governmental employment taken from 1947 census, Government of Iraq, Direc or General of Census, 1950. Data on permanent army staff not included.)

ous chapter. But at least it may serve as a first-order estimate for comparisons with the ancient past.

While direct comparisons with antiquity are not possible, there are relevant data from Girsu (part of ancient Lagash), deep in the southern part of the Mesopotamian plain. Including a 50 per cent allowance for lands not directly accounted for, it has been determined from the archives of the Bau temple there that its holdings were about 66 sq. kms. Grouped around the temple, and presumably dependent upon it for land, were some 1,200 persons and their families. If the 250 or more slaves are assumed generally not to have had families, and if the 100 or so fishermen and their families are considered to have been exploiting a supplementary resource (which never was significant in the lower Diyala region), the pursuit of agriculture on the temple's

23

land must have been supporting about 4,500 persons.[3] This is 1.46 hectares per person, approximately the same ratio which has been obtained for the contemporary scene.

It must be borne in mind that the figure of about 1.4 hectares per person includes not only cultivated but also fallow and uncultivable areas, and that the former necessarily is somewhat smaller than the combination of the latter two categories. Probably it is reasonable to assume, in other words, that substantially less than 0.7 hectares per person must actually be sowed to a crop during any given year for minimal subsistence needs under the conditions offered by the fallow system in southern Mesopotamia. Yet we have shown earlier that each "agricultural worker"—defined as including not only men but also women and boys—can cultivate at least three hectares in any given year with a technology that still has not been improved appreciably by the products of the industrial revolution. Assuming four such "workers" per family, a family of six still can produce three times its minimal needs in basic subsistence products. The margin between these figures serves not only to meet periodic crises but also to maintain members of the society who have been freed from a direct role in subsistence production. Whether extracted as a crop-share in lieu of land rent, as interest payments, as taxes, booty, or as voluntary contributions to a religious center, this or a similar margin of surplus has served to sustain the growth of all of the great urban civilizations of the Mesopotamian past.

This calculation of the average sustaining capacity of the irrigated area invites attention to the further problem of population density within the settlements themselves. Ideally, this might be done by comparing town and city areas as shown on the aerial photographs with their recorded populations in the 1957 census. But the available mosaics are too small in scale for this to be practical, and in any case the prevalence of dense palm groves around most towns makes a determination of their boundaries from the air very difficult.

For the most urbanized end of the settlement continuum, data are available from Baghdad on the basis of the 1947 census. The suburban districts which sprawl along wide new avenues radiating from Baghdad are the products of an important conjunction of social and economic forces having many counterparts elsewhere in the world, but none that are apparent in Iraq's earlier history. Hence it is more useful for present purposes to deal exclusively with the seventy quarters comprising the old city between its traditional north and south gates. Particularly along their eastern boundaries a few of these quarters extend beyond the former city walls and include minor areas of modern low-density occupance; in addition, the density of numerous other old quarters is reduced by the increasingly high incidence of non-residential buildings. But to a degree at least, these factors must be compensated for by the abnormal crowding brought about by the steady drift of rural population into the city and by the emphasis on multistory construction that has been engendered by the high cost of Baghdad real estate.

For the seventy old quarters of the city, population densities range from 34.7 to 330. At least on the basis of the 1947 census, the average density was 102.2 persons per hectare (253,485/2,479 hectares). The mean density, perhaps a more significant figure in view of the tendency of government buildings to cluster in certain restricted areas, was 137.2 persons per hectare.[4]

No comparable data on density of settlement are available for smaller towns or villages scattered over the Iraq countryside. Perhaps it may be excusable, therefore, to cite evidence from the neighboring province of Khuzestan, which at least reflects an ethnically mixed population including a large Arabic-speaking minority, and which occupies a geographical extension of the Mesopotamian plain providing essentially similar ecological conditions to those in the Diyala area.

An important recent epidemiological study of Khuzestan includes demographic data and maps of 55 villages.[5] Fully 42 of these are walled enclosures of a type which earlier must have predominated over much of the Mesopotamian countryside because of the superior security they afford against local raiding and theft of livestock. Within the entire group of villages, a survey disclosed 2,274 "housing units" containing 5,965 rooms. It must be noted, however, that slightly less than half of these rooms were found to be utilized for human habitation: 24 per cent were stables, 21.5 per cent storehouses, 4.4 per cent kitchens, and 0.3 per cent shops. Hence, although the mean number of rooms per housing unit was 2.6, only 1.3 were dwelling rooms. The mean number of persons per dwelling room was 3.9 (standard deviation 0.6), eloquent testimony to the depressed condition of the Near Eastern peasant cultivator, and mean family size accordingly about 5.1.[6] Calculating the areas of the villages and utilizing the demographic data supplied, it appears that the range in density for this entire group is from about 96 to 395 persons per hectare and that the mean is approximately 223 persons per hectare. Granting that the special conditions of tenant farming tend to minimize the land occupied by non-productive forms of land use, it is nonetheless interesting to note that there is absolutely no evidence of lesser population densities obtaining in small agricultural settlements than in urban centers in spite of the necessity of accommodating large numbers of livestock in small settlements. Generalizing from what is admittedly very limited evidence, we might reasonably conclude that densities of settlement on the contemporary Mesopotamian plain range from 125 to 250 persons per hectare, and that there is little or no evidence of a positive correlation between larger settlement size and greater density.

It remains to consider the processes by which the contemporary patterns of settlement have become dominant. If sedentary agriculture today is virtually universal in the area, if irrigation extends virtually to the natural limits imposed by the volume of water available in the Diyala River, and if a shift is in progress from extensive subsistence crops to intensive production for the market, nevertheless it must be stressed that all of these are relatively recent features. To a substantial degree, of course, they are related to the decline of nomadic, feuding tribal units as the pre-eminent forces on the rural scene, and this in turn to the imposition of political stability by a rising central power in Baghdad. But all of these developments are inextricably intertwined with one another rather than forming a simple cause-and-effect series, and in any case they probably have not advanced as a regular formation but only with many brakings, internal contradictions, and reversals. The more explicitly political details of the process, concentrated in Baghdad as the capital of an Ottoman pashalik, are not within the purview of the present study.[7] But here we must dwell at least briefly on the rural aspect of the military pacification and agricul-

tural growth which the lower Diyala region has undergone since the days of Ottoman suzerainty.

The concept of the rural economy, not merely as the helpless pawn in political struggles but as something of independent worth, something to be noticed and nourished by princes, dawns slowly in the historical record. Early European travelers' accounts, like most of those of the medieval Islamic geographers, pass quickly from city to city with little more than a word for the length and tribulations of the road between. Rarely before the mid-nineteenth century do even the most meticulous journals seek to portray a continuous countryside, including the empty steppe of the nomad, the roads and caravansaries of the merchants and pilgrims, and the waxing and waning enclaves of cultivation within a single interacting whole. And by then, of course, this widened awareness cannot be understood merely as an exercise in practical political economy but must be seen as part of the conscious stream of modern scholarship.

In the case of the Diyala region, perhaps our first useful modern reference dates from a German visitor in 1574. Traveling northward to Mosul from Baghdad, he recalls seeing well-cultivated fields, and then, rejoining the Tigris, "several towns, so that I expected to find nothing else but a land rich in grain, wine, honey. . . ." Farther still, however, the land became an empty, arid waste, so that his party was obliged to camp in the open without benefit of the shelter that even a village would afford. His itinerary is somewhat unclear,[8] but it would appear that the pattern of discontinuous enclaves of settlement and cultivation, so well attested in later times, was already present.[9]

Almost a half-century later, one of the most insightful of the early visitors, Pietro della Valle, left a record of having ridden northeast across the Diyala plains toward Persia along the old Khurāsān road.[10] Crossing the Diyala (which he was apparently the first to identify with the river Gyndes of Herodotus' account) at the village of Buhriz, he described the landscape with characteristic acumen:

> I found this countryside, through which we journied from Babylonia, very flat. With the exception, however, of several inhabited places which were very few in number, many parts of it were swampy and many others arid and desolate. But this land

25

is not desolate by nature, for while it is not culti-vated one sees many kinds of plants and wild roots growing well everywhere.

Although travelers continued, and indeed became more numerous (see chap. 8 for their descriptions of towns in the Diyala region), after these few, brief impressions of the countryside the record of similar impressions becomes silent for nearly two centuries.

In the late eighteenth and nineteenth centuries, such impressions reappear in quantity, now convey-ing a flood of descriptive information on the rural economy that previously had been thought to be beneath a visitor's (or possibly merely a cultivated reader's) notice. A French diplomat journeying from Delli ᶜAbbās to Baghdad, for example, pauses to notice the village of Dukhāla, a way-station eight hours north of his destination on the Tigris:

> The inhabitants of Doc-Khalir follow the Persian religion. The village is of little extent; it is sur-rounded by gardens almost all planted in date-palms. Cotton, sesame, rice, and all the ordinary cereals are grown in the irrigated fields of the vicin-ity.[11]

A decade later we hear again of Dukhāla, an English passenger on the river this time noticing its reputa-tion for agricultural productivity and referring to several neighboring towns as well:

> At half past three P.M., the village of Sindia, surrounded by groves of date trees; . . . At half past six a fine expanse of water, and a village called Suedia on the left bank, surrounded with planta-tions of date, apricot, fig and mulberry trees; at eight o'clock the village of Monsourg on the left bank, and at midnight the district of Dokhara, said to be the most productive in the pashalic of Bagdad.
>
> At five in the morning of the 13th, the village of Swadia on the right bank. From this village al-most the whole of the remainder of the way to Bag-dad, both banks of the Tigris are covered with en-gines and melon-gardens.[12]

Presumably the "engines" referred to here were the donkey- or mule-driven water wheels (*sharrads*) which still are found in the area, although they are no longer in use along the banks of the Tigris. Viewed from the river, of course, the cultivated fields and orchards crowding the banks would tend to domi-nate the scene. The more accurate view, of relatively limited enclaves of cultivation hugging the rivers and major canals and surrounded by wastes, came

from the interior. Except for an insignificant fringe immediately along the Tigris banks, all of the agri-cultural production described above was dependent upon the single artery of the Khālis canal. Claudius Rich has left us an appraisal of it in 1813, noting that it

> supplies sixty-two villages, most of which are now become mere nominal ones, with water for agri-culture; the Tigris itself being unfit for that pur-pose. The principal of these villages are Yenghijeh, twenty miles from Bagdad, on the banks of the Tigris, now almost abandoned on account of the great oppression under which the peasantry labour; Howeish, a village of a hundred houses, famous for its fruit gardens, three miles from Yenghijeh, and also on the Tigris; Dokhala, close to Howeish; Hophopa, about six miles from Howe-ish in the desert; Mansooria, six miles from Howe-ish on the Tigris; Saadia, three and a half miles from Mansooria, also on the Tigris; Sindia, Doltova, and several villages on the Diala.
>
> Near Mansooria some cotton is grown; the rest of the cultivation is barley, corn, and grass.[13]

Twenty-four years later the English topographer H. B. Lynch found approximately the same limits of cultivation. Passing beyond the gardens and date groves along the Tigris immediately north of Bagh-dad, he describes "an unbounded horizon for miles" across a barren plain to the village of Jadīda. Here begin the villages of the Khālis canal, he notes, "and vary the road for about sixteen miles farther north, to the village of Sindiya, the highest or last of the villages of Khālis." From thence to the ᶜAdheim River he records only patches of cultivation, carried on by "Abū Keshmeh" Arabs living in tents and reed huts and hence surely at least seminomadic.[14]

A roughly contemporary account of a journey to Kirkūk at first retraces this road, and then branches away toward Delli ᶜAbbās to the northeast:

> The part of the plain which we passed in the morning, was under good cultivation, the ground being well watered by numerous canals, which, to our great discomfort, were destitute of bridges. One of these canals, called Khalis, might have been entitled to the name of a river, if it had not been running out of a stream, instead of flowing into it. . . . Other parts of the plain were entirely barren, or covered with a dry brush-wood, which furnishes fuel to the villages. At different points over the plain we could descry the sites of numer-ous villages, by the clusters of date-trees which surrounded them; and we saw here and there, a

26

solitary *Iman* ... Delli Abbas itself is a lonely khan in the midst of the desert.[15]

A particularly well-informed and full account of conditions in the southern part of the region just prior to the middle of the nineteenth century is provided by the memoirs of Commander J. F. Jones, I.N. He describes permanent settlement as having been altogether lacking along the left bank of the Tigris from the mouth of the Diyala all the way to Kūt, and at the time of his journey into the interior of the region in 1848 even its nomadic occupants, the Shammar Toqah, had been drawn to the environs of Baghdad by a dispute over repressive rates of taxation. Hence, upon leaving Kūt, he records traversing one hundred miles of territory without sight of another human being outside of his own party.[16] He continues:

> As we approach the Diyaleh river traces of the fixed abode of man are becoming visible in a partial cultivation, but so impoverished is this once prolific province that the agricultural district does not extend ten miles south of the capital. The insecurity of property is evident in the circumscribed extent of the fields beyond the southern bank of the Diyaleh river. These, however, exhibit goodly crops of wheat and barley, and tend at least to show the richness of the soil and the capabilities of the province as a granary alone. The vestiges of the ancient canals to the east and north-east of Ctesiphon tell a tale of former fertility that contrasts sadly with the meagre patches that are observable, few and far between, in its present neighbourhood, and the wire-drawn irrigants of the modern race,—that an infant can step across,—compared with the stupendous conduits of antiquity, heighten the picture of decay before us.[17]

He records similar impressions not only for the empty wilderness east and southeast of the lower Diyala but also for the desert plain lying to the north of Baghdad, between the Tigris and Diyala rivers. Travel in both cases was by armed caravan only, with overnight halts at enclosures like Khān Banī-Saʿad to which water not infrequently had to be carried by the traveling party itself.[18]

With the increasingly numerous itineraries of later decades in the nineteenth century we learn of elements of change beginning to be introduced into this pattern, very slowly at first and then with gathering speed. As late as 1875 the sequence and description of towns along the road to Delli ʿAbbās remained virtually unchanged, with fields and gardens clustering around scattered villages or hugging the banks of the rivers, and apparently with great empty tracts remaining between the Tigris and the Diyala. Delli ʿAbbās, for all its position as a caravansary on a great pilgrim route, still was "a very unpretending place, built of mud and sun-dried brick, and with a khan of the most miserable kind."[19] Five years earlier, the Černik Expedition had recorded the entire population of the lands between the Diyala and the Tigris as only 21,600, all members of the Jerboah Arab tribe.[20] But the Černik Expedition also had noted the first installation of a new and significant type of agricultural enterprise, a capitalized estate utilizing two steam-driven pumps to irrigate lands along the lower Diyala near its confluence with the Tigris.[21] And at about the same time the town of ʿAzīzīya appears as a new Turkish administrative subdistrict governed by a Turkish *kaimakam*.[22] We have already seen the testimony of Felix Jones that permanent settlement was altogether lacking in this region less than thirty years earlier.

By the years immediately preceding World War I, this picture had been modified further still. Along the Tigris below Baghdad, not merely one but a number of small permanent towns had come into existence that were connected with telegraph lines, sometimes staffed with a few Turkish officials, and occasionally garrisoned with contingents of *Zaptié* (civil police). In part, these towns are to be explained as fueling stations of the new river-steamer trade, serving as shipping points for wild licorice and trading entrepôts for the surrounding tribesmen, but unsupported by a firm basis in agriculture. Of ʿAzīzīya, for example, it was said in 1916 that "there is no cultivation in the immediate neighbourhood owing to the lack of irrigation, and the supplies of the town are drawn from the neighbouring Shammar Toqah tribe."[23] On the other hand, some cultivated land was beginning to appear along the riverbanks,[24] and sporadic cultivation even is mentioned in interior depressions east of the lower Diyala.[25] By this time, evidence of an expansion in the zone of sedentary cultivation is found in the existence of a narrow strip of *sharrad* (animal-operated, water-hoist) irrigation of both winter and summer crops upstream from Baghdad along both banks of the Tigris to beyond the mouth of the ʿAdheim River[26] and downstream as

27

far as Salmān Pāk.[27] Although still relatively rare, occasional references are made in the itineraries of this period to canals supplied with irrigation pumps, harbingers of what was increasingly to dominate the scene along the Tigris. After this modest beginning, the availability of cheap fuel and empty, well-drained, high-lying land along the rivers encouraged the very rapid growth of this mode of agriculture during the 1920's and 1930's with no further government stimulation than the extension of tax-remission privileges.[28] At present, as has been noted earlier, pump-fed canals account for more than two-fifths (44.9 per cent) of all irrigated land in the region.

Within the network of gravity-flow canals stemming from the foot of the Jebel Hamrīn gorge a contemporaneous, if less rapid, expansion was taking place. The limits of cultivation dependent on these canals can be approximately reconstructed as they must have been around 1872 and clearly had widened by the end of World War I to a position intermediate between their relatively stable nineteenth-century limits and where they are at present (Fig. 1). The actual process by which the canals themselves were extended is not clear. Since government interest after World War I seems to have centered first on installation and control of canal headworks and on replacement (in 1927–28) of the traditional, annually renewed earth and brushwood weir across the Diyala just below the Jebel Hamrīn by a permanent structure,[29] it seems likely that most of the lengthening of canal tails was carried on in small accretions by individual landowners. In any case, control over water distribution and responsibility for major canal maintenance was established only gradually. Well before this time, Baʿqūba had emerged as the major town for the large and growing enclave of irrigation agriculture that these canals served. Its population in 1910 was estimated at 4,000–5,000, and it was connected by telegraph and indifferent roads (frequently equipped with culverts to facilitate the movement of Persian pilgrims) not only with Baghdad but also with smaller towns of the interior.[30] Still, as late as 1907 Herzfeld had noted that the Baʿqūba dates "are neither highly valued nor exported, although they constitute an important, next to bread the most important, source of subsistence for the population."[31] The development of Baʿqūba as a major, specialized producer of dates and fruit for

the Baghdad market was a future trend which could not then be envisioned.

It is also worth noting that the main group of nomadic tribesmen in the area, the Shammar Toqah, were themselves settling down and becoming cultivators during and after this period. In contrast with their behavior in Jones's time, by 1908 it could be said of them that they "grow wheat, barley, maize, and sesame, and breed cattle and camels. They live mainly in tents and sometimes wander in spring."[32] This transition also is illustrated by their changing geographical distribution. At the end of World War I they were concentrated in the new cultivated zone along the left bank of the Tigris from Salmān Pāk to Kūt, and in a smaller cluster, well to the north across the Nahrawān wilderness, on the tails of the Mahrūt canal.[33] In more recent years this process has proceeded even further. Nomadic herdsmen have disappeared altogether from the region, largely because the spread of cultivation has barred access to summer forage and water for their herds along the major watercourses. Flocks today are entirely in the hands of sedentary cultivators, and forage crops and supplementary feeding on stubble, grain, and young shoots of barley have begun to compete with open grazing as the major source for their maintenance. Although a scattering of tents still may be seen in the spring on the empty lands of the Nahrawān district, elsewhere their use as dwellings has been given up almost entirely. Moreover, a trend toward "detribalization" is now well advanced. Such reciprocal obligations of the sheikhs to their followers as the maintenance of a *madhīf* (guest house) are rarely if ever observed, in contrast with conditions on the middle and lower Euphrates, and the descendants of the old tribal leaders increasingly have assumed the aspect (prior, at least, to the Revolution of July, 1958) of absentee landowners dealing through local agents with a largely landless peasantry. In the eyes of many peasant farmers the old bonds of tribal solidarity undoubtedly continue to dominate, but cases are becoming common wherein groups of related families periodically move from one landowner's domain to another in an effort to improve their conditions of tenure.

A final demographic trend may be tentatively suggested, if by no means conclusively demonstrated, from the available data on the expansion of settle-

28

ment during the past century or so. The accounts of nineteenth- and early twentieth-century travelers are entirely silent on the possible existence of a dispersed rural population living in small hamlets, such as those in which the bulk of the population resides today. While to a degree this may reflect the preoccupation of early travelers with larger settlements, the absence of any reference to outlying groups of houses even in fairly detailed military itineraries seems to imply, at least in part, a recent increase in the dispersion of the sedentary rural population. If so, it may have been related to the advent of peaceful conditions in the countryside during the period since World War I, which removed one of the important inducements for agriculturalists to cluster together in the protection of a large village or town. But if so, the constantly recurring contrast between the urban part of the plain in the south and the villages of the north still awaits a convincing historical or ecological explanation.

Briefly to recapitulate these findings, it seems fairly clear that a number of interrelated trends have contributed to the emergence of the present agricultural regime during the past century or so. Population, and with it the extent of the irrigation zone, have expanded very substantially. The extension of irrigation itself has been an increasingly artificial process, involving the excavation of new canal tails along the lines of old levees, the installation of weirs and canal

regulators, and the widespread introduction of diesel pumps. Pastoral, nomadic tribesmen have dwindled and finally disappeared, tending to join the ranks of sedentary cultivators as the latter became more numerous and strong enough to dominate access both to permanent waterways and to the superior pasturage which adjoined them. With the declining power of the tribes, the authority of the central government has virtually ceased to be questioned locally. Its authority is manifest not only in a rapidly growing communications net that radiates from the capital, but also in increasing control over social and economic activities on the local scene like water distribution, conditions of land tenure, education, and the administration of justice. The rise of authority is paralleled, furthermore, by a centripetal tendency for opinion-making and decision-forming to be localized in Baghdad, and by the extraordinary growth of Baghdad as a cosmopolitan center.

But while all of these developments combine to transform many features of the countryside, nonetheless it is still possible to say for the most part that cultivation remains primitive in technique, extensive rather than intensive in its approach to land use, and predominantly oriented toward production for subsistence rather than for a market. Throughout the Diyala area the hamlet and the village, rather than the town or city, remain the characteristic units of settlement.

PART 2

THE CHANGING PATTERNS OF ANCIENT OCCUPANCE

4

THE FORMATION OF WALLED TOWNS (4000-2100 B.C.)

THE PREVIOUS chapters have attempted to summarize contemporary patterns of land use and settlement on the Diyala plains, both as those patterns interact with a complex (and not entirely stable) natural milieu and also as they change more rapidly in response to shifting historical forces which for the most part originate outside the area. In many respects the data have been found inadequate even for this task. Yet the major objective of this study is to offer such an account covering a six-thousand-year period. It will be apparent at once that at best we can hope to trace through time the emergence of an abridged and highly tentative version of the patterns that have been encountered on the present scene.

The primary source of information for this undertaking are the findings of an intensive (but not exhaustive) archaeological surface reconnaissance of the Diyala region which was initiated in 1937 and carried to completion in 1957–58. An account of the methods and assumptions of the survey, while perhaps useful for the specialist, is not germane to the undertaking itself and hence has been left to an appendix (Appendix A). The main substance of the findings is summarized in a sequence of maps (Figs. 2–6) which records the major changes in settlement patterns through a succession of five major phases divided into fifteen periods of somewhat irregular length. In a sense, this and the following four chapters may be regarded as an extended commentary upon the maps, intended to explain some of their doubtful features

and to draw conclusions about changing modes of land use which otherwise may not be readily apparent. Perhaps more important, these chapters seek to interpret the evolving patterns of irrigation agriculture and urbanization to be deduced from the results of the survey in the light of the historical sources.

This account begins with the earliest agricultural occupation of the Diyala region that is presently known, probably at around 4000 B.C. But before describing the development of patterns of settled life thenceforth, it may be noted that by that date the evolution of agriculture as a mode of subsistence had continued for a time at least two-thirds as long as has elapsed since. And while these beginnings of Near Eastern agriculture remain poorly understood, at least it is clear, not merely that they preceded the widespread, permanent settlement of the Diyala plains, but that they served as indispensable preconditions for it.

In the eighth millennium B.C. or even earlier, there is the first evidence of incipient herdsmen and agriculturalists beginning an unprecedented process of experimentation with, and modification of, some specific features of the environmental zones they occupied. In a variety of distinctive local circumstances, faced with shifting combinations of potential domesticates and other natural limitations or stimuli, a new, creative, and yet broadly similar response emerged everywhere. Its essence was the increasingly

33

sophisticated and intensive exploitation of the food resources of a particular region, probably with rapid improvements in subsistence technology (e.g., ground stone implements for husking and pulverizing vegetal foods, employment of microliths in complex composite tools, etc.) as a major contributing feature.

With agriculture came the possibility of predictable harvests and the storage of food supplies. Population growth and increasing sedentism, linked consequences of these significant new conditions, are reflected in the growth and coalescence of the earlier enclaves of experimentation, and in the formation of the first of those innumerable nucleated villages whose mounded ruins dot the Near Eastern countryside. Surely the transition from food-gathering to food production is one of the handful of crucial transformations that set off the whole human career, and regionally distinctive examples of it are to be found not far distant from the lower Diyala plains. With research on the problem still in a highly selective, exploratory phase, ancient settlements whose occupations fell in this transitional period already have been described in the rolling, dissected Assyrian piedmont to the north,[1] eastward into the Kurdish intermontane valleys leading in serried steps up the flanks of the Iranian plateau,[2] and even to the southeast, on the margins of the Mesopotamian plain itself.[3] But at least at present there is no evidence that any of the steps in the initial transition were represented in the Diyala region. In that sense, the beginnings of agriculture can be thus dismissed as antecedent to the present study.[4]

1. THE ᶜUBAID PERIOD

At present, human occupation of the Diyala region only comes into focus in the ᶜUbaid period, at a time which can be ascribed to around the beginning of the fourth millennium B.C. Settlements of the periods intervening between the introduction of ceramics in the early seventh millennium B.C. and the early fourth millennium are found not far outside the region to the north and west,[5] but the characteristic pottery of these periods never has been observed in either excavated or surface collections from the alluvium. This discontinuity, coinciding with the geological boundary between the alluvium and the Miocene land surface of Upper Mesopotamia and with the approximately similar line of demarcation between contemporary dry and irrigation agriculture, suggests the coincidence of a cultural and an environmental barrier. The immediate antecedents of the earliest known occupation of the Diyala plains, it would appear, lay not with the original hearth of village farming in the uplands but with later, more rapidly developing townsmen who had worked out techniques of irrigation in the heart of the southern alluvium.[6]

The ᶜUbaid period is not well represented in the lower Diyala region, either in comparison with most later occupations of the same area or with the contemporary occupation of the central portion of the lower Mesopotamian plain that adjoins the Diyala basin to the south. In all, only twenty-two sites provide evidence of ᶜUbaid remains, consisting in almost half of these cases of no more than one or two sherds obtained in much larger and later surface collections. Not a single example was found anywhere on the Diyala plain below the Jebel Hamrīn of a site where the ᶜUbaid occupation appeared to have been terminal, as occurs in the adjoining region of Akkad to the south at Ras al-ᶜAmiyah,[7] Tell ᶜUqair,[8] and elsewhere. In no case were remains representative of the ᶜUbaid period so numerous and widely distributed on the surface of a later site as to suggest an extensive ᶜUbaid settlement. Moreover, while ᶜUbaid sherds occur at Tell Asmar, Tell Agrab, and Khafājah in stratigraphic context,[9] all were in secondary association with later materials rather than a primary ᶜUbaid deposit. Since virgin soil was found directly beneath Protoliterate remains in all exposures at these sites, it appears that the bulk of their growth in size and population occurred only subsequent to the ᶜUbaid period. In short, while the present limited findings are subject to modification in detail with future survey and excavation, it seems clear that the ᶜUbaid occupation of the region consisted of only a small number of village settlements. Three millenniums or more after the beginnings of village agriculture in neighboring areas to the north and east, there is still no sign here of the presence of that next major impulse which soon was to lead rapidly toward urbanization.

It will be observed in the accompanying map (Fig. 2) that the villages of the period, although small in number, were not widely or uniformly distributed. With the exception of Khafājah (421), all of the sites lie at a considerable distance east of the present course of the lower Diyala. With one exception, to be

34

mentioned presently, the ʿUbaid sites are south of 33°30′ N. Lat., at a distance of more than 60 kms. from the only present source of gravity-flow canal irrigation, the Jebel Hamrīn outlet of the Diyala River. Considered without reference to subsequent developments, the distribution of these sites cannot explain the means by which irrigation was accomplished under the circumstances. All the same, it is possible to identify several short linear enclaves of settlements running toward the present western edge of the great north-south band of seasonal swamp called the Haur es-Subaicha.

The northernmost of these lines consists of Abū Yiwālik (397) and possibly an adjoining site (396). A short distance to the southwest is another line, consisting of Abū Zambīl (384), Abū Rāsain (530), and three smaller sites (531, 534, 535). Paralleling these lines farther to the west as a longer one that seems to commence with Tell Asmar (244) and pass southeast through Tell Agrab (515) to a third settlement (634). In addition, a group of sites in the southeast corner of the region form another linear pattern that centers on Abū Dibis (842) and includes two other settlements (818, 851). Finally, there is a suggestion of a line that commences at Khafājah (421) and terminates at Abū Jāwan (685), with a third possible site (577) between these two important settlements of later periods. The remaining four sites for which definite evidence of a beginning in the ʿUbaid period has been obtained (12, Tell Dhibaʿi [268], 344, Abū Kubeir [517], 648, Khashim Wāwi [628]) do not seem directly related to the foregoing linear patterns or to each other, although all but the first of them fall in the same approximate area.

This arrangement of sites only becomes intelligible when considered as a forerunner of the more extensive and better documented pattern of early watercourses which had emerged by the end of the Early Dynastic period. In broadest outline, this latter pattern is that of an anastomosing network of watercourses, capable of depositing alluvial materials far more widely over the floodplain of the Diyala than the single entrenched channel of the present river. It will be observed that no branch of the suggested proto-Diyala of that period seems to have followed the river's present lower course. Instead, the predecessor of this course lay somewhat farther to the west and joined the Tigris through a complex series of mouths. In

fact, one branch bifurcated from the main stream at about 33°30′ N. Lat. and flowed southeast for 110 kms. before finding its way into the Tigris, constituting a tributary of the "Yazoo" type, described earlier as a normal feature of stream junctions in a floodplain. To be sure, several lengthy segments of watercourses in the network are reconstructed in Figure 2 without evidence for contemporary occupation along their banks, but the suggested reconstruction is supported by the positions of towns and villages of later periods. Just as the enclaves of settlement expanded and in some cases coalesced by the end of the Early Dynastic period, so it would appear that in later times these enclaves apparently expanded still farther.

Returning to the ʿUbaid period, we may conclude that most of the small village settlements characteristic of that occupation lay relatively close to a natural network of watercourses that largely antedated man's appearance as a cultivator, not only because the over-all pattern of settlement was so sparse and primitive but also because it more closely defines a natural pattern of stream channels in a floodplain than does a canal distribution system. Of course, minor modifications of the basic stream patterns must have been attempted almost from the beginning. For example, some of the short lines of settlement referred to above may have followed natural overflow channels leading into the back-swamp, but other such channels may have been constructed in order to take advantage of the especially favorable conditions for primitive cultivators which the edges of the swamp afforded: the possibility of small-scale basin irrigation in the wake of receding swamp waters, the accessibility of good forage for animals, and perhaps also the availability of woody vegetation and other swamp products. The gradual (but not necessarily continuous) expansion that most of the enclaves of settlement underwent supports the supposition that modifications in the network of watercourses and drainage channels were introduced by the early inhabitants. Probably beginning in those areas most immediately favorable to a complex of subsistence pursuits that included irrigation agriculture, settlements must have been forced to spread gradually into adjoining zones which needed either preliminary drainage or perhaps a somewhat longer and more complex system of canals in order to be irrigated

35

successfully. If this reconstruction is correct, a part of the explanation for the restricted distribution of ᶜUbaid sites in the Diyala region is that cultivators of that period located their villages within a narrow range of local conditions (such as small to moderate differences between stream and bank elevations) which occurred only within a restricted geographical area.

An additional explanation of the pattern of distribution derives from the greater frequency of ᶜUbaid remains in the central part of the Mesopotamian plain than in the Diyala region,[10] and from the existence of presently known pre-ᶜUbaid levels only in the extreme south (Hajī Mohammed and Eridu).[11] Both of these observations suggest that the southern part of the Diyala basin was more heavily settled because it was from still farther south, in the heart of ancient Sumer, that the earliest agricultural inhabitants came. Some support for this interpretation derives from the aforementioned absence of ceramics with northern affinities within the entire Diyala region. In the preponderance of baked clay sickles and greenish overfired wares, the known ᶜUbaid pottery in the area looks southward, while a single ᶜUbaid site (12) visited in the survey—nearby but on the northern slope of the Jebel Hamrīn—lacks these features and is to be associated with the northern ᶜUbaid cultural province that depended on rainfall farming.

Briefly to summarize, the ᶜUbaid occupation apparently consisted of small settlements which tended to cluster loosely in linear enclaves in the southern part of the lower Diyala basin. No direct estimates of population are possible, either for the region as a whole or for any of its component villages, save that it must have been relatively much smaller than in most later periods. In some cases the settlements are so closely grouped (e.g., 384, 530, 531, 534, and 535 form a line less than nine kms. in length) that some collaboration on irrigation tasks and even a degree of political integration may be implied. More frequently, however, the villages were ten to twenty kms. apart, a separation which, in view of their apparently small size, does not support the hypothesis that close political or economic bonds existed between them.

It seems clear that the ᶜUbaid villages trace out an essentially natural pattern of watercourses, although modifying this in detail as time went on. The restricted part of the basin they occupy probably is to be explained as a result of selection by these earliest sedentary cultivators of the zones where stream regimen and soil conditions were optimal for simple irrigation through short breaches in levee banks, and where nearby swamps offered important additional subsistence advantages. There is some suggestion, based on limited distributional evidence, that the ᶜUbaid farmers entered from, or at least had their primary affiliations with, areas farther south in the Tigris-Euphrates floodplain. In most cases the ᶜUbaid village sites seem to have continued into later periods (although stratigraphic proof of this so far is lacking), and it is particularly noteworthy that ᶜUbaid remains underlie most or all of the larger Early Dynastic towns.

2. THE WARKA AND PROTOLITERATE PERIODS

Although better represented than the ᶜUbaid period, the Warka and Protoliterate periods which follow it do not play a conspicuous quantitative part in the surface collections of the survey. Probably this reflects a limitation in the "index fossil" approach used throughout, in that the ceramics of those periods contained little that was distinctively different from those of the Early Dynastic period and so could not easily be recognized. Some types, like the widely noted Warka "red" and "gray" wares, seem to be virtually absent. Others, such as beveled-rim bowls and clay nails for wall mosaics, occur fairly frequently in collections from a few of the larger sites but are lacking elsewhere. Another kind of obstacle is presented by jar profiles, in that profiles characteristic of this phase seldom can be identified from small surface sherds. In the end, the identification of remains of the Protoliterate and Warka periods rests primarily on a variety of dish of somewhat doubtful attribution (cf. Appendix B).

Because of these problems, and because the occupational levels of these periods were covered in every case with extensive later debris, no more can be said about the size of Warka and Protoliterate settlements on the basis of the survey's findings than could be said of the ᶜUbaid period. However, it has been found in soundings at several of the large Early Dynastic town sites that the underlying Protoliterate remains

36

rest directly on virgin soil. Although still inconclusive, this suggests "that during the Protoliterate period there occurred a considerable increase of the population and that most of the urban centers became more densely populated."[12] And to a degree at least, this apparent increase in the size of individual towns seems to have been paralleled by an increasing number of outlying village settlements also.

Perhaps the most important expansion took place in the western part of the region, along the ancient watercourse flowing between the present beds of the Tigris and Diyala rivers. It will be recalled that the ᶜUbaid occupation here consisted of only three widely-scattered sites located along one channel within a total distance of thirty-five kms. above its apparent confluence with the Tigris. In the Warka and Protoliterate periods settlement was extended thirty kms. farther upstream, commencing with Tell al-Halfayah (169) and including two other sites (214, 229) also. Below Khafājah a small and perhaps questionable ᶜUbaid site (577) seems not to have continued in use, but both Khafājah (421) and the site apparently adjoining the outlet of this particular channel at Abū Jāwan (685) remained in occupation and probably expanded. Moreover, eight new settlements were founded along this reach during the interval (433, 441, 458, 463, 465, 576, 579, 599), marking a clear and substantial increase in the density of occupance. Branching off from the lower part of this watercourse, two new channels connecting with the Tigris are suggested by four additional sites (556, 558, 563, and 568), and the three apparent outlets for the Diyala now documented along the Tigris combine to suggest a course for the latter river somewhat to the north of its present position.

Above Khafājah accompanying settlements make it possible for the first time to approximate the upper course of a long "Yazoo tributary" which branched off from the Diyala and flowed far to the southeast before finding its way into the Tigris. Perhaps bifurcating from the Diyala near a previously mentioned site (214), it can be traced for thirty kms. to the southeast on the basis of three further mounds (220–22, 446, 455) which must have adjoined it within this distance. On the other hand, a long intervening stretch below the last of these remains undocumented before this stream can be detected again immediately above its outlet, and in this stretch a

site with a possible ᶜUbaid occupation (Khashim Wāwi [628]) may even have been abandoned. The three ᶜUbaid sites (818, 842, 851) which marked the confluence of this watercourse with the Tigris seem to have continued to be inhabited, but there is no evidence of the founding of new settlements between them or upstream from them during the immediately following periods.

The picture of relative stability in the number of settlements that holds in the southeastern part of the region also applies farther north to the considerable group of earlier settlements east and southeast of Tell Asmar. Here we have previously identified fourteen sites as having been occupied during the ᶜUbaid period. Only three newly founded villages (354, 364, 380) can be shown to have originated during the Warka and Protoliterate periods, none of them suggesting substantial additions to the network of watercourses previously in use. And eight of the fourteen ᶜUbaid sites did not provide specimens datable to these subsequent periods. Some of these ᶜUbaid sites certainly must have continued in occupation, but four of the eight cluster along a line below Abū Zambīl (530, 531, 534, 535) and thus suggest that at least this immediate area temporarily ceased to be occupied or cultivated.

Elsewhere, the modest beginnings of a northward spread of settlement can be detected. Two new villages were founded in the little valley north of the Jebel Hamrīn (Aq Tepe [7], 14), where a small ᶜUbaid site previously was abandoned. Eighteen kms. southwest of the Jebel Hamrīn outlet appeared another small, isolated settlement (18). Farther south, but similarly isolated, lay two other new little enclaves (77 and 160, 162).

In short, according to the evidence obtained in the survey, the number of occupied sites increased from 22 to 43 during the Warka and Protoliterate periods, although the pattern of expansion was quite irregular and perhaps even included some local abandonment. To be sure, if remains of these periods were easier to recognize, an additional number of new settlements undoubtedly would be found beneath the later debris of Early Dynastic towns. This substantial numerical increase was mainly a consequence of the appearance of new settlements in the western part of the region. There the occupied area was extended and the average distance between sites along the lower Diyala shrank to about five kms., certainly implying greater social and economic contact and perhaps a degree of political unity between them.

Two new Diyala outlets on the Tigris in that region are another important innovation, perhaps reflecting the capacity of nearby cultivators to open channels six to eight kms. in length. Judging from the durability of these channels through many later periods, however, they might also have been natural escapes cut by the Diyala in winter flood, of which the Warka and Protoliterate period settlers merely took advantage. In any case, fairly dense clusters of settlement already had appeared in the ᶜUbaid period (albeit on a smaller scale), so that some of the watercourses assumed to have served as axes of settlement at that time were possibly also partly artificial in origin.

Thus in a sense the changes in settlement distribution that were introduced by the Warka and Protoliterate periods were a matter of degree and not of kind. The enclaves established earlier were consolidated and extended, and new ones appeared farther to the north. The bulk of the growth in cultivated areas occurred in a region of little importance previously, although archaeological soundings suggest that some of the larger settlements grew rapidly in size even where they cannot be identified as the hub of an expanding network of outlying villages. In the light of present evidence we can only conclude that the crucial social and cultural changes leading to the subsequent emergence of fortified Early Dynastic towns went on primarily within the town centers themselves. At any rate, they find little apparent reflection in the disposition of the remaining, smaller settlements over the countryside.

3. THE EARLY DYNASTIC PERIOD

In comparison with all preceding (and some subsequent) periods, the Early Dynastic period is well understood and sharply defined. Its town architecture, both public and private, has been extensively sampled at Tell Asmar, Tell Agrab, and Khafājah.[13] An unprecedented bulk of its ceramics, derived from carefully excavated stratigraphical contexts, have been studied and published.[14] Remains of the Early Dynastic period are sufficiently distinctive so that many types stand out clearly in surface collections, making possible the easy identification of Early

Dynastic occupational levels even where there is a thick overburden of later debris. Finally, on more than one-fifth of the 97 observed sites with apparent Early Dynastic levels, these levels either were terminal or constituted the most extensive occupation. With confirmation from this source of the same range of village and town sizes that is suggested by later settlements, it is possible to compose provisional estimates not merely of the size of individual settlements but also (although admittedly with much greater uncertainty) of the gross population and cultivated area (see Appendix A).

Both in number and size of settlements the Early Dynastic period seems to have witnessed a substantial growth over preceding periods, yet its occupation for the most part remained within the area which had been settled earlier. The enclaves of settlement which first had appeared in Protoliterate times in the northern part of the region now underwent a considerable expansion (24 settlements north of 33°30′ N. Lat., as compared with 6 in Protoliterate times), but there was little change in the outlines of the main zones of settlement farther south. Moreover, essentially the same pattern of watercourses is traced out by Early Dynastic sites as had been known earlier, although a possible new Diyala outlet to the Tigris (at 590) and a new lower branch of the Tell Asmar stream (connecting 253, 357, 359) may reflect some combination of human and natural agencies leading to changes in detail. Hence it is sufficient to present some salient characteristics of Early Dynastic sites in tabular form (Table 10) without describing their disposition along watercourses.

A consideration of the data in Table 10 in light of the geographical distribution of Early Dynastic sites (see Fig. 2) suggests a number of generalizations as to prevailing modes of settlement. In the first place, it is clear that by the Early Dynastic period—if not earlier—we are dealing with a hierarchy of towns and villages that differed greatly from one another in size, internal complexity, and political influence. At one end of the scale were fairly large towns, already known from excavations at three sites: Tell Asmar, Tell Agrab, and Khafājah. Although for the most part less imposing in their modern aspect than these three, seven other sites in the foregoing table fall into the same range of surface areas that these sites define: Abū Rāsain (109), Tell Dhibaᶜi (264–67), Abū Zambīl

38

(384), Tulūl Abū Yiwālik (397), Tell Abū Jāwan (685), Tell Abū Dibis (842), and a large ruin nearly at plain level and hence unnamed (851).[15]

Fortification walls apparently encircled the three excavated sites and were identified provisionally from surface indications at two of the others as well (109, 842); hence it is not unlikely that circumvallation was generally associated with centers of this size and importance. While in a narrow sense purely defensive in function, town walls also provided the only possible basis for political independence or expanding territorial claims. In short, the larger towns probably may be identified with the primary political rivalries of the period within the region, and with the major constituent forces in coalitions directed against other regions under the unstable hegemony of one or another of its component towns.

The character of the leadership exercised by the larger towns is an historical problem whose details lie beyond the scope of this study.[16] It is worth noting, however, that excavations in the region to date have exposed numerous temples belonging to the Early Dynastic period[17] but no structures which might be described as palaces until perhaps the very end of that period. Elsewhere in southern Mesopotamia monumental palaces have been excavated at Kish[18] and Eridu,[19] belonging to the early Early Dynastic III and the late Early Dynastic II periods, respectively. Moreover, smaller structures which may still imply "palace"-like functions are known at Fara for the Early Dynastic III period.[20] In the lower Diyala basin, the Northern "Palace" (actually a "Woman's House," probably a textile workshop) at Tell Asmar possibly is to be attributed to pre-Sargonid Akkadian conquerors, and at any event was constructed only at the very end of the Early Dynastic (i.e., Protoimperial) period.[21] On this obviously provisional basis, it seems that the continuous exercise of secular authority was somewhat slower to make its appearance in the Diyala region than in the more urbanized regions of Sumer and Akkad to the south. But whatever the forms of leadership they exercised, the dominant hierarchies of temple compounds like the Temple Oval at Khafājah—which is itself fortified—certainly are not inconsistent with the assumption of periodically hostile relations between at least the major towns.

The distribution of the larger towns is of some interest. Five of them are clustered in the area immediately east and southeast of Tell Asmar (244, 264–67, 384, 397, 515), together with five smaller towns (253, 355, 359, 366, 520) and thirty-one still smaller settlements which perhaps may be described as villages. Together these sites comprise a built-up area of perhaps 133 hectares out of a total of 384 hectares for the region as a whole below the Jebel Hamrīn. The built-up area along the stream roughly

TABLE 10

EARLY DYNASTIC SITES IN THE LOWER DIYALA REGION

1. Early Dynastic sites that probably were inhabited prior to that period:*
   7 (trace), 14 (tr.), 18 (tr.), 77, 160, 162, 169, 214, 221, 229, 244, 267, 344 (tr.), 354 (tr.), 364, 384, 396 (tr.), 397, 421, 433, 441, 446, 458, 463, 465, 515, 517, 530, 531, 534, 556, 558 (tr.), 563, 568, 576, 579, 599, 634, 648, 685, 818, 842, 851.

2. Early Dynastic towns classified by size:
   Large towns (more than 10 hectares in area):
   109 (Abū Rāsain, 13.5 ha.†), 244 (Tell Asmar), 264–67 (Tell Dhibaʿi, 10.6 ha.‡), 384 (Abū Zambīl), 397 (Tulūl Abū Yiwālik), 421 (Khafājah), 515 (Tell Agrab, 10.8 ha.), 685 (Tell Abū Jāwan), 842 (Tell Abū Dibis), 851.
   Small towns (4–10 hectares in area):
   7 (Aq Tepe), 16 (Tell Ousha?), 24 (Tell Yahūdī), 71 (Tell al-Dhahab), 113 (Abū Salabikh, 6.2 ha.), 162 (Tell Abū Tibbin), 169 Tell al-Halfayah), 229 (Tell Halāwa), 253, 355 (Tulūl Shilbiyāt), 359 (Abū Khusan saghīr, 4.0 ha.), 366 (Tell Sebʿe), 446 (Abū Obayya), 462, 520 (6.0 ha.), 558 (Tell Rishād), 568, 590 (Tulūl Mujailiʿ), 810 (Tell al-Lami).
   Villages (less than 4 hectares in area):
   9, 14, 18, 31, 45 (?), 46 (?), 56, 77, 80 (?), 102, 105, 122, 158, 160, 176, 192 (?), 214, 221, 225, 259, 261, 262, 270, 276, 278, 297, 298, 341, 342 (?), 344, 345 (?), 350, 354, 357, 362, 364, 368 (?), 370, 372, 381, 396, 419, 429, 433, 441, 450, 458, 463, 465, 489, 517, 521 (?), 530, 531, 534, 556, 563, 576, 579, 581, 599, 633, 634, 637, 648, 818, 835.
   In Total: 96 sites, aggregating approximately 384 hectares of settlement. This includes 10 large towns occupying perhaps 181 hectares, 19 small towns occupying 116 hectares, and 67 villages occupying 87 hectares.§ Approximately 77 per cent of known settlement was in towns.

3. Early Dynastic sites subsequently abandoned or with only traces of an Akkadian occupation:‖
   Large towns:
   109 (Abū Rāsain), 264–67 (Tell Dhibaʿi), 515 (Tell Agrab).
   Small towns:
   113, 359, 520.
   Villages:
   9, 45, 46, 80, 102, 105, 176, 192, 262, 270, 276, 278, 341, 342, 345, 362, 368, 396, 429, 517, 521, 534, 633, 634, 637.
   In Total: 31 sites, approximately 78.4 hectares of settlement.

* "Trace" or "tr." denotes occurrence of a single earlier sherd in surface collections. The problems of distinguishing pre-Early Dynastic pottery, adumbrated on p. 36, make even a tentative assessment of the extent of earlier settlement inadvisable.

† Site areas are given in this table in cases where the subsequent partial or complete abandonment of the town makes its size during the Early Dynastic period reasonably certain (see Appendix A).

‡ Topographic data for Tell Dhibaʿi are inadequate to show whether this was one large settlement or several smaller adjoining ones.

§ As discussed in Appendix A, total areas given here are based on the assumption (modified in certain instances where additional data are available) that known areas of these sites at later periods are approximately equivalent to their Early Dynastic area. At village sites whose occupation has been indicated as questionable ("?"), the only present evidence for the provisional assignment of an Early Dynastic date is the finding of a small number of worked flint blades on their surfaces. The absence of more extensive early finds suggests that settlements at this time were small at best, and the arbitrary figure of 0.5 ha. has been assigned in each case. Admittedly some of these sites may have been earlier than the Early Dynastic period, and on others the flints may have been brought in at a later time as strays.

‖ At some of these sites, visited only in the 1937 survey and hence not examined for the full group of dating criteria used in the final reconnaissance, it is probable that evidence of a continuing later occupation exists but was not recorded. Included in this group are: 46, 192, 264, 345, 368, 520.

39

approximating the lower Diyala's present course was only slightly less extensive: two large towns (421 and 685), seven smaller ones (169, 229, 446, 462, 558, 568, 590) and eighteen villages, comprising roughly 130 hectares. It seems, in other words, that while the Tell Asmar region may have held a priority in original settlement, its pre-eminence as a zone of clustered towns and surrounding villages was substantially reduced by the end of the Early Dynastic period.

The remainder of the lower Diyala basin contrasts in different ways with the zones around Tell Asmar and Khafājah. The enclave of settlement at the southeast corner of the basin included only five sites during the Early Dynastic period, but two of these were important towns (842, 851). A third, somewhat smaller, town also was present, and the built-up area of settlement in the enclave may already have been as much as 50 hectares. Although failing significantly to expand its limits after the ᶜUbaid period, in other words, this enclave was perhaps more urbanized than any other part of the region. In the northern part of the basin, the opposite situation prevailed. Of nineteen known or probable settlements in separate enclaves below the Jebel Hamrīn, only one (109) may be counted among the larger towns. To be sure, five smaller towns also were present (16, 24, 71, 113, 162), but as is described more fully in Appendix A a disproportionate number of the smaller sites in this zone probably were overlooked because of more extensive cultivation and more superficial coverage in the survey. The northern part of the basin, then, reflects the comparative lateness of its initial settlement in that it remained pronouncedly more rural throughout the Early Dynastic period.

Aside from the large towns, virtually nothing is known of the physical layout of Early Dynastic settlements in the lower Diyala region. The smaller towns or villages have failed to stimulate the interest of either the professional archaeologist or the illicit digger, so that no comparisons can yet be drawn with the artifacts and architecture of the main centers. Even the range of activities within the smaller settlements remains obscure, although together they comprise more than half of the built-up area of the period as given in Table 10 (and this does not take into account the relatively more complete coverage of large sites in the survey). Were all of them occupied by homogeneous agricultural villagers, for example,

with the larger rural landholders tending (as at present) to gravitate toward the towns? Or were some of them the rural installations of private estates such as those that are attested in slightly later documents,[22] perhaps with an attached manor house commanding the site in which the leading family of the district resided? What, in any case, was the relation of the numerous small settlements to the large towns? Were the latter visited as religious sanctuaries, markets, dispensaries of justice, or avoided except in times of crisis as essentially predatory and hostile collectors of tribute or taxes from defenseless rural districts?

Even so obvious a question as to whether the Early Dynastic villages and smaller towns generally were fortified cannot be answered at present; they may well have needed to be if organized military campaigning was complemented on a lesser scale by petty nomadic raids and banditry. No traces of circumvallation around them were observed in the course of the survey, but it could be argued that this reflects only the less imposing construction to be expected around smaller settlements. Nor were walls noted in the surface reconnaissance around later settlements, yet even one as modest in size at Tell Abū Harmal was found upon excavation to be surrounded by an impressive and well-built wall.[23] However, that wall did not antedate the Larsa period.

We are compelled, then, to describe the relations between the main towns and their smaller neighbors on the limited and problematical basis of their respective geographical distributions, as illustrated in Figure 2. The main towns, it will be observed, do not form the hubs of radiating canal networks along which the subsidiary villages are strung. Instead, towns and villages alike occur at intervals along what we have argued earlier can best be interpreted as an anastomosing network of essentially natural watercourses. While local improvements and changes in this system do seem to have occurred, it had persisted in essentials since the beginnings of agricultural settlement and would continue for more than two millenniums after the Early Dynastic period, a stability which contrasts sharply with the rapid and continuous mutability of later—essentially artificial—irrigation systems. The subsistence requirements for the existing, still comparatively small, population could have been met with flood irrigation based on

40

temporary dams and small ditches to direct the water, supplemented with, or perhaps increasingly replaced in time by, small canal systems that grew slowly by accretion but that never were extended more than a few kilometers inland from the streams. In the context of Mesopotamian conditions, it has recently been shown that this kind of irrigation is well within the capabilities of local groups without state intervention.[24] Elaborate control works to regulate the water supply certainly were not necessary for so rudimentary an irrigation system. Hence it is difficult to see the emergence of the towns as a consequence of any monopolistic control of the water supply of surrounding villages, and still more difficult to imagine the growth of their political institutions as a consequence of a need for a bureaucracy concerned with canal management.[25] In short, no clear and consistent dependency of political developments on irrigation practices is deducible from the distribution of the major towns.

It appears instead that the disposition of the large towns along watercourses is quite irregular, the product of a number of interacting local variables. Perhaps the only significant generalization that can be made is that they tend to be placed on separate branches of a stream, or at least on separate reaches of a long-continuing branch, and the juxtaposition of two of the large sites (842, 851) is an exception even to this rule. One distinct pattern is represented by the line of settlement beginning with Abū Zambīl (384, 530, 531, 534), which already had come into existence in ʿUbaid times. Here the major town lay nearest the parent stream, in a position seemingly best suited to expand its irrigated area at the expense of downstream users. However, the growth of Abū Rāsain (109) and Tulūl Abū Yiwālik (397) cannot be explained by invoking a similar privileged position; both were established somewhat below the sources of the branches on which they apparently lay, and neither could draw from downstream populations whose villages became less attractively situated for irrigation as the towns expanded. Still another explanation suggests itself in the case of Tell Abū Jāwan (685) and the large site at the mouth of a lower stream bed (851). Perhaps the importance of these sites, lying at the junctions of two tributaries with the assumed ancient course of the Tigris River,[26] can be understood in terms of the commerce for

which they served as shipping points and entrepôts. But it will be observed that none of the other large towns seems to have been placed at a stream junction. Tell Asmar (244) and Khafājah (421), in particular, are some distance above the branching points where, from a commercial or even political and military point of view, they might most advantageously have been situated.

Finally, it is worth noting that with rare exceptions the large towns occur in relative isolation, i.e., with few smaller settlements closely adjoining them. This would seem to suggest that the bulk of the agriculture in their immediately surrounding areas was carried on by their own inhabitants. Hence it underlines the predominantly agricultural orientation of the society as a whole, and lends support to the view that extensive surpluses could not be drawn regularly from outlying villages for the support of non-agricultural elites and specialists in the major towns.

On the basis of data and assumptions which are set forth in Appendix A, a provisional estimate may be given of the sedentary population of the Diyala plains during the Early Dynastic period. With an approximate density of 200 persons per hectare, the 384 hectares of recorded town and village settlement would have supported a population of about 77,000 persons, not more than 20 per cent or so of the present population (exclusive of Baghdad). Such a population in turn would have needed only a fraction of the land area cultivated today. Utilizing the figure of 1.4 hectares of cultivable land (about half of it lying fallow at any given time) per person, established in Chapter 2, it would appear that no more than some 1,100 square kilometers of land devoted to irrigation agriculture were sufficient for subsistence purposes. The enclaves surrounded by swamp or wasteland symbols shown in Figure 2 exceed this area by a generous margin (enclosing 1,900 instead of 1,100 sq. kms.). Their limited extent lends support to the conclusion, already indicated by the placement of sites in semi-isolated clusters rather than continuous zones, that only a fraction of the land and water resources of the region were regularly utilized during Early Dynastic times.

Two other aspects of these calculations deserve to be noted. In the first place, even in the case of the largest of the Early Dynastic towns in the region, a computation first of their population (assuming 200

41

persons per hectare) and then of the lands needed for subsistence (assuming 1.4 hectares of fields per person) shows that, with no allowance for the procurement of food from surrounding subsidiary towns, an area of around 90 sq. kms. would have been sufficient. Conceived of as a circular zone around the town, this would imply a radius of only a little more than 5 kms. More probably, the zone was elongated along the watercourses, so that the distance from the permanent streams to the limits of cultivation was always considerably less.

Finally, it is interesting to compare the gross estimate for the irrigated area in the region in Early Dynastic times with the modern irrigated area that is dependent on the Diyala River—presumably the only important source of irrigation water available in antiquity. Previously it has been noted that the area irrigated today by gravity-flow canals from the Diyala is approximately 2,958.5 sq. kms., with an additional 537.5 sq. kms. of pump irrigation along the lower Diyala. The total water resources of the river below the Jebel Hamrīn gorge are probably adequate at most for around 4,000 sq. kms.[27] Thus it appears that less than one-third or at least the present usable flow was necessary for irrigation during the Early Dynastic period. To be sure, problems of a technical nature may have limited the water supplies or area of land that could be commanded for irrigation purposes. However, it is still very difficult to see in these figures any evidence that "population pressure," in the sense of land or water shortage in relation to existing subsistence needs, was an important and widespread factor on the historical and social scene.

To sum up briefly, the Early Dynastic period seems to have witnessed a substantial increase in the number, and probably also in the size, of settlements. At the same time, the sites of this period remain grouped in enclaves virtually the same as those occupied earlier. The network of watercourses relied upon for irrigation also had changed little since ᶜUbaid and Protoliterate times. Among the settlements a hierarchy in size is clearly apparent, and it probably coincides roughly with differences in political importance and function. The larger towns fall in a range of from 10 to 33 hectares and in some—and perhaps all—cases were surrounded by walls. Presumably they constituted the main political centers of the region around which the more numerous smaller towns and

villages were grouped in varying relations of dependence. It does not appear, however, that the main towns generally were in a position to control or monopolize the supplies of irrigation water by serving as the hubs of extensive radiating networks of branch canals for the settlements over which they held suzerainty. Instead, the arrangement of sites evokes the image of beads of different sizes strung along a string, each settlement claiming a larger or smaller share of the surrounding land for agriculture practiced by its own citizenry.

Finally, both the restricted enclaves in which sites occur and the very rough calculations of population and land use based on the extent of ruins combine to suggest that only one-third or less of the available land and water were utilized for irrigation agriculture during the Early Dynastic period. Particularly in the northern part of the lower Diyala basin, the population must have remained sparse and non-sedentary by modern standards. Even considering the primary concentration of settlement in the Nahrawān wilderness area now beyond the cultivation limits, the total population appears to have been less than one-fifth of what it is at present.

4. THE AKKADIAN AND GUTIAN PERIODS

Under the conditions of relatively sparse settlement that the Diyala plains offered, considerable movement of population was possible without displacement of the existing sedentary population. While the lands most suitable for easy, small-scale irrigation perhaps were largely taken, a glance at Figure 2 shows that in Early Dynastic times large tracts remained which would have afforded excellent grazing and with access to streams to assure water for flocks and marginal irrigation as well. This is the ecological niche, it may be assumed, into which semi-nomadic tribesmen naturally would have moved, whether from the great sweep of the Fertile Crescent extending westward into Syria or from the foothills of the Zagros Mountains to the east. Such movement may well have been a relatively continuous one, extending far back into prehistoric times, but it is necessary to distinguish the slow infiltration of small extended-family groups or displaced villages of marginal dry-farmers from the periodic appearance of much larger groupings whose tribal organizations had political over-

42

tones. The former represented no real threat to the established settlements; politically fragmented and with few resources, they soon would have drifted into a dependent symbiosis with the towns and then disappeared as a separate cultural stratum. The great tribal groupings, however, were also a substantial military force and hence from time to time had profound political consequences.

The Akkadian conquest of Mesopotamia, initiated by Sargon and renewed by his successors, was the first and most dramatic of these consequences. Earlier patterns of territorial aggrandizement on the Mesopotamian alluvium had been short-lived; the resources of a single city-state and the charisma of its ruler were not able to maintain for long the unstable coalitions of the principalities upon which they were based. By contrast, as one authority recently has suggested, "our extant evidence certainly suggests that the political organization of the Akkad Dynasty amounted to something of a real revolution in Mesopotamian history. We are in almost total ignorance of the causes which led to this new development; to speak of the particular personal gifts and abilities of the Akkadian kings is only to paraphrase the native traditions and to underscore our real lack of historical information. The fact nevertheless remains that it was the Akkadian rulers who were the first to establish a unified administration over all of Mesopotamia and much of its surrounding regions. . . ."[28]

Whether the term "unified administration" implies a fuller and more sophisticated degree of centralized control than in fact existed until considerably later times is a problem of interpretation for the specialist.[29] The temporary breakdown of the system upon the death of each ruler tends to indicate this. The pattern, however, was clearly an unprecedented one, involving the placing of garrisons, the destruction of city walls in order to deprive potential rebels of their strongpoints, the appointment of Akkadian administrators for conquered towns, and possibly the holding of local ruling families as hostages.[30] And it is difficult to believe that much of the stimulus for this pattern did not stem from the non-urban, essentially tribal, modes of organization with which much of the Akkadian element in the population still must have been familiar.[31]

There are hints that the Diyala plains played an important strategic role during the Akkadian dy-

nasty, perhaps being more closely integrated with the heartland of the alluvium than it had been previously or would be again until long afterward. A fortress named after Rimush, the second king of the dynasty, has not been precisely located but presumably lay close to Ischali (ancient Neribtum [442]) since it is mentioned frequently in texts from there.[32] Moreover, the final ruler in the Agade line, Shū-Durul, bore the name given to the Diyala River at the time,[33] perhaps indicating a special concern with the area.[34]

The patterns of settlement occurring on the Diyala plains during the Akkadian period can be dealt with more briefly than their Early Dynastic predecessors. For the most part they merely continue the latter, although Table 11 indicates that almost a third of the individual occupation sites were new. The totals given for the Akkadian period, 97 sites aggregating perhaps 403 hectares of ruins, are virtually the same as those given for the Early Dynastic period. On the other hand, since the bulk of Akkadian pottery is less distinctive than Early Dynastic types and since Akkadian levels generally were covered by thick debris, it is difficult to estimate the extent of the underlying Akkadian settlements from the available surface data. Possibly many of the Akkadian sites recorded in Table 11 as towns were only villages during that period, although subsequently they grew in size. If so, then both the settled area and gross population of the region may have shrunk considerably after the Early Dynastic period. This seems probable in light of the historic events of the period, and would help to explain the abandonment, not solely of Early Dynastic villages, but even of several of the larger towns; however, it cannot be shown conclusively with the archaeological evidence available at present.

Although less well-known than the Early Dynastic period, Akkadian levels in the lower Diyala basin have been sampled fairly extensively stratigraphically. The largest exposures to date are at Tell Asmar, where successive levels containing both monumental architecture and private dwelling units have been exposed.[35] There were also extensive Akkadian deposits on the Early Dynastic Mound "A" at Khafājah, but these have been almost entirely denuded; all that remains at present are very shallow traces of monumental foundations[36] and fragments of contemporary ceramics which have been left behind on the surface as the uppermost levels eroded away.[37] Finally, Ak-

43

kadian levels were probed in small soundings at Tell Abū Harmal[38] and Tell al-Dhibaʿi.[39] Beyond the fact that the former apparently was an open and undefended small settlement, no information is yet available on the associated objects or architectural findings.

The only extension of the zone of settlement in Akkadian times which apparently reflects a change in the basic pattern of watercourses occurs in the environs of modern Baghdad (see Fig. 2). Four new sites (302, 307, 411, 413) form a line suggesting a new Diyala outlet to the Tigris, farther to the northwest

TABLE 11

Akkadian or Gutian Sites in the Lower Diyala Region

1. Early Dynastic sites apparently continuing into the Akkadian period:*
   Large towns:
   244 (Tell Asmar), 384 (Abū Zambīl), 397 (Tulūl Abū Yiwālik), 421 (Khafājah), 685 (Tell Abū Jāwan), 842 (Tell Abū Dibis), 851.
   Small towns:
   7, 16, 24, 71, 162, 169, 229, 253, 355, 366, 446, 462, 558, 568, 590, 810.
   Villages:
   14, 18, 31, 56, 77, 122, 158, 160, 214, 221, 225, 259, 261, 297, 298, 344, 350, 354, 357, 364, 370, 372, 381, 419, 433, 441, 450, 458, 463, 465, 489, 530, 531, 556, 563, 576, 579, 581, 599, 648, 818, 835.
   In total: 65 sites, approximately 294 hectares of settlement.

2. Newly established Akkadian or Gutian sites:†
   Large towns:
   421 (Khafājah, mounds B–D), 442 (Ischali).
   Small towns:
   100 (Tell Abū Sekhūl), 102 (Abū Hilāl), 116 (Tell Saʿad), 398, 411 (Tell al-Dhibaʿi), 536, 628 (Kashim Wāwi).
   Villages:
   159, 213, 217, 222, 302, 305, 307, 340, 343, 380, 413 (Tell Abū Harmal), 422, 439, 443, 455, 512, 535, 541, 821, 824, 825, 846, 860.
   In total: 32 sites, approximately 109 hectares of settlement.

Total (sections 1 and 2): 97 Akkadian or Gutian sites, aggregating approximately 403 hectares of settlement. This includes 8 large towns‡ occupying about 170 hectares, and 24 small towns occupying about 137 hectares.§ Seventy-six per cent of known settlement was in towns.

3. Sites largely or wholly abandoned during or immediately after the Akkadian periods:‖
   Large towns:
   244 (Tell Asmar), 421 (Khafājah A), 685 (Abū Jāwan).
   Small towns:
   355.
   Villages:
   14, 221, 302, 372, 576, 824, 825.

* This description indicates that evidence was found supporting a span of occupation that continued from the Early Dynastic into or through the Akkadian or later periods. It is not meant to imply that no hiatuses may have occurred within this span.

† This category includes three sites which may have shifted only slightly and gradually in location: 102, 421 (Khafājah), 396–97 (Tulūl Abū Yiwālik). Since no newly founded Akkadian settlement can be shown from the available surface data to have been larger than a village, the areas given here for large and small towns may refer only to later periods.

‡ It is assumed here that Khafājah A was abandoned before the occupation of Khafājah B, C, and D began.

§ Cf. note‡, Table 10.

‖ This category reflects the absence in surface observations and collections of evidence for an occupation during the Ur III or Isin-Larsa periods. It does not preclude the possibility that briefer hiatuses in occupation may also have occurred on the sites not given on this list.

than any previous junction. It is not clear, of course, whether the new channel was cut artificially, or by an abnormally heavy flood discharge, or by some combination of the two. However, its total length is slightly less than ten kms., well within the capabilities of local groups of modern villagers without machinery or outside resources. Moreover, the settlements themselves are all very small, and the Akkadian levels in at least the two excavated examples (Tell al-Dhibaʿi and Tell Abū Harmal) only can be described as suggesting open and undefended little villages.[40] Accordingly, it seems more reasonable to regard this new stream branch or canal as a product of purely local efforts than as evidence of the intervention of a major outside power.

Finally, it is necessary to consider briefly the circumstances surrounding the end of the Akkadian period. At the large towns upon which excavations in the main have concentrated, the picture is undeniably one of extensive destruction and abandonment. There are neither surface sherds nor architectural remains to indicate a later occupation of Mound "A" at Khafājah. Tell Agrab had been abandoned in Early Dynastic times and remained uninhabited throughout the Akkadian period. At Tell Asmar the picture is clearest. Commenting upon a widespread layer of rubbish and ashes, Frankfort observes:

> The obvious inference is that some of the Akkadian buildings had been deserted and had stood in a ruinous state for a rather long period before they were rebuilt and again inhabited during the 3rd dynasty of Ur. This presents a definite contrast to the case of the private houses, which, as we have proved, were continuously inhabited all through this intermediate period. We were therefore driven to the conclusion that the large building in Figure 20 [the "Northern Palace"] was of a public nature, in which case its desertion and ruin can be ascribed to the period of anarchy after the wild Gutium mountaineers from the east had overthrown the last king of the dynasty of Akkad. It will be remembered that tablets dated to the reign of this last king, Shudurul, were found among the private houses; and we may thus suppose that the populace continued to live in Eshnunna although the palace of its local ruler was deserted.[41]

So far as present archaeological information goes, it supports the historical thesis that the larger towns underwent a period of crisis and dissolution in connection with Gutian invasions at the end of the Akkadian period.

On the other hand, it seems certain that the tempo of sedentary agricultural life as a whole was less severely affected than the dynastic or religious institutions which were supported by its surpluses. Much of the dwelling area in Tell Asmar remained occupied, while in Khafājah it may only have shifted to an immediately adjoining area across the river or outside the older wall (Mounds B, C, D). Comparable phases of destruction were not noted in the admittedly small-scale soundings at villages like Tell al-Dhibaᶜi and Tell Abū Harmal. Moreover, only nine of the ninety Akkadian small towns and villages were not occupied during Ur III or Isin-Larsa times. While this obviously cannot confirm the absence of a general hiatus in settlement during the Gutian period, it does suggest that any lapses were of relatively short duration and were not accompanied by a widespread reshuffling of the population.[42]

To summarize briefly, the Akkadian period for the most part saw a continuation of patterns already well established in Early Dynastic times. Some reduction or displacement of population is indicated by the abandonment of several of the large Early Dynastic towns and numerous smaller towns and villages. A slightly larger number of settlements in turn were newly founded, but there are some grounds for believing that most or all of these were relatively small. In that case, some reduction in total population must have occurred so that the region assumed a slightly more rural aspect. The only significant extension of settlement probably involved stream changes or new canal construction, but only in one small area and on a modest scale that might have been carried on by co-operating local villagers without outside resources. Finally, it appears that the larger towns of the region suffered badly from the effects of war and outside invasion at the end of the Akkadian period, although settled life in the villages, and even in the residential quarters of the towns, may have continued with no more than brief interruptions.

45

5

REGIONAL AUTONOMY, SUBJUGATION, AND DECLINE (2100-626 B.C.)

THE SECOND major phase into which the record of changing patterns of settlement in the lower Diyala region is divided is illustrated in Figure 3. It is a phase in which the region at first attained at least local political independence at times under the leadership of ancient Eshnunna, but subsequently the region tended to fall increasingly under the domination of one or another outside power. In consequence, in the Old Babylonian period the beginnings of a decline are evident not only in the average size of settlements but in the total population living in nucleated towns and villages. By the latter part of the Cassite period the region was no longer merely subject to the hegemony of a neighboring Babylonian state, but instead had become a buffer area periodically sacked, divided, and contended for by Babylonian, Elamite, and Assyrian forces. In Middle Babylonian times, probably as a result of the Assyrian campaigns, the total sedentary population seems to have been reduced to a fraction of what it had been during earlier periods of relative independence and prosperity, and much of the area must have gone out of cultivation entirely and been given over to nomadism.

Nevertheless, the persistence of linear enclaves of sites in the same positions indicates that essentially the same network of watercourses continued in existence throughout this phase, as during the pre- and protohistoric periods, although, to be sure, their accompanying levees are too deeply buried beneath later deposits to be detected on the surface. For this reason

the enumeration of the sequence of periods in Figures 2 and 3 is continuous rather than separate. Few of the individual settlements of the prehistoric period continued to be occupied as late as the Middle Babylonian period, but the succession of shifting settlements indicates little change either in the position of the major streams or in the limited and local character of the irrigation regimes they supplied. Only at the very end of this long span of time are there hints of possible natural changes affecting the basic environmental equilibrium in which the area had remained for more than three millenniums.

5. THE THIRD DYNASTY OF UR AND THE ISIN-LARSA PERIOD

With the restoration of Sumerian hegemony under the Third Dynasty of Ur the lower Diyala region emerges for the first time into the full light of recorded history. Building inscriptions and archives from such sites as Tell Asmar, Khafājah, Ischali, and Tell Abū Harmal furnish local dynastic sequences which can be placed more or less securely in the chronological fabric of Lower Mesopotamia as a whole. They also provide the foundation for interpretive studies not merely of the political history of ancient Eshnunna, which occupied at least the central part of the region, but also of the institutional framework of temple administrations and private commerce.[1]

In briefest outline, these textual sources first disclose Eshnunna under the administration of gover-

46

nors appointed by the kings of Ur, and then attaining a precarious independence toward the end of that dynasty. Subsequently Eshnunna at times seems to have controlled relatively distant towns like Sippar and Rapiku on the Euphrates, while at other times it became a vassal to overlords like Shamshiadad I of Assyria and even may have been sacked on one occasion by Anumutabil of Der. Finally it passed under the suzerainty of Babylon during the later years of the reign of Hammurabi.[2] While helping to establish an interpretive framework for the period, these political events are not directly within the purview of the present study. Here we are concerned instead with changing patterns of settlement in and around the kingdom of Eshnunna as they are interpreted from the results of reconnaissance and excavation.

Archaeological materials representing the Ur III period are not well known in the region. At Tell Asmar (244) the pertinent levels may contain admixtures from earlier and later periods,[3] while at Tell al-Dhibaʿi (411) only a few sparse remains, not yet described in detail, are assigned provisionally to the period.[4] Elsewhere, contemporary levels remain undug or at least unrecognized.

Remains are much more abundant for the Isin-Larsa period that follows. Stratified building levels at Tell Asmar, Khafājah, and Ischali in most cases can be assigned unequivocally to definite reigns on the basis of stamped bricks or tablets bearing date formulae.[5] Extensive building levels belonging to this period also have been excavated at Tell al-Dhibaʿi[6] and at Tell Abū Harmal (413).[7]

All of the known sites that apparently were occupied during the Ur III or Isin-Larsa periods are recorded in Table 12. A comparison of their geographic distribution and size with conditions obtaining during earlier periods suggests aspects of both continuity and change in the general pattern of settlement.

The primary theme is one of continuity, for the basic pattern remained very similar to what it had been previously. With one exception, to be noted presently, settled communities were not established in any important area that previously had been unoccupied or devoted only to pastoralism. Like the sites that were abandoned during the Akkadian period, those which were newly occupied during Ur III or Isin-Larsa times for the most part are distributed in an apparently random fashion among the major

enclaves of settlement which already had become distinguishable by Protoliterate times. Even the range of variation in community size seems to have remained substantially unaffected by changing political fortunes. For example, while the political successes won by Eshnunna are reflected in its substantial growth (from probably less than 10 to 24 hectares), even at the peak of its fortunes it never exceeded the maximum areal extent which other towns in the region had attained as early as the Early Dynastic period. And the total area of village and town ruins increased only slightly, from 403 to 462 hectares. Quite possibly this increase is not a significant one in view of the incompleteness and imprecision of the data. In any case, it was insufficient to alter the basic condi-

TABLE 12

THIRD DYNASTY OF UR AND ISIN-LARSA SITES
IN THE LOWER DIYALA REGION

1. Akkadian sites continuing into (or subsequently reoccupied during) the Ur III and Isin-Larsa periods.
   Large towns:
   244 (Tell Asmar), 384 (Abū Zambīl), 397 (Tulūl Abū Yiwālik), 421 (Khafājah B & D), 442 (Ischali), 685 (Tell Abū Jāwan), 842 (Tell Abū Dibis), 851.
   Small towns:
   7, 16, 24, 71, 100, 102, 116, 162, 169, 229, 253, 366, 398, 411, 419, 446, 462, 536, 558, 568, 590, 628, 810.
   Villages:
   18, 31, 56, 77, 122, 158, 159, 160, 213, 214, 217, 222, 225, 259, 261, 297, 298, 305, 307, 340, 343, 344, 350, 354, 355, 357, 364, 370, 380, 381, 413, 422, 433, 439, 441, 443, 450, 455, 458, 463, 465, 489, 512, 530, 531, 535, 541, 556, 563, 579, 581, 599, 648, 687, 818, 821, 835, 846, 860.
   Ninety sites, approximately 382 hectares of settlement.
2. Newly established Ur III or Isin-Larsa period sites:*
   Small towns:
   33 (Abū Harmal), 46 (Tell Mandak), 192 (Bdeir), 247 (Tell al-Wān), 515 (Tell Agrab), 639 (Abū Trachīya al-Jenūbi), 728 (Umm Zifrāyeh).
   Villages:
   58, 105, 123, 152, 165, 166, 212, 220, 256, 258, 260, 306, 341, 345, 368, 396, 425, 429, 435, 481, 496, 498, 520, 522, 534, 545, 610, 637, 730, 751, 813, 849.
   Thirty-nine sites, approximately 80 hectares of settlement.
In total: 129 sites, aggregating approximately 462 hectares of settlement. This includes 8 large towns occupying 176 hectares, and 30 small towns occupying 151 hectares. Seventy-one per cent of known settlement was in towns.
3. Sites largely or wholly abandoned during or soon after the Isin-Larsa period:†
   Large towns:
   244, 384, 397, 421, 442, 685.
   Small towns:
   71, 162, 398, 411, 515, 810.
   Villages:
   56, 58, 122, 213, 221, 225, 261, 302, 340, 344, 345, 350, 354, 355, 357, 368, 381, 413, 463, 520, 535, 581, 599, 648, 860.
   Thirty-seven sites, approximately 178 hectares of settlement.

* This category includes the following Early Dynastic sites at which no evidence of an intervening Akkadian or Gutian occupation was obtained through surface collections: 105, 341, 368, 396, 429, 515, 520, 534, 637. At Tell Agrab (515), Delougaz (1952: Table 3) lists a hiatus during the Akkadian period, although purchased seals said to have come from the site have been described as Akkadian in style (Frankfort, H. 1955. *Stratified Cylinder Seals from the Diyala Region. Oriental Institute Publications,* 72. Chicago. Plates 90–92). In addition, it includes the following sites with traces of an early (E. D.?) occupation which were visited only in the 1937 reconnaissance and hence not examined for the full range of dating criteria used in the final survey: 46, 192, 345, 368, 520.

† This category reflects the absence of evidences of the Old Babylonian period in excavations or surface observations and collections. It does not preclude the possibility of briefer hiatuses elsewhere.

47

tion observed in Early Dynastic times—that only a fraction of the available waters of the Diyala River were utilized for irrigation.

Against this broad and basic continuity, two new developments stand out in minor relief. Perhaps the more significant is the onset of a trend toward a more dispersed and rural mode of settlement, one indication of which is the declining proportion of the total built-up area occupied by towns (exceeding four hectares in extent) as opposed to smaller villages. This process had begun already at the end of the Early Dynastic period and continued through Isin-Larsa times, leaving approximately 71 per cent of built-up areas classifiable as towns during the latter period in contrast to 77 per cent during the former. This change is so small in absolute terms as possibly to be only an artifact of observational error, but subsequently it assumes undeniable importance and hence may have been underway before the end of the third millennium B.C. Whatever the magnitude of the change, at least the available data indicate the stagnation or decline of most or all of the larger towns of the region save for Eshnunna itself, and this at a time when the number of smaller communities was continuing to increase. Among the larger settlements Ischali alone, apparently not having been founded before the Akkadian period,[8] may run counter to this trend. But no large towns that first made their appearance in the Ur III or Isin-Larsa periods have been identified, and in addition the total number of large towns suffered a steady attrition after the Early Dynastic period. This point may be seen more clearly by considering separately the new settlements of Ur III and Isin-Larsa date. Not only are no large towns present among them, but only 49 per cent of their aggregate area falls in settlements classifiable even as small towns.

At the same time, it should be stressed that this apparent dispersion of settlement does not reflect necessarily the general impoverishment or decline of the region in economic terms. The political successes of Eshnunna were accompanied not by an enlargement and enrichment of the capital alone but also by important temple-building activities undertaken in the name of Eshnunna's rulers at nearby subject towns like Ischali.[9] Even in still smaller towns and villages like Tell Abū Harmal and Tell al-Dhibaꜥi, the limited information available suggests a more pros-

perous, active, and diversified economic scene than can be recorded for any previous period. Thus it is possible that the reduction in the number of large towns is of primarily political significance, related in some way to the centralization of administrative authority in Eshnunna.

The second new feature of the Ur III and Isin-Larsa periods was a substantial expansion of one of the linear enclaves of settlement, which previously had remained relatively stable in size for as long as two millenniums. This took place in the southeast corner of the lower Diyala basin, along the banks of the lower end of a watercourse which Thorkild Jacobsen had identified provisionally with the River Daban of cuneiform sources.[10] Previously the region to the northwest of this enclave, separating it from the larger settled zones around Tell Asmar and Khafājah, had supported little or no permanent population. One possible explanation for the puzzling absence of earlier settlement is the proximity of the region to the assumed contemporary course of the Tigris, perhaps leading to uninviting conditions of seasonal or permanent swamp like those which Felix Jones noted a century ago at nearby Tell al-Deir (Deir al-ꜥĀqūl, 791) under similar conditions.[11] Of course, because of the local topography the Daban also might have maintained a swampy regime along the middle reaches of its course even without receiving increments from the seasonal overflow of the Tigris, and soil salinity or other local conditions also may have impeded the earlier spread of irrigation agriculture.

Whatever the explanation for the previous avoidance of the region, the establishment of new settlements there during Isin-Larsa times must have been associated with some new effort at swamp drainage and/or canal construction, an effort which succeeded in more than doubling at least the length of the adjoining enclave to the southeast. To be sure, most of the new sites (481, 496, 498, 637, 639, 728, 730, 751) were small, but some corresponding growth in the political importance of the southeastern part of the basin at least would be understandable. Evidence is provided by the brief existence at this time of an independent dynasty at Malgium, which is generally supposed to have been located in this region.[12]

It remains to describe briefly the effect on the region around Eshnunna of its incorporation into the Old Babylonian kingdom under Hammurabi. While

48

the political events surrounding the end of Eshnunna's independence at the close of the Isin-Larsa period are not within the scope of this discussion, both the archaeological survey and excavations suggest that its demographic consequences were widespread and catastrophic.

The picture obtained from excavations is a fairly uniform one of extensive destruction. While a client ruler may have governed at Eshnunna for Hammurabi, and while Eshnunna briefly reclaimed its independence before a final conquest by Samsuiluna,[13] the uppermost levels discovered in most of the excavations there belonged to the late Larsa period at the time of Ibiqadad II and his immediate successors.[14] At Khafājah, Old Babylonian remains are found only in Dūr Samsuiluna on Mounds "B" and "C," where the omission of reference to an older name and the fact that it is described as having been "built" by Samsuiluna[15] suggest that the site previously had been abandoned for a period after a late Larsa occupation. Even in smaller sites, evidence is found of devastation. Tell Abū Harmal, possibly the religious-administrative center for a small agricultural district in the late Larsa period, was entirely destroyed by fire at about the time of Hammurabi's conquest of Eshnunna.[16] The nearby small town of Tell al-Dhibaʿi also was destroyed by fire in late Larsa times, and subsequently was left abandoned for a period.[17] At Tell Agrab, too, the Isin-Larsa settlement apparently was not succeeded by an Old Babylonian occupation.[18] Among those sites in the Diyala region which have been excavated, only at Ischali is it possible that the transition between control by Eshnunna and the supremacy of the First Dynasty of Babylon was not a violent one. Old Babylonian pottery was found in the uppermost strata there,[19] although the extent of the contemporary settlement is not known.

The impression gained from excavations of widespread destruction at the end of the Isin-Larsa period finds additional support in the results of reconnaissance. Particularly at the large town sites, Old Babylonian remains are sparse or absent in the surface collections in comparison with Larsa sherd types and it is interesting to note that the only two such sites where this observation may not hold (842, 851) occur together at the southeastern end of the region. Thus, in comparison with ten towns exceeding ten hectares in area during the Early Dynastic period,

eight in the Akkadian period and eight in the Isin-Larsa period, only three at most continued into the Old Babylonian period.[20] But even at smaller towns and villages there is evidence of considerable disruption, comparable to that preceding the Akkadian period and leading to a substantially larger number of sites abandoned and not quickly reoccupied than seems to have been the case during the Gutian invasions (cf. Table 11). Moreover, if it is borne in mind that representative Old Babylonian sherd types in surface collections are very difficult to distinguish from those of the Cassite period (pp. 50–51), the possibility must be recognized that a number of additional sites here assumed to have been occupied continuously from Larsa into Cassite times were in fact only reoccupied during the Cassite period after an Old Babylonian hiatus. Indeed, this is what did happen at Tell Abū Harmal[21] and Tell al-Dhibaʿi,[22] and it is quite possible that it happened fairly generally.

One other aspect of the destruction at the end of the Larsa period deserves mention. A whole group of sites which had lined the watercourse running from Eshnunna to Tell Agrab and beyond in the Larsa period (340, 350, 354, 355, 515, 520) were subsequently abandoned and not reoccupied even during the Cassite period. Two alternative explanations for this strictly local abandonment present themselves. One is that poor drainage conditions developed like those obtaining in the Haur Agrab which occupies roughly the same area today. With over-irrigation along the newly settled levee of what we have provisionally identified as the Daban immediately to the west possibly having been a contributing factor, increased salinity and leaching may have reduced the attractiveness of the region for the cultivators of the time.

A second explanation stems from the observation that the Eshnunna–Tell Agrab stream was perhaps first supplemented, and then replaced, by parallel watercourses slightly farther to the west (see Fig. 3). While the evidence is inadequate, it is tempting to speculate that the earlier settlements had to be abandoned as a result of a change in the course of the stream—a change which might have come about, for example, during a destructive flood of the Diyala area like the flood which occurred in the thirty-seventh regnal year of Hammurabi.[23]

In summary, the Third Dynasty of Ur and the Isin-Larsa period saw for the most part a continua-

49

tion of pre-existing patterns of settlement, with a substantial expansion in only one of the major occupied enclaves. Some evidence was noted for a modest increase in both the number of sites and in the assumed total population of the region as a whole, but with the exception of Eshnunna this seems to have been achieved primarily by the formation of small villages rather than by the further growth of previously existing large towns or the appearance of new ones. At the end of the Larsa period, both excavations and reconnaissance combine to indicate that there was a substantial disruption of settlement, with most of the large sites and many of the smaller ones temporarily or permanently abandoned.

6. THE OLD BABYLONIAN PERIOD

Very much less is known of the lower Diyala basin under the hegemony of the First Dynasty of Babylon than during the preceding period. One reference occurs to a brief period of revolt during the reign of Samsuiluna, and to the subsequent construction by that king of a new stronghold at Khafājah.[24] Eight years later we learn that he was still in control of the area, naming his thirty-second regnal year after operations he had conducted to deepen and/or realign the Diyala and Daban watercourses.[25] Other than this, historical records so far have not been found. And while several excavations have been carried on in Old Babylonian levels of sites within the region, for a variety of reasons described below they have contributed little to an understanding of the character of representative sites or settlement patterns during the period. Moreover, even the results of our reconnaissance are of limited utility because of special problems concerning the interpretation of Old Babylonian surface materials. A number of circumstances, in other words, make the discussion of the period that is possible here less comprehensive and less securely founded than that for at least the Early Dynastic, Akkadian, Ur III, or Isin-Larsa periods which its debris overlies.

The earliest excavations of Old Babylonian strata in the lower Diyala region in fact were the earliest archaeological excavations conducted there. Perhaps preceded by J. F. Jones in 1848,[26] A. H. Layard dug briefly in Tell Mohammad (414) in 1850.[27] Layard found several hollow bronze balls or maceheads bearing the inscription: E.GAL Ha-am-mu-ra-bi "(prop-

erty of) the palace of Hammurabi," but other objects and architectural finds are not described or illustrated sufficiently to be assigned a date. Further knowledge of the length of its occupation has not been obtained since the site of Tell Mohammad has been largely built over as a result of the expansion of modern Baghdad, but a brief description and plan of the ruins fortunately was prepared before that time.[28] For purposes of the present study, the available data are sufficient only to indicate that a moderately large town existed here, but whether before, during, or after the Old Babylonian period cannot be ascertained.[29]

While they were undertaken only at the more recent end of a span of eighty or more years from the time of Layard's work at Tell Mohammad, a span during which archaeology had come of age as a scientific discipline, the Oriental Institute's excavations during the thirties at Tell Asmar and Ischali are also relatively uniformative about the Old Babylonian period. As noted earlier, only the badly denuded uppermost levels in these mounds are assignable to the period of the supremacy of Hammurabi and his successors. In the case of Dūr Samsuiluna, exposures to date have been inadequate to disclose more than a small portion of the layout of this redoubt,[30] although the securely dated ceramics obtained from them have contributed to the period-criteria utilized in the survey. Finally, a more recent clearance of the uppermost levels of Tell al-Dhibaʿi merely cut through a succession of small villages, which apparently could be assigned on the basis of ceramics only "to the end of the Old Babylonian period, including the early part of the Cassite period."[31] In short, the period of Babylonian supremacy under Hammurabi and his successors in the Diyala area is poorly represented archaeologically, particularly with regard to the special concern of this study for gross changes in representative site plans.

The problems which limit the interpretation of survey data are of a different order. Many Old Babylonian sites are known in the area, but except in the case of a terminal occupation during the Old Babylonian period it is frequently impossible to identify them with confidence. As described more fully in Appendix B, Cassite surface remains are distinguished principally by a large solid-footed chalice (type 7:A). While this is apparently absent in Old Babylonian strata, most other Old Babylonian ceramic features (at least insofar as they can be derived from broken surface pottery where full vessel profiles are seldom available) merely continue into Cassite times without perceptible change. Remains of the Cassite period, in other words, can be identified easily, but positive criteria are lacking to establish the presence or absence of Old Babylonian remains underlying them.

This problem is posed even more urgently by the known sequences at Tell Abū Harmal (413) and Tell al-Dhibaʿi (411), where the small Cassite settlements represent reoccupation of older mounds after an Old Babylonian hiatus. If these sites are fairly representative, and there is no reason to believe they are not, then the survey data may lead to a substantial overestimation of the size and importance of the whole Old Babylonian occupation of the region. In addition, changes in the distribution of sites which in fact took place only under Cassites may be wrongly attributed to the Old Babylonian period. Unfortunately, these difficulties cannot be overcome with the evidence in hand; among other things, they serve to illustrate the limitations of a reconnaissance that is not paralleled by an extensive program of archaeological soundings.

The available data on settlement in the Old Babylonian period are summarized in Table 13 and mapped in Figure 3. In spite of deficiencies in the evidence, described above, an examination of the size and distribution of the sites identified there suggests a few observations about the character of settlement during this period.

There is, in the first place, an obvious continuity of occupation in most of the settled areas. The network of watercourses traced out by Old Babylonian sites is substantially the same as that known earlier, although it is changed in a few places either by natural stream movements, by canal construction, or both.

Several local changes in the position of watercourses deserve special comment. The abandonment of sites along the westernmost branch of the Diyala above Khafājah (through Tell Halāwa, 229) during or soon after the Old Babylonian period suggests that this branch silted up or went out of use, possibly as a natural consequence of the slow rise of the Tigris levee. The bulk of the Diyala's flow shifted to the more easterly channel, passing down to a new point of bifurcation about 6 kms. north of Khafājah. Since

a number of Old Babylonian sites between and including Khafājah and Ischali also were not reoccupied during Cassite times, a shift, in this case slightly to the west, also seems to have taken place in the lower portion of the same watercourse. Another noticeable change was the abandonment of sites along the lower reaches of two watercourses which previously led out into the Haur es-Subaicha; these are the lines running southeast from Tell Sebʿe (366) and Abū Zambīl (384). Possibly agricultural productivity here was adversely affected by a substantial expansion of the zone of leached soils accompanying the Haur, such as might have occurred if the overflow of

TABLE 13

SITES OF THE OLD BABYLONIAN PERIOD
IN THE LOWER DIYALA REGION

1. Isin-Larsa sites continuing into (or subsequently reoccupied during) the Old Babylonian period:
    *Large towns:**
      244 (Tell Asmar), 442 (Ischali), 685 (Tell Abū Jāwan), 842 (Tell Abū Dibis), 851.
    Small towns:
      7, 16, 24, 33, 46, 100, 102, 116, 169, 192, 229, 247, 253, 446, 462, 536, 558, 568, 590, 628, 639, 728.
    Villages:
      18, 31, 77, 105, 123, 152, 158, 159, 160, 165, 166, 212, 214, 217, 220, 222, 256, 258, 259, 260, 297, 298, 305, 306, 307, 341, 343, 344, 364, 370, 380, 396, 397, 419, 422, 425, 429, 433, 435, 439, 441, 443, 450, 455, 458, 465, 481, 489, 496, 498, 512, 522, 530, 531, 534, 541, 545, 556, 563, 579, 610, 637, 687, 730, 751, 810, 813, 818, 821, 835, 846, 849.
      Ninety-nine sites, approximately 284 hectares of settlement.
2. Newly established Old Babylonian sites:
    Large towns:
      414 (Tell Mohammad).†
    Small towns:
      142 (Abū Khazaf), 264 (Tell Dhibaʿi "C"), 295, 421 (Khafājah B), 508 (ʿAlwat al-Badʾīya), 575.
    Villages:
      20, 97, 115, 133, 197, 203, 274, 283, 284, 285, 288, 289, 291, 293, 296, 321, 345, 389, 390, 392, 399, 400, 410, 412, 417, 418, 427, 430, 431, 446, 447, 487, 499, 566, 577, 622, 624, 646, 715, 741, 742, 773, 776, 825, 837, 838.
      Fifty-three sites, approximately 96 hectares of settlement.
   In total: 152 sites, aggregating approximately 380 hectares of settlement. This includes six large towns occupying perhaps 97 hectares, and 28 small towns occupying 143 hectares. Sixty-three per cent of known settlement was in towns.
3. Sites largely or wholly abandoned during or soon after the Old Babylonian period.‡
    Large towns:
      244, 442, 685, 842.
    Small towns:
      7, 24, 33, 100, 169, 229, 421, 446, 536, 558, 568, 628.
    Villages:
      18, 31, 77, 158, 160, 212, 214, 217, 256, 259, 274, 298, 307, 321, 343, 344, 364, 370, 380, 419, 422, 425, 430, 433, 439, 441, 455, 458, 462, 487, 512, 522, 530, 531, 534, 541, 545, 556, 563, 579, 687, 715, 741, 825, 835, 837, 849.
      Sixty-three sites, approximately 183 hectares of settlement.

* Sites 244, 442, and 685 are each estimated to have occupied ten hectares, while the remaining two sites are estimated to have occupied their maximal area. These estimates are quite uncertain, for reasons given in the text.

† Cf. p. 50. The period of occupation of this site is extremely questionable. An area of 24 hectares is assumed, using the dimensions of the mound itself rather than the somewhat doubtful "Stadtgebiet" of 80 hectares identified by Herzfeld (Sarre, F., and Herzfeld, 1920: II, 95).

‡ This category reflects the absence of evidence of the Cassite period in surface collections or excavations. It does not preclude the possibility that brief hiatuses in occupation between the Old Babylonian and Cassite periods may have occurred in other sites as well.

51

a particularly disastrous flood found its way into the depression. Whatever the cause, the net loss of settled area in this instance may have been as much as 200 sq. kms.

In all of the foregoing cases, however, it can only be said that the changes took place during or soon after the Old Babylonian period. Not even a tentative assessment is possible of when in that period they occurred, nor whether they took place simultaneously, nor even whether they were relatively rapid, catastrophic events or only very slow and gradual transitions.

A different pattern of change is to be found north of these abandoned lower reaches. There a number of new settlements made their appearance along a curiously curving arc, presumably the line of a new canal or stream course, which ultimately rejoined the levee of the older watercourse flowing through Tulūl Abū Yiwālik (397) and perhaps became a substitute for the latter. Sites included in this group are: 203, 283, 284, 285, 286, 288, 289, 291, 293, 294, 295, 296, 297, 389, 390, 392, 394, 399, and 400. It is noteworthy that all were small villages, although they are perhaps more closely spaced than any contemporary group of settlements.

Further upstream along the same watercourse, there is evidence in the location of new sites for a southward displacement of the bed of the channel for about 4 kms. As with shifts on the lower Diyala near Khafājah, the absence of Cassite sherds along the older channel indicates only that this displacement occurred during or immediately after the Old Babylonian period, since Old Babylonian sherds cannot be distinguished from those of the Cassite period along the newer channel. Similarly, the beginning of the curving arc of new, closely spaced villages cannot be firmly assigned to the Old Babylonian period or to the Cassite period.

Aside from purely local changes in zones of occupation, two more general trends may be pointed out. The first affected the average size of the settlement unit. On most of those sites where excavations have been conducted, it has already been observed that a considerable decline or even abandonment seems to have taken place during the Old Babylonian period. With the exceptions of Dūr Samsuiluna and Tell Mohammad, no substantial building is known that was undertaken in the area by Hammurabi or his suc-

cessors, and the town areas given in Table 13 for the larger settlements during this period probably are overly generous. Thus, while a considerable increase in the total number of settlements may have occurred, the proportion of known settlement consisting of towns occupying four hectares or more fell slightly, from 71 per cent in the previous period to 63 per cent.

Somewhat more clearcut is the decline in average settlement size. After attaining its highest level, four or more hectares, in the Early Dynastic and Akkadian periods, it dropped only slightly, to 3.5 hectares, during the Isin-Larsa period; during Old Babylonian times, however, it fell more precipitately, to 2.4 hectares. From an area inhabited primarily by town-dwellers, much of the lower Diyala basin was on the way to becoming a district of villagers.

Hand in hand with the dispersion of settlement went an apparent reduction in the permanently settled population. The minimum amount of this decline is suggested by the difference between 462 hectares of built-up Isin-Larsa settlement, and the 380 hectares that are recorded for the Old Babylonian period; this represents a diminution of approximately 17 per cent. In fact, however, the extensive destruction and abandonment that have been reported within Old Babylonian towns indicate that the amount of the decline must have been much greater. Moreover, the difficulties in distinguishing Old Babylonian from Cassite remains almost certainly have led to the inclusion in Table 13 of a substantial number of sites as Old Babylonian which were not occupied before Cassite times. Taking these factors into account, a decline in total population over the preceding period of one-third to one-half appears to be a more reasonable estimate.

In summary, the Old Babylonian period saw a substantial disruption in settled life, probably at least partly in consequence of the conquest of the lower Diyala region by Hammurabi. Total population declined considerably, in some cases probably dispersing from towns into smaller villages, in other cases perhaps abandoning an agricultural way of life, at least temporarily, for nomadism, and in still other cases possibly being drawn out of the region altogether.[32] On the other hand, local changes in the position of watercourses may reflect new canal construction and the colonization of new areas on at least a modest scale, coupled with partial or complete abandonment

52

of adjoining zones. Some of these changes, and perhaps most of them, may have been initiated by Cassite rulers, since Old Babylonian remains are difficult to distinguish when they underlie those of the succeeding period. For the same reason, it has not been possible to identify the effects of the end of Babylonian hegemony on gross patterns of settlement.

7. THE CASSITE PERIOD

As far as is known, the lower Diyala region did not play an independent role during the period of Cassite domination of Babylonia. It was a border district astride the routes taken by invading Assyrian and Elamite armies and probably shifting or contradictory in its relations with outside powers. No building inscriptions have been found directly attesting Cassite activities in the area, and Cassite interests find expression in fluctuating boundaries of political authority that were renegotiated periodically with the Assyrians in accordance with the success or failure of a particular campaign.[33] Yet ultimately the region seems to have suffered more from the unchecked power of a rising Assyria than from the more evenly balanced forces that had contended for it earlier.

Archaeological excavations to date are fairly uninformative. Aside from small exposures at Tell Abū Harmal (413)[34] and Tell al-Dhibaⁱ (411),[35] Cassite remains in the region have not been examined *in situ*. Moreover, in both of these instances the Cassite levels, representing the final occupation, were severely denuded by erosion, and in any case represented the remains only of small villages. Both sites are thought to have been abandoned after the early part of the Cassite period, although textual evidence for the period of their occupation is lacking.

The difficulties of distinguishing Old Babylonian from Cassite remains have been described in the previous section. The result is a tendency to overstate the number and size of sites of the Old Babylonian period, and to render impossible a separation between changes introduced in the layout of settlements and watercourses in Old Babylonian times and changes that occurred only under the Cassites. In consequence, no independent description can be given here of the innovations of the Cassite period; they are included in—and perhaps represent a majority of—the changes noted in the previous section. Even the relatively small number of sites listed in Table 14 as new-

ly founded during the Cassite period, for the most part, have been identified only by a small minority of secondarily deposited Cassite sherds which had been brought up by surface disturbance through thick levels of later debris. Hence the possibility exists that some of these sites had Old Babylonian or earlier levels as well whose distinctive ceramic types were overlooked. A further consequence is that no comparison of general demographic patterns with those of the Old Babylonian period is possible, and that no firm basis exists for contrasting the total population of the region during the two periods.

On the other hand, it is clear that the problem arises primarily from the absence of positive ceramic

TABLE 14

CASSITE SITES IN THE LOWER DIYALA REGION

1. Old Babylonian sites continuing into (or subsequently reoccupied during) the Cassite period:*
   Large towns:
      590 (Tulūl Mujailiᶜ), 851.
   Small towns:
      16, 46, 102, 116, 142, 192, 247, 253, 264, 295, 508, 575, 639, 728.
   Villages:
      20, 97, 105, 115, 123, 133, 152, 166, 197, 203, 220, 222, 258, 260, 283, 284, 285, 288, 289, 291, 293, 296, 297, 305, 306, 341, 389, 390, 392, 396, 397, 399, 400, 410, 412, 417, 418, 427, 429, 431, 443, 447, 458, 462, 465, 466, 481, 489, 496, 498, 499, 566, 577, 610, 622, 624, 637, 646, 730, 742, 751, 773, 776, 810, 813, 818, 821, 838, 846.
   Eighty-five sites, approximately 202 hectares of settlement.
2. Newly established Cassite sites:
   Small towns:
      149 (Tell Hant), 189 (Abū Barabich).
   Villages:
      23, 76, 78, 163, 193, 195, 286, 294, 303, 411, 413, 471, 633, 638, 738, 772, 861.
   Nineteen sites, approximately 32 hectares of settlement.
   Trace only:†
      81, 87, 88, 99, 118, 137, 138, 158, 159, 160, 165, 262, 269, 320, 370, 375, 394, 411, 413, 435, 446, 450, 470, 509, 511, 530, 541, 556, 563, 609, 619, 647, 739, 741, 774, 775.
   In total: 104 sites, aggregating approximately 230 hectares of settlement. This includes two large towns occupying 42.5 hectares, and 16 small towns occupying 86 hectares. Fifty-six per cent of known settlement area was in towns.
3. Sites largely or wholly abandoned during or soon after the Cassite period:‡
   Large towns:
      851.
   Small towns:
      16, 102, 116, 142, 149, 189, 192, 247, 253, 264, 295, 575, 639, 728.
   Villages and Traces:
      23, 46, 76, 78, (81), (87), (88), 97, 105, 115, 123, 138, 152, 158, 160, 163, (165), 166, 193, 220, 258, 260, 262, 269, 283, 284, 285, 286, 294, 295, 296, 297, 305, 306, 320, 341, 345, 370, 375, 394, 396, 397, 399, 400, 410, 411, 412, 413, 417, 418, 431, (435), 443, 446, (450), 458, 462, 465, 466, 470, 481, 489, 496, 498, 499, (509), 511, 530, 541, 556, 563, 577, 609, 610, 619, 622, 624, 633, 637, 638, 646, 647, 730, 738, 739, 741, 742, 751, 772, 773, 774, 775, 776, 810, 813, 818, 821, 838, 846, 861.

* Some in this category in fact may not antedate the Cassite period. Cf. pp. 50–51.

† Cf. discussion in text, p. 54.

‡ At sites recorded in parentheses evidence was found for an occupation during the Neo-Babylonian period. While the ill-defined Middle Babylonian period is not represented, there may have been some continuity of occupation at these sites from Cassite into Neo-Babylonian times.

indexes for the Old Babylonian period. Cassite remains are easily and unmistakably identified from the ubiquitous solid-footed chalices (type 7:A), and hence permit a close comparison of demographic patterns with those of the Isin-Larsa, Akkadian, and earlier periods.

Before discussing these comparisons, however, one aspect of the distribution of Cassite sherds may be mentioned which is puzzlingly different from those of earlier and later periods. At a considerable number of sites—those listed in Table 14 as containing a trace of Cassite materials—a very few, usually widely scattered, Cassite solid-footed chalice bases were found, but other evidence of a Cassite occupation was lacking. In the case of sites which were occupied during earlier periods, this might be accounted for by assuming that a few Cassite graves were dug into the flanks of previously abandoned mounds and subsequently exposed through surface erosion. At many sites of this category, however, no other evidence for a pre-Parthian occupation could be found than one or two of these distinctive bases.

Clearly, the interpretation of the latter group that is most consistent with the general practice of the survey is that small Cassite settlements are covered by heavy later overburdens of cultural debris. This leaves unexplained our failure to find other rim and base forms characteristic of the Cassite period, as well as the occasionally somewhat scattered distribution of these sites with reference to the major lines of Cassite settlement. On the other hand, if we regard some of these Cassite sites as temporary encampments away from the major stream and canal courses, their erratic distribution would find its explanation in the increasing importance of nomadism at the expense of settled life.

Another possible interpretation may be that in some cases these heavy, solid bases were picked up on the surfaces of abandoned mounds by later inhabitants of the region and carried back to their villages, much as seems to have happened during Sassanian and Islamic times in the case of microlithic flint cores. What secondary purpose the Cassite chalice bases might have served is not clear, but the possibility remains that their distribution reflects both contemporary and non-residential use and dispersal in later periods. For this reason, sites listed in Table 14 as providing only a trace of Cassite occupation are dis-

regarded in the observations to follow, although some undoubtedly were occupied by small (and probably shifting) settlements during the Cassite period.

Table 14 records the salient distributional data for the Cassite period. It indicates a substantial decline in both the density of settlement and the degree of urbanization of the region. In spite of the ease of recognizing Cassite remains and the somewhat improved preservation (and lesser submergence through alluviation) that is expected of a later period, the total area of known Cassite ruins is only approximately half that of Isin-Larsa times and only 60 per cent of that even of the Early Dynastic period. While 71 per cent of the estimated area of Isin-Larsa settlements lay in towns larger than four hectares in extent (and even higher percentages in earlier periods), only 56 per cent of the estimated Cassite area lay in towns. Moreover, even if the sites with only a trace of Cassite occupation are excluded, the average size of settlement fell from 3.6 hectares during the Isin-Larsa period to 2.25 hectares.

Most of these changes, it will be observed at once, differ only in detail from what has already been described for the Old Babylonian period. Although our data do not permit a direct comparison, it is tempting to speculate on whether the density and extent of settlement dropped in Old Babylonian times to a level at which they remained fairly steady or whether instead they reached an even lower level during the Old Babylonian period and subsequently experienced a modest resurgence.

The latter alternative is possible because of the confusion of Old Babylonian with Cassite dating criteria. It finds some slight support in the early Cassite reoccupation of abandoned mounds at the only two sites in the region where these chronological horizons have been sampled by excavation. In addition, the admittedly apocryphal Agum-kakrime inscription claims for that early Cassite ruler that he was "the king of the wide country of Babylon, who caused to settle in the country of Eshnunna the widely spread people."[36] If this historical detail is trustworthy in spite of its doubtful context, it also suggests some resettlement of the lower Diyala region under Cassite auspices after an earlier hiatus. But even in aggregate it must be admitted that the available evidence is quite insufficient to establish the fact of a Cassite re-

54

surgence without further excavations or the discovery of new historical texts.

As Table 14 shows, the end of the Cassite period was marked by a more decisive phase of destruction and abandonment than had occurred previously in the area. Of the 104 known Cassite sites, only 32 seem to have survived into Middle Babylonian times. Unfortunately, the chronological placement of this catastrophe remains in doubt, due in large part to the poorly understood ceramic stratigraphy of the period. It may have occurred only gradually, beginning as early as Tukulti-Ninurta I's defeat of Kashtiliashu IV and temporary conquest of Babylon,[37] and culminating during the last years of the Cassite dynasty under the combined blows of Assyrian and Elamite forces.[38] On the other hand, it may also have been the effect of a single, very destructive raid which cannot now be identified. Still another alternative is that it occurred only after the fall of the Cassite dynasty itself, on the assumption that "Cassite" ceramic types noted in the surface reconnaissance persisted for some time into the Middle Babylonian period. This last alternative is most compatible with the degree of settlement and prosperity in the region reported by Shamshiadad V after his fifth campaign in 814 B.C.,[39] and perhaps indicates that that ruler's claims to have carried out widespread destruction are not unfounded.

It may be noted that all of these possibilities have been phrased in terms of the adjacent, sedentary, known centers of political power. But while the destructive role of Assyria and Elam is well established in the existing records and hence is not to be denied, we must admit that still more powerful, if less clearly identifiable, forces also were at work. The late second millennium B.C. was, after all, a time of profound displacements of population within the Eurasiatic heartland, displacements having their Near Eastern reflection in the rise to dominance over parts of the area of Indo-European-speaking mounted warriors with horse-drawn chariotry. In neighboring Iran, in particular, it must have been during this period that the numerous groups of mounted barbarians known to us from the famed Luristan Bronzes and from later Assyrian annals first arrived upon the scene. Perhaps at times in combination with the Assyrians or Elamites, and at other times acting independently or even in opposition to them, these unsettled groups of hill folk no doubt played a substantial part in the destruction

and depopulation of the Diyala plains. As sedentary life came near to flickering away, the local annals and archives which might have recorded this process seem to have disappeared altogether. It remains for another generation of archaeologists to painstakingly re-establish, from fragmentary material remains, the specific contribution of the hill folk to the general decline.

In résumé, it is difficult to distinguish the Cassite occupation of the lower Diyala region from the Old Babylonian period which preceded it. In contrast with still earlier periods, a substantial reduction took place in the average size of settlement and presumably also in the density of population. There is some reason for believing that the decline was most precipitate during the Old Babylonian period, and that at least a slight increase in the sedentary population occurred under the Cassites. Subsequently, the region seems to have suffered the fate of a weak intermediary between powerful Cassite, Elamite, and Assyrian forces contending over its territories. Still further disruption must have been caused by politically fragmented but militarily potent groups of mounted barbarians raiding down into the plains from their newly occupied strongholds in the Iranian uplands. At the end of the Cassite period, or at any rate within a few centuries thereafter, a general phase of abandonment reduced at least the sedentary population to its lowest level since the ᶜUbaid period.

8. THE MIDDLE BABYLONIAN PERIOD

Only a brief and inadequate treatment of patterns of settlement in the lower Diyala region between the fall of the Cassite dynasty and the onset of the Neo-Babylonian period can be provided with the data from the survey. Throughout southern Mesopotamia this is an interval during which historical as well as archaeological sources are largely silent, and in the absence of comparative material it is extremely difficult to evaluate the results of archaeological reconnaissance in a particular area.

One serious problem which has already been alluded to is that of the duration of the Middle Babylonian period. Since we are concerned here with the interpretation of survey data on the basis of ceramic surface collections, this has reference primarily to ceramic types in securely dated archaeological context. Unfortunately, even an approximate terminal date for the characteristic Cassite solid-footed chalice is not known, while the first appearance of types regarded here as mainly Neo-Babylonian is equally uncertain. Hence, of the five centuries in political history separating the Cassites and the Neo-Babylonian kings, it is quite possible that a substantial portion was characterized by ceramic features regarded in the present study as characteristic of the preceding and following periods.

Underlying the problem of duration is one of definition. At the outset of the survey, no ceramic features which occurred exclusively during the Middle

TABLE 15

MIDDLE BABYLONIAN SITES IN THE LOWER DIYALA REGION

1. Cassite sites continuing into Middle Babylonian times:*
    Large towns:
        (590).
    Small towns:
        (508).
    Villages:
        20, (81), (87), (88), (99), (118), 133, 137, 159, (165), 195, 197, 203, (222), 288, 289, 291, 293, (303), 389, 390, 392, (427), (429), (435), (447), (450), 471, (509), (566).
    Thirty-two sites, approximately 50 hectares of settlement.
2. Newly established Middle Babylonian sites:†
    Villages:
        25, (339).
    Two sites, approximately 3 hectares of settlement.
In total: 34 sites, aggregating approximately 53 hectares of settlement. This includes one large town occupying 10 hectares, and 1 small town occupying 4 hectares. Twenty-six per cent of known settlement area was in towns.
3. Sites largely or wholly abandoned during or soon after the Middle Babylonian period:
    Villages:
        20, 159, 203, 289, 291, 293, 389, 390, 392, 471.

* Parentheses indicate that occupation during this period is inferred only from the presence of dating criteria for Cassite and Neo-Babylonian periods. See discussion on this page.

† Parentheses indicate that occupation is inferred only from presence of Neo-Babylonian dating criteria, although surface remains were regarded generally as being earlier during inspection of the site.

Babylonian period could be identified from excavation reports. Gradually, a modest handful of such features came to be recognized, most of them occupying an intermediate typological position between accepted Cassite and Neo-Babylonian dating criteria and serving to differentiate a small group of sites distinct from both. But the new criteria could not be applied retrospectively to surface collections already made, and in any case cannot be documented with the results of stratigraphic sequences. Therefore, it has been necessary to include in the category of presumed Middle Babylonian sites not only those where the newly identified features were found but also those where the presence of both Cassite and Neo-Babylonian ceramic types suggests the possibility of an occupation spanning the interval between these

periods. In short, the description of any individual site as having been occupied during the Middle Babylonian period rests on variable and insecure criteria. Even at best, the span of a particular occupation cannot be assumed with confidence to have overlapped such political events as the campaigns of Shamshi-adad V, rendering very difficult the attempt to identify named towns with archaeological sites.

With the qualifications mentioned, sites assumed to have been occupied during part or all of the Middle Babylonian period are listed in Table 15. In comparison with the 462 hectares of total settlement in the Isin-Larsa period and 230 hectares in the Cassite period, only 50 hectares can be recorded for the Middle Babylonian period. Compared with 129 Isin-Larsa sites and 104 Cassite sites, only 34 Middle Babylonian sites can be identified.[40]

Whatever the deficiencies in detail of our data for this period, the general validity of this picture of very sparse permanent settlement seems incontrovertible. It is supported not only by the large number of sites whose terminal occupation is characterized by "Cassite" pottery (albeit perhaps dating from after the end of the Cassite dynasty proper), but also by the continuing sparseness of settlement during the Neo-Babylonian period when uncertainty as to dating criteria is not a problem. For an interval during the first third of the first millennium B.C., in other words, external pressures seem to have forced the large-scale abandonment of settled irrigation agriculture as the prevailing mode of life, and probably to have reduced the total population of the region very substantially as a consequence.

There are several noteworthy features about the geographical distribution of Middle Babylonian sites in relation to those of earlier periods. The first is that it defines the same basic network of watercourses that had been known since prehistoric times. Rather than remaining within a perimeter of irrigation and cultivation which shrank northward toward the Jebel Hamrīn outlet as population declined—the process which occurred during Ottoman times (see Fig. 1)—at least some enclaves of settlement remained relatively far to the south. This suggests that the Diyala as a whole still pursued the regimen of a branching network rather than following a single incised bed for most of its length as it does at present, and that irri-

56

gation had not yet come to depend on long, artificially maintained canals as opposed to the earlier pattern of local ditches and flooding.

The persistence of some enclaves did not mean, however, that the abandonment of formerly cultivated areas proceeded everywhere at a uniform rate. Some formerly important areas apparently were given up almost completely, such as the large region extending southeast from Tell Asmar to the edge of the Subaicha depression. Of the many branches previously in use below that city, there is evidence in Middle Babylonian times for only a single, somewhat doubtful, watercourse pursuing a course directly southward

from its ruins. Equally striking is the abandonment of the long line of settlements farther to the southeast, along the banks of the watercourse provisionally identified as the Daban. Finally, we note that by Middle Babylonian times at least three former outlet channels leading from the lower Diyala into the Tigris River apparently had disappeared. Insofar as these gross differences may reflect natural as well as historical factors, they provide at least a hint that tectonic or other processes were already at work by the Middle Babylonian period, tending to alter the landscape gradually in the direction of its present appearance.

6

RESETTLEMENT AND URBANIZATION
(626 B.C.–A.D. 226)

THE EARLIER chronological units into which this report is divided are numbered continuously, from the ʿUbaid period as no. 1 to the Middle Babylonian period as no. 8. They are grouped into two successive phases on the basis of internal discontinuities connected with the Gutian invasion, but essentially they represent a single pattern of subsistence and settlement. At least in part as a result of the increasing subjection of the region to hostile outside forces which did not encourage its internal economy, traces of settled life had almost disappeared in the lower Diyala region by the end of Middle Babylonian times.

The third major phase embraces a transformation of this pattern, and not merely a cyclical return to the levels of its earlier, more successful episodes. For perhaps the first third of the new phase the qualitative nature of this change is not evident. The data of a surface survey, at least, reveal only the lineaments of a slow recovery from the nadir of the Middle Babylonian period, during which population and agricultural output probably rose considerably but still failed to reach the levels that the region had known in Early Dynastic or Isin-Larsa times. Then, with the advent of the Seleucids and their Parthian successors, a tremendous increase in settlement took place, accompanied by the first appearance of truly urban centers. Although not attaining the limits later reached during the Sassanian period, a considerable extension in the zone of irrigation also ensued which must have brought agriculturalists on the Diyala plains face to face with the entirely new problem of

chronic water shortages. And just as the earlier decline of the region is only understandable in relation to developments outside its boundaries, so these impressive changes cannot be viewed as a purely local outgrowth. They are the products, in a particular and favored locality, of new and wider modes of imperial organization that emerged from the contact of oriental monarchies with Hellenism.

1. THE NEO-BABYLONIAN PERIOD

As with the Middle Babylonian period, the period corresponding to the latter part of the Neo-Assyrian Empire and the Second Dynasty of Babylon is little known in the Diyala area. Place names that can be definitely identified with the region do not occur in Neo-Babylonian building inscriptions, nor are Neo-Babylonian stamped bricks (ubiquitous west of the Tigris) to be found on the surface of mounds in the Diyala basin. Apart from the discovery of a few figurines illustrated by Layard,[1] which may be of either Neo-Babylonian or Achaemenian date, excavations in the region have not probed strata belonging to this period.

Particulars for the known Neo-Babylonian sites are given in Table 16, and their geographic distribution may be seen in Figure 4. While the number of sites is not large enough to support a detailed reconstruction, in general it suggests that at least the major watercourses remained in approximately the positions they had occupied earlier. One possible exception is a portion of the Tigris course that forms a part of the southern boundary of the region. Too few Neo-

58

Babylonian sites are known to indicate clearly that the position of the Tigris River had changed, but it is noteworthy that two Neo-Babylonian sites (672, 832) lie substantially closer to the present bed of the Tigris than any older sites in the same district along its left bank. Thus it is possible that along this reach of the river there had been some displacement of the bed toward the southwest.

It is apparent from Table 16 that a modest increase in both the number of settled places and the total population of the region occurred during the Neo-Babylonian period. While not approaching even the sharply reduced figures for Cassite settlement, some recoil is evident from at least the extremely low sed-

TABLE 16

NEO-BABYLONIAN SITES IN THE LOWER DIYALA REGION

1. Middle Babylonian sites continuing into the Neo-Babylonian period:
   Large towns:
   590 (Tulūl Mujailiᶜ).
   Small towns:
   508.
   Villages:
   25, 81, 87, 88, 99, 118, 133, 137, 165, 195, 197, 222, 288, 303, 339, 427, 429, 435, 447, 450, 509, 566.
   Twenty-four sites, approximately 40 hectares of settlement.
2. Newly established Neo-Babylonian sites:
   Villages:
   29, 36, 107, 120, 121, 126, 139, 140, 143, 145, 146, 157, 170, 171, 186, 215, 223, 232, 238, 321, 457, 479, 495, 604, 629, 672, 687, 795, 832.
   Twenty-nine sites, approximately 35 hectares of settlement.
In total: 53 sites, aggregating approximately 75 hectares of settlement. This includes one large town occupying 10 hectares, and one small town occupying four hectares. Nineteen per cent of known settlement area was in towns.
3. Sites largely or wholly abandoned during or soon after the Neo-Babylonian period:
   Large towns:
   590.
   Villages:
   25, 29, 99, 107, 118, 120, 126, 133, 143, 146, 197, 222, 232, 288, 303, 427, 429, 447.

entary population of the Middle Babylonian period; specifically, there is a gain from 33 to 53 known sites and from 53 to 75 hectares of built-up settlement. On the other hand, it appears that these increases were entirely a product of the appearance of new villages, most of them very small, rather than resulting from the formation of larger towns. Moreover, most of the newly founded sites are scattered widely along the pre-existing network of watercourses rather than forming compact new groups in limited areas. Inconclusive as they admittedly are, these observations tend to corroborate the impression gained from the negative evidence of historical records that little attention was directed to the improvement or resettle-

ment of this region by most of the later Assyrian and Neo-Babylonian kings.[2]

2. THE ACHAEMENIAN PERIOD

The slow regeneration of settled life in the lower Diyala region, begun in the Neo-Babylonian period, continued during Achaemenian times. Table 17 indicates an increase from 53 to 57 known sites and from 75 to 100 hectares of built-up settlement. More important, it suggests that this expansion was a result primarily of the formation of several new towns, in contrast to the smaller villages which made their

TABLE 17

ACHAEMENIAN SITES IN THE LOWER DIYALA REGION

1. Neo-Babylonian sites continuing into the Achaemenian period:
   Small towns:
   508.
   Villages:
   36, 81, 87, 88, 121, 137, 139, 140, 145, 157, 165, 170, 171, 186, 195, 215, 223, 238, 321, 339, 435, 450, 457, 479, 495, 509, 566, 604, 629, 672, 687, 795, 832.
   Thirty-four sites, approximately 44 hectares of settlement.
2. Newly established Achaemenian sites:
   Small towns:
   37, 116, 149, 198, 588, 698.
   Villages:
   11, 76, 82, 114, 119, 228, 239, 326, 331, 465, 470, 638, 682, 693, 734, 742, 776.
   Twenty-three sites, approximately 56 hectares of settlement.
In total: 57 sites, aggregating approximately 100 hectares of settlement. This includes seven small towns occupying 38 hectares. Thirty-eight per cent of known settlement area was in towns.
3. Sites largely or wholly abandoned during or soon after the Achaemenian period:
   Small towns:
   37, 149, 508.
   Villages:
   76, 81, 87, 137, 139, 140, 165, 170, 186, 195, 228, 238, 321, 326, 331, 339, 465, 470, 479, 509, 629, 638, 687, 742.

appearance during the Middle Babylonian and Neo-Babylonian periods. While attaining a population level that appears to have been still less than half that of the Cassite period, total settlement during the Achaemenid period at least doubled from what it had been in Middle Babylonian times.

It must be conceded that this estimate is a minimal and perhaps somewhat misleading one. The Old Babylonian, Cassite, and Middle Babylonian periods had been times of abandonment, and accordingly a high proportion of their settlements was left in ruins and not reoccupied afterward. As a result, it may be assumed that they are disproportionately well represented in the findings of an archaeological surface reconnaissance. In contrast, the Neo-Babylonian and Achaemenian periods were a time of resettlement, anticipating the wave of city-building and the expan-

59

sion of cultivation that were introduced by the Greeks. Remains of these periods accordingly are to be found deeply buried beneath the debris of the immense ruined sites associated with the Seleucid, Parthian, and Sassanian periods. Quite possibly, therefore, both the number of sites and the total area of town and village settlement recorded for the Neo-Babylonian and Achaemenian periods need to be increased.

On the other hand, it seems reasonably certain that the broad outlines of the Achaemenian settlement pattern summarized in Table 17 are not an under-estimate to the point of serious distortion. At least some Achaemenian sherd types, as well as some of the Neo-Babylonian period, are highly distinctive and hence not easily overlooked during surface recon-naissance even when heavy later occupations reduce them to a minority of what remains on a site for ar-chaeological collection. Furthermore, while negative arguments are always less convincing than positive ones, the absence of contemporary cuneiform ar-chives reported to come from the area, or of unambig-uous historical references to important towns located in it, strongly suggests that the former extent of settled occupation had not yet been regained. More-over, it may be noted that a very limited extent of permanent Achaemenian settlement also has been ob-served in Khuzestan, where the immediate vicinity of the capital at Susa apparently stands out alone as an enclave of intensive cultivation.[3] At least until the capture of Babylon introduced a substantial new con-centration of sedentary agriculture, in other words, there are hints that the subsistence basis of the Achaemenian realm as a whole remained highly dis-persed, non-intensive, and perhaps even predomi-nantly pastoral. Such, at any rate, appears to have been the condition of the Diyala plains, amid the ruins of former towns and villages which periodically had prospered on irrigation for several millenniums.

Some slight hints are furnished by records of or about the Achaemenid rulers as to the extent to which the partial resettling of the area by sedentary cultiva-tors was the result of royal policy. Cyrus the Great claimed to have restored the images of the deities to their accustomed homes in Eshnunna and Meturnu, among other places, and at the same time to have brought together the scattered inhabitants of these towns.[4] On the other hand, no evidence of an Achaem-enid occupation was found at Eshnunna (Tell Asmar) during many seasons of excavations at the site. Possibly its original location had been forgotten during the preceding centuries of unrest; alternatively, of course, Cyrus may have constructed only a small shrine on a ruined mound which remained aban-doned.

A second reference to the area that is even more difficult to evaluate occurs in the anecdote recorded by Herodotus, according to which Cyrus undertook to punish the Gyndes (Diyala) River for the drown-ing of one of his sacred horses by laboriously diverting it into 360 separate channels, "making it so weak that even a woman could get over in future without diffi-culty and without wetting her knees." Conceivably this might be an allegorical description of the recon-stitution or enlargement of an irrigation network, although it is difficult to believe that Cyrus for so mundane a purpose would have failed to press toward his major objective of Babylon for a whole season. Without the capture of Babylon, after all, control of the region might be lost at any time. But in any case, no dense grouping of new Achaemenid sites, such as might have been expected if substantial irrigation projects had been completed, was found in the survey of the lower Diyala basin.

The distribution of newly founded Achaemenid settlements generally follows the earlier pattern of watercourses and presupposes no substantial changes in that pattern. Perhaps the most significant expan-sion in the settled area occurred in the southeastern part of the region, where a large enclave of settlement along the presumptive course of the lower Daban had been abandoned in Cassite times and not resettled heretofore. Three of the new sites (638, 742, 776) are scattered at wide intervals along the same line that had been followed during the Cassite period, suggest-ing that this watercourse still followed a natural river regime and hence was able to maintain its position even in the absence of periodic de-silting by sedentary cultivators along its banks. Moreover, the consider-able distance between these sites also seems to indi-cate that satisfactory irrigation still was possible based on local flooding and small-scale canalization in a limited area rather than on the construction of great integrated networks of weirs and canals.

In addition to the new sites along the lower Daban, several new settlements are to be observed southwest

60

of this line (693, 698, 734). At one of them, Sumāka or formerly Uskāf Banī Junayd (734), restricted exposures of Achaemenid strata, made by the Diyala Basin Archaeological Project, constitute the only evidence of the occupation of the region during this period that has been obtained in proper archaeological context. Encroaching further upon the position of the modern Tigris, these sites suggest that the movement of this river course toward the southwest, posited for the Neo-Babylonian period, continued into later times as well.

In general, in spite of a few of these abrupt local changes, the resettlement that continued during the Achaemenid period followed the lines of a much more ancient pattern of watercourse that remained virtually intact. And if we remain in some doubt as to the full extent of settlement in relation to earlier and later periods, at least it seems clear that even the moderate scale of land utilization of the time of the hegemony of Eshnunna was not equaled. There was no more than a dim foreshadowing of the explosive developments to come.

3. THE SELEUCID AND PARTHIAN PERIODS

The epoch that was introduced with the conquests of Alexander witnessed a transformation of the lower Diyala region far beyond the scope of any that had occurred. While still falling short of the later Sassanian and Abbasid achievements, the Seleucid and Parthian rulers of the area at least seem to have been responsible for introducing most of the basic innovations in settlement and irrigation which characterized the better-known later developments. It is to be regretted that the long span of more than half a millennium between Alexander's victory at Gaugamela and the coronation of Ardashir in A.D. 226 must be treated here as a single unit, since this may tend to obscure our understanding of the sequence and tempo of the crucial changes that were effected. However, the absence of good criteria for distinguishing Seleucid from Parthian types in ceramic surface collections leaves no alternative with respect to the archaeological reconnaissance upon which this account primarily is based.

Several aspects of the broader Hellenistic milieu that swept the Orient are particularly pertinent for this study, although they can only be briefly outlined here. Perhaps, above all, the intensive program of urbanization that is associated with Alexander and his successors finds reflection in the microcosm of our region. Seleucus I alone is credited with having founded not less than 75 cities,[5] while it is even said of Arsaces, the founder of the Parthian dynasty, that he filled Persia with cities.[6] With the forced transportation of much of the population of Babylon to the new capital at Seleucia on the Tigris, the population of the lower Diyala region must have been directly exposed for the first time to the influences of one of the great cosmopolitan centers of the ancient world.[7] The city of Ctesiphon was established directly across the river, originally as a camp for Parthian soldiery but subsequently as a trading entrepôt and as the great winter capital of the Arsacid dynasty.[8] Also within the Diyala region lay the city of Artemita, alternately described as Greek or Parthian in composition,[9] which Keppel was probably first among modern visitors to associate with the ruins of Karastel (74) near Baʿqūba.[10] Another center that was probably of urban dimensions and that occurs in classical sources is Scaphae,[11] probably the Lower Uskāf (826) of the Arabic sources.[12] As will be seen in Table 18, there were still other settlements of comparable size that apparently escaped the attention of at least those classical authors whose works have survived.

Another facet of both Seleucid and Parthian patterns of imperial control that is pertinent for the lower Diyala region was their stress on improvement of communications and commerce. The royal road from Seleucia to Bactria passed directly through the region, leading to the establishment of a network of village way stations along the great overland route that led northward through Artemita and thence northeast to Ecbatana (modern Hamadān).[13] Possibly at least a part of the expansion in settlement that the region subsequently witnessed is to be attributed to its proximity to the central artery of imperial administration and trade.

A third relevant feature of the Parthian period in particular was the relatively stable and peaceful conditions it imposed over a large area. Except for invasions at relatively long intervals, warfare with the Romans for the most part took place along the line of the Euphrates or in Armenia and did not lead to the destruction of towns or irrigation works in the

61

TABLE 18

SELEUCID AND PARTHIAN SITES IN
THE LOWER DIYALA REGION

1. Achaemenian sites continuing into the Seleucid or Parthian period:*
   Small urban centers:
   223 (Tulūl Khaṭṭāb, 56 ha.), 776 (50 ha.).
   Large towns:
   682 (Tulūl Abū Jāwan), 734 (Sumāka).
   Small towns:
   116, 198, 215, 588, 672, 698.
   Villages:
   11, 36, 82, 88, 114, 119, 121, 145, 171, 239?, 435, 450, 457, 566, 604, 693, 795, 832.

2. Newly established Seleucid or Parthian sites:
   Cities:
   74 (Karastel [Artemita?]), 666 (Salmān Pāk [Ctesiphon]), 814 (100 ha.), 826 (Tulūl al-Shuʿailah).
   Small urban centers:
   497 (Abū Jilāj), 627 (Tell Tabl), 791 (Tell al-Deir).
   Large towns:
   53 (12 ha.), 157, 218 (10 ha.), 246 (Tell Amlah), 275 (Tell al-Dīmī), 287 (Tell Borākhān al-saghīr), 300, 329 (Tell Umm al-Tarish), 338 (Tell Jimʿa), 358 (Tell Salāma), 607 (Tulūl Midr Rumaili, 18 ha.), 608 (Abū Sūqa), 618 (10 ha.), 663 (Tulūl Bāwi), 664 (Tulūl Bāwi), 711 (Tell Zuhra al-Sharqī), 756 (10 ha.), 770 (15 ha.), 799 (Jemdet Shahrazād), 833 (Tell al-Mlaich, 18 ha.), 836, 843 (10 ha.).
   Small towns:
   30, 45, 61, 69, 89, 108, 112, 125, 156, 234, 257, 269, 292, 304, 327, 335, 460, 476, 478, 492, 499, 510, 560, 567, 571, 580, 582, 584, 596, 605, 610, 617, 631, 662, 667, 671, 678, 763, 764, 767, 772, 779, 817, 850.
   Villages:
   1, 6, 8, 19, 28, 29, 32, 38?, 39, 52, 54, 57, 62?, 63, 64?, 67?, 75?, 85?, 92, 94, 111, 114, 117, 120, 128, 141, 144, 146, 155, 161, 165?, 170, 175, 194, 203, 214, 216?, 227, 232, 240, 242, 243, 248, 251, 262, 286, 294, 295, 311, 316, 323, 333, 342, 349, 353, 359, 375, 410, 415, 426, 440, 456, 459, 461, 484, 487,494, 495, 502?, 507, 513, 557?, 561?, 569, 595, 603, 612, 623, 633, 661, 668?, 669, 670, 673, 679, 680, 684, 738?, 745, 796?, 798, 810, 811, 812, 824, 829, 844, 858.

   In total: 199 sites, aggregating approximately 1,507 hectares of settlement. This includes four cities occupying about 430 hectares, five small urban centers occupying about 255 hectares, 24 large towns occupying about 345 hectares, 50 small towns occupying about 285 hectares, and 116 villages occupying about 172 hectares.

3. Sites largely or completely abandoned during or soon after the Parthian period:†
   Cities:
   814.
   Small urban centers:
   223, 776.
   Large towns:
   53, 218, 607, 618, 756, 770, 833, 843.
   Small towns:
   30, 45, 61, 69, 89, 108, 156, 215, 234, 257, 304, 327, 460, 476, 560, 580, 582, 584, 588, 596, 607, 610, 617, 631, 662, 671, 678, 698, 772, 779, 817, 850.
   Villages:
   6, 11, 36, 39, 63, 64, 75, 82, 88, 92, 94, 114, 116, 117, 119, 120, 121, 146, 161, 170, 171, 214, 227, 240, 243, 251, 262, 286, 294, 323, 342, 349, 410, 415, 426, 435, 440, 456, 457, 459, 461, 484, 487, 494, 495, 566, 569, 595, 604, 612, 623, 672, 679, 680, 684, 693, 795, 811, 824, 829, 832.
   One hundred and four sites, approximately 568 hectares of settlement.

---

* At many low and sprawling settlements of the Seleucid-Parthian and later periods it proved possible to distinguish relatively small portions of the site, often only individual small hummocks, to which Achaemenian debris was confined. This accounts for the substantial increases shown in the areas of some settlements between the Achaemenian and Seleucid-Parthian periods. See Appendix C for details.

As noted above (p. 39, n.), areas are given for individual sites only in cases where the occupation during this period was maximal or terminal, permitting its extent to be measured directly from observations of surface debris. Gross areas for groups of sites include these areas and areas of Sassanian sites with Seleucid-Parthian admixture in surface collections.

Site numbers followed by a question mark are small; their sparse surface remains allowed only a provisional dating to the Seleucid-Parthian period.

† This listing includes only those sites which could be definitely assigned to the Seleucid or the Parthian period.

62

heart of the empire. Moreover, even the sporadic Roman attacks upon Ctesiphon itself (prior to that of Julian in the Sassanian period) advanced and withdrew along a route to the west of the Tigris so that their effect on the Diyala region in the northern and eastern hinterlands of Ctesiphon must have been slight. Internal dynastic rivalries, to be sure, not infrequently led to fighting within the region; the final defeat of the pretender Molon by Antiochus III (220 B.C.), for example, seems to have occurred there.[14] But the objective of hostilities of this sort was the destruction of opposing armed forces rather than the systematic devastation of the region at large—whose continuing prosperity, after all, was to the advantage of all contending parties. In consequence, records of raids upon individual towns or cities become relatively rare, contrasting, for example, with the emphasis on such campaigns in Assyrian annals. An attack on Apamea by the Elamites within a few months of the onset of Parthian hegemony in Mesopotamia in 141 B.C. is a rare exception, only possible because at that time Mithradates I was engaged in the defense of another part of the empire.[15] In short, while the warlike character of the Parthian period generally is taken for granted, there are good grounds for believing that conditions within the Diyala region were relatively less disturbed by open hostilities and brigandage than they had been at any time previously. Probably a considerable part of the ensuing prosperity here finds a sufficient explanation.

The relevant archaeological record for the Diyala region itself is fragmentary or obscure. Excavations at Ctesiphon, while potentially most promising, have heretofore dealt mainly with building levels of the Sassanian period, and in any case only preliminary reports are yet available in which the ceramics are not described.[16] The earliest reference to Ctesiphon is in the time of Molon, who wintered in what was then (221 B.C.) merely a village by that name.[17] Pending further excavations, its subsequent development as a capital is unclear. It is said to have been strengthened with additional inhabitants and walls and made "the crowning ornament of Persia" by Pacorus (d. 38 B.C.),[18] but presumably its employment as a garrison post—and possibly even as a royal winter residence—antedated this expansion. While well situated from the point of view of commerce and communications, its growth as a metropolitan center clearly is explicable only as a consequence of wider Arsacid policy and not as the culmination of urbanization trends within the Diyala region alone. As Strabo observes, "Because of Parthian power . . . , Ctesiphon is a city rather than a village."[19]

For purposes of the present study, it is fortunate that Parthian levels in the neighboring city of Seleucia have been more extensively excavated and published. The ceramics have received a particularly full treatment,[20] providing the main basis for the selection of Parthian dating criteria used in the archaelogical reconnaissance of the Diyala region. In addition, soundings have been conducted by the Iraq Directorate General of Antiquities at Tell Abū Thar,[21] a small Parthian mound in the suburbs of Baghdad (starred mound southeast of Tell al-Dhibaʿi [411]; see reference map), and Parthian levels were encountered in the deep trench excavated at Sumāka (734) by the Diyala Basin Archaeological Project.

The most important and obvious impression to be drawn from Table 18 is of the immense expansion in Seleucid and Parthian times. In comparison with the Isin-Larsa period, the apogee of population and settlement trends in earlier antiquity, more than a threefold increase in settled area appears to have taken place.[22] While part of this increase is to be accounted for by the modest addition of individual sites, from 130 in Isin-Larsa times to 199 in the Seleucid and Parthian periods, in far larger part it reflects a process of urbanization that was unknown in the earlier period. As Table 18 indicates, this was true not only in the major centers of Seleucid and Arsacid power but throughout the region; in fact, it is assumed here that Ctesiphon itself attained exceptional size only in the Sassanian period,[23] while Seleucia is outside the region covered by this inquiry. But a whole new class of urban settlements appeared elsewhere in the Diyala region, and both the size and number of large towns also underwent a considerable expansion. This expansion is reflected in an increase in the average size of settlement from 3.5 hectares in the Isin-Larsa period to 8.8 hectares in Seleucid and Parthian times, and in a decline over the same period of the proportion of the total settled area consisting of villages and small towns (occupying less than ten hectares) from 62 to 30 per cent.

These comparisons thus far have been made, it will be observed, only with the earlier period of greatest expansion. If instead the Seleucid and Parthian settlements are contrasted with their immediate Achaemenian predecessors, the contrast becomes even more marked. More than a fifteen-fold increase in at least the recorded area of built-up settlement (although possibly less in reality, due to the tendency of rapidly expanding urban centers to mask the smaller communities out of which they had grown) was accompanied over this shorter span by a decisive shift from settlement exclusively in villages and small towns to a pattern in which these community types probably were occupied by only 30 per cent of the region's inhabitants.

The magnitude of these changes, in fact, is such as to pose several interpretive problems. In the first place, a calculation similar to that attempted earlier (supra, p. 41), first of population and then of total cultivated area from the data in Table 18 on the total area of built-up settlement, would seem to indicate that 4,500 sq. kms. of irrigable land were necessary as a subsistence base for the Seleucid and Parthian population of the region. This is the maximum area, if not somewhat more than the maximum area, for which the Diyala alone is sufficient as a source of irrigation water. Hence, if the Diyala is assumed to have been the only important source, it leaves no allowance for the substantial expansion that took place in Sassanian times. Moreover, it does not accord with the distribution of Seleucid and Parthian sites that may be observed in Figure 4, for there it is apparent that a number of large subareas within the Diyala region either were still unsettled or at best very lightly settled until the end of the Parthian period. Clearly, not only the data on settlement given in Table 18 but also the estimates of population and cultivated area that are calculated from them require closer scrutiny before the character and full extent of the changes in the Seleucid and Parthian periods can be properly evaluated.

A possible approach to this problem is to claim that the area of settlements given in Table 18 is a substantial overestimate. In the first place, the Seleucid and Parthian sites, being younger, are relatively less submerged beneath a rising blanket of alluvium than those of earlier antiquity. Second, there are a few sites whose attribution to the Parthian period is questionable or which may have been primarily non-residential in character.[24] These slightly reduce the total

63

area of settlement, although admittedly their effect is negligible. Third, it must be conceded that at many large sites which attained their greatest dimensions in the Sassanian period, our surface reconnaissance provides little basis for determining the probable limits of pre-Sassanian settlement. Since Parthian ceramic types are much more varied and distinctive than those of the Sassanian period, an approximately equal number of Parthian and Sassanian dating criteria in a given surface collection might be obtained even where a large Sassanian town or city was preceded only by a relatively small Parthian village. If this occurred in a significant number of instances, a substantial reduction in the total of built-up area given in Table 18 would be in order.

However, the data in Table 18 on sites whose occupation was terminated in the Parthian period serve very clearly to minimize the probable extent of at least the latter discrepancy. In the case of these terminal sites, there is no difficulty in assessing accurately the areas of occupation during the Seleucid and Parthian periods, and it is noteworthy that the total area of terminal Parthian settlement alone substantially exceeds the total estimated area of all Isin-Larsa settlement (568 hectares as compared with 462 hectares). Moreover, the proportion of terminal Parthian settlements to the total for the Parthian period is approximately 3/8, almost identical with the Isin-Larsa period, although the latter was followed by a substantial and general retraction rather than expansion. In addition, it is evident from a breakdown of sites not occupied after the Parthian period that in at least some cases individual communities attained dimensions in the Seleucid or Parthian periods already comparable with those of most Sassanian cities. In spite of what may have been the greater propensity for large rather than small settlements to persist into later times, 54 per cent of the terminal Parthian sites are classifiable as cities or large towns exceeding 10 hectares in area. In short, while some reduction in the total of 1,507 hectares of settlement may be justified for purposes of computing the population of the region, on the basis of non-residential sites or overestimates of the extent of Parthian occupation at sites that continued into later periods, these factors are seemingly of a very modest order.

Another possible source of an excessive estimate for the Seleucid-Parthian period can be still more readily disposed of. A number of clear and unequivocal dating criteria for surface collections of the Seleucid and Parthian periods are available, documented by the ceramic findings of fairly extensive stratigraphic excavations. Confidence in the attribution of a Seleucid or Parthian dating on the basis of surface collections is further increased by the independent evidence of coins.[25]

Thus there is no apparent reason to doubt that the area devoted to city, town, and village settlements underwent a manifold increase after the Achaemenian period, and that the unprecedented extent of Seleucid and Parthian ruins in comparison with those of earlier periods is a valid observation and not an artifact of the archaeological reconnaissance itself. But what of the population inhabiting these many new settlements—did it undergo an increase in proportion to the increased area of ruins? There are two lines of argument which suggest that it did not.

The first involves the probable effect on oriental urban densities of the new concepts of city planning associated with Hellenism. In the absence of extensive excavations in Hellenistic sites in Mesopotamia, one can only assume that an appreciable reduction in density would have been brought about, at least temporarily, by the more diversified range of public works and buildings associated with Greek cities. Moreover, the grid of wide streets seen in the Seleucia town plan would, if this feature were widely repeated, also act to reduce density. In a broader sense, of course, the quantitative effect of these factors depends less upon differences between ideal Greek and Babylonian town plans than on the extent to which Greek cultural patterns were followed outside of a handful of major Greek centers like Seleucia. As Rostovstev notes, only further excavations can answer this question. But since he also records tantalizing hints of how far Greek patterns may have succeeded in predominating,[26] it would be prudent to assume that some general reduction of density may have occurred as a result.

A second reason for not assuming an increase in population fully equivalent to that in area of ruins arises from the probability of sequent, as opposed to fully contemporary, occupation of many Seleucid and Parthian communities. Since the period considered as a unit for purposes of surface reconnaissance lasted approximately 560 years, a very long time span in

64

comparison with most of our other periods, it is not unreasonable to suppose that the proportion of sites which was not occupied simultaneously was relatively larger than in the case of, for example, the Ur III and Isin-Larsa period, which lasted perhaps 325 years. Since the Neo-Babylonian and Achaemenian periods were much briefer still, this factor would tend even more to heighten the contrast between them and the Seleucid-Parthian period.

The possibilities for sequent occupance are dependent not only on the duration of the period but also on its character. The policy of urbanization which the classical sources are virtually unanimous in attributing to the Seleucid and Parthian rulers implies, after all, both the colonization of new cities and towns and the relocation of smaller rural communities in and around the newly formed centers. Moreover, at least during the Sassanian period, tax rates and collections decreased with increasing distance from the royal towns, allowing the founding, expansion, or decline of such towns to be regarded as an aspect of the interplay for power between the ruling dynasty and the landed nobility.[27] Since roughly similar conditions and motives may be reasonably inferred for the Parthian period as well, powerful forces would have been at work leading to a heightened rate of both town formation and abandonment.

It should be understood, of course, that these qualifications upon the probable extent of population growth during the Hellenistic period are not intended to deny that it did occur on a very impressive scale. For the first time in history something approaching the modern population of the Diyala region (exclusive of Baghdad) must have been attained. Must we visualize this greatly enlarged population continuing to depend for its subsistence on irrigation maintained by small-scale gravity-flow canals stemming from one of the Diyala's numerous natural channels? As the maps of earlier distributions of settlements in the area indicate, such had been the preponderant pattern in earlier antiquity. But as Figure 4 shows, many of the larger Seleucid and Parthian sites tend to concentrate instead along the Tigris River flanks of the region. This suggests that the Tigris was assuming increasing importance—either as an artery of commerce in bulk or as a supplementary source of irrigation water or both.

With the construction of Seleucia and Ctesiphon,

the lower Diyala region was transformed from its earlier condition as a perilously independent minor kingdom or a border district contended for by invading forces to one of the most populous and vital regions of a great empire. While long-distance trade was principally in luxuries, some net flow of subsistence products also may have occurred into the cities of the region from more remote districts. The extent to which part of the population may not have depended on food produced locally cannot, of course, be quantified with the relatively crude data of a survey.

In addition, it is not unlikely that a calculation of subsistence limits on the basis of Diyala water alone would fail to take into account the lifting of water from the Tigris as a significant secondary source. With only the hand-operated $sh\bar{a}d\bar{u}f$ having been common in much of earlier antiquity, water could not have been drawn profitably from the deep bed of the Tigris. But with the introduction of pulleys and animal traction in Assyrian or later times this became comparatively easy.[28] As a supplementary subsistence source that helps to explain the density of Seleucid and Parthian population, we must visualize a newly created fringe of date gardens along the Tigris, particularly in the vicinity of Ctesiphon.[29]

An additional corollary of increasing urbanization and population density was the formation of broad zones, rather than narrow enclaves, of settlement. The city of Artemita, for example, occupied about 1.5 sq. kms., roughly five times as great an area as any of the towns of earlier antiquity. Even if the population of Artemita at any one time was somewhat less dense than that of earlier towns, it is clearly only one of several urban communities in the region, each of which must have housed 20,000 or more people. Assuming that the bulk of its subsistence needs was met from its own immediate hinterlands, an irrigated area slightly more than 19 kms. in diameter would have been required for subsistence, more than twice as large as had been necessary during earlier periods.

This problem was accentuated still further when a number of large, adjacent communities were closely spaced along a watercourse, as was the case particularly in the southeastern corner of the Diyala area. Under these circumstances, effective irrigation came to depend more and more on the construction of large and fairly lengthy lateral canals to conduct water from the major watercourses to the distant limits of

65

cultivation. And in some regions, as particularly in the immediate hinterlands of Ctesiphon, the dense distribution of sites and population seems to presuppose, for the first time in the history of the region, the formation of a virtually continuous zone of cultivation and settlement that embraced several networks of streams and canals rather than a single arterial watercourse and its minor effluents.

Moreover, the increasing construction of lateral canals must have had substantial effects on the regimes of the parent streams. Increasing withdrawals of water undoubtedly led to greater silt deposition in the major channels, and would also have reduced the capacity of periodic floods to scour the beds and thus maintain a natural equilibrium. Hence an increasing amount of attention to the arterial watercourses themselves is implied by the Seleucid and Parthian expansion, probably taking the form of attempts to dredge and straighten channels in order to maintain flow. Not surprisingly, some of the larger Parthian watercourses still can be followed on the surface as relatively straight and narrow levees (albeit low and badly eroded in comparison with those of later times); examples of this include the long ridge running southeast through site 156, the levee leading southeast to site 679, and a number of levees in the Ctesiphon area.

These, incidentally, are the oldest canal levees unambiguously recognizable today on the Diyala plains. Others, including those of the major watercourse systems of earlier antiquity, must have continued to be used periodically for later canal branches, and hence must underlie some of the major levee deposits shown by long tongues in the surface contours on the reference map. But no canals or watercourses which were abandoned earlier than these of the Parthian period can be followed from surface contours alone. The approximate courses of all earlier canals have to be inferred primarily from the evidence of contemporary sites which presumably adjoined their banks, and only secondarily from the congruence of these approximate courses with broad, gently sloping levees known to have been used later but reasonably certain to be very ancient in origin.

Before completing this brief survey of the Seleucid and Parthian periods, some discussion is necessary of a few specific features of the system of watercourses reconstructed in Figure 4. Among these is the position of the Tigris, which for the first time can be accurate-

ly fixed at least at a few points. The dry meandering bed shown south and west of the present Tigris course in the vicinity of the ʿAdheim River mouth was abandoned only in the thirteenth century (see *infra*, p. 91). But numerous large sites along its banks indicate that this was the main Tigris channel at least as early as the Seleucid period. Prior to that time there were also a very few large sites, suggesting that probably this was the position of the river through most or all of man's earlier occupation of the Mesopotamian alluvium. However, since not more than one early site for any given period was located which lay along this entire section of the river, no attempt has been made to reconstruct this portion of the course in maps for earlier periods.[30]

A second fixed point along the Tigris is its passage between Seleucia and Ctesiphon. Above these ruins no clear topographic evidence of its earlier course remains until the aforementioned dry bed is encountered 60 kms. to the north-northwest; presumably all traces of old channels and oxbows have been blurred or eliminated as a result of more recent floods and the expansion of Baghdad itself. But below Seleucia and Ctesiphon there are both topographic and historical indications that the river broadened at its junction with the Nahr al-Mālik, the Yūsifiyah canal of today.[31] Then its course is lost from sight again for 40 kms. or more, and the illustrated loop which places sites 693, 698, and 779 directly along its banks is a frankly speculative reconstruction based only on difficulties of tying in those sites with canals emanating from the Diyala.

Since in Islamic times the river flowed past Deir al-ʿĀqūl, "the Convent of the [river] Loop,"[32] and since an inspection of its extensive present-day remains that are called Tell al-Deir (791) indicates that the Parthian and Sassanian phases of occupation were even more important than that of the Islamic, it is probably safe to assume that the Tigris flowed just to the northeast,[33] at least in the Parthian period. And then finally, the identification of Islamic Lower Uskāf with Ptolemaic Scaphae permits a tentative position to be established for the Tigris not far from the southeastern limits of the Diyala region. If the rather impressionistic Ptolemaic map of Mesopotamia in that period can be relied upon,[34] Scaphae in fact lay on the right, or southwest, bank of the Tigris, and hence was outside the Diyala basin altogether as it

66

was then constituted. This, however, required either the reconstruction of a meander loop substantially wider than any now known along the middle portion of the Tigris, with an inexplicable corresponding increase in the bed width of the Tigris itself (*supra*, p. 10), or the assumption that the surface of the alluvial plain was distorted by tectonic movement. In the absence of substantiating evidence for either of these possibilities, the course of the river has been reconstructed in Figure 4 as passing to the south of Scaphae and continuing more or less along the line later taken by the Nahrawān canal. It should be stressed, of course, that the entire reconstruction below Ctesiphon is an abstraction which omits the changing meander pattern that the river undoubtedly followed.

Another feature of the system of Seleucid-Parthian watercourses needing separate discussion is an apparent shift in the westernmost branch of the Diyala that took place during this interval. Following approximately the line of the modern Muradīya canal 9 kms. west of the present bed of the Diyala, this branch had remained uninterruptedly in use since the prehistoric period. The distribution of Seleucid and Parthian sites along the crest of its levee and a few short, right bank offtakes indicates that it remained in use for most of the Parthian period. But subsequently it was abandoned, and apparently remained so for many centuries. Although intensive date and fruit cultivation makes topographic reconnaissance of the area difficult, the Diyala seems to have burst through directly to the south along roughly its present course near a cluster of sites (48–55) which currently are being undercut by the deeply entrenched stream. Possibly this new course resulted from the digging of a canal that ran southward to Baʿqūba, whose Aramaic name suggests that it came into existence as a town at least by the Sassanian period and possibly earlier. Such a canal, if allowed to run out of control, might have served to divert the stream into the new bed it has occupied ever since. At any rate, sites which remained in use afterward along the old stream levee farther to the west must have depended on a series of newly constructed lateral canals leading southwest from the main stream, like those of the Sassanian period whose levees still can be traced on the surface.

While the fact of this shift is beyond dispute, its timing is not. The interpretation that it took place in late Parthian rather than early Sassanian times rests primarily on a low but still visible canal levee running from Tell al-Tayyān (234) southeastward past Medar (492). Since these and other sites along this course were occupied by at least the late Parthian period, and since the head of this levee cannot be traced west of the present course of the Diyala, it is assumed that the canal was constructed only after the Diyala had shifted to its new bed. Unfortunately, the canal intersects with the great Nahrawān levee below Medar, so that its further course cannot be followed on the ground or by means of aerial photographs. However, the location of Parthian sites and of adjoining canal levees (which concededly may not antedate the Sassanian period) suggests that the Medar canal could have extended originally as far as Scaphae (826) on the Tigris. This is the reconstruction—admittedly inconclusive—that is shown in the map for the Seleucid and Parthian periods. If correct, it indicates that the lower part of the great Nahrawān canal of the Sassanian period already had been substantially anticipated by Parthian canal construction.

A third and final problem of local interpretation concerns the possible existence in Seleucid or Parthian times of what is now the upper part of the Khālis canal. The district served by this canal occupies the northernmost part of the lower Diyala basin. Since there was insufficient time during the field reconnaissance to examine any sites along its course, its age remains uncertain. On the basis of its relative "youth" from the viewpoint of canal morphology[35] and of a plausible reconstruction of its sequence of growth (p. 108, *infra*), however, it may be regarded provisionally as having been constructed only at a later period.

Briefly to recapitulate, the Seleucid and Parthian periods saw an immense expansion in the built-up area of settlement that was recorded by the survey, coupled with the formation of many new towns and cities. While for a number of reasons our estimates are not directly comparable with those of earlier antiquity, it appears certain that total population substantially exceeded any previous level, and was many times as large as it had been during the preceding Achaemenian period. On the other hand this expansion was still uneven, leaving parts of the lower Diyala region with few or no permanent communities and other parts densely settled.

Around the larger cities and in those areas with numerous, closely spaced, smaller settlements, a substantial extension of the cultivated zone apparently took place, based on new lateral canal construction. In consequence, the regime of the major Diyala branches undoubtedly also changed, assuming gradually an increasingly "artificial" character for that network as a whole. Probably at this time significant supplies of water also were obtained from the Tigris by lifting devices, permitting intensive garden cultivation along its banks. Additional food may have been brought into the area through commerce or taxation, for the support of at least the upper strata in its urban population.

Thus three major developments are implicit in the results of the survey: extensive urbanization, population growth, and the gradual transformation of the irrigation system in the direction of a more intensive, large-scale, artificially maintained, and regionally interdependent enterprise. It is obvious that all of these developments are not to be understood as products of the isolated evolution of the Diyala region alone. Instead they are at least in part a consequence of the wider and wider integration of society in classical antiquity. The major stimulus for the grandiose new patterns of subsistence and settlement lay not in the remote Akkadian or Babylonian past, but in the interplay of Hellenistic influences with the power and resources of a great Persian Empire.

68

7

THE LIMITS OF AGRICULTURAL EXPANSION
(A.D. 226-637)

THE FOURTH major phase in the historical demography and ecology of the lower Diyala basin was its culmination. In the number of occupied sites, in the breadth of settlement and cultivation, in the dispersion of urban construction, and above all in the massiveness of state-initiated irrigation enterprises upon which those other features largely depended, maxima were reached far in excess of anything before or since. In the process there gradually emerged a new and more comprehensive approach to the utilization of land and water within the region as a whole, an approach which promoted stability and vastly increased prosperity but which also left the rural agriculturalist increasingly dependent on the intervention of a regime which was itself unstable. Even before the political demise of the Sassanian dynasty the economic benefits that earlier Sassanid rule had conferred upon the region had been vitiated by oppressive taxation, devolution of authority into the hands of the landed nobility, and military disaster.

Many of the detailed characteristics of Sassanian rule lie outside the scope of this study, but some of its more general features, directly relevant to the development of the Diyala area, deserve brief mention. As a whole, it was stronger and more centralized than that of the preceding Parthian period, with the nobility more closely dependent on positions at court and with the progressive growth of an organized state bureaucracy. However, the increased firmness of royal control was not a phenomenon that manifested itself immediately and uniformly. In fact, it only emerged gradually[1] and with marked fluctuations during the course of the dynasty.

Particularly noteworthy for present purposes is the repeated description of Sassanian kings as having founded cities in many parts of their realm, a continuation of Seleucid and Parthian practices recounted in the previous chapter. Only to a degree, however, may the retention of this policy be viewed as a continuing stimulant to commerce and regional growth. More frequently it had become an instrument for the consolidation of royal power at the expense of the nobility in newly rewon territories,[2] a forced and artificial transfer of populations that may have reaped as large a harvest in social and economic disruption as it did in enhanced commercial, craft, or financial strength from the creation of new urban centers. Moreover, as a policy it remained closely linked to the continuing drain of hostilities with Rome. Hence, even the transformation of the irrigation system of Khuzestan,[3] accomplished through the forced labor and resettlement of the 70,000 captives taken by Shapur I after defeating the Roman emperor Valerian near Edessa, must be counterbalanced against the onerous cessions of territory in the west that in turn were demanded of his two immediate successors.[4] And within the Diyala region itself, the removal of a body of the skilled and cosmopolitan citizenry of Edessa and Alexandria to Dastagird and Daskara by Chosroes II was quickly counterbalanced by their flight when a campaign by Heraclius provided opportunity.[5]

Within the Diyala area as it was then constituted,

69

two instances of the royal founding of cities can be documented which subsequently will be shown to have had profound effects on the distribution of population and on the irrigation system. The first involved the founding of Buzurg-Shapur, later known as ᶜUkbarā,[6] by Shapur I (A.D. 241–72); its population included many prisoners from successful Syrian campaigns,[7] although apparently not any large contingent of the Roman legionnaires captured with Valerian.[8] The second case was the resettling of the exiled population of Syrian Antioch by Chosroes I Anōsharwān in a new city named Weh-Antiokh-i-Khosrau, a city painstakingly patterned after its namesake and thenceforth placed directly under the protection and patronage of that ruler.[9] But whatever differences there may have been in the sources from which the new populations were drawn, it is significant that in these as in most other instances elsewhere in the Sassanian realm the formation of cities was undertaken by kings whose wealth and power had been augmented through highly successful military campaigns.

A second aspect, then, of the Sassanid period was the periodic resumption of imperial hostilities with Rome, which undoubtedly had pervasive effects on the lower Diyala basin. To be sure, for the most part this did not involve direct penetration of the Diyala area itself. After having been stormed three times in the course of the second century A.D. during the declining years of Parthian power, Ctesiphon was subsequently taken only once by invading forces prior to the rise of Islam, by the emperor M. Aurelius Carus in 283. Moreover, Roman forces were extensively deployed on the left bank of the Tigris, in the Diyala area proper, only on two occasions: during the disastrous retreat of Julian in 363 after the burning of his fleet had prevented the return of his army over the route by which it had advanced, and in Heraclius' more destructive foray into the northern part of the area in 627–28.

In many respects, however, the course of developments in the Diyala area was more continuously, if indirectly, set by the varying military fortunes of Sassanian armies with Byzantium on the western and northwestern frontiers. From the accounts of Julian's advance against Ctesiphon, for example, the destructive, long-term effects of Sassanian-Roman hostilities become evident even along the Middle Euphrates and Nahr al-Mālik, deep inside the normal frontier. Persian defensive measures included widespread destruction of dikes and flooding[10] and, at the same time, the damming-up of major waterways to prevent their use for Roman transport.[11] Julian's army, for its part, not only took by storm the major cities and strong points along its line of march, but also burned the abandoned smaller towns and villages whose occupants had fled and even sent out small parties to destroy herds and crops.[12] In the case of the larger cities, Roman campaigns were particularly decisive. Seleucia, with perhaps 80,000 inhabitants prior to that time (cf. infra, p. 175, n. 7) had been virtually obliterated by Avidius Cassius in A.D. 165, and Septimius Severus found it abandoned thirty years later.[13] Reconstituted by the first of the Sassanian kings as Weh-Ardashir,[14] the smaller settlement within the older ruins was again sacked by Carus in 283 and remained deserted even eighty years later at the time of Julian's visit.[15]

In sum, there was repeated, widespread destruction not only of towns and urban centers but of basic agricultural facilities upon which recovery would depend. Both as a natural movement of people seeking protection and as a conscious Sassanian policy, it is understandable that attention thenceforth was directed primarily to the development of Ctesiphon as a capital and of the Diyala area as an agricultural region, rather than to the regions and towns exposed to the military threat on the right bank of the Tigris.

This finds at least partial corroboration in reconnaissance data. While the widest extent of human occupation in the Diyala area occurred in the Sassanian period, it was the conclusion of a survey west of the Tigris River in the area of ancient Akkad that the most extensive settlement there had taken place in Parthian times and was followed by a substantial retraction.[16]

One other general feature of Sassanian rule is relevant to our discussion of developments within the Diyala region. The middle years of the Sassanian period witnessed a steady growth in the powers and freedom of action of the landed nobility at the expense of the king and his officialdom. This trend, however, was arrested by the sanguinary fighting precipitated by the rise of the Mazdakite movement, and the tax reforms initiated by Kavadh (A.D. 488–531) and extended and codified by Chosroes I Anōsharwān (531–579) substantially erased the favored position

70

that the nobility had enjoyed. In the sequel, the revenues available to the Sassanian ruler greatly increased, permitting the maintenance of a royal army without the traditional dependence on the contributions of the nobility—and also permitting the underwriting of civic enterprises on a vastly greater scale than had been known. Thus, under Chosroes I we learn of the construction of forts to improve security on the roads, of the repair of bridges, of the reconstruction of ruined villages, and of the improvement and extension of canals and irrigation works.[17]

Already under Kavadh, the Sawād, i.e., roughly the territory of ancient Babylonia, alone contributed more than 214,000,000 dirhems in annual taxes under the new and more stringent schedule, a sum perhaps very roughly equivalent to $73,000,000 at the present level of U.S. currency. Although marked fluctuations may have occurred subsequently, tax revenues for the same area from the Sawād by the eighteenth regnal year of Chosroes II Parvez (590–628) probably had increased to approximately 240,000,000 dirhems, and before the end of that king's reign to more than 340,000,000 dirhems, an increase of about 60 per cent in less than a century.[18]

While total revenues prior to the reform are not known, it seems clear that they were only a fraction of these figures. Herein lay the source of at least the financial capacity of the later Sassanian rulers not only to increase the opulence of royal life at Ctesiphon and Dastagird but to assume an unprecedented responsibility for agricultural planning and economic well-being. This attitude finds concise expression in a maxim attributed by Masʿudī to Chosroes I Anōsharwān.

> Royal power rests upon the army, and the army upon money, and money upon the land-tax [kharāj], and the land-tax upon agriculture, and agriculture upon just administration, and just administration upon the integrity of government officials, and the integrity of government officials upon the reliability of the vizier, and the pinnacle of all of these is the vigilance of the king in resisting his own inclinations, and his capability so to guide them that he rules them and they do not rule him.[19]

Like the historical and documentary record, the archaeological record for the Sassanian period is relatively more complete than for the Parthian period. Exposures to date have not been extensive enough to reveal many details of city-planning, although some of the grandiose public buildings of Ctesiphon have been measured and described.[20] Excavations conducted by the Diyala Basin Archaeological Project have exposed Sassanian levels at Sumāka (734) and the remains of a Sassanian weir at Al-Qantara (718) (Figs. 18–19), while from sites like Qasr-i-Shīrīn and Kish there are full accounts of Sassanian architecture in regions adjacent to the Diyala area.[21]

From the viewpoint of the present study, however, present knowledge of the Sassanian period remains seriously deficient with regard to ordinary household ceramics. In part, the problem is one of an impoverished technical and stylistic repertoire. Perhaps as a consequence of the contemporary emphasis given to metalwork, it has been noted that most of the excavated material "is so poor, both artistically and technically, that it cannot be regarded as instructive, and is consequently of little value for exact dating."[22] But also it seems undeniable that the potentialities of domestic refuse for cultural and chronological understanding have been neglected for those of public architecture in sites like Ctesiphon. In consequence, the dating criteria used in the surface reconnaissance rest to an unusually large degree on types provisionally established from the surface collections themselves and on unpublished vessels or sherds in the Iraq Museum. Quite possibly, the partial circularity of method that is imposed by this deficiency has led in some cases to the confusion of early Sassanian with late Parthian remains, or, more significantly, of late Sassanian remains with those of the Early Islamic period. In general, however, the conspectus of Sassanian ceramic forms and surface treatments as utilized in the reconnaissance seems sufficiently consistent to indicate that future seriational studies will affect detailed interpretations of the survey data but not the major conclusions derived from them.

Table 19 summarizes the findings of the survey for the Sassanian period. It makes abundantly clear the full extent of further growth in settlement beyond the levels already attained in the Parthian period: there are slightly more than twice the number of individual Sassanian sites and about the same proportion of increase in the the total built-up area of settlement. For all of the stress in Sassanian state ideology on the legitimacy of descent of the dynasty from Achaemenian kings,[23] it is worth pointing out that at least in the Diyala area the Sassanian period saw not merely a

71

TABLE 19

SITES OF THE SASSANIAN PERIOD IN THE LOWER DIYALA REGION

1. Parthian sites continuing into, or reoccupied during, the Sassanian period:

Cities:

74 (Karastel [Artemita?], 150 hectares), 338 (Tell Jim'ah, 100 ha.), 666 (Salmān Pāk [Ctesiphon, including Asfānabr], 540 ha.), 734 (Sumāka), 791 [Tell al-Deir, 100 ha.], 826 (Tell al-Shu'aila, 100 ha.).

Six sites, approximately 1,390 hectares of settlement.

Small urban centers:

497 (Abū Jilāj, 55 ha.), 627 (Tell Tabl).

Two sites, approximately 99 hectares of settlement.

Large towns:

157 (10 ha.), 223 (Tulūl Khattāb, 20 ha.), 246 (Tell Amlah, 16 ha.), 275 (Tell al-Dīmī, 13 ha.), 287 (Tell Borākhān al-Seghīr), 300 (12 ha.), 329 (Tulūl Umm al-Tarish, 18 ha.), 358 (Tell Salāma, 20 ha.), 450 (11 ha.), 492 (Medar, 27 ha.), 608 (Abū Sūqa, 10 ha.), 663 (Tulūl Bāwi, 15 ha.), 664 (Tulūl Bāwi, 18 ha.), 682 (Tulūl Abū Jāwan, 17 ha.), 711 (Tell Zuhra al-Sharqī), 799 (Jemdet Shahrazād), 802 (14 ha.), 833 (Tell al-Mlaich, 18 ha.), 836 (10 ha.).

Nineteen sites, approximately 297 hectares of settlement.

Small towns:

125, 234, 269, 292, 295, 335, 478, 499, 510, 567, 571, 605, 667, 672, 738, 763, 764, 767.

Eighteen sites, approximately 110 hectares of settlement.

Villages:*

1, 8, 19, 28, 32, 38?, 53, 54, 57 (2), 108, 111, 112 (2), 128, 141, 144, 145, 155, 165?, 175, 194, 203, 216?, 232, 242, 300, 311 (2), 316, 323, 333, 353, 359, 375, 434, 502, 507, 513, 557?, 584, 588, 603, 633 (2), 661, 669, 670 (6), 673, 745, 796, 798, 801, 810, 843, 844, 858.

Sixty-two sites, approximately 90 hectares of settlement.

Mainly non-residential:†

52, 62?, 67?, 85, 668 (2)?

Six sites, approximately 6 hectares.

2. Newly Founded Sassanian Sites:

Cities:

41 (Bint al-Emīr, Eski Baghdad [Daskara]), 252 (Tell Abū Ja'ari, 150 ha.), 620 ('Abertā‡, 150 ha.).

Three sites, approximately 444 hectares of settlement tabulated 1 additional site (Weh-Antiokh-i-Khosrau, or Rūmīyā) known but unlocated.

Small urban centers:

363 (Tulūl Rughāth), 700.

Two sites, approximately 89 hectares of settlement.

Large towns:

15 (Tell al-Hafa²ir 27 ha.), 167, 219 (16 ha.), 250 (2), 407 (12 ha.), 467, 472 (Fleye, 17 ha.), 480 (Tell Abū Chit, 18 ha.), 538 (14 ha.), 544, 601 (15 ha.), 613 (Tell Abū Fahadah), 689, 704 (Tell Abū Khansīrah, 25 ha.), 705.

Sixteen sites, approximately 302 hectares of settlement tabulated; 6 additional sites§ known.

Small towns:

7, 37, 44, 129, 206, 208, 237, 247, 274, 288, 290, 324, 328, 332, 379, 424, 477, 500, 504, 533, 543, 578 (2), 593, 609, 619, 625, 626, 647, 658, 676, 708, 712, 717, 722, 724, 727 (2), 777, 828, 839.

Forty-one sites, approximately 246 hectares of settlement.

Villages:

4 (4), 5, 9, 13, 17, 18, 21, 34, 35, 40, 47, 48, 49, 50, 51, 55, 59 (3), 60, 66 (2), 72, 73, 80, 83 (2), 86, 91, 93, 95, 101 (4), 110, 126, 130?, 131, 132, 135, 136, 138, 143, 148, 150 (2), 151 (6), 153, 154, 168, 173 (2), 174, 177 (2), 178, 180, 190, 196?, 199 (2), 200, 201, 205, 206, 207, 208, 209, 210, 224, 226, 228 (2), 230, 233, 235, 241, 245, 248 (4), 249, 250, 254 (4), 258, 259, 260, 263 (2), 265, 266, 271, 272, 278 (3), 279, 281, 299, 310 (6), 312, 315, 317, 319, 320, 322, 325, 328, 330, 334, 336, 337 (2), 344, 345, 346, 350, 352, 357, 361, 367, 368, 371, 374, 376, 385, 387, 388, 394, 398, 408, 416, 420, 425, 428, 432, 433, 444, 451, 469, 473, 475, 486, 488, 491, 501, 505, 506, 511, 512, 516, 519, 523?, 525 (2), 526, 527, 528, 529, 532, 537, 540, 542, 546, 549 (2), 559?, 565, 570, 572, 574, 583, 586, 587, 589 (3), 591, 594, 597, 598, 611, 614, 630, 632, 638, 659, 660, 674, 675, 676 (2), 701, 707, 715, 716, 725, 732?, 735, 737, 740 (3), 744, 746, 747 (4), 756, 782, 788, 790 (2), 793, 797 (2), 803, 815, 816, 821, 822, 831, 841, 846, 848, 854, 862.

Two hundred and forty-six sites, approximately 350 hectares of settlement.

Mainly non-residential:

2?, 3, 42, 84, 104, 211?, 225, 313, 348, 409, 438 (2), 468, 562, 564?, 775.

Sixteen sites, approximately 66 hectares.

In total: 437 recorded sites, aggregating approximately 3,489 hectares of built-up area. This includes 9 cities aggregating 1,834 hectares, 4 smaller urban centers aggregating 188 hectares, 35 large towns aggregating 600 hectares, 59 small towns aggregating 356 hectares, 308 villages aggregating 439 hectares, and 22 non-residential sites aggregating 72 hectares. Of the 3,417 hectares of primarily residential area, 59 per cent was urban, 28 per cent was in towns, and the remainder was in smaller villages.

3. Sites abandoned or partly abandoned during or soon after the Sassanian period:‖

Cities:

74, 252, 338, 620, 666, 791, 826.

Small urban centers:

497.

Large towns:

15, 157, 219, 223, 246, 275, 300, 329, 358, 407, 450, 472, 480, 492, 538, 601, 608, 663, 664, 682, 704, 802, 833, 836.

Other:

1, 2, 3, 4, 5, 7, 8, 9, 13, 17, 18, 19, 21, 28, 32, 34, 35, 37, 38, 40, 42, 44, 47, 48, 49, 50, 51, 52, 53, 54, 55, 57, 59, 60, 62, 66, 67, 72, 73, 80, 83, 84, 85, 91, 93, 95, 101, 104, 108, 110, 111, 112, 125, 126, 128, 129, 131, 132, 135, 136, 138, 141, 143, 144, 145, 150, 155, 165, 173, 174, 175, 177, 178, 180, 190, 193, 194, 199, 200, 201, 203, 205, 207, 208, 209, 211, 216, 224, 225, 226, 228, 230, 232, 234, 235, 241, 242, 245, 247, 248, 249, 258, 259, 260, 263, 265, 266, 269, 271, 272, 274, 278, 279, 281, 288, 290, 292, 295, 299, 310, 311, 312, 316, 317, 319, 322, 323, 324, 325, 328, 330, 332, 333, 334, 335, 336, 337, 344, 345, 346, 348, 350, 352, 353, 357, 359, 367, 374, 375, 376, 387, 388, 394, 398, 408, 409, 416, 420, 424, 425, 428, 434, 438, 451, 468, 469, 473, 475, 477, 478, 486, 488, 491, 499, 500, 501, 502, 504, 505, 506, 507, 510, 512, 513, 519, 525, 526, 527, 528, 529, 537, 540, 542, 543, 546, 557, 562, 564, 567, 570, 571, 572, 574, 578, 587, 588, 589, 591, 593, 598, 603, 605, 609, 611, 614, 625, 630, 633, 638, 647, 661, 667, 668, 669, 670, 672, 673, 676, 701, 707, 715, 716, 732, 735, 738, 740, 744, 746, 756, 763, 764, 767, 775, 777, 790, 796, 798, 801, 803, 810, 815, 821, 843, 846, 848, 858.

In total: Of the primarily residential sites aggregating 3,418 hectares, 1,969 hectares or approximately 58 per cent were subsequently abandoned.

---

* Numbers in parentheses indicate that more than one site of same class is subsumed under the preceding site-number, as opposed to a single settlement. Where sites of different classes (e.g., a town and several smaller villages) are subsumed under a single site-number, that number is listed separately in the different categories. Question marks indicate that the sites to which they pertain could only be assigned roughly to the Parthian and/or Sassanian period because of sparse or absent surface ceramics or an inadequate collection.

† For discussion of this category see p. 73.

‡ The question of a possible Parthian or earlier occupation of this site was not fully explored; it hence remains open.

§ Probably also to be included under this heading are the following six towns: Shahrābān, Ba'qūba, Bājisrā, Nahrawān, Jarjarāyā, and Humānīya. Shahrābān

(Le Strange, G. 1905:62), Jarjarāyā (cf. p. 91) and Humānīya (Obermeyer, J. 1929:192 ff.) are mentioned in contemporary sources or credited with a Sassanian origin in Islamic accounts. The locations and names of the others less positively suggest the same conclusion. For Nahrawān there is the further evidence of a number of Sassanian bullae collected at the site (modern Sifwah) by Herzfeld (1948:44).

‖ In this listing an attempt has been made to estimate the actual proportion of the surface area of each site which was not occupied after the Sassanian period. Such a calculation is obviously hazardous from surface inspection alone but may serve as a first approximation in the absence of other evidence.

revival but a vast transformation of the old imperial tradition. The surviving remains of settlement, at least, are of the order of *thirty-five times* as dense and widespread as for the Achaemenid period. This was a time when a single city, Ctesiphon, embraced a larger area within its walls than the total area of the 130 known sites in the entire basin during the Isin-Larsa period, the apogee of earlier antiquity.

Several features of Sassanian settlement patterns, in addition to this marked increase in the gross number and area of occupied sites, are evident in Table 19, and each is somewhat different from its counterpart in the Parthian period. One is that the size of individual urban centers apparently increased substantially. In the case of Ctesiphon the extent of the enlargement is difficult to determine, since the size of the Parthian capital is not yet known (cf. *supra*, p. 62). Nevertheless, the impression of the excavator of Ctesiphon is perhaps worth noting: during the Sassanian period "the city spread far beyond its original boundaries."[24] This expansion, of course, is largely attributable to royal favor and policy, as was the formation of such other urban centers as ᶜUkbarā and Weh-Antiokh-i-Khosrau. On the other hand, ᶜAbertā (620) and Uskāf (734) also flourished and expanded greatly before the end of the Sassanian period, even though neither is referred to in surviving traditions and records of Sassanian rule. Uskāf, in particular, grew to cover an area not much less than that of Ctesiphon itself.

A second difference between the Sassanian and Parthian periods is related to the first. The distribution of settlements of different sizes underwent a shift in Sassanian times, obviously at least in part as a consequence of the continuing trend toward urbanization. Thus Parthian cities are thought to have occupied perhaps 431 hectares, 28.5 per cent of the total settled area of that period, while by the Sassanian period the cities that could be recorded in the survey covered perhaps 1,834 hectares, about 52 per cent of a much larger built-up area. But at the same time, both the number and the proportion of Sassanian villages increased slightly over what they had been during the Parthian period, rising in number from 50 to 70 per cent of all known sites and in the proportion of the total built-up area they occupied from 11.5 to 12.5 per cent. In effect, this means that further urbanization was accomplished at the expense of the

towns and small urban centers rather than by concentrating the more dispersed village population—and presumably rural population in general—in newly founded cities. To be sure, the number and aggregate area of settlements classifiable as towns also grew, but at a substantially slower rate; Sassanian towns and small urban centers included only 33 per cent of all settlement, in contrast to 59 per cent in Parthian times.[25]

A further general feature of Sassanian settlement on the Diyala plains is not apparent from Table 19 but only from a detailed examination of Appendix C. With very few exceptions, Sassanian sites are low and sprawling, with irregular shapes and indefinite contours. Not infrequently, occupational remains extend in thin bands for considerable distances along old canal levees or crop up sparsely at intervals separated by apparently uninhabited areas. While surface evidence alone must remain inconclusive, all of this is not suggestive of a "feudal" society, with peasant villages hugging the flanks of the high, fortified seats of a landed nobility. Instead, it seems to imply a considerable degree of internal peace and central control, with major fortifications limited to those maintained around the capital city for defense against dynastic upheavals or Byzantine incursions involving large bodies of troops. On this reconstruction, the class of very small and generally isolated Sassanian sites composed almost entirely of bricks and mortar (e.g., 2, 84, 409, 564, 668; unfortunately, brick-robbing has denuded most of them past recognition, and none has been excavated) perhaps are to be interpreted as as rural guardhouses or road-patrol posts maintained by the central authority. Larger walled enclosures also occur (e.g., 52, 67, 211, 274, 562), but their outer walls are only of unbaked brick and the absence of any structural debris within the enclosures also suggests that they were not primarily strongholds but rather caravansaries or temporary collecting points for agricultural commodities. Of course, the Diyala plains were virtually the heartland of Sassanid strength, so that the absence of rural fortifications and the implied high degree of royal control may be quite uncharacteristic of regions further from the capital.

Since it was suggested in the previous chapter that irrigation requirements for the subsistence of the region's inhabitants already were being met not merely

73

from the Diyala but from the Tigris, the enormous further expansion in Sassanian settlement clearly presupposes not only the emergence of chronic water shortages in some areas but also the successful further development of alternative water supplies derived from the Tigris. Before considering the nature and effectiveness of the most important of these new sources directly, it is necessary to scrutinize more closely the figures on extent of settlement given in Table 19, and both to relate them to alternative sources of water and to modify them for reasons similar to those advanced during the discussion of the Seleucid and Parthian periods.

It may be noted, in the first place, that a number of sites and a considerable proportion of the total built-up area apparently lay either across the Tigris or along its banks. As Yaᶜqūbī observes, "The cities on the east bank of the Tigris consume the water of this river; those on the west bank consume the water of the Euphrates, which is conducted to them by a canal derived from this river, the Nahra-Mālik."[26] Particularly in the case of Ctesiphon (666) and Sikara (Tell al-Deir, 791), which together account for 640 hectares of settlement, this constitutes an important reduction in the demands on Diyala water. In the case of Ctesiphon, furthermore, its role as the Sassanian capital must mean that a substantial part of its population was able to draw (through taxes, rents, trading monopolies, and administrative fees) upon the subsistence resources of a far larger area than the Diyala plains alone. In addition, several of the large settlements along the Tigris not included in the survey and not included in the totals given in Table 19 may be disregarded for the same reason. These include Weh-Antiokh-i-Khosrau, Sābāt, Shekunsib, Humānīya, and Jarjarāyā.[27]

On the other hand, some additional consumption of Diyala water occurred at known sites that were not recorded (Shahrābān, Baᶜqūba, Bājisrā, Nahrawān), and in the region behind ᶜUkbarā that now lies on the western bank of the Tigris (although ᶜUkbarā itself, like cities further downstream, undoubtedly relied in the main on Tigris water obtained with lifting devices). While no accurate summarization of these various reductions and increases can be given, it would appear that perhaps 500 hectares of the total Sassanian area of settlement as given in Table 19 may be deducted from the total as dependent primarily on

the utilization of Tigris waters by means of lifting devices. Also to be deducted are the sites which, to judge from surface inspection at least, were not primarily of a residential character. These included the small walled enclosures and forts mentioned earlier, possible fire-temples (e.g., 468), and a large site apparently devoted to the specialized production of pottery (775). As indicated in Table 19, the aggregate area of such sites is about 72 hectares.

Taking account both of this category and of communities relying on the lifting of Tigris water, it would appear that an adjusted total of occupied Sassanian settlement within the Diyala area whose subsistence needs could only be supplied by local agriculture dependent on gravity-flow canals might be about 2,900 hectares. At 200 persons per hectare of built-up town or city, and at 1.4 hectares of cultivable land per person, this implies the cultivation of about 8,100 square kilometers of land—approximately the entire potential area of cultivable land on the lower Diyala plains. And, indeed, it is possible to confirm independently that virtually the entire land surface must have been utilized for agriculture during the Sassanian period.

Three converging lines of reasoning argue for at least a relatively complete utilization of the irrigable area that was available in the lower Diyala basin. The first stems from the wide distribution of Sassanian sites, in comparison with that of all other periods. Taking account of the differing degrees of completeness of the survey in different areas, the Sassanian pattern is a strikingly extensive and continuous one that appears to omit no major subarea within the basin. To be sure, it is possible that such uniform coverage in part reflects the occupation of a succession of different areas rather than their simultaneous use, but in all areas settlement persisted long enough for substantial accumulations of residential debris to form at the larger sites.

Second, a comparison of Sassanian with Early Islamic settlement patterns makes clear that a substantial retraction occurred before the Islamic period both in the extent and density of occupation. Yet even for the early Abbasid period calculations from tax revenues tend to indicate that an area of 5,000 to 6,000 sq. kms. was cultivated (cf. *infra*, p. 102). While conceding that the period of maximum use may have been brief, this suggests that a substantially larger

74

figure, approaching the estimated limit of 8,000 sq. kms. is not unreasonable for the Sassanian period.

Third, it is instructive to consider the triangular area on the left bank of the Diyala immediately above the Jebel Hamrīn. This shallow valley, sloping gently northward to the Diyala, had been only thinly occupied during all of earlier antiquity. A few ancient villages or hamlets were to be found along ephemeral watercourses that drain the area during the winter rains, while along the river itself lay a handful of small towns.[28] But subsistence in earlier periods must have been based primarily on dry-farming or herding, as it is today. In the Sassanian period, however, a massive program of irrigation was undertaken, fed by a large canal whose banks still can be traced running southward from its main offtake not far below Jalūlā. This canal approaches the Jebel Hamrīn diagonally from its upper side, and the "uphill" slope of the adjoining land indicates that its bed must have been dug progressively deeper as the canal continued southward to the abrupt, low folds of the Jebel Hamrīn itself. At that point, the canal became a *qanāt* or vented tunnel which pierced the Hamrīn and emerged above the alluvial plain to the south, and the spoilbanks of the vertical shafts between which the *qanāt* was dug constituted the only evidence in the Diyala area for the utilization of this essentially Persian technique. At the foot of the northern slope of the Hamrīn, not far from the point at which the canal became a *qanāt*, sprang up a large Sassanian town (15) whose well-preserved and regular outlines imply a planned and artificial origin rather than a slow process of natural growth. Undoubtedly other towns and villages came into existence, at least briefly, on the alluvial plain that was served by the *qanāt* to the south of the Jebel Hamrīn, although time did not permit an extension of the survey to this area.

Apart from the far more intensive use that was made of this little area during the Sassanian period, it is the planned, large-scale aspect of its new irrigation and settlement pattern that is significant for the Diyala region as a whole. The new canal and *qanāt* differed from earlier approaches to irrigation not only in their greater cost but also in the need to complete their construction prior to obtaining any substantial advantages from their use. Unlike canal extensions in the alluvium, which can be managed profitably as a series of small accretions, this system contributed little to irrigation until it had been carried through and beyond the Jebel Hamrīn. The justification for such an effort, it would seem, was not to be found in a purely local effort to improve cultivation but in a state decision to open new lands at the expense of the royal treasury. As such, surely it reflects a shortage of lands in the lower Diyala basin which could be commanded directly from the river at lesser cost. In short, this too suggests that most of the irrigable area in the lower Diyala region was simultaneously under cultivation (on an alternate fallow system) for at least a part of the Sassanian period. Perhaps this argument is individually no more conclusive than those based on site distributions and comparisons with Islamic tax revenues, but the three together do seem to justify the assumption that a cultivated area 8,000 sq. kms. in extent, for the first and only time covering essentially the entire land surface of the region, was at least approached at times during the Sassanian period.

Such times may have been brief, of course. The Sassanian period lasted more than four hundred years, almost as long a span as the Seleucid-Parthian period, so that some short-lived settlements may have been sequential rather than contemporary. And as also with the Seleucid and Parthian periods, it is likely that the normal flux in settlement patterns was accelerated by Sassanian royal policy. Enforced urbanization, it would appear, must have been followed in at least some cases by a further reshuffling of population with each new dynasty. Towns and estates in the hands of the nobility must have shifted not only in response to shifting favor at court but as a result of the decimation of the nobility during the Mazdakite uprising. Further redistribution must have occurred as a result of new, large-scale programs of canalization which the later Sassanid tax reforms made possible. We can assume, in other words, that an unusually high rate of settlement formation and abandonment was induced by the waxing and waning of the powers of control of the state.

But while taking all these qualifications into account may emphasize the brevity of the period of virtually continuous cultivation of the region under the Sassanians, it does not negate the distributional evidence that there were at least times of an incipient land shortage for the first time in the region's history. On the other hand, 8,000 sq. kms. is approximately twice the area which can be irrigated with the waters of the Diyala alone. Hence we must discuss next how this was accomplished. Fortunately, at least all the major elements in the Sassanian canal network are still clearly traceable in surface contours, permitting this question to be answered with reasonable completeness and confidence.

Two especially noteworthy examples of large-scale canal construction below the Jebel Hamrīn can be traced to the Sassanian period. The first began at the foot of the Hamrīn gorge on the right bank of the Diyala and ran southwest, approximately the course of the modern river (see Fig. 5); although virtually destroyed by the subsequent entrenchment and meandering of the Diyala, isolated sections of this levee still can be traced with the aid of air photographs and on the ground. Then, north of Baᶜqūba, the canal swung first west and then southwest again, apparently crossing the modern course of the Tigris (which then lay farther to the west) and terminating in several branches in the vicinity of Buzurg-Shapur or ᶜUkbarā.

With all of its associated smaller settlements, the construction of this canal apparently was a central component in the founding of ᶜUkbarā by Shapur I (A.D. 241–72). Like the new pattern above the Jebel Hamrīn, we see here on a still larger scale the centrally directed planning and execution of an integrated system of new cities and canals.[29] And it is interesting to observe that only the foundation of the city finds a reference in the surviving chronicles of Sassanian rule;[30] apparently the provision of adequate supplies of irrigation water could simply be taken for granted as part of king's responsibilities in establishing a new city bearing his name.

The second example is the so-called Kātūl al-Kisrawī, or Cut-of-Chosroes, the giant feeder-canal which solved the problem of chronic water shortages by supplementing the flow of the Diyala with a large additional supply obtained from the Tigris in the vicinity of the later city of Sāmarrā. Before turning to some of the topographic details of this impressive engineering achievement, a brief inquiry is desirable concerning the circumstances surrounding its construction. Curiously enough, no contemporary record has survived describing its construction or attributing it to one or another of the Sassanian rulers. However, as Jacobsen observes, there is little reason to

doubt the later Islamic tradition recorded by Yāqūt[31] and Qazwīnī[32] which attributes it to Chosroes I Anōsharwān (A.D. 531–79). The financial capacities of that king for such a project, together with his general attention to the improvement of the agricultural economy, have already been indicated (supra, p. 71). Since the Kātūl crosses and cuts off the canal to Buzurg-Shapur constructed by Shapur I, and since the latter canal was in use long enough to establish a substantial levee, a dating to the time of Chosroes is surely approximately correct. Morever, it was Chosroes I Anōsharwān who established the Upper, Middle, and Lower Nahrawān administrative districts, the earliest mention in the chronicle of Tabarī of the great Nahrawān canal system fed by the Kātūl al-Kisrawī.[33] Significantly enough, the chronicle of Tabarī associates the setting up of the new districts with Chosroes' establishment of Weh-Antiokh-i-Khosrau for the former inhabitants of Syrian Antioch, thus offering a parallel with the case of Buzurg-Shapur in that construction of the canal would have been conceived as an integral part of the founding of the city. Finally, a direct mention of an encounter on the banks of the Nahrawān during the short reign of Chosroes' immediate successor[34] serves to confirm that the Kātūl must have been in use no later than his time.

A map of the upper part of the Kātūl al-Kisrawī is given in Figure 7. Elsewhere the complex and still somewhat obscure features of this impressive engineering work have been described in detail.[35] Moreover, we are fortunate in having an account of the operation of the entire Kātūl-Narhawān system three centuries or so later than its initial installation in the Sassanian period, from which components of its plan, since destroyed, can be deduced.[36] In the very limited period which could be devoted to its examination during a field study concerned primarily with the Diyala area proper, further information on the design and sequence of the inlets of the Kātūl was unobtainable, and we can only briefly recapitulate earlier findings.

The name Kātūl al-Kisrawī apparently applied originally to what is now the Nahr al-Rāsāsi, which leaves the Tigris north of the later palace of Al-Mutawakkil in Sāmarrā and follows a fairly direct southeasterly course across the alluvial fan of the ᶜAdheim River to a junction with the Diyala River below

Ba'qūba. This is joined below Tell al-Dhulu'iyya (867) by a branch of comparable or even larger size flowing east from its inlet on the Tigris just above the river's great eastward bend south of Sāmarrā. The latter branch, apparently the Nahr al-Yahūdī of Ibn Serapion, is the only one of three "lesser Kātūls" still largely preserved, and its inclusion in the original installation seems assured by the Sassanian and Early Islamic dating of construction along its banks. The Nahr al-Yahūdī in turn had a second inlet, the Al-Māmūnī of Ibn Serapion, a still larger branch whose upper portion has been cut away by the northward movement of the Tigris.

The third of the "lesser Kātūls" has entirely disappeared. Unlike the others, which were cut through the gently rolling downlands of tertiary conglomerate on which Sāmarrā stands, the Abū-l-Jund ran across the upper end of the alluvial plain slightly farther to the south. It is said to have been "dug" by Hārūn-al-Rashīd.[37] On the other hand, the Islamic tradition attributing the original construction of the Kātūl to Chosroes is preserved in an anecdote which refers to a similar canal in what may be the same district. Thus it appears that the Kātūl may have depended upon several inlets almost from its inception, although the reasons for this multiple construction are not apparent.[38]

In the absence of excavated sections across the Kātūl, or of careful leveling between soundings dug at intervals along its bed, it is difficult to determine the volume of discharge of the feeder-canal. As derived from principles of contemporary canal design, the following observations are pertinent with respect to its flow:

> From the present width we estimate the capacity of the feeder [i.e., the Kātūl] to have been about 250–300 cumecs [cubic meters per second], which is far in excess of apparent requirements. However, the slope which is about 10 cms./km. is more nearly that for a canal of the required capacity, say 50–100 cumecs. If the discharge for which the section seems to have been excavated, namely 300 cumecs, had ever passed down the Nahrawān feeder for long periods at a slope of 10 cms./km., there would be more evidence of scour and meandering.[39]

To be sure, if the great feeder-canal was completed only some years after the fall of Syrian Antioch (in 540), and if it was not properly maintained during the troubled and largely leaderless years after the death of Chosroes II Parvez (in 628), we might still imagine that less than a century elapsed during which it provided a very substantial water surplus to Sassanian settlements in the southern part of the Diyala area. Its Islamic performance will be considered in the next chapter.

Having indicated earlier that an area at times perhaps approaching 8,000 sq. kms. of land was cultivated by means of gravity-flow canals during a part of the Sassanian period, and that this maximum was approximately twice as large an area as the Diyala could supply with irrigation water, an independent estimate of maximum flow in the Kātūl can be derived from the probable irrigation requirements for 4,000 sq. kms. Present design practice on the Diyala plains[40] calls for 40–50 sq. kms. of field irrigation per cumec (cubic meter per second) of canal flow and 10 sq. kms. of orchard irrigation per cumec. Averaging these two types of cultivation at about 40 sq. kms. per cumec, 100 cumecs would have been the maximum discharge of the Kātūl which could have been applied to supplement the Diyala for irrigation. Of course some residual flow from the tail of the Kātūl-Nahrawān system into the Tigris may have been desirable for purposes of maintaining a navigable channel. Considerations arising from the condition of the feeder-canal bed and from the water requirements the Kātūl was intended to serve both indicate, in other words, that only a fraction of its full design capacity was ever carried or needed.

The passage of the Kātūl across the present course of the 'Adheim River presents another problem to which allusion has been made. Although its flow is insignificant for most of the year, the 'Adheim occasionally floods very destructively. Moreover, its bed is deeply incised in a wide alluvial fan which the Kātūl had to cross. Under present conditions, then, a crossing would require large works and would be subject to periodic undercutting and diversion into the Tigris.

This problem, too, could not be investigated directly during the reconnaissance, but there are three reasons for believing that it was less serious during the Sassanian period than present conditions would indicate. In the first place, the shift of the adjoining section of the Tigris to the north and east during the thirteenth century (see *infra*, p. 91) shortened the

77

course of the ᶜAdheim by perhaps 10 kms. while maintaining the same difference in elevation between its outlet and its headwaters. The incision of the lower bed thus can be explained by the increased slope it assumed subsequent to the Sassanian period, and the destructive, scouring effects of ᶜAdheim floods upon the Kātūl crossing would have been correspondingly lessened at that time.

Second, as Jones observed, the radiating network of canals fed from the ancient Band-i-ᶜAdheim (many of the tails of which can be seen in Fig. 7) serves to disperse the waters of that stream, while the former dam of this name must have exercised a major influence in controlling floods.[41] Since the sites and canals in this area have not been examined, it is not clear whether they are to be attributed to the Sassanian period or, as Herzfeld maintains,[42] only to the Islamic period.

Third, a former alternative branch of the ᶜAdheim diverges to the left from the present course and, after bifurcating again, joins the present Khālis canal north of Baᶜqūba. The age of this branch is not known from an inspection of adjoining sites, nor is it clear whether it carried the entire flow of the ᶜAdheim or merely a part of it. On the example of the broad sequence of stream patterns of the Diyala area, it is probably that the ᶜAdheim originally had several branches, thus distributing its flow widely over its alluvial fan. In Jones's day, the disused branch was known as the "Nahr Rathan,"[43] recalling the Abbasid administrative district known as Upper and Lower Rādhān and suggesting that it still was in use after the Sassanian period.[44]

In sum, it appears that only a portion of the flow of the ᶜAdheim may have passed directly into the Kātūl during the Sassanian period, that even that portion may have been further dispersed by canals and regulated by a weir, and that, in any case, channel conditions would have been far less destructive than they are at present due to the subsequent shift of the Tigris. Under the circumstances, it is reasonable to suppose that the Kātūl crossed the ᶜAdheim fan without elaborate works or serious danger of diversion. Depending on its volume of flow, the Kātūl might even have been able to transport the high silt load introduced periodically by ᶜAdheim floods without needing extensive cleaning.

The transfer of the waters of the Kātūl from the right bank to the left bank of the Tāmarrā-Diyala system seems to have been handled in an essentially similar fashion. In a junction south of Baᶜqūba that is still visible in aerial photographs the two were brought together, apparently without intervening control works, and then flowed south for approximately 30 kms. There are a number of right-bank branch-canal offtakes along this section of the course, all of which were extended across the much older levee of the Tāmarrā farther to the west (supra, p. 67) in order to water the region along the Tigris where Baghdad later was founded. Some of these branches may have been connected with one another by feeder-canals running parallel to the parent stream (see map), but the greater channel width and pronounced meander pattern of the easternmost bed indicate that the bulk of the water both from the Kātūl and from what now is called the Diyala passed down this single channel. Then, assuming Ibn Serapion's account to apply also to the late Sassanian period, the main canal was directed to the southeast below the large town or city of Nahrawān (modern Sifwah [308-9]), while what was known as the Diyala was withdrawn from its right bank as a modest branch canal which watered the district along the present lower course of the river.[45]

It was only below the town of Nahrawān that the main feeder-canal was known in Islamic times as the Nahrawān canal, while between that town and Baᶜqūba it was called the Tāmarrā. The Kātūl which is attributed by its name to Chosroes is, then, merely that section of the feeder that runs from Sāmarrā to Baᶜqūba. This is fully consistent with the findings of the survey. The river course called the Tāmarrā that ran between Baᶜqūba and Nahrawān already had come into existence in late Parthian times and probably needed only further diking or deepening at the time the Kātūl al-Kisrawī was laid out. (It has been noted that the great branching system of canals below Nahrawān already seems to have been substantially anticipated in late Parthian times [supra, p. 67].)

Because of the dense, continuing occupation along its banks in later times, few features of the Nahrawān course below the town of Nahrawān can be distinguished (at least in a topographic survey unaccompanied by soundings) and definitely attributed to the Sassanian period. An outstanding exception is the

78

massive Sassanian weir at Al-Qantara (718) not far north of the city of Uskāf. Its fallen remains beneath a later Islamic counterpart were uncovered in excavations by the Diyala Basin Archaeological Project. To judge from the continuity of construction in this locality, it is probable that the upper weir reported by Ibn Serapion to have existed below the town of Nahrawān[46] also had a Sassanian predecessor. No doubt because of extensive brick-robbing in a region which continued to be inhabited even after the rupture of the Nahrawān itself, no trace survives of this upper weir. Its position, however, can be fixed with reasonable accuracy from topographic inspection, aerial photographs, and the direct evidence of contemporary itineraries, and it is noteworthy that the silt banks of a number of large Sassanian branch canals flowing in the direction of Ctesiphon have their origin just above this point (313). There is little doubt, in other words, that a weir in this position played an integral part in maintaining and regulating the flow of water to the capital, its suburbs, and hinterlands as early as the Sassanian period. The weir at Al-Qantara, on the other hand, seems not to have been accompanied by a special concentration of newly constructed Sassanian branch canals.[47] This gives the impression—which only more intensive study could document—that the lower weir may have been in use only for a relatively much shorter time during the Sassanian period.

In addition to the weirs, other construction is associated with the canal. The responsibility of Chosroes I Anōsharwān for bridges is acknowledged by Tabarī (supra, p. 71), and such a bridge at Nahrawān figures in the campaign of Heraclius.[48] Moreover, at least in the vicinity of the weir at Al-Qantara and below Uskāf, and probably all along the Nahrawān course, occasional traces can be seen of canal headworks carefully constructed of baked bricks whose measurements indicate that they are of Sassanian date. A full report of these, as well as of the lower weir at Al Qantara, is in preparation; individual examples are shown in Figures 20–21. But even these summary observations make clear that the completion of the gigantic Nahrawān system by Chosroes I Anōsharwān involved much more than the construction of an impressively long and large feeder-canal. Among the ramifying series of ancillary operations, bridges, branch-canal headworks, and weirs can be identified

as integral parts of the vast undertaking which finally provided a solution to the chronic and growing problem of water shortages in the region.

The outlet of the lower Nahrawān canal into the Tigris during the Sassanian period, as well as in later times, is a final topographic problem that must remain somewhat obscure. Undoubtedly part of the difficulty arises from the slow but continuing westward shift of the Tigris, a process we have traced through many previous periods and which probably still is going on today. In addition, more rapid changes in the meander pattern of the river must have necessitated fairly frequent adjustments in the position of the Nahrawān outlet or outlets. Depending on the volume of water available from the Kātūl, the tail of the Nahrawān may have been either a considerable stream or one reduced to an insignificant flow by withdrawals for irrigation purposes along its course. Many of the larger right-bank branches, in fact, may have been joined directly with the Tigris themselves, both to promote drainage and to reduce silt accumulation in their beds by maintaining a relatively large flow.

There may have been a temptation to utilize any excess supplies that were available in the tail of the Nahrawān by constructing new left-bank branches above its confluence with the Tigris, the branches to parallel the river and re-enter it farther downstream. That a whole series of such extensions was constructed is evident not only from Islamic accounts which place the final Nahrawān outfall almost as far downstream as Kūt-al-ᶜAmāra (forty kms. southeast of the limits of the survey),[49] but also from old canal levees shown on modern maps of the intervening region. To a considerable degree, however, these branches must have depended on additional waters channeled in as outflow from the Haur es-Subaicha or from small, intermittent streams reaching the foot of the Iranian highlands to the northeast, rather than on Tigris or Diyala waters obtained via the Kātūl-Nahrawān canal. In any case, the extent to which these supplementary tails had developed before the end of the Sassanian period is not yet known, and for purposes of this study the Nahrawān system is regarded as having terminated where present traces of its main channel are lost at about 45°15′ E. Long.

With the advent of the Kātūl al-Kisrawī the alleviation of earlier water shortages must have been

79

most marked in the lower part of the Diyala basin, the region not only farthest removed from the source of Diyala waters at the foot of the Hamrīn gorge but also characterized by greatest urban growth. Perhaps the upper part of the basin benefited more indirectly, being permitted to utilize water longer or more freely for irrigation after the Nahrawān was in operation than before the completion of its connection with the Tigris. At the same time, it should be pointed out that evidence is lacking for the centralized bureaucratic management of water consumption that would have been necessary to allocate supplies between different major canals and regions.

References to royally appointed irrigation officials do not occur in surviving sources on the Sassanian period, and the few sluice gates at the heads of Sassanian and Islamic branch canals cleared by the Diyala Basin Archaeological Project apparently were designed without closing mechanisms. This suggests that consumption controls were ordinarily of a more rudimentary and decentralized order. Probably they involved regulations as to periods when water could be withdrawn for actual irrigation, while both main and branch canals were kept as full as river levels would permit through the winter growing season.

Whatever the indirect effects of the opening of the canal on the northern part of the basin, no consequent change in the canal network can be demonstrated from the results of the survey. The Rūz canal is known to have been functioning not long afterward, since at the end of Chosroes II Parvez' reign it was regarded by Heraclius as a potential line of defense against his advance on Dastagird from the northeast.[50] On the other hand, the incompleteness of the survey coverage along the upper portion of this canal leaves open the possibility that it had been continuously in use from an early historic, or even prehistoric, period. It was extended, at any rate, during the Sassanian period, leading to a substantial lengthening of branch-canal tails far to the south that earlier had been supplied only by means of a long feeder running southeast from the Gukha or Mahrūt; but there is no evidence as to when in the Sassanian period this was accomplished.

Far more important, at least in the light of present knowledge, was the watercourse now known as the Mahrūt. This large and widely branching stream or canal, identified by Jacobsen[51] as the Gukha of con-

temporary sources, previously had watered the largest part of the northern half of the basin; in Parthian times it even seems to have extended as far as Scaphae on the Tigris. During the Sassanian period some of the region served by its more westerly branches came to be supplied instead by a new canal, just as the Rūz took over some of its functions on the east. The new canal on the west was the predecessor of the lower part of the Abbasid Jalūlā (the present Khurāsān), which at that time apparently had its offtake near Baʿqūba. But there is nothing in the survey data to connect this shift to the construction of the Kātūl al-Kisrawī, and it may have taken place as much as several centuries earlier.

It is worth noting that there are historical hints of an increasing intensity of settlement in the northern part of the basin, even if they cannot yet be documented with reconnaissance data. Dastagird, for example, became the permanent Sassanian capital only under Chosroes II Parvez[52] although founded much earlier,[53] and it has already been pointed out that Syrian and Egyptian captives were resettled in that vicinity by the same ruler (supra, p. 69). Elsewhere we are told that the nearby village of Shahrābān, together with eighty subsidiary villages or smaller settlements, was founded by a daughter of one of the Chosroes.[54] Since this increase seems to have come only at the very end of the Sassanian period, perhaps our failure to find more traces of an expansion in Sassanian settlement within the region served by this canal reflects its brief floruit before a nearly total disruption.

The events surrounding the end of the Sassanian period need not be recounted here except insofar as they reflect the deterioration of the central authority upon which the prosperity of the Diyala basin had come to rest. Ten kings reigned in the brief period of nine years between the murder of Chosroes II and the Arab seizure of Ctesiphon, and behind the façade of a continuity of royal blood throughout the line, the real rule was increasingly an object of contention between parties of the nobility. We hear of a "new feudalism," marked by the domination of generals and governors in whose hands many districts became virtually autonomous. From an empire which had reached its greatest extent since the Achaemenids only thirty years previously, it deteriorated precipitately into a headless, floundering organism with nei-

80

ther the will nor the capacity even to maintain the agricultural system on which its wealth had been based.[55]

This disintegration finds a clear reflection in the Diyala area. A computation of the settlements not soon reoccupied after the Sassanian period (Table 19) indicates that they comprise 58 per cent of the entire recorded area for the period. Admittedly the abandonment of some of the sites may antedate the terminal phase of the period, being related instead to earlier episodes in the shifting relations between king and landed nobility (supra, p. 75) or to purely local conditions. But, on the whole, it seems fair to conclude that nearly half of the total settled area in the Diyala basin was abandoned at least temporarily at around the end of the Sassanian period. Only the breakup of the Cassite occupation of the area was a greater calamity, and it probably occurred over a longer span of time and surely involved a much smaller number of people.

The effects of the abandonment are particularly noticeable in the northern part of the area, along the erstwhile branches of the Diyala stemming from the Jebel Hamrīn gorge. In many districts there the abandonment seems to have been complete, and to have lasted without respite up until the beginning of the twentieth century. Such was the case, for example, in virtually the entire watershed formerly served by the Gukha canal, as is shown both in the results of survey and in the testimony of Yāqūt.[56] It also seems to have been true along the right bank of the Tāmarrā or Diyala, in the region traversed by Shapur's canal to Buzurg-Shapur or ʿUkbarā, and along at least some of the branches of the Jalūlā canal on the left bank of the Nahrawān channel between Baʿqūba and Nahrawān town. The extent of abandonment was greatest, of course, in the most urbanized and densely settled regions, like the one still accurately described as the "Nahrawān wilderness," east and north of the Nahrawān and south of the present tails of the Khurāsān and Mahrūt canals.

Upon closer inspection it becomes evident that the pattern of abandonment differs in detail from region to region, suggesting that a number of locally variable factors were responsible rather than a single great calamity. In the case of the empty lands along the lower Nahrawān, much of the land today is classified as too saline for productive irrigation agricul-

ture, or even for economical reclamation. Perhaps this indicates that a disastrous rise in ground-water took place, as it might well have done after the opening of the Kātūl al-Kisrawi brought an end to water shortages and thus removed the most immediate constraint against overirrigation. Moreover, the propensity for excessive runoff to accumulate in this area would only have been encouraged by the growth of new levees of silt deposits along the Nahrawān and its branches. Such deposits impeded natural drainage toward the southeast, into the great depression known as the Haur es-Subaicha, the more especially so since a southward extension of the Rūz canal intersected with those levees to further restrict drainage.

Explanations in terms of rising salinity do not hold, however, for the upper reaches of canals stemming from the Jebel Hamrīn gorge, for there increased gradients would always have led to adequate drainage. Perhaps in these areas we may think of the destructive effects of Heraclius' campaign and of the departure of forcibly resettled foreigners with his retreating army. Alternatively, it may be that a combination of natural and human factors induced the Gukha or Mahrūt canal to begin to silt, at a time when the centralized authority of the state was no longer sufficient to compel its proper maintenance. We have noted earlier that encroachments on the former Mahrūt watershed began during the Sassanian period, both from the direction of the newly constructed Jalūlā or Khurāsān canal on the west and from the newly extended Rūz canal on the east. Reduced below a certain critical size by these gradual encroachments, the Gukha or Mahrūt ultimately may have lost the capacity to scour its own bed and thereafter silted up very quickly.

Still another situation occurs on the tails of the Rūz canal as well as on some of the branches emanating from near the weir on the Nahrawān canal above Uskāf. It was observed in the survey that terminal Sassanian and early Islamic settlements in those areas often neatly alternated with one another along the same canal branches. Since in most cases the early Islamic sites were newly settled after Sassanian times, this suggests that the Sassanian abandonment was associated with a social upheaval sufficient to break off the tradition of residence at most of the Sassanian sites; on the other hand, the early Islamic occupation along the same watercourses, and with roughly com-

81

parable population density, suggests that the interval of disuse could not have been very long. Social or political disturbances also furnish a likely explanation for the abandonment of the canal leading southward from Nahrawān to Ctesiphon, a watercourse whose banks must have been used as a highway by many armed bands as anarchy spread.

Finally, there is a hint that decisive topographic changes elsewhere may have exercised an influence within the Diyala basin. Bilādhurī has left an account of the origin of the so-called Great Swamp between the lower Tigris and Euphrates which attributes its appearance in large part to a particularly severe flood late in the reign of Chosroes II Parvez:

> According to the account in Bilādhurī, King Parvez himself superintended the repair of the dykes, sparing (he writes) neither men's lives nor money, "crucifying forty dyke-men, at a certain breach, in one day, and yet was unable to master the water." The Swamps, thus formed, became permanent, for during the succeeding years, when the Muslims were over-running Mesopotamia and destroying the Persian monarchy, the dykes naturally were left uncared for. "Then breaches came in all the embankments, and none attended, for the Dikhans [the Persian landlords] were powerless to renew the great dykes, and so the Swamps lengthened and widened."[57]

Topographically, what the formation of the swamps involved was the shift of the lower Tigris from a course not unlike its present one to one which turned directly south near Kūt-al-ʿAmāra, down the Shatt al-Hai. Whether or not the tectonic instability of the Mesopotamian plain that recently has been adduced[58] was a factor in this change, its effect was to foreshorten radically the course of the Tigris, probably leading to decisive changes in the regime far upstream. Although we cannot reconstruct the precise effects, this makes more comprehensible the statements of Ibn Rusta[59] and Yāqūt[60] that the southern part of the Gukha district (here a synonym for the Middle and Lower Nahrawān?) was laid waste in connection with the movement of the Tigris.[61]

In short, a whole constellation of processes can be identified which contributed to the breakup of the Sassanian rural economy. Salinization, silt accumulation in the canals, and the destructive effects of floods and changes in river courses all were combined with administrative collapse, political upheaval, and,

ultimately, invasion and occupation by outside forces. What is crucial, however, is to recognize the interdependence of these trends. With the advent of truly gigantic irrigation systems, local self-sufficiency was no longer possible. Small changes in canal pattern and regime, or the failure to carry out routine maintenance procedures, now could exercise a profound effect on the livelihood of groups who were too far downsteam to correct conditions themselves and who had no access to other irrigable lands. The maintenance of central state initiative had become a prerequisite, in other words, not only for the further extension but even for the continuation of the prosperity of the region. When that initiative was retarded or destroyed, a host of problems quickly became more serious and, combining with one another in ways which might exhibit considerable local variation, constituted a threat of unprecedented proportion to the existing order. In comparison with numerous periods of political instability in antiquity, the dissolution of Sassanian power and the Islamic invasion in themselves were neither as long nor as pervasive a disruption as their profound consequences in the Diyala countryside would suggest.[62] The difference was that the immense expansion in settlement and irrigation which the Seleucids, Parthians, and Sassanians had brought about came at the expense of the capacity to adapt on the local level to a wide range of natural and political conditions.

To summarize very briefly, the Sassanian period seems to have reached the limits of territorial expansion which ancient technology made possible within the region. Proceeding along lines already laid down in the Seleucid and Parthian periods, it went on to witness more than a doubling of at least the physical remains of settlement and to exceed in one city the total built-up area known for the whole basin in more remote periods of antiquity. Some of this growth, it seems clear, is a reflection of prevailing practices of arbitrary resettlement and urbanization rather than a simple index to prosperity, but enough remains to indicate that virtually the entire cultivable area was brought under the plow and commanded by a vast network of new canals. The construction of these canals seems to adumbrate a new and radically different outlook. They imply the engineering competence to plan, and the political and financial power to execute, a fundamental reshaping of the landscape and

82

its water resources in the endeavor further to enlarge and stabilize the revenues of the state. Their primary weaknesses, it would appear, were organizational and not material: the powerful, centralized administrative apparatus that was needed for their maintenance turned out to be less durable than the irrigation works themselves.

As in the Seleucid and Parthian periods, much of the new advance in the Diyala basin was a consequence of relations with the West. While the irrigation technology itself must have been local and ancient, the imperial machinery which activated it was both loaned and borrowed freely. Moreover, its specific application to the intensive improvement of the Diyala area is only understandable as an aspect of continuing hostilities with Rome and Byzantium. But however important external stimuli may have been, the development of the area was not merely a passive response which later reversed itself. Patterns of settlement and irrigation were qualitatively and permanently transformed, and even the desperate crises at the end of the Sassanian and Abbasid periods failed to return them to their earlier condition. Both in their problems and their policies, Sassanian irrigation and settlement patterns strikingly anticipate the modern scene and differ equally strikingly from all save perhaps the immediately preceding centuries of earlier antiquity.

8

ISLAMIC REVIVAL AND DECLINE
(A.D. 637–1900)

WE HAVE seen that the conditions under which the Diyala area was most extensively irrigated and settled were those imposed by a strong, centralized government prepared to commit huge sums to agricultural development and maintenance—and in turn to benefit from an even greater increase in revenues. With the dissolution of Sassanian power, the Arabs who quickly occupied the region came into possession of an impressive engineering and agricultural establishment in a state of temporary crisis. While certain districts seem never to have been reclaimed, the early centuries of Islam saw the repair and renewal of most of this establishment under an efficient administration whose powers had not yet been eroded by internal rivalries and corruption. Perhaps as early as the middle of the ninth century, however, the declining political authority of the caliphate began to be reflected in a neglect of the rural economy and in an increasingly rapacious and short-sighted exploitation of the peasantry. This was inevitably accompanied by a gradual recrudescence of the crisis in the irrigation system and in the dense array of settlements that irrigation agriculture supported, leading to a further deterioration in the resources and powers of the regime. Having very quickly attained the stature of a great empire, by the middle of the tenth century the Abbasid caliphate had been reduced to a petty state commanding little more than a purely formal allegiance beyond the lower Mesopotamian plain. Great as was the destruction wrought by the Mongols two hundred years or more later, that destruction was merely a climactic

episode in a much deeper and longer phase of decline —which in fact has come to an end only within the last century.

It is beyond the scope of this study, and the competence of the author, to review the voluminous literature on the social and economic history of the caliphate. Neither is the well-documented network of relations between the Abbasid capital at Baghdad and its many far-flung dependencies a necessary part of our theme, nor the details of changing political forces within Baghdad itself. More pertinent, although still somewhat tangential, would be a discussion of the bureaucracy and administrative establishment, particularly as its general features may have affected the several districts into which the Diyala region was divided. Fortunately, discussions of many aspects of this subject are available elsewhere,[1] so that here we may deal almost exclusively with the Diyala plains as a separate entity. Perhaps, however, a brief description of the decay of the administration and rural economy in the Sawād (essentially ancient Babylonia) as a whole, especially as reflected in the decline of tax revenues, may help to identify the forces at work in the Diyala basin as well.

It will be recalled that annual receipts from the head tax and land tax of the Sawād had approximated 340,000,000 dirhems for a time toward the end of the Sassanian period (supra, p. 71). Under the Caliph ᶜUmar ibn al-Khattāb (634–44), revenues for the Sawād were fixed at 128,000,000 dirhems, an abrupt decline of 62 per cent.[2] By the time of Muᶜāwiya (661–80) they had sunk further still, only being main-

84

tained at a level of 100,000,000 dirhems upon threat of dismissal of the governor of the province in spite of renewed efforts to restore lands to cultivation that had been flooded since the closing days of the Sassanian period.[3] With minor fluctuations they then remained at about this level for a considerable period; at any rate, ʿUmar ibn ʿAbd al-ʿAzīz (717–20) is said to have collected 124,000,000 dirhems.[4] Soon afterward, if not already during his reign,[5] the decline began again, the income from the province reaching only 108,457,650 dirhems in Qudāma's records for A.D. 819[6] and falling to 87,000,000 dirhems a quarter of a century later.[7]

Much of this decline, of course, does not reflect a decrease in agricultural production so much as the increasing diversion of state revenues to corrupt civil servants and to private landholders. Occasional vigorous efforts to reverse this process seemingly were effective for no more than a few years at most. But it is essential to note that total agricultural production and state revenues ultimately were linked with one another. Under the conditions of large-scale state-financed irrigation which had been imposed over much of the Sawād by the Sassanians, only unified, competent administration and a continuing high level of capital investment in maintenance would permit gross production to remain indefinitely at its earlier figure. And private entrepreneurs were unprepared to supplement declining state revenues in filling these needs. Both the widespread political upheavals which continued in the wake of the victorious Arab armies, and the absence of a landed aristocracy independent of court intrigues, discouraged them from long-term investments and focused their interests instead on short-term windfall profits. Ultimately then, the decline in state revenues tended to be reflected in a parallel decline in agricultural production as well. This problem, to be sure, only emerged as a cumulatively decisive one after an interval of two to three centuries of Islamic rule, an interval during which at least the bureaucratic traditions of Sassanian agricultural administration were maintained without serious disruption.

Later figures are somewhat obscured by periodic reliance on tax-farming and debasement of the coinage, but the general trend is unmistakable. In 893 about half of the Sawād was leased out for 2,500,000 dinars,[8] implying a total income of perhaps 75,000,000

dirhems.[9] By 918/19 the gross income from the Sawād was only 1,547,374 dinars, around 31,000,000 dirhems.[10] Again the level of collections seems to have stabilized—at no more than 10 per cent or so of the Sassanian figure. According to Ibn Hauqal, in 968 Ibn Fadl leased out all of the Sawād for 42,000,000 dirhems. A few years later the Būyid Sultan ʿAdud al-Daulah offered only 30,000,000 dirhems for the right to farm these claims.[11] Then, after a surely brief and somewhat questionable rise at the time of the Caliph Nāsir (1180–1225), they plunged still further with the widespread destruction that accompanied the Mongol invasion. Mustawfī reports that 3,000,000 dinars, or only 18,000,000 dirhems, was listed as due in 1340. He admits that actual payments of the permanent impost were much less even than this, although they probably were supplemented by additional collections in the major towns.[12] In short, as von Kremer rightly affirmed, "One fact appears to emerge with certainty from the list of tax-payments of Sawād province; it is the decline of the agricultural economy, while simultaneously the grandees of the state, the members of the ruling families, established for themselves widespread latifundia."[13]

Behind the bare outlines of this late Abbasid financial decline lay a more general decay in the fabric of administration which has been vividly illuminated for us by contemporary writers. This widely noted process is described in particularly clear and graphic terms by Miskawaih's "The Experiences of the Nations." He recounts the rise of a pretender from whose exactions the Diyala area suffered, for instance, in terms which reflect not only the political weaknesses to which the caliphate had become prone even before the middle of the tenth century but also the hardships wrought on the countryside by the interminable disputes for power:

> When Hārūn b. Gharīb learned of Radī's accession to the Caliphate, he was residing in Dīnawar, which is the chief town of the district Mah al-Kūfah, he being minister of public security, *kharāj* and Estates for Mah al-Kūfah, Masabadhan, Mihirjanqadhaq, and Hulwān. These were the only regions out of the Eastern provinces which remained in the hands of the Sultan after the conquests of Mardawij. Hārūn b. Gharīb supposed himself to have a better right to be ruler than any one else; so he wrote to all the commanders in the capital promising that if he came to the capital and

85

were made commander-in-chief and administrator-general, he would remit to them their pay intact, and keep none of it back. He started for Baghdad and reached Khaniqīn; this gave great offence to Ibn Muqlah, Mohammad b. Yāqūt, the Saji, Hujari, and Mu'nisi troops; these all made representations to Radī, who replied: I dislike the man; prevent him from entering Baghdad, fighting him, if he makes it necessary.

On Saturday 7 Jumada i, 322 [April 24, 934] Abū Bakr Ibn Yāqūt summoned Abū Ja'far Ibn Sherzād, and introduced him to Radī, who made him the bearer of a message to Hārūn b. Gharīb, bidding him return to Dinawar; he sent with him a letter also. Ibn Sherzād started at once, and found that Hārūn had advanced to the bridge of Nahrawān. He repeated the message and delivered the letter. Hārūn replied that the revenue of his province was not sufficient for the troops who had now joined him—Ibn Sherzād took this message and delivered it to Radī in the presence of the vizier Ibn Muqlah and the Chamberlain Mohammad b. Yāqūt. They offered to give him the administration of the whole Khurāsān Road, and to let its revenue be devoted to his needs in addition to what he already received. Radī said: His best plan would be to reduce the numbers of his troops —Ibn Sherzād, accompanied by Abū Ishāq Qarārītī returned with this reply. When they had delivered their message, he refused, declaring that this addition would not satisfy the troops. Then he said: And who made the son of Yāqūt worthier of the offices of Chamberlain and Commander-in-chief than me? People know that at the end of Muqtadir's time he used to sit in front of me and obey my orders. Who made him to be nearer the Caliph than me, who am a relative and kinsman of the Commander of the Faithful, whereas Ibn Yāqūt is the son of one of his slaves?—Qarārītī observed: If you were to do your duty as a kinsman, you would not be in rebellion against him.— He replied: Were you not an envoy, I should have had you assaulted. Be off!—Hārūn then started collecting money, and collected the revenue of the Khurāsān Road, arresting the Sultan's officers; he collected the money with great violence and cruelty, though the time was near the commencement of the financial year.

As his acts became more and more arbitrary, Mohammad b. Yāqūt started at the head of the troops which were in the capital, and encamped at Nahrabīn; as a final effort he sent Ibn Sherzād once more with a civil message, promising to make an agreement with him about the number of men whom he should retain, and that he would consider their requirements as shown by the rolls for a

kharāj year, and if the revenue of his provinces was sufficient for his pay and theirs, he should return to Dīnawar; but if it were insufficient, then Mohammad b. Yāqūt would order the deficit to be made good from the districts of the Nahrawāns.[14]

In the sequel, the proffered concessions in this particular case were never taken up because of Hārūn's subsequent assassination by his slave, but the affair is illustrative of the repeated tendency to compromise the resources and authority of the caliphate with a whole succession of disaffected claimants and military commanders at the expense of the rural economy.

The callous disregard as to the economic well-being of the peasantry that was displayed at times, and its tragic consequences, is illustrated by the calculated breaching of the Nahrawān canal by Ibn Rā'iq in 937, in an unsuccessful attempt to defend his emirate against Bachkam's advance from Wāsit upon the capital.[15] With the diversion of the Nahrawān into the lower Diyala all of the densely settled area that had depended on the Nahrawān was suddenly confronted with a desperate water shortage for which temporary emigration was the only possible solution. Even in Baghdad, not directly dependent upon Nahrawān water, this calamity was reflected in an ensuing scarcity of grain, and this in turn was further aggravated by fighting between rival bodies of Turkish and Dailemite mercenaries:

This year [946] prices rose so high that people had absolutely no bread and ate the dead, or grass or any creature that had died a natural death or carrion. When a horse dropped dung a number of persons collected and searched the dung for barleycorns to pick out and eat. Cotton-seed would be taken, moistened with water and spread on an iron plate, which was then put on the fire till it was dry, and the seed was then eaten; this produced tumours in the intestines of which most of the eaters died, whereas the survivors looked like corpses. Men, women and children would stand on the highroad perishing of famine and crying *Hunger, hunger*, till they collapsed and died. If any one found a little bread he would hide it under his clothes, else it would be snatched from him. So many were the corpses that they could not be buried in time, and the dogs devoured their flesh. The poor migrated in vast numbers and continuous lines to Basrah to eat dates, and most of them perished on the road; those of them who reached the place died after a short time. A woman of the Hashim family was found who had stolen a child and baked him alive in an oven. She had partly eaten him and was seized eating the remainder; she was put to death. Houses and plots were sold for loaves, some of the loaf being assigned to the broker as commission. Another woman was caught killing children and eating them, and the practice became common, so that many women were executed for this offence. When the civil war was over and the new crops came in prices fell.[16]

When, after twenty years out of cultivation, Muʿizz al-Daulah finally succeeded in closing the breaches, it is reported that "Baghdad became prosperous, fine bread being sold at twenty ratls the dirhem. Hence the populace approved of the regime of Muʿizz al-Daulah and liked him personally."[17] But later breaches occurred, accompanied by new abandonments. Along the Nahrawān, the increasing neglect of essential maintenance tasks, which, unlike the smaller branches, were the responsibility of the central government,[18] thus led eventually to the cessation of cultivation and settlement in what had been one of the most prosperous areas under the control of the caliphate. Yāqūt (ca. 1224) eloquently describes the final outcome:

It is now in ruins and all its cities and villages are mounds and can be seen with standing walls. The destruction of this canal was caused by the differences among the Sultans and the fighting between them at the time of the Saljūks. None of these Sultans was interested in construction and building, their only aim was to collect taxes and consume them. It was also on the route of their armies, so the population left their lands and it continued to go to ruin.[19]

Two centuries before this occurred the general process of deterioration which culminated under the Saljūks had been perceptively set forth by Miskawaih:

In this year, the Dailemites mutinied against Muʿizz al-daulah violently, and indulged in fierce abuse and vituperation of him. He promised to remit their pay to them by a fixed term, and was compelled to oppress the citizens and extort money from improper sources. He assigned to his officers, his household and his Turks as fiefs the estates of the Sultan, the estates of the persons who had gone into hiding, e.g., those of Ibn Sherzād, and the rights of the Treasury on the estates of civilians. Thus most of the Sawād was locked up, and became inaccessible to revenue-officers, only a little being liable to taxation and farmed. Most of the bureaus therefore became superfluous and idle, as were the bureaus of control; and all the officers were united in one.

When the administration is based on unsound principles, the fact though it may be at first concealed manifests itself in course of time. It is as when a man diverges from the high road; a slight divergence may go unnoticed at the first, but if it continues he loses his direction, and the further he travels the further astray he is; and he becomes conscious of his error when it is too late to repair it. One such error committed by Muʿizz al-daulah was that he allocated most of the districts of the Sawād in fief while they were out of cultivation and before they had returned to it, so that their value was reduced; in the next place the viziers were complaisant to the assignees, took bribes, in some cases receiving gratuities themselves, in others letting themselves be influenced by intermediaries. Thus the fiefs were assigned at variable rates. As the years passed, and the land came into cultivation, in some cases the amount due as tax rose owing to the increase in the produce, in others it was reduced owing to the fall in prices; for when these fiefs were assigned to the army prices were abnormally high owing to the famine which had been described. Those who made a profit retained the fiefs which they held, and it was not possible to exact full payment according to the assessments. Those who lost returned their fiefs and received others instead so as to make up their deficits. The evil increased till it became the practice for the soldiers to ruin their fiefs and take others of their own selection in exchange. Thus they succeeded in being always the gainers and pocketing a profit. The fiefs which were given back were bestowed on persons whose sole aim it was to appropriate all that they found there, and render an account only of part. They would take no steps to put them into cultivation. The assignees would then return to those fiefs which had got mixed together, and obtain fresh assignation of them on the basis of their present value when that value was reduced to the lowest possible figure. The original deeds rotted away as the years passed, the old assessments became obsolete, the canals went to ruin, the sluices got out of order, misfortune fell on the cultivators, whose circumstances were wretched, some of them migrating and exiling themselves, others patiently enduring wrongs for which no redress could be obtained, while others were content to surrender their lands to the assignees in order to escape injury from them and satisfy them. Thus cultivation was at a standstill, the bureaus were closed, the arts of finance-clerk and revenue-farmer disappeared; those who were skilled in them became extinct, and a generation arose which knew nothing

87

of either. When any one of them undertook business of this sort, he proved himself a clumsy novice. The assignees did no more than put their lands under the control of their slaves and bailiffs, who kept no account of what passed through their hands, and devised no improvements nor methods of increasing the produce. They merely embezzled their masters' property by various forms of knavery. Their masters recouped themselves for their losses by fining their agents and iniquitous treatment of those with whom they had dealings. The officers of irrigation departed because the territory was no longer in the hands of the Sultan, and the business connected therewith was confined to the drawing up of estimates of what was required for the irrigation, which was then apportioned to the assignees, who however neglected the payment of their shares; if they paid them, the money was embezzled and not expended on the purposes for which it was levied. The inspectors were indifferent to catastrophes, their principle being to "take the limpid and leave the turbid," and to have recourse to the government on which they could make new demands while handing back the fiefs which had gone to ruin in their possession. The administration of each district was committed to a powerful Dailemite favourite, who made thereof his residence and private estate; these governors were surrounded by dishonest agents, whose aim and object was to defer, to keep things going, and to put off from year to year. The lands not included in the fiefs were assigned to two classes of men to farm. One of these consisted of generals and other officers of the army, the others of civil functionaries and men of business. The officers were anxious to amass wealth, pocket profits, lodge appeals, and demand abatements. If payment of tax were strictly demanded of them, they became enemies, bent on resistance, with ample means; they caused disintegration of the empire, and furnished rebels. If they were treated with leniency, their greed became all the fiercer and stopped at no limit. The civilians on the other hand displayed greater skill than the soldiers in making the government pay and greater ingenuity in enriching themselves at its expense. Further they made common cause in their operations, offered gratuities, and entrenched themselves in secret influence, whereas all people ought to be governed by the same rule. As the years passed, they became independent in their provinces, and were subject to no interference in their dealings with others. Among the latter the weaklings might be fined or their contributions altered and their benefits reduced in accordance with their quality and means, whereas the contributions of others

who were able to defend themselves would be abated, for which purpose the assignee would take a secret profit from them. Such persons would be welcomed by the assignee as a help to him in times of stress, and when he was under government scrutiny, whilst he would have no mercy on the weaklings. It ceased to be the fashion to present any balance-sheet to the bureaus or issue any instructions to a finance-minister; to hear any complaint or to accept the suggestions of any clerk. In the scrutiny of the revenue-farmers the examiners limited themselves to mentioning the original terms of the contract, the amount realized and the amount in arrear, without inquiry into the treatment of the subject populations, and whether justice or injustice had been meted out to them, or notice being taken of precautions against putting land out of cultivation, measures for restoring waste lands to cultivation, taxes improperly collected, fines that were purely iniquitous, additions to the assessments according to no register, and items put down as expenditure which represented no reality. If any of the clerks called attention to any such point, if he was a man of importance he was "guaranteed," dismissed, ruined and put to death, being sold by the Sultan for a trifling sum. If he were a poor and indigent individual, he would be pacified with a small sum and transfer his support to the opponent. He was not to be blamed, as the Sultan neither protected him when he was in fear, nor assisted him if he spoke.

This is a summary of the situation as regards the revenue. The expenditure on the other hand was multiplying, the business of the bureaus was at a standstill, and the offices of control were idle. To this there were added other matters which it would take long to explain, and of which one would lead on to another. I have therefore confined myself to indications in lieu of dilating.

Further Muᶜizz al-daulah indulged his fancy in the matter of his retainers, to whom he was liberal in the matter of fiefs and increases, and whom he lavishly enriched and aggrandized. He was therefore unable to lay by anything for the evil day, or ever to show a surplus in his accounts. His expenses were continually on the increase and his resources diminishing till there was a deficit against him which he never confined within any limit, but permitted to increase at an enormous rate. As the years passed this led to stoppage of the pay of the Dailemites, who became envious of the more fortunately situated Turks. Necessity compelled him to attach the Turks more closely to himself, promote them higher and higher, and rely on their aid against the Dailemites. His favours being bestowed on the former while neglect befell the latter, disaffection resulted, and indeed with both; the Turks being stimulated by greed, whereas the Dailemites were goaded by want and poverty. They were on the look out for insurrections, which this procedure fomented, and wherein it brought about the occurrences which we hope to describe.[20]

On the basis of general accounts such as these of the decline in the later days of the caliphate, we can consider more directly the changing character of settlement on the Diyala plains. As a first step, it is useful to deal exclusively with the major towns and cities of the region to which the contemporary Arabic geographers refer. By supplementing the available written descriptions of different periods with data from archaeological surface reconnaissance (where this has not been prevented by overlying modern settlements), the histories of individual cities and smaller provincial centers may be compared at least roughly with one another through a succession of chronological phases. Then as a subsequent step they also will be compared with the more complete but less graphic data of the surface reconnaissance for the great majority of sites in the region which are not otherwise known.

Baghdad. Although only the eastern part of Baghdad lies within the Diyala area proper, the history of both parts of the city obviously must be considered together. The following remarks are in general terms in order to skirt the inevitable controversies about specific details of the history of the city, and they are based for the most part on the full account of Le Strange.[21]

The first undisputed reference to a settlement at Baghdad concerns a successful raid dispatched by the Arab general Khālid ibn-al-Walīd during the caliphate of Abū Bakr, at the very end of the Sassanian period. Apparently it was at that time the scene of a monthly market on the west bank of the Tigris.

The Round City of Mansūr was founded on the west bank in a.d. 762 and completed four years later, an army of 100,000 craftsmen from Syria and Persia as well as Iraq reputedly having been employed in its construction. In its original plan it was encircled by a double defensive wall four miles in circumference, but before the death of Mansūr in 775 suburbs had extended outward from each of its four gates and a settlement had also come into being on the east bank of the Tigris.

Under Mahdī and Hārūn-al-Rashīd the eastern quarter, Rusāfah, grew to rival (at least in grandeur) the Round City and its suburbs on the west bank, a geographical shift consummated by the virtual destruction of the Round City in Maʾmūn's successful two-year struggle to depose his half-brother, the Caliph Amīn (813). A second siege of Baghdad, lasting for about a year, followed the flight of the Caliph Mustaʿīn to escape the tyranny of his Turkish bodyguard at Sāmarrā. By the time of the caliph's defeat and death in 866, there had been extensive devastation of the northern part of East Baghdad in turn, and the rebuilding which followed was concentrated south of Mustaʿīn's city wall, in the area which still forms the heart of modern Baghdad. In 884, not long before the final return of the caliphate from Sāmarrā, it is reported that West and East Baghdad occupied 41.8 and 27.9 sq. kms., respectively,[22] although subsequent accounts make clear that East Baghdad in particular was largely taken up with palaces and government offices.

In the two and a half centuries of Būyid and Saljūk supremacy which followed, the increasing political insignificance of the caliphs was accompanied by their increasing preoccupation with palace construction. Almost annual occurrences of widespread destruction are reported to have been caused by floods, conflagrations, or civil unrest, and from around the end of the eleventh century onward increasingly frequent mention was made of quarters of the city that were appropriately described as *kharābāt*, "ruins."[23] As Claude Cahen has observed:

> The impression is that, with not only inundations and fires contributing but also with the changes of residence, destructions and reconstructions of princes, etc., for a unified city there was progressively substituted, after the beginning of the century, a group of semi-autonomous quarters separated by fields of ruins or empty lands or gardens: this would explain the duplication, indeed the multiplication, of certain *sūqs* [bazaars] and of congregational mosques. Socially there was accentuated also the differentiation between these quarters, even their mutual hatred, their state of masked war, for example between shīʿite Karkh and the outlying sunni quarters. The most animated zones meanwhile were preserved on the eastern bank of the Tigris, centers of the caliphate and sultanate, residences of the aristocracy, and popular quarters that continued to maintain themselves.[24]

89

As a further cause of deterioration during the declining days of the caliphate, Baghdad also sustained a third and a fourth siege. The former, in 1136, led to the abdication of Mansūr Rashīd and the plundering of the western quarters, while the Saljūk Sultan Muhammad was forced to break off the fourth siege (in 1157) and retreat along the old Khurāsān road into Persia. Ibn Jubayr's account, twenty-seven years later,[25] describes West Baghdad as being for the most part in ruins, although he implies that a considerable population still resided there and although the markets of East Baghdad were almost entirely supplied from cultivated lands on the opposite bank. In East Baghdad itself, more than a quarter of the area was estimated to have been occupied by the palaces of the caliph, while large additional areas were devoted to nobles' palaces, tombs, and public buildings.

In Yāqūt's time (ca. 1224) the city had partly decomposed into separate walled quarters, and the palace of the caliph is said to have occupied a third part of its whole area. Shortly afterward it was besieged and stormed by the Mongols under Hulagu in 1258, brutally and abruptly completing a process of deterioration that had set in much earlier. Most of the remaining private quarters as well as the public buildings were destroyed in a general conflagration, and a large proportion of the inhabitants was massacred. Its precarious subsequent history of sharply diminished influence and size prior to independence and recent expansion, under successive Ilkhanid, Turkoman, Persian and finally Ottoman suzerainty, has been fully described elsewhere[26] and hence need not be recounted here.

Sāmarrā. Lying athwart the inlets to the Kātūl al-Kisrawī, Sāmarrā is relevant to this study both for the part it plays in the history of the caliphate and for the extreme example of urban formation that it furnishes. Founded by the Caliph Al-Muᶜtasim in 835, its replacement of Baghdad as the capital for a period of 58 years was a consequence of political rather than economic factors. Originally having been established to curb the excesses of the Turkish bodyguard by removing them from Baghdad, its isolation left Muᶜtasim and the next six caliphs in turn virtually prisoners at the mercy of that guard. The growth of Sāmarrā, in short, was not linked to any economic superiority of its location, but rather to the lavish and artificial building programs indulged in by titular

rulers while the affairs of the empire were dealt with by their subordinates.

Herzfeld estimates the population of Sāmarrā in the time of Al-Mutawakkil at 1,000,000 inhabitants, considerably smaller than that of Baghdad.[27] The city proper was built on low bluffs east of the Tigris. Eventually it came to extend for seven leagues along the river and to include a considerable area on the western bank as well, a vast urban zone that was at once more dispersed and less controlled by defensive considerations than Baghdad. Its growth, however, neither followed an over-all plan nor proceeded by continuous small accretions. Instead it expanded as a series of separately planned quarters undertaken by successive rulers, each consisting primarily of an enormous palace with surrounding pleasure grounds and adjoining residences for retainers. Not surprisingly, most of it fell rapidly to ruin when the caliphate was permanently reestablished in the older capital. To a degree, the continuing survival of a small town at Sāmarrā owes less to the natural advantages of its location than to other considerations— particularly the importance of shrines established in the ruins as a terminus for Shīᶜite pilgrim traffic. In any case, since the town is situated outside the Diyala region its history ceases to be pertinent for this study with its abandonment as the Abbasid capital.

Writing at the end of the ninth century, Yaᶜqūbī has left us a valuable and lengthy account of the appearance of the city within a few years after the removal of the seat of government.[28] The results of topographic, archaeological, and epigraphic studies on the site and its surrounding region have been comprehensively summarized by Herzfeld.[29] A more specialized study also has been undertaken, primarily from the Arabic textual sources, of the irrigation system of Sāmarrā and its environs.[30]

ᶜUkbarā. Founded early in the Sassanian period, ᶜUkbarā lay along the left bank of the Tigris on what came to be the main post road northward from Baghdad to Sāmarrā, Mosul, and the Syrian provinces. Usually it is mentioned together with Awānā, a sister-city on the opposite bank and a short distance downsteam, and the smaller town or village of Busrā, on the east bank 7 kms. downstream. All three were frequented by vacationers from the capital. Toward the close of the tenth century Muqaddasī describes

90

ᶜUkbarā as a large, populous town surrounded by excellent vineyards and vegetable gardens.[31]

As late as 1168 Benjamin of Tudela claimed to have found ᶜUkbarā still a thriving city, with a Jewish community numbering 10,000 persons.[32] In Yāqūt's great geographical compilation, only a half-century later, it is described as a small town, while in the Marāsid it is reported that the place was abandoned not long afterward when the Tigris left its bed between ᶜUkbarā and Awānā for a course farther to the east. Since Al-Mustansir (1226–42) was responsible for the construction of new canals to irrigate the districts cut off from their normal supplies by the movement of the Tigris, the shift by which ᶜUkbarā was taken out of the Diyala basin must have occurred around 1230 or even earlier.[33]

Al-Madāin. Of the seven cities or towns subsumed under this name by Moslem authors, five survived until the time of Yaᶜqūbī,[34] at the end of the ninth century. Those on the east, or Diyala, bank of the Tigris were Al-Madīna-Al-ᶜAtīka, the former Ctesiphon, Asbānbur or Asfanabr, and Rūmīya, the town patterned after Syrian Antioch by Chosroes I Anōsharwān. The Caliph Mansūr resided for a time in the latter settlement prior to the construction of Baghdad, but the admiration which many Islamic authors profess for the grandeur of nearby Sassanian architectural monuments failed to protect most of them from destruction through brick-robbing.[35] Even before the foundation of Baghdad as the seat of the Abbasid caliphate, al-Madāin had been superseded by newly established Arab military colonies at Kūfa, Basra, and Wāsit, to the first of which the great gates of Ctesiphon were carried after the city was taken from the Sassanians. At the end of the ninth century al-Madāin was still a prosperous town, with two congregational mosques and a market,[36] and it remained inhabited into at least the eleventh century. Serving only as an encampment at the time of Hulagu's invasion in 1258,[37] it is described as entirely in ruins by Mustawfī in 1340.[38] The modern town of Salmān Pāk thus is of more recent origin, and its growth probably is to be explained by the continuing pilgrim traffic to the tomb of one of the Companions of the Prophet, Salmān the Persian.

Deir-al-ᶜĀqūl. Having occupied approximately a square kilometer in the Parthian and Sassanian periods, the Islamic settlement here was found during the survey to be limited to an area of about 20 hectares. Apparently it was built around a Christian monastery, and was reckoned as the chief town of the Middle Nahrawān district.[39] Yet as late as the time of Muqaddasī, at the end of the tenth century, it still lay on the west bank of the Tigris,[40] across the river from the lands watered by the Nahrawān. At the time of Ibn Rusta, a century earlier, the town had a congregational mosque, a market, and a control barrier across the Tigris, apparently for customs purposes.[41] To Muqaddasī it was the finest river town between Baghdad and Wāsit,[42] but by the time of Yāqūt a westward shift in the bed of the river left it in the midsts of a low-lying plain a mile or so from the eastern banks. Cultivation and settlement still continued, however, for Mustawfī describes it in 1340 as "A small town . . . having a close climate on account of its palm-groves."[43] The surface collection made at the site found little to reflect an occupation during the Ilkhanid period, and in any case settlement there must have come to an end soon after.

Humānīya. Also having originated in pre-Islamic times, Humānīya nonetheless remained unnoticed by the geographers who have bequeathed us their ninth- and tenth-century itineraries. Yāqūt, however, described it as a village of the size of a city,[44] suggesting that it had expanded late in the Abbasid period at a time when most similar settlements were declining or being abandoned. One or more minarets still were standing in its ruins at the time of Felix Jones' survey of the Nahrawān canal in the mid-nineteenth century,[45] perhaps implying that it also differed from most similar towns in that for a time it continued to be inhabited in spite of the unsettled conditions associated with the coming of the Mongols. It lay on the right bank of the Tigris, across the river from the Diyala area, until the oxbow loop it occupied was cut through in the latter part of the nineteenth century.[46]

Jarjarāyā. This was a town of the Lower Nahrawān district that is said to have been inhabited by the descendants of Persian nobles.[47] Described by Muqaddasī in the tenth century as having a congregational mosque, it was in ruins by the time of Yāqūt, some years before the Mongol Conquest.[48]

Nahrawān. A clear description of the town of Nahrawān at the beginning of the tenth century is given by Ibn Rusta. Since his account continues with

91

a description of the great Khurāsān highroad to Persia, along which this town was the first stopping-place, it is worth including here in full:

> From Baghdad to Nahrawān a journey of four leagues, through uninterrupted date-plantations and cultivated fields, along Musallā, past the Nahr Bīn and Nahr Būq [canals], until arriving at the town of Nahrawān through which a watercourse flows. On its west bank are bazaars, a congregational mosque, and water-wheels [nāʿūrah] which irrigate its fields. There is a congregational mosque and a bazaar also on the east bank, and around the mosque are caravansaries for pilgrims passing through the town.

> From Nahrawān to Deir Tirmah a journey of four leagues through date-plantations and a continuing series of villages, until one comes to Deir Tirmah through which a large canal flows.

> From Deir Tirmah to Daskara a journey of eight leagues over a level plain, villages to the right and left. But these places are in ruins, abandoned by their inhabitants out of fear of the bedouins. The population has been compelled to seek refuge in a building with high walls on the summit of a tell to the left that served as a prison, it is said, in the time of certain Sassanian kings. Continuing further across the flat plain, to the right a desert, to the left palms and cultivated fields, the route leads to Daskara. This is a large town, with a castle built by one of the Sassanian kings. It is surrounded by a high wall, but in the interior there are no buildings; the only gateway enters from the west side.

> From Daskara to Jalūlā a journey of seven leagues, the route traversing sand dunes and encountering running water and date-palms. It passes through Jalūltā, where there is an important watercourse crossed by a stone bridge built by the Sassanians. Occasionally the level of the water rises above the bridge, and it is then impossible to move [on foot]. However camels can cross it, not without difficulty, and continue to a bridge known as Tazaristān, over which passes a lead aqueduct. Very near to this is the town of Hārūnīya. Finally, through a pass between two hills, one comes to Jalūlā.[49]

Unfortunately, other sources of information on Nahrawān are less adequate. The town is said to have contained a large Jewish community.[50] From the observations of the archaeological survey, it was apparent that the eastern part of the town was substantially the larger, although this may in part be due to less extensive brick-robbing there. Moreover, there was no evidence in the ceramic surface collection that

occupation along the west bank continued much after the ninth century.

In Muqaddasī's time, late in the tenth century, the eastern part was certainly at least the more populous, and its mosque was then the only one in use.[51] Subsequently, the town disappears from view altogether and presumably fell into ruins, while the Khurāsān road shifted northward to cross the Tāmarrā-Diyala near Baʿqūba instead of at Nahrawān. This shift antedates the completion of Yāqūt's geographical dictionary in 1224. In fact, having been transcribed into Mustawfī (1340) from *Risāla i Malikshāhiyya*, it must have occurred before or during the time of the Saljūk Sultan Malikshāh (1072–92).[52] Perhaps, then, little remained of either part of Nahrawān by the end of the eleventh century, although the surface collection indicates a continuing small occupation well into Ottoman times. At any rate, Mustawfī said it was in ruins in 1340.[53]

Daskara. Ibn Rusta's description of Daskara has been given together with that of Nahrawān and the Khurāsān road. Eighty years or so later, Ibn Hauqal noted that it possessed a strong castle,[54] and Muqaddasī described it still as a small city with a congregational mosque and a solitary market.[55] Presumably all this had grown up outside the great square, walled enclosure, while the latter served as a halting-place for caravans, offering a modicum of protection against the local banditry to which Ibn Rusta had alluded. To Yāqūt, two hundred and forty years later, the place had sunk to the status of "a village on the Khurāsān Road close to Shahrābān." Perhaps instrumental in its decline was the domination of the area for a period by the Ghuzz, who are reported to have successfully raided Daskara, Hārūnīya, and Bājisrā in 1048.[56]

Shahrābān. Also founded in the Sassanian period, Shahrābān continued into later times as a small town not important enough to attract the traffic of the Khurāsān road,[57] nor consequently of the medieval geographers. While never becoming prominent, it seems to have survived, in periodically changing circumstances but at any rate without substantial interruption, the long interval between the decline of the caliphate and the gradual return of prosperity in the late nineteenth century.

In 1617, perhaps the earliest European visitor to have left an account of it describes passing through

92

the village of Techiá and "then through another which may be called a town because of its size, and was named Shahrābān."[58] One hundred and sixty years later it was still a "large town" with gardens of dates, lemons, oranges, pomegranates, figs, and raisins.[59] Not long afterward, its fortunes were found to have declined considerably. An early-nineteenth-century account records laconically that it was a "tolerably important village, although half in ruins."[60] And a visitor in 1818 has left a more lyrical, but essentially corroborative, description:

> Sharaban (or Shahr-e-Van) is a small town or village which the inhabitants say was in former times a large city more magnificent than Bagdad. Not a vestige of this past grandeur remains. . . . The ground it covers is pretty extensive, and its appearance rather imposing. Like other towns and villages of the pashalick, it is built without a surrounding fortification; but each house has its own encircling high wall, entered by a gate; which walls, when connected in the circuit of the town, give the whole a demonstration of strength nearly equal to the circumvallation of a Persian town, bating the absence of towers. The general appearance has the advantage of being more open, from the trees and gardens which intersect the place in a variety of directions. Besides the date, limes grow in great perfection; and farther around, wheat, barley, tobacco, and cotton diversified the fields. Sharaban is watered by a small stream running along a deep bed, whose abrupt banks at one part are surmounted by a picturesque mosque, shooting up its grey minarets over the expanding and feathery branches of date and other trees. These groves spread through the town; and under their shadowy boughs we found the few shops which compose its little bazar, enjoying a more delightful canopy from the piercing heat of the sun than the richest arcades of ornamented masonry could have afforded.[61]

Another account, from approximately the same period, provides some supplementary details. Shahrābān, we are told, "has one mosque with a well-built minaret, and two khans [caravansaries], but nothing else worthy of notice. . . . The population may be estimated at about two thousand five hundred, of whom two-thirds are Soonnees, and the remainder Sheeahs, there being neither Jews nor Christians here. The language is Turkish, although Arabic is still understood, and the Aga of the place is subject to Bagdad."[62]

Even these relatively unprepossessing conditions were subject to substantial deterioration in that they invited military occupation and plunder. The condition of the town next was noted by a traveler in 1824, shortly after the withdrawal of an invading Persian force:

> We reached Shehreban at eleven o'clock P.M., and found it almost entirely deserted. It is a place of considerable extent. We wandered through the desolate streets some time, without finding any house with inhabitants, till we came to a caravanserai, where we met a man who told us that all the inhabitants had left the place, which had been sacked and ruined by the Coords. . . .
>
> In the evening, we visited Shehreban, or rather its ruins, as there was scarcely one entire house remaining. A winding stream of water, occasioned by a cut from the Diala, traverses nearly every house. This stream has been occasionally embanked with masonry, of which many portions remain that appear ancient, and may have been built during the time of the former city. There are also numerous bridges of bricks, forming communications with the different streets, but, apparently, not older than the modern town.
>
> No remains of ancient buildings exist, and the present town bids fair to add its heap of ashes to its predecessor. It was for some time in the hands of the Persians. The works they have left here, and at the other places we have passed, give abundant proof of their expertness in spoliation. The spectacle it presents is truly wretched. The roofs of many of the houses are fallen in; the wood having been probably used for fuel.
>
> This town was not many months back one of the most populous and thriving in the Pashalick of Bagdad; now the whole population consists of about three families.[63]

These depradations still had left their mark two decades later. An eye-witness account of 1844 indicates little change in the picture of desolation it had afforded earlier:

> Took up our quarters in the best house the place afforded, but a miserable hovel. . . . The Shehraban canal bisects the village, and is lost a little to the south of it. . . . Many mounds covered with broken pottery, and the remains of numerous canals crossing each other in fantastic lines, mark it as the former abode of a numerous and industrious population. The now barren and densely heated plain, highly cultivated as it no doubt was, afforded in bygone times some pleasant retreats, under the shelter of its groves, from the scorching heats of summer, which we, alas! feel and must bear, without a hope of relief. The date-

tree, so luxuriant and fruitful in the neighborhood of Baghdad, is here a stunted and a forlorn object. A headless minaret stands in the center of the village, a fit emblem of its fallen condition.[64]

Not long subsequent to this report, the slow regeneration of Shahrābān must have begun. Eight years after Jones's visit, it is reported that there were still only about a hundred houses in the town, but the presence of four Jewish families and the construction of an excellent caravansary[65] suggest that a newly established network of commerce and communications was beginning to connect it with the capital. The survival of Shahrābān until the present day, although now under the Arab name of Miqdādiya, has been indicated in the census data presented in an earlier chapter.

Not far from Shahrābān lay the town of Hārūnīya. First mentioned by Ibn Rusta (see above, p. 92), it assumed increasing importance with the decline of Daskara and the northward shift of the perimeter of cultivation and the Khurāsān road. In the early seventeenth century it still could be described as a town,[66] but subsequently it was abandoned completely. According to one account this was brought about by the blocking of its canal in an earthslide.[67] Since a glance at the map indicates that no earth movement in that vicinity could have been of more than minor proportion, the settlement must have been moribund even without this final disaster.

Barāz-al-Rūz. As at Shahrābān, there is continuity at Barāz-al-Rūz from Abbasid times into the modern period. Its origin is obscure, but Yāqūt records that the Caliph Muᶜtadid (892–902) built a palace there.[68] Mustawfī notes that in 1340 it paid over annually the fairly modest revenue of 20,000 dinars to the Baghdad treasury.[69] Apparently continuing to prosper in the late eighteenth century, it was described as a large town under the control of Baghdad.[70] At the time of Felix Jones's surveys in the mid-nineteenth century, the Rūz canal seems to have terminated in the immediate vicinity of the town,[71] although as late as the Ilkhanid period it had extended more than 50 kms. farther to the south (see *infra,* p. 106). The present name of the town is Balad Rūz.

Baᶜqūba. Although probably founded in the Sassanian period, Baᶜqūba was little mentioned until the Khurāsān road shifted northward to pass through it instead of Nahrawān. In Yāqūt's time (1224), it was a large village, "as large as a city," with several public baths and mosques, as well as a market. It was densely surrounded by irrigated orchards, and the dates and lemons in particular were proverbial for their excellence.[72] Slightly more than a century later, both Mustawfī and the epitomizer of Yāqūt reckoned it the chief town of the district along the Khurāsān road, although the former noted that it was more malarial than Baghdad because of its numerous palm-groves.[73]

At the beginning of the nineteenth century, the same general description continued to apply to the settlement, although probably it had shrunk in size during the interval. A traveler on the road to Kermānshāh reports that it was "a small village . . . , surrounded by date-palms, lemon trees, pomegranate trees and other fruit trees."[74] At about the same time it was described fulsomely, but probably less accurately, as a "large town renowned for the agreeable temperature of its climate, the abundance of its pastures and the exquisite flavour of its dates. . . . many villages are subordinate to it, and it is ruled by a *zabet* who is appointed by the pasha every two or three years."[75] At any rate, an eye-witness description of around 1820 supports the more jaundiced impression:

> It [Baᶜqūba] is a large straggling village, formed of mud-built dwellings, gardens, date-grounds, etc., all intermingled, with a poor bazar and two small mosques. The inhabitants do not exceed two thousand, all of whom are Arabs, and nearly half of these Sheeahs or of the Persian sect. The place is under the command of Yusuf Aga, who is dependent on Assad Pasha of Bagdad; its produce is purely agricultural, and this very scanty."[76]

What followed at Baᶜqūba closely paralleled events in Shahrābān. A visitor in 1824 reports that it had been laid in waste almost entirely during the immediately preceding occupation by the Kurdish army of Mohammad Ali Mirza, governor of Kermānshāh.[77] Ten years or so later it was described as "little better than a heap of ruins, in a jungle of date and pomegranate-trees."[78] By 1845, a French traveler tells us that the bazaar and one of the mosques were functioning again, but that the town, "formerly of great importance, being the point where several much frequented roads meet," had been reduced to seven or eight hundred houses. In spite of flourishing gardens and fields in its vicinity, he regarded it as having been

94

brought "to a state of decay from which there is little chance of its ever recovering."[79]

Less than thirty years later (in 1872–73), Turkish civil administration and the pacification of the region were beginning to restore the institutions of town life. "The place is the seat of a qāʾimmaqām [official], and has solidly built houses and a mosque. The palm gardens here, as also in Kharnābāt [a short distance to the north] are larger and more distinguished than those of the land between the Tigris and Euphrates rivers."[80] By the end of the century, Baʿqūba could accurately be described not only as increasingly prosperous but also as increasingly bound up in an economic nexus stretching far beyond its immediate hinterlands:

> The heart of the town is formed by a small bazaar with many fruits and vegetables, American coffee, Indian tea, French sugar and English textiles, in addition to the usual native products. But the bazaar is surrounded by a wide district of expansive gardens with characteristic gate-cottages, and at the eastern exit from the town there is a large and handsome caravansary that is full of Shīʿite pilgrims almost throughout the year.[81]

(The more recent development of the town as a regional capital has been described in Chapter III.)

A short distance to the south of Baʿqūba lay Bājisrā, a smaller town closely associated with it. Possibly the latter is the same settlement which today is known as Buhriz, probably after Mujāhid al-Dīn-Buhriz, an engineer who, in 1140, made the last serious attempt to repair and re-open the Nahrawān canal.

ʿAbertā. Although not attaining the maximum limits of the Sassanian settlement, ʿAbertā remained a considerable city in the Early Islamic and Sāmarrān periods. Presumably it was during this time that it produced a number of learned men and tradition-bearers, as Yāqūt records. Its decline in size coincided with an even sharper decline in rural settlement around it, induced by periodic breaches of the Nahrawān farther upstream and by other less dramatic but no less effective aspects of the general deterioration of the agricultural regime. Soon after the beginning of the twelfth century ʿAbertā had become the last settled outpost in a virtually abandoned countryside, and it must have depended precariously upon an irregular trickle in the great bed of the Nahrawān

canal alongside the town. Still, a century later Yāqūt described it as a large village with a flourishing market[82] and considerable quantities of fourteenth-century Chinese glazed pottery found in its uppermost levels during excavations show that it even survived for a time the Mongol conquests.

In later phases ʿAbertā was reduced to a walled settlement about four hectares in extent, perched on a high central mound and surrounded by more than a square kilometer of ruins. Its market, surely, no longer dealt in agricultural commodities. Instead the town must have served primarily as a way-station along a secondary caravan route from Persia, offering some protection against banditry within a modest wall of re-used bricks and rubble, and perhaps trading illegally in luxury commodities destined for the Baghdad market.

Uskāf-Banī-Junayd. Since extensive excavations were conducted in a number of locations at Uskāf by the Diyala Basin Archaeological Project, a full description of the stratigraphy and architecture of portions of this city must await a later, more specialized study. For purposes of a general discussion of settlement, however, some of the findings may be briefly summarized.

As it had been in the Sassanian period, Uskāf was apparently the largest city in the Diyala basin outside of the capital during Early Islamic and Sāmmarān times. Having left densely built-up debris that today covers approximately 4 sq. kms., according to Yāqūt it was occupied by the Banī-Junayd whose lords were noted for their hospitality.[83] In spite of the continuation of Islamic settlement within about as large an area as earlier, it is noteworthy that, at least in the central part of the site, settlement was resumed only after an interval of abandonment at the end of the Sassanian period. Nevertheless, the construction of an impressive palace decorated with stucco on one of the abandoned central mounds overlooking the Nahrawān, apparently even before the end of the seventh century, suggests that this interval was not a very long one. Similarly, on the opposite bank of the Nahrawān a mosque was built over abandoned Sassanian rubble, either at the same time or at any rate no later than the Early Abbasid period. In all probability the great number of learned men said by Yāqūt to have come from Uskāf were products of this period of renewed prosperity and vitality.

As at ʿAbertā, the post-Sāmarrān occupation at Uskāf was sharply diminished in size. Since no effort seemingly was made to wall in this later settlement, its remains cannot readily be distinguished from those of the Early Islamic city. However, systematic examination of ceramics on the surface of the site suggests that it covered an area of only about 20 hectares, a twentieth of the widest earlier limits; as at ʿAbertā, this final zone of occupation lay near the center of the city and must have been surrounded on all sides by mounds of ruined rubble. In the final phase of construction, dating to the end of the eleventh century, an unimpressive little minaret was added to the mosque on the west bank, while the rooms of the palace on the east were divided up with thin, poorly built partition walls. Not long afterward, permanent settlement came to an end. Perhaps final extinction may be traced to the termination of all flow in the Nahrawān, but both the results of surface reconnaissance and the testimony of Yāqūt suggest that the dwindling occupation persisted somewhat longer on the east bank than on the west. Today, even the original name of the city no longer is known by the rare catch-crop farmers and herdsmen who are its only visitors.

Brief and uneven as these accounts of individual settlements in the Diyala basin have been, they nevertheless suggest certain general observations about the history and character of at least its more important towns and cities during the Islamic period. Particularly noteworthy is the artificiality of new urban development. Baghdad and Sāmarrā both were consciously constructed as capitals rather than assuming that status as a result of prior economic or political pre-eminence. While the forced resettlement of conquered populations no longer seems to have played a major part in the urbanization process, the armies of laborers and craftsmen employed on the new capitals were brought together by huge expenditures from the state treasury and, probably, by a measure of duress as well.

As creations of state policy, these metropolises were also its victims. They were subject at times to abrupt transfer of governmental functions, costly and arbitrary internal rebuilding, social and commercial disruption as a result of political decline, and periodic waves of violent military destruction. Yet for all of the vicissitudes of their formation and subsequent history, Baghdad and Sāmarrā both seem to have exceeded Seleucia and Ctesiphon substantially in size and population, just as the latter two were far larger than all their predecessors. Moreover, Baghdad, at least, somehow survived as a city of this new and special, politically decisive, character through the long dark age following the collapse of the caliphate. Viewed from the political capitals, it thus appears that urbanism in the Diyala basin has been a cumulative rather than a merely cyclical phenomenon.

This observation is only underlined if we refer in addition to the smaller urban centers accounted for above. Most, or perhaps all, of them antedate the Islamic period, and many may have reached their greatest extent in Sassanian times. With interruptions of varying length and severity at the end of the Sassanian period, they afterwards experienced a brief resurgence in early Abbasid times or even earlier. But thenceforward they suffered a fairly uniform decline in size and prosperity. Well before the supposed *coup de grâce* of the Mongol conquest, most centers appear to have been severely reduced and impoverished by the exactions of tax-farmers, the conflicting claims and sanguinary destruction of Saljūk armies, and the decay of the imperial administration.

Seen in this light, the great size attained by Baghdad and Sāmarrā stands out in even sharper historical relief. To articulate one of the general themes of this study, the Diyala plains had emerged as an area settled with numerous towns that were roughly equal in size and importance; political dominance was transitory, and based more often on alliances between such towns than the enduring dominance of one of them. But with the Islamic period we see the full crystallization of a different pattern. The Diyala region had become a permanently backward and subservient hinterland whose agricultural wealth and human resources were largely drawn off to sustain a great urban capital that had grown up on its Tigris margin.

We are not concerned solely with urbanization as it is reflected in Baghdad and the major provincial towns. In fact, the decline or destruction of many of the major centers, and the progressive economic and administrative deterioration to which it was linked, merely provide an interpretive framework for the central focus of this chapter upon basic changes in

96

irrigation and settlement throughout the Diyala basin. For a direct understanding of the latter, we must depend primarily on the results of archaeological survey. While lacking the chronological precision possible with written documents, surface reconnaissance at least allows the reconstruction of a sequence of change in some of the basic conditions of life on the local level, thus complementing Arab chroniclers whose major interest was the fluid political scene in the capital itself.

Any attempt to reconstruct a sequence of change archaeologically must rest on a periodization of the surface remains within the long Islamic phase of occupation. To a degree, this has been made possible by reference to publications of ceramic finds, particularly at Sāmarrā[84] and Wāsit,[85] but the material presently in hand has several defects for this immediate purpose. The brief span of occupation of the Sāmarrā palaces, for example, defines the floruit of several notable ceramic types, but it fixes neither the beginning nor the end of their periods of use. Hence we are left with an early Islamic period that ostensibly covers two centuries and unfortunately lumps together the Omayyads and early Abbasids, and a subsequent Sāmarrān period of little more than half a century.

It seems only reasonable to suppose under the circumstances that the ceramic styles known as Sāmarrān considerably antedate the move to the new capital, probably coming into vogue not later than the zenith of power and prosperity reached under Hārūn-al-Rashīd (786–809). Moreover, since the date of the first general abandonment of the Nahrawān districts has been fixed at 937 (supra, p. 86), it can be shown from the surface collections that essentially the same groups of ceramic types remained common through at least the first third of the tenth century. Thereafter they were gradually replaced, both at Wāsit and in the Diyala area, but in the ensuing proliferation of new local styles of utiltarian glaze-ware few parallels can be drawn to published sources until the last century or so of Abbasid rule. For this interval of about two centuries, the dating of the surface collections rests largely on ceramic types (or stylistic variations) whose validity cannot yet be fully demonstrated stratigraphically.

The inference that the chronology as a whole is approximately correct, however, is indicated by collections which can be tied (with the aid of air photographs) to superimposed canal courses, and by the conformity of the sequence of settlements reconstructed with the aid of such types to the sequence that can be projected from historical records. Subsequently, the problems of dating are substantially reduced with the advent of new techniques of painted decoration under glaze (probably around A.D. 1150 in rural areas like the Diyala basin), and remain relatively simple through at least the fifteenth century when our record of settlement fades away almost completely.

1. EARLY ISLAMIC AND SĀMARRĀN PERIODS

As applied to the analysis of archaeological surface collections, these two periods together cover a span of perhaps three centuries. A separation between them obviously would be desirable, but it has been avoided here (except for special purposes) for several reasons. In particular, the deficiencies just cited in the available evidence combine to render somewhat obscure both the temporal and typological distinctions between the two periods. Moreover, the ceramic dating criteria finally worked out during the survey were not all apparent at its beginning, so that many sites can only be classified as having been occupied during the Early Islamic or Sāmarrān periods. Accordingly, Table 20 lists jointly all sites that are described in the Site Catalogue (Appendix C) as having been occupied during either or both of these periods, although in a separate section sites are tabulated which appear to have been abandoned before the Sāmarrān period.

This procedure assumes, in effect, that virtually no new settlements were established in the Diyala basin during the ninth century. By attributing Omayyad or early Abbasid origins to all sites found to have been occupied during Sāmarrān times, it probably exaggerates the extent of Early Islamic settlement and inevitably offers too sharply drawn a picture of declining population afterward. But it may be pointed out that such evidence as we have is not inconsistent with this reconstruction. The tax revenues from the Sawād as a whole (supra, p. 85) indicate a decline in collections of perhaps 30 per cent between the Omayyad period and the time of Ibn Khurradādhbah (ca. 844). While in part reflecting a diversion into private hands rather than a decline in the cultivated

97

area, this hardly suggests that conditions of economic abundance continued everywhere without qualification. Again, the vigorous program of building undertaken during the eighth century at Uskāf-Banī-Junayd and at the weir across the Nahrawān a short distance above the city was not duplicated afterward. Finally, it seems only reasonable to suppose that the bulk of building activities was diverted elsewhere from the time of Mansūr on, first to the construction of Baghdad and subsequently to Sāmarrā.

TABLE 20

SITES OF THE EARLY ISLAMIC AND SĀMARRĀN PERIODS
IN THE LOWER DIYALA REGION

1. Important cities and towns that are identified in contemporary Arabic sources (for descriptions see pp. 89–96):*
Baghdad, (6,400 hectares [Le Strange 1900:325]); Sāmarrā, (6,800 ha. [Herzfeld 1948:137]); ᶜUkbarā, (130 ha.); Busrā, (5 ha.); Al-Madāin (Taq-i-Kesrā, Salmān Pāk, 665–666 [100 ha.?]); Deir al-ᶜĀqūl (791), (20 ha.); Humānīya, (20 ha.?); Jarjarāyā, (20 ha.?); Nahrawān (Sifwah, 308–309), (25 ha.); Daskara (Eski Baghdad, 41), (20 ha.?); Shahrābān (20 ha.?); Barāz-al-Rūz (Balad Rūz), (20 ha.?); Baᶜqūba (10 ha.?); Bājisrā (Buhriz ?), (5 ha.?); ᶜAbertā (620), (100 ha.); Uskāf-Banī-Junayd (Sumāka, 734), (400 ha.).

2. Sassanian sites continuing into, or reoccupied during, the Early Islamic or Sāmarrān periods (not including those given above):
Small urban centers:
627, Tell Tabl (44 ha.); 700 (40 ha.); 826, Tulūl al-Shuᶜailah (35 ha.).
Three sites, approximately 119 hectares of settlement.
Large towns:
167 (20 ha.); 287, Tell Borākhān al-saghīr (20 ha.); 363, Tulūl Rughāth (20 ha.); 371, Tell Mukherīj (16 ha.); 467 (25 ha.); 544 (25 ha.); 613, Tell Abū Fahadah (11 ha.); 632, Tell Jubayl (10 ha.); 689 (20 ha.); 704, Tell Abū Khansīra (16 ha.); 705 (20 ha.); 799, Jemdet Shahrazād (18 ha.).
Twelve sites, approximately 221 hectares of settlement.
Small towns:
237, 379, 533, 578, 619, 626, 658, 708, 717, 722, 724, 727 (2), 771, 777, 828, 839, 867.
Eighteen sites, approximately 114 hectares of settlement.
Villages:
83, 86, 130, 148, 153, 154, 168, 173, 196 (?), 200, 210, 228, 233, 248, 252, 254 (4), 263, 271, 288, 313, 315, 320, 361, 368, 385, 394, 432, 433, 444, 511, 516, 523 (?), 532, 542, 549 (2), 559 (?), 565, 583, 584, 586, 594, 597, 659, 660, 673, 674, 711, 725, 737, 738, 740 (3), 744, 745, 747 (4), 782, 788, 793, 797, 816, 822, 831, 841, 844, 854, 862.
Seventy-four sites, approximately 103 hectares of settlement.

3. Newly founded Early Islamic–Sāmarrān sites:
Small urban centers:
514, Tell Jaᶜara (50 ha.); 641, Tell Zuhra (40 ha.); 675, Tell al-Drāzi (56 ha.).
Three sites, approximately 146 hectares of settlement.
Large towns:
551, Tell Daimat al-ᶜOda (12 ha.); 592 (10 ha.); 642, Tell Mirhij (21 ha.); 649 (14 ha.); 655, Tell Mujassas (25 ha.); 710, Tel Maᶜbūd (12 ha.); 756 (10 ha.); 804, Mayyah al-Sharqī (19 ha.).
Eight sites, approximately 123 hectares of settlement.
Small towns:
90, 183, 268, 301, 318, 360 (?), 372, 373, 406, 454, 490, 493, 521, 539, 553, 555, 573, 600, 606, 650, 681, 683, 686, 736, 743, 750, 759, 761, 762, 766, 769, 778, 805, 807, 823, 834, 855.
Thirty-seven sites, approximately 213 hectares of settlement.
Villages:
43, 124, 127, 179, 181, 182, 184, 185, 188, 202, 204, 207, 231, 236, 273, 277, 280, 282, 347, 351, 356, 365, 369, 377, 378, 382,

* Because of later occupation, extending up to the present time, the areas of many of these sites are impossible to determine accurately. Areas shown with a question mark are frankly speculative.

Both of these new cities were of a quite unprecedented size. Each was apparently on the order of ten times as large as Ctesiphon, and each substantially exceeded the entire area of built-up settlement in the Diyala region during the Sassanian period. In this respect, they indicate not merely a quantitative but a qualitative advance in urban scale and complexity as compared with the earlier period, just as the Sassanian capital signified for its time a qualitative advance in urbanization over conditions in earlier antiq-

TABLE 20—*Continued*

383, 386, 391, 393, 395, 401, 402, 403, 404, 405, 423, 448, 452 (?), 453, 462, 464 (?), 482, 483 (?), 485, 518, 524, 536, 547, 548, 550, 552, 554 (4), 585, 602, 615, 616, 621, 635, 636, 640 (2), 643 (3), 644 (6), 645 (2), 651, 652, 653 (3), 654, 656, 677, 688, 690, 691, 692, 694, 695, 696, 697 (3), 699, 702, 706, 709, 713, 714, 718, 719 (2), 720 (2), 721, 723 (2), 726, 728, 729, 731, 733, 739, 746 (3), 748, 749, 752, 753, 754, 755, 757, 758, 760, 765, 768, 774, 780, 781, 784, 785, 786, 787, 789, 792, 794, 800, 806, 808, 809, 815, 819, 820, 827, 830, 833, 834, 840, 845, 847, 850, 852 (3), 853, 855 (2), 856.
One hundred and sixty sites, approximately 264 hectares of settlement.

In total: Not including Baghdad and Sāmarrā, 329 recorded sites, aggregating approximately 2,198 hectares of built-up area. This includes 4 cities aggregating 730 ha., 6 smaller urban centers aggregating 265 ha., 28 large towns aggregating 499 ha., 57 small towns aggregating 337 ha., and 234 villages aggregating 367 ha. Excluding Baghdad and Sāmarrā, 45.5 per cent of settlement area was urban and 38 per cent was in towns. Note that Baghdad and Sāmarrā each occupied several times as large a built-up area as all other contemporary settlements in the Diyala basin together.

4. Sites largely or wholly abandoned before the Sāmarrān period:
Large towns:
167, 287, 363, 467, 544, 592, 613, 649, 689, 705, 756, 826.
Twelve sites, approximately 210 hectares of settlement.
Other:
43, 83, 90, 130, 148, 153, 154, 168, 173, 196 (?), 200, 248, 254 (4), 263, 282, 315, 320, 356, 361, 365, 368, 373, 377, 378, 379, 383, 391, 423, 433, 444, 448, 452, 453, 454, 462, 511, 516, 518, 521, 532, 539, 542, 549 (2), 573, 578, 583, 584, 586, 594, 600, 602, 616, 619, 635, 640 (2), 643 (3), 658, 659, 673, 681, 690, 712, 722, 724, 725, 739, 745, 746 (2), 747 (4), 768, 774, 782, 793, 808, 820, 827, 831, 833, 839, 840, 841, 845, 850, 853, 854, 862, 867.
Ninety-eight sites, approximately 218 hectares of settlement.

5. Sites largely or wholly abandoned soon after the Sāmarrān period:
Cities:
620 (ᶜAbertā), 734 (Uskāf).
Two sites, approximately 476 hectares of settlement. In addition, most of Sāmarrā itself must have been abandoned with the return of the Caliphate to Baghdad.
Smaller urban centers:
514, 627, 641, 675, 700.
Five sites, 230 hectares of settlement.
Large towns:
655, 799, 826.
Three sites, 53 hectares of settlement.
Other:
86, 124, 202, 204, 268, 271, 288, 308, 351, 360 (?), 372, 382, 385, 482, 483 (?), 493, 523 (?), 524, 536, 539, 554 (4), 555, 559 (?), 565, 585, 597, 615, 621, 636, 645 (2), 653 (3), 654, 656, 660, 674, 677, 688, 692, 702, 706, 708, 709, 711, 714, 717, 718, 719 (2), 720 (2), 721, 728, 729, 733, 737, 738, 740 (3), 743, 744, 746, 748, 749, 750, 752, 753, 757, 758, 762, 765, 766, 788, 792, 797, 816, 823, 844, 847, 852 (3), 856.
Ninety sites, approximately 204 hectares of settlement.

In total: Not including Sāmarrā, 210 sites aggregating approximately 1,382 hectares of settlement abandoned before the Late Abbasid period. This was 62.5 per cent of all settlement during the Early Islamic and Sāmarrān periods.

uity. Given the separate periods of florescence of each of these cities as capitals, of course, it is clear that the bulk of their inhabitants were drawn from one to the other by the flow of political events, so that the maximum population of either must have been very nearly as large as the aggregate population of both at any one time.

It is apparent from contemporary descriptions that the bulk of the inhabitants of Baghdad and Sāmarrā were officials, service and military personnel, merchants, and artisans who were wholly dependent for their food on agricultural production by others in rural areas. The evidence suggests, in other words, a new emphasis on facilities for the transport of commodities in bulk and a highly efficient taxing system to sustain the regular flow of wealth to the cities. It suggests also that both cities drew their support from an immense agricultural hinterland of which the Diyala basin was only a minor constituent.[86]

At the same time that we trace the expansion of the newly-founded capitals until they attained unprecedented size, the actual conditions of settlement in the countryside deteriorated. Having reached a maximum in the Sassanian period, over-all density of settlement on the Diyala plains afterward declined sharply. Part of this decline may reflect an actual siphoning off of population from provincial towns and villages into the capital cities. But for the most part the decline in the Diyala region at large antedates their construction, for the total built-up area (excluding Baghdad and Sāmarrā) in Early Islamic times as given in Table 20 is only 64 per cent of the same total for the Sassanian period. The greatest degree of urbanization prior to modern times, in other words, came not as a concomitant of the greatest intensity of land usage but as the sequel to a decline in provincial settlement, irrigation, and agricultural production. To phrase the matter more generally, a broad contrast emerges even within the confines of this relatively small region between the preponderantly agrarian-based civilization of the Sassanian period and the increasingly urban, mercantile orientation of Islam. This conclusion was already evident in the brief historical sketches given earlier of Baghdad, Sāmarrā, and the other towns in the Diyala region that are mentioned prominently in Arabic sources; it finds additional corroboration in the data of the survey.

Considered in relation to their geographic distribution (Fig. 6), the sites recorded in Table 20 are not widely and uniformly scattered. There are fairly large areas which had been intensively occupied earlier and which seem to have been entirely avoided by settled cultivators. In the case of the region north and northwest of ʿAbertā, it has been suggested that salinization of the soil was a factor in explaining the sparsity of settlement, but in other regions of reduced occupation, as, for example, along what is now called the Mahrūt canal, the greater slope of the land at least would have reduced sharply the dangers of having to abandon cultivation for this reason. Moreover, since adequate supplies of water now were available for the whole basin through the construction of the Kātūl al-Kisrawī, it is difficult to attribute the sparsity of settlement there to a water shortage. Perhaps, as Ibn Rusta's account (supra, p. 92) suggests, the area had been abandoned because of nomadic raids, although we may wonder whether such raids were a sufficient cause of depopulation or only one of its symptoms. In any case, there is no apparent environmental reason in this case for the avoidance of settlement which the results of survey so clearly reflect.

By way of contrast, we may consider a part of the Middle and Lower Nahrawān districts which is shown at a greater scale in Figure 8. This region has not been reoccupied since the final failure of the Nahrawān in about A.D. 1150. Remains of the Islamic period are virtually undisturbed on a land surface which has received only a very slight alluvial increment after the abandonment of irrigation. Hence traces of settlement just prior to that time can be mapped almost completely, essentially without the losses encountered in earlier periods as a result of submergence beneath the rising land surface or later cultural debris. As a result, overestimates of their individual areas (see pp. 124–25) probably are not balanced by the diminution or disappearance of other sites, leading to a substantial overestimate of the total area of built-up settlement.

We can arrive at the same conclusion in another way. A total cultivable area of about 1,450 sq. kms. is shown in Figure 8. According to the procedures of the survey which have been followed for earlier periods, settlements of the Early Islamic and Sāmarran periods within this area were calculated to have occupied 1,155 hectares, fully 53 per cent of the total recorded for the entire region outside of the capital cities. Such a total of built-up settlement is slightly more than twice as large as could be maintained with the available land at our earlier estimate of density. At least in part this discrepancy must stem from overestimates of site areas of the kind described above. In addition, it may have been aggravated by the reshuffling or urban and rural populations through tax and resettlement policies, a practice that began in earlier periods (*supra*, pp. 65, 75, 81) and continued in Islamic times, as indicated by Miskawaih's long description of the decay of Abbasid administration. Tending to hasten the cycle of formation and abandonment for many towns and villages, this rapid reshuffling in response to political and military pressures increases the possibilities of confusion between sequent and contemporary settlement and contributes to an overestimate of the latter.

But with all these reservations taken into account, we are left with the impression of exceedingly dense and prosperous settlement along the Middle and Lower Nahrawān, strikingly different from the situation not only along the Mahrūt canal but also in many other parts of the Diyala basin. The visitor to the almost continuous ruins along the Nahrawān today is not surprised to find that Ibn Serapion, writing of the Nahrawān canal in its heyday, describes its banks in this region as being lined with beautiful villages and domains that lay contiguous to one another.[87]

Complementing the thickly clustered settlements along the Nahrawān and its principal branches was a well-functioning irrigation system. Figure 8 illustrates the irrigation regime in the neighborhood of ᶜAbertā and Uskāf-Banī-Junayd at its prime, with relatively straight, short branches carrying water from the Nahrawān into nearby fields. From the absence of spoil-banks along its entire length in this sector, we may assume that the main canal maintained a sufficient flow to scour its own bed and so avoid becoming clogged with silt that would require periodic removal. Since villages begin very near the heads of most of the branches, it is apparent that the level of flow in the Nahrawān was sufficient to command all but the highest part of its levee for irrigation purposes. This, of course, made irrigation possible with only short branches, and thus kept the whole problem of de-silting to a minimum.[88] The weir at

Al-Qantara, it is true, was used during this period to provide a stable level of supply for two large new branch canals serving an area below Uskāf which formerly had been fed directly from the Nahrawān, but this was probably only a local problem brought about by the exceptional water requirements of the Uskāf urban area; in part, it may also have arisen as a result of an excessive scouring by the Nahrawān of its bed below the weir. The general pattern of the branches, in any case, is clearly one that would have facilitated irrigation and drainage and that makes more understandable the intensive utilization of land which the abundant ruins suggest.

Further light on the character of settlement and the extent of agricultural production is provided by Ibn Khurradādhbah's record of Abbasid tax revenues in about A.D. 844. For districts east of the Tigris and within or adjoining the Diyala basin, his figures are given in Table 21. Because of the very large proportion of the total revenues which was received in kind, we may assume that taxes on fields producing wheat and barley normally were paid directly with the grain itself at a fixed rate. In addition, of course, a proportion of the receipts from the head tax, and from taxes on date and vegetable gardens, probably was paid in grain.

Unfortunately, the boundaries of the districts cannot be determined, although their general location is fairly clear in most cases. Lacking a comparison of the areas of different districts, no comparisons can be drawn between them as to their respective agricultural yields. But for the lower Diyala plains as a whole, whose maximum cultivable area we have estimated previously as about 8,000 sq. kms., some further progress is possible with Ibn Khurradādhbah's data.

As a first step, three districts given in Table 21 need to be eliminated from the total in order to reflect the production of the lower Diyala basin by itself. To begin with, Rustukbādh and Jalūlā lay—at least for the most part—above the Jebel Hamrīn, on the right and left banks of the Diyala respectively.[89] Rādhānain is more questionable. It is assigned by Le Strange[90] to the region between Al-Madāin and the Nahrawān canal, a location which seems impossible in view of the canal network of the time and the better-known position of surrounding districts. Instead, the district is regarded here as occupying the alluvial

100

fan of the lower ᶜAdheim river, one of whose two branches was known as the Nahr Radhan until recent times (*supra*, p. 78). These three districts together produced 23.5 per cent of the total revenues recorded in Table 21. More important, they contributed 19,340 metric tons of wheat and 17,546 tons of barley to the total receipts in kind. Since they are provisionally assumed to fall outside the lower Diyala basin, their grain receipts must be subtracted from the totals in the table before a computation of the total production of the basin can be made.

Second, there is the question of tax rates. Those quoted by Ibn Khurradādhbah, and presumably applying to the imposts he describes, are said to have been laid down by the Caliph ᶜUmar ibn al-Khattāb (634–44). The land tax was assessed on each owner at a rate which varied according to the crops grown. For each *jarīb* (about 0.1592 ha.) in cultivation under the fallow system,[91] barley required an annual payment of 2 dirhems, wheat 4 dirhems, vineyards 6 dirhems,

and date-palm gardens 8 dirhems.[92] In addition, a head tax was imposed on a tributary population numbered at 500,000 persons (Christians and Magians). Elsewhere we are told that the population was divided into three categories, with the upper class paying 48 dirhems annually, the middle class 24 dirhems, and the lowest class 12 dirhems.[93] Obviously the contribution to total revenues stemming from the head tax cannot be fixed unless more is known not only of the basis for division into classes[94] but also the size of religious minorities compelled to pay the head tax.

The rates of land tax can be calculated for different crops. Two dirhems per *jarīb* of barley can be converted (see *infra*, p. 180, note 7; Table 21, note) to an equivalent of 13.7 kg. of tax per *jarīb*. Similarly, four dirhems per *jarīb* of wheat can be converted to a tax of 21.2 kg. of wheat per *jarīb*. Average barley yields in the Diyala area were shown in Chapter II to be 1,396 kg. per hectare, while wheat yields averaged 1,132 kg.[95] Approximately halving these yields

TABLE 21

ABBASID TAX REVENUES FROM THE LOWER DIYALA REGION, *ca.* A.D. 844

Districts (See Fig. 6)	Market Towns	Barns	Tax in Wheat	Tax in Barley	Tax in Silver
26. Buzurjasābur	9	263	2,500 khurr*	2,200 khurr†	300,000 dirhems
27. Rādhānain	16	362	4,800	4,800	120,000
28. Nahr Būq	......	......	200	1,000	100,000
29. Kalwādhā and Nahr Bīn	3	34	1,600	1,500	330,000
30. Madīna ᶜAtīqa and Jāzir	7	116	1,000	1,500	140,000‡
31. Rustukbādh	......	......	1,000	1,400§	170,000‖
32. Mahrūdh and Silsil	......	......	2,000	2,500#	250,000**
33. Jalūlā and Jalūltā	5	76	1,000	1,000	100,000
34. Dhibain	4	230	700††	1,300	40,000
35. Daskara and Rustākain	7	44	2,000	2,000	70,000‡‡
36. Barāz-al-Rūz	7	86	3,000	5,500§§	120,000
38. Nahrawān	21	380	4,700	3,500	600,000
a) Upper	......	......	2,700‖‖	1,800	350,000
b) Middle	......	......	1,000	500	100,000
c) Lower	......	......	1,000	1,200	150,000##
Totals:	79	1,591	24,500 (85,600)***	28,200 (71,000)***	2,340,999
Total Revenues converted to Dirhems			13,352,500	10,011,000	2,340,999
				26,704,499	

* 1 khurr of wheat = 2,925 kg. (Hinz, W. 1955. Islamische Masse und Gewichte, p. 42).
† 1 khurr of barley = 2,437.5 kg. (De Goeje, M. J. 1889. Pp. 9–10).
‡ Qudāma gives 246,000, MS B gives 250,000 (DeGoeje 1889. P. 9).
§ This includes millet as well as barley.
‖ Qudāma: 246,000 (De Goeje 1889. P. 9).
Qudāma: 1,500 (De Goeje 1889. P. 9).
** Qudāma: 150,000 (De Goeje 1889. P. 9).
†† Qudāma: 1,900 (De Goeje 1889. P. 10).
‡‡ Qudāma: 1,800 wheat, 1,400 barley, 60,000 silver (De Goeje 1889. P. 10).
§§ Qudāma: 5,100 (De Goeje 1889. P. 10).
‖‖ Qudāma: 1,700 (De Goeje 1889. P. 10).
Qudāma: 1,700 wheat, 1,300 barley, 53,000 silver (De Goeje 1889. P. 10).
*** Expressed in metric tons.

(Source: De Goeje, M. J. 1889. Pp. 9–10. Kitâb al-Masâlik wa'l-Mamalik, auctore Abu'l-Kâsim Obaidallah ibn Abdallah Ibn Khordâdhbeh. Accedunt excerpta e Kitâb al-Kharâdj, auctore Kodâma ibn Djaᶜfar. Bibliotheca Geographorum Arabicorum, 6. Leiden.)

to take account of the fact that the tax was based on fallow fields as well as those in cultivation and assuming that there has been no significant change in agricultural productivity, it follows that the probable output of barley per *jarīb* of land forming the tax base was approximately 111 kg., and that of wheat 90 kg. Thus the tax on barley would have been about 12 per cent of potential yield, and that of wheat about 24 per cent of potential yield.[96] But in addition, as we have noted, the higher taxes on vineyards and orchards and perhaps even head taxes on non-Muslims often must have been paid in grain since, of the total revenues recorded in Table 21, 88 per cent were received in wheat and barley. Thus a reasonable, probably conservative, estimate may be that one-fourth of the yearly barley crop and one-third of the wheat were taken annually in taxes.

Again using the figures obtained earlier for contemporary yields per hectare, these over-all rates of taxation serve as a basis for estimating the total area of cultivation. Payments of tax in barley, as amended to include only those districts within the Diyala basin proper, are shown in Table 21 to be 53,454 metric tons. This would have required a growing area (including fallow land) of approximately 76,500 hectares, or a total area devoted to barley of around 306,000 hectares. Similarly, the amended total tax in wheat of 66,260 tons implies a growing area of 117,000 hectares, and a corresponding area in wheat of around 350,000 hectares. Furthermore, this total of about 6,600 sq. kms. of cultivable land must include a part of the Lower Nahrawān (and possibly also the Barāz-al-Rūz) district southeast of the Diyala basin proper, along supplementary lower outlets of the Nahrawān or its branches extending toward their junction with the Tigris almost as far downstream as the modern town of Kūt. The canal branches and accompanying settlements in this large area were not covered by our archaeological reconnaissance, but from the dating of the upper portions of the main branches serving the area it seems certain that their major development began only with the Islamic period.

In short, within the Diyala basin itself it would appear that the cultivated area had shrunk from around 8,000 sq. kms. toward the end of the Sassanian period to perhaps 6,000 sq. kms. in the mid-ninth century. Moreover, this had occurred in spite of the appreciable extension of irrigation and settlement in certain

districts, e.g., the Abū-l-Jund canal, constructed (or at least enlarged) by Hārūn-al-Rashīd and said by Ibn Serapion to have been the finest and best cultivated of the "lesser Kātūls,"[97] and probably also the Dhib or Khālis. Herein is reflected both the enduring effect of the late Sassanian abandonment and the weakness of their successors at a crucial point. At the peak of their power and prosperity, and faced with far heavier fixed requirements of revenue for the maintenance of agriculturally unproductive urban centers, the Abbasid caliphs were unwilling or unable to regain the ground that had been lost since Sassanian times in the vital rural economy.

2. LATER ABBASID (POST-SĀMARRĀN) PERIOD

Although the revenues of the mid-ninth century already reflect a decline in cultivation and settlement from maxima reached in the Sassanian period, a much more serious decline was imminent. The sharp reductions in total tax receipts from the Sawād and the accompanying deterioration at all levels in the administration already have been indicated briefly. It remains to describe in greater detail the effects of these changes within the Diyala basin in particular.

Tax revenues for districts in the Diyala region in 918–19, scarcely seventy-five years after those of Ibn Khurradādhbah, are given in Table 22. While several administrative boundary changes make interpretation more difficult (see notes in Table), a serious decline in the receipts from most districts is strikingly evident. To be sure, it is accompanied by a new reliance on tax payments exclusively in currency, but in view of other conditions we may wonder whether this technical advance does not mask an increasing inability of the bureaucracy to transport and redistribute the huge volume of payments in kind it had handled successfully earlier. Similarly, the regrouping of administrative districts, apparently in all cases a combining of formerly separate entities that was accompanied by substantial losses in revenue, seems to point not only to the weakening of central authority but to an increasing scarcity of trained governmental personnel. Seen in this light, the increasing tendency to replace state collectors with the extortions of private tax-farmers becomes an understandable and almost necessary development.

The one exception to the serious shrinkage in reve-

102

nues shown in Table 22 is provided by the Middle and Lower Nahrawān. Perhaps the slight decrease in the Lower Nahrawān indicates that in spite of a decline in the general rate of return new lands were continuing to be taken under cultivation near the tails of the canal. But the maintenance of Middle Nahrawān district revenues with relatively small loss suggests that even the older areas of settlement in the agricultural region served by this great artificial watercourse for a time escaped the unhappy conditions prevalent elsewhere. As a result, the contribution of these districts to the total revenues received by the caliph from the Sawād increased to 6.5 per cent, virtually trebling what it had been at the time of Ibn Khurradādhbah. This, of course, was cut off at a stroke when Ibn Rāʾiq breached the Nahrawān less than two decades later.

Subsequent records of Abbasid tax receipts from the Diyala region are not available to trace the process of deterioration. Nor do any contemporary writers whose works have survived recount what must have been a tragic and harrowing series of regressions, occasionally punctuated with brief promises of returning prosperity. At best an abstract and impersonal record is furnished by the changing patterns of irrigation and settlement recorded in the archaeological survey, but at present there is little else to go on.

As summarized in Table 20, by the end of the Sāmarrān period (or, more probably, the early years of the tenth century) 62 per cent of all recorded settlement outside Baghdad had been abandoned. Some regions, e.g., that between the Upper Nahrawān canal and Al-Madāin, seem to have been deserted fairly quickly and completely, but more frequently the process was one of attrition, in which the population of at least the larger communities sought for a long time to remain, or repeatedly returned, and in any case dwindled away slowly.

Table 23 makes clear that relatively few new settlements were formed after the Sāmarrān period, while the accounts previously given of individual towns suggest that most of them declined in size and importance only gradually during the ensuing centuries. It is probable that by the end of the Abbasid period only a portion of the 937 hectares of recorded town and village sites outside the capital were occupied. If so, the catastrophic effects of the Mongol conquest must be regarded as largely limited to major cities like

Baghdad, for little would have remained in the Diyala countryside at least that would have offered resistance to or attracted the interest of an invading army of mounted nomads.

The interaction of human and natural forces in the reduction of settlement and irrigation nowhere is clearer than along the Middle and Lower Nahrawān. The sequence of Figures 8 and 9 contrasts the pattern of occupation of Early Islamic and Sāmarrān times with the post-Sāmarrān period in a region which, as we have seen, had effectively resisted the general decline until the first interruption of its main water supply in A.D. 937. Perhaps most obvious is the sharp reduction which occurred in population density as re-

TABLE 22

ABBASID TAX REVENUES FROM THE LOWER DIYALA REGION, A.D. 918-19

District	Revenue in Dinars (1 dinar = 16+ dirhems)*		Approximate Percentage of Revenues of A.D. 844 (Table 21)†
		(per cent)	
1. Bādurayā, Kalwādhā, and Nahr Bīn	10,392	(27.3)‡	2.5
3. Bahorasir, Rumakān, ʾYghār Jaktyn, Jāzir and Madīna ʿAtīqa	75,576	(19.2)§	19
13. Nahr Būq and Lower Dayr	20,590		58
14. Buzurjasābur	24,300		16
15. Rādhānain	30,035		11
16. Rustukabādh	13,666		19
17. Upper Nahrawān and Samatnāj	46,480		30
18. Middle Nahrawān	40,327		78
19. Lower Nahrawān	60,532		86
20. Silh and Manāzil‖	159,089		26
Total:#	480,987**		

* This equivalence is given by von Kremer, A. 1888:287.

† Computed by converting payments-in-kind in Table 21 into silver payments, using the equivalences given by de Goeje (infra, p. 180, n. 7), and dividing total A.D. 844 payments into A.D. 918-19 payments (the latter also converted into dirhems).

‡ The percentage in the parenthesis represents the proportion of the total revenue from this district assumed to come from the Diyala area. Bādurayā is on the west bank of the Tigris and is listed separately by Ibn Khurradādhbah in 844. The proportion of the combined payments of the two districts (payments-in-kind converted into currency plus currency payments) for that year that was contributed by the district in the Diyala area is given in the parentheses and is assumed to apply also to the tax-year of 918-19.

§ Similar to the case discussed in previous note, this district represents a combination of several earlier districts—of which only Madīna ʿAtīqa and Jāzir were on the left bank of the Tigris and grouped as a single district in Ibn Khurradādhbah's account. The figure in the parentheses is the proportion of the total taxes for these districts contributed by the two in the Diyala area. It is assumed to apply also to 918-19.

‖ These districts do not appear in the Ibn Khurradādhbah account. On the other hand, several districts there (32-36, Table 21) do not appear in this listing, although archaeological survey, itineraries, etc., indicate clearly that the area in which they were continued to be occupied. Hence it is assumed here that Silh and Manazil simply combined Mahrūth and Silsil, Dhibain, Daskara and Rustākain, Barāz-al-Rūz, and possibly Jalūlā and Jalūltā, and the comparison of revenues in 844 and 918-19 is computed on this basis.

This total is meant to include only the revenues from the Diyala area. Hence only those portions of tax-revenues from districts 1 and 3 assumed to come from the left bank of the Tigris (notes ‡ and §, above) have been included.

** This equals 31 per cent of total revenues from the Sawād for that year.

Source: von Kremer, A. 1888. Pp. 312-13. Ueber das Einnahmebudget des Abbasiden-Reiches vom Jahre 306 H (918-19). Denkschriften der Kaiserlichen Akademie der Wissenschaften, Vienna. Phil.-Hist. Klasse. Vol. 36.

flected in areas of built-up settlement. Within the 1,450 sq. kms. of cultivable land shown, the gross area of ruins declined from 1,155 hectares to 148 hectares, approximately one-eighth of the former figure. From this alone, even in the absence of any other

TABLE 23

SITES OF THE LATER ABBASID (POST-SĀMARRĀN) PERIOD IN THE LOWER DIYALA REGION

1. Important cities and towns identified in contemporary Arabic sources (for descriptions see pp. 89–96):
Baghdad (5,400 ha.); Sāmarrā (100 ha.?); ᶜUkbarā (130 ha.); Busrā (5 ha.); Deir al-ᶜĀqūl (791), (20 ha.); Al-Mādāin (Taq-i-Kesrā, Salmān Pāk, 666), (20 ha.?); Humānīya (20 ha.?); Jarjarāyā (20 ha.?); Nahrawān (Sifwah, 308–9), (25 ha.); Daskara (Eski Baghdad, 41), (20 ha.?); Shahrābān (20 ha.?); Barāz-al-Rūz (20 ha.?); Hārūnīya (20 ha.?); Baᶜqūba (30 ha.?); Bājisrā (10 ha.?); ᶜAbertā (620), (4 ha.); Uskāf-Banī-Junayd (Sumāka, 734), (20 ha.?).

2. Early Islamic–Sāmarrān sites continuing into, or reoccupied during, the later Abbasid period (not including those given above):
Large towns:
371, Tell Mukherīj (16 ha.); 551, Tell Daimat al-ᶜOda (12 ha.); 632, Tell Jubayl (10 ha.); 642, Tell Mirhij (21 ha.); 704, Tell Abū Khansīra (16 ha.); 710, Tell Maᶜbūd (12 ha.); 804, Mayyah al-Sharqī (19 ha.); 826, Tulūl al-Shuᶜailah (10 ha.).
Eight sites, approximately 116 hectares of settlement.
Small towns:
183, 210, 237, 273, 301, 318, 406, 490, 553, 555, 606, 626, 650, 686, 727 (2), 736, 759, 761, 769, 771, 777, 778, 805, 807, 828, 834, 855.
Twenty-eight sites, approximately 156 hectares of settlement.
Villages:
127, 130, 179, 181, 182, 184, 185, 188, 207, 228, 231, 233, 236, 252, 277, 280, 313, 315, 347, 356, 369, 386, 393, 394, 395, 401, 402, 403, 404, 405, 432, 485, 547, 548, 550, 552, 644 (6), 651, 652, 691, 694, 695, 696, 697 (3), 699, 713, 723 (2), 726, 731, 754, 755, 758, 760, 780, 781, 784, 785, 786, 787, 789, 794, 800, 806, 809, 815, 819, 822, 830, 834 (2), 855 (2).
Eighty sites, approximately 127 hectares of settlement.

3. Newly founded sites of the later Abbasid (Post-Sāmarrān) period:
Small towns:
22, 27, 70, 864.
Four sites, approximately 17 hectares of settlement.
Villages:
8, 65, 96, 98, 134, 147, 190, 191, 194, 255, 445, 577, 657, 783, 857 (2), 859 (3), 863, 865, 866.
Twenty-two sites, approximately 37 hectares of settlement.

In total: Not including Baghdad, 158 recorded sites aggregating approximately 937 hectares of built-up area. This includes 2 cities aggregating perhaps 230 hectares, 20 large towns aggregating perhaps 361 hectares, 34 small towns aggregating 182 hectares, and 102 villages aggregating 164 hectares. Excluding Baghdad, perhaps 25 per cent of all settlement was urban and 58 per cent appears to have been in towns.

4. Sites appearing to have been largely or wholly abandoned during or at the end of later Abbasid times:
Important cities and towns:
Baghdad, ᶜUkbarā, Busrā, Al-Mādāin, Jarjarāyā, Nahrawān, Daskara, Uskāf.
Other large towns:
632, 642, 704, 710, 804, 826.
Six sites, approximately 88 hectares of settlement.
Small towns and villages:
207, 228, 252, 277, 280, 313, 315, 318, 347, 356, 369, 386, 394, 402, 432, 485, 490, 547, 548, 552, 606, 626, 644 (6), 650, 651, 652, 686, 691, 694, 695, 696, 697 (3), 699, 713, 723 (2), 726, 727 (2), 731, 736, 754, 755, 758, 759, 760, 761, 769, 771, 778, 780, 781, 783, 784, 785, 786, 787, 789, 794, 800, 805, 806, 807, 809, 815, 819, 822, 828, 830, 834 (2), 855 (3), 857 (2), 859 (3).
Eighty-six sites, approximately 93 hectares of settlement.

In total: Not including Baghdad, 100 sites aggregating approximately 421 hectares of settlement were abandoned. This was 45 per cent of all settlement during the later Abbasid period.

data, it might be deduced that later resumptions of flow in the Nahrawān were too brief and precarious to encourage more than a small proportion of the original emigrants or others seeking land to venture back into the deserted area.

But we are not limited to purely demographic data. Since it has been possible to work out sequences of branch-canal superposition from air photographs and ground observation, the sequence of maps also contrasts the networks of branch canals appropriate to the Early Islamic–Sāmarrān and the later Abbasid periods. Herein can be seen some of the more complex and ramifying changes in the irrigation regime that the temporary cessation of the Nahrawān had produced.

Before considering the branch-canal system in this area as a whole, however, it may be noted that there is evidence from sections across the Nahrawān bed (excavated by the Diyala Basin Archaeological Project) that the flow in the main canal itself never returned to its former volume. Not only was there a gradual in-filling of the bed, but in addition the quay walls at Uskāf in time came to be constructed in what earlier had been the main channel. With this reduction of flow almost certainly went a decline in the normal level of the water in the canal (Figs. 18, 20, 22).

Probably contributing to such a decline in relative level of water with respect to the surrounding land was the ongoing process of alluviation as the silt in the irrigation water was left behind in the fields; a number of erosion cuts observed during the survey and excavations suggests that the land level might have risen by more than a half-meter through alluviation between the end of the Sassanian period and the total abandonment of the Nahrawān area at around A.D. 1150. But at best the loss of command through alluviation of land along the banks of the Nahrawān was slow and undramatic, while that which resulted from shrinkage of the canal's volume was abrupt and decisive.

Three principal results of the increasing difficulties of commanding the land with the prevailing water supply can be observed in Figure 9. One was the need to rely more and more heavily upon the weir above Uskāf as a source of irrigation water, substituting the artificially maintained level it offered for the sharply reduced level in the canal from that point downstream to the outfall of the Nahrawān. Related to

104

this was an increasing dependence on branch canals instead of on the Nahrawān itself; in the final phase we find the Nahrawān closely paralleled along both banks for 25 kms. or more by branch canals. These new branches drew supplies from above the weir and substituted for the Nahrawān as sources for a great number of branch canals farther downstream which originally had been connected directly with the Nahrawān.

Furthermore, a comparison of Figures 8 and 9 makes clear that population declined much more sharply along the upper portions than along the tails of virtually all of the branch canals shown. Close to the Nahrawān, it would appear, the level of water was now insufficient for regular irrigation even with the aid of the weir, forcing cultivators farther and farther out, onto the slopes of major depressions like the one shown in an enlarged detail from a 1:50,000 aerial photograph (Fig. 10). Under such conditions, as the results of soil surveys plotted in Fig. 9 demonstrate, conditions for stable, productive irrigation agriculture were least promising. Unlike the coarse-textured, easily drained sediments closer to the Nahrawān, the soils in the areas which now became most important for settlement tended toward the surface-leaching associated with gilgai depressions,[98] or complementary saline conditions on adjoining raised land surfaces. In fact, almost all of the area in which the bulk of post-Sāmarrān settlement was concentrated has been classified as unsuitable for agricultural use under the more intensive practices favored by modern redevelopment schemes.

These three closely related changes in regime—the elongation of branches, the increased dependence on the weir, and the forced reliance on less suitable soils —combined to present the agriculturalists of the time with unprecedentedly difficult conditions. With a population reduced to perhaps one-eighth of its former level, it now was necessary to clean and maintain a far more extensive network of branch canals. In particular, those which ran alongside the Nahrawān below the weir could attain no more than the modest slope of the Nahrawān itself although they had only a tiny fraction of its cross-sectional area. Hence they silted up rapidly and must have required onerous effort to keep clear; even today, their spoilbanks run for many kilometers as raised ridges higher than the summits of all but the highest tells.

The dependence on the weir in itself might not have been a source of difficulty, except that it came at a time when the central government was increasingly unwilling or unable to maintain this huge facility as it had done in the past. Particularly under their newly reduced circumstances, the local inhabitants had neither the financial capacity nor the skills to make good the damages wrought by yearly floods or ordinary deterioration, and yet they were increasingly forced to depend upon their own resources for this crucial task. Finally, of course, the impoverished soils which were supporting an increasing proportion of the total cultivation continued to reduce the reserves of the local population.

This, in short, was an originally prosperous agricultural region now in a state of chronic crisis. With its water supply periodically cut off entirely, with its best soils no longer commanded by the available level of water without lifting devices, with many of its towns and villages nearly deserted, the remaining population faced immensely greater problems of irrigation maintenance than ever before. When to these was added, as we have already heard, the destructive effects of Saljūk armies using the banks of the canal as a roadway in the marching and counter-marching that accompanied court intrigues in Baghdad, both the possibilities and the incentives for continued settled life gradually disappeared altogether. The particular unrepaired breach in the vicinity of Nahrawān town which finally led to general abandonment around the middle of the twelfth century thus is a minor incident in a broad tide of deterioration that beset not only the administration in Baghdad but the whole rural economy as well.

The retraction of settlement, however, did not proceed at the same pace throughout the Diyala basin as it did in the Nahrawān districts. The accounts of major towns mentioned in contemporary itineraries have made it clear that some survived without apparent interruption until modern times while others still flourished at least under the Mongols, if not later. In general, those which outlasted the Abbasid period lay either on the old post roads along the Tigris or on the Khurāsān road to Persia. What commerce there was to sustain these arteries and their way stations during the final impoverished years of the caliphate is not clear, although the movement of pilgrims, then as now, may have been an important factor. But in addition to the road and river towns, there were two canal networks, in the area covered by the survey, where the last centuries of the Abbasid period saw a somewhat different course of events.

One of these consisted of the branching tails of the Rūz canal, south of the town of Barāz-al-Rūz. This dendritic network had reached its greatest limit in Sassanian and Early Islamic times, and in the latter period one branch appears from air photographs to have been extended far to the southeast, probably joining one of the tails of the Nahrawān not far above Jarjarāyā. After the Early Islamic period, as Figure 8 shows, large sections of some of these tails were abandoned and the zone of settlement retreated northward. Further losses during the Late Abbasid period were not large, however, although on a few sites the terminal ceramic assemblage suggests that they did not survive the Mongol invasion. A larger area seems to have been abandoned during the Mongol or Ilkhanid period, and after that time occupation along the Rūz probably never extended farther south than 33°30′ N. Lat. until this century.

Thus after one substantial retraction in the ninth or tenth century, irrigation persisted somewhat longer on the lower tails of the Rūz than on the Nahrawān. Then, after a slight retraction that perhaps coincided with the Mongol invasion, a second major abandonment during the Ilkhanid period confined most subsequent settlement to the vicinity of Barāz-al-Rūz. In the case of this canal, in other words, decline proceeded upward from the tails, while on the Nahrawān the tails of at least a few of its branches were among the latest zones to be inhabited.

Also worth attention in contrast to the Nahrawān is the antecedent of the present Khurāsān canal. This appears to have been the Nahr Jalūlā of the contemporary sources,[99] a name which one of the high spoil-banks south of Baʿqūba still retains. Apparently dug during the Sassanian period (supra, p. 80), this must be the "large canal" which Ibn Rusta reported as bisecting Deir Tirmah early in the tenth century (supra, p. 92). As far as can be determined from the results of survey, this canal survived the declining years of the caliphate and even the Mongol invasion with little or no retraction of its length or shrinkage of accompanying settlement. It may even have been somewhat extended after the final breach of the Nahrawān in order to drain into the great dry trench

of the Nahrawān below the breach and provide at least a modest flow for household purposes in the few remaining settlements like ʿAbertā.

At some point, either during the Late Abbasid period or, more probably, after its end, the inlet of the canal near Baʿqūba became too high to receive Diyala water; hence the canal was extended upstream to take off the Diyala just below the Jebel Hamrīn, just as it is found today. This action probably was precipitated by the entrenchment of the Diyala in its bed following the final breaching of the Nahrawān, a process which the artificial paving of the bed of the stream reported by Yāqūt[100] may have been intended to prevent.

Thus we see a considerable variety of different local responses to the political and economic disintegration of the Abbasid caliphate even within a relatively small region like the Diyala plains. Some areas went abruptly and completely out of cultivation, their former inhabitants emigrating, becoming nomads, or failing to survive the change. In other areas the effect was less pronounced and more gradual; a slow, if cumulatively important, retraction still left a considerable amount of land settled and in cultivation at the time of the arrival of the Mongols. Finally, in a few other, exceptionally favored areas, town and village life continued with little perceptible change.[101] But behind this variation, of course, lay a general and progressive devolution of authority and responsibility at the capital, so that at the end there remained neither the inducements nor the means to capitalize on the surviving enclaves of prosperity and rebuild outward from them. Thus the deterioration of Baghdad before Hulagu Khan appeared upon the scene mirrors in microcosm what had happened to the Diyala hinterlands. Its breakup into separate quarters and the abandonment of many formerly important areas within its defenses paralleled the decline of the countryside. In spite of their former grandeur, neither city nor countryside offered an effective impediment to the spreading chain of Mongol conquests.

3. ILKHANID AND LATER PERIODS

The appalling slaughter of the inhabitants of Baghdad which accompanied the sack of the city by Hulagu Khan claimed a major share of the attention of contemporary writers. Although much reduced in size and wealth, Baghdad surely was still one of the great cities of its day, and the detailed horror of its cold-blooded destruction[102] produced an impression which time has not erased. Yet by the time of Hulagu, as we have been at some pains to show, the relation of the city to its hinterlands was no longer a close and mutually beneficial one. With its swollen size, relative to the few and struggling towns left in the countryside, the city continued to extract much of what little tax and profit still could be obtained from the rural peasantry; but in return it gave less and less of the just administration, the underwriting of irrigation and other improvements, and the military protection which had originally justified urban growth.

Hence the destruction of much of Baghdad must not be permitted to epitomize the total effect of the Mongol invasion upon the countryside. However terrible at times, Ilkhanid policy was by no means unvaryingly brutal and repressive. The encouragement of dissident minorities and the rewarding of defectors were political tactics assiduously employed by the Mongols; their repeated success reflects not only the bankruptcy of the Abbasid cause but also the awareness among many subjects of the caliph of real and acceptable alternatives under Mongol rule. If, having shown resistance, Baghdad was for a time virtually leveled, and if every male inhabitant of Wāsit was put to the sword, it is still worth remembering by way of contrast that towns like Hilla, Kūfa, Basra, and Najaf opened their gates to the invaders and readily came to terms. Again, it bears on at least the attitude of the Mongol conquerors that Hulagu queried the assembled Doctors of Law in the Mustansirīya College after the sack of the city as to whether a just, unbelieving ruler was not preferable to an unjust Moslem ruler.[103] We may doubt whether the Ulemas would have replied in the affirmative under any other circumstances, but the propounding of the question hardly suggests that the Mongols were determined on a policy of senseless extermination and destruction.

With regard to the impact of the Mongol onslaught on the Diyala countryside in particular, we are handicapped by the absence of documentary or archaeological evidence on what conditions were like in the years immediately before it. Yāqūt's geographical dictionary contains entries for only the most important towns, and few of these are informative on the actual extent of settlement at the time. Tax accounts, if any were available, would provide a surer perspective on the condition of the rural economy, but nothing comparable to the ninth- and tenth-century records is known.

While an archaeological survey can compensate in part for these lacunae, its principal defect is that it deals with relatively broad time periods within which conditions may have changed drastically. What is crucial in this case is not comparison of the total extent of post-Sāmarrān settlement with that of the Ilkhanid period, but rather a comparison of *terminal* Abbasid settlement with that of the immediately succeeding decades under the Mongols. Lacking such data (or even the means to obtain them at present), a meaningful comparison of the Late Abbasid and Ilkhanid periods is extremely difficult to draw.

Table 24 summarizes the recorded sites where Ilkhanid and later settlements occurred. It is apparent at once that relatively few new sites were founded and that there had been a considerable decline from the level of the later Abbasid period taken as a whole. While no estimate of the size of the larger towns mentioned by Mustawfī can be obtained from the available sources, a comparison with the previous period, on the less complete basis of only those sites visited in the survey, suggests a decline from 562 hectares to 190 hectares of settlement. When it is recalled, however, that the entire Nahrawān region below ʿAbertā went out of cultivation a century or more before Hulagu, to take account of that area alone at least 148 hectares need be subtracted from the former figure. On this admittedly insecure basis we are left with Ilkhanid settlement outside of the capital apparently representing slightly less than half (46 per cent) of that which may have been present upon the arrival of the Mongols. That there was a substantial reduction thus seems undeniable, but at least it appears to have been far less devastating than the putative massacre of 800,000 or more of Baghdad's Moslem residents would suggest.[104]

The distribution of the remaining occupation of Ilkhanid times has already been largely indicated in the preceding section. Apart from a few remaining enclaves of permanent settlement like Deir al-ʿĀqūl and Humānīya along the Tigris, a polarization into two major zones had occurred that was without precedent in the earlier history of the area. One of these, of course, lay around Baghdad; the pre-eminence which the city quickly regained in spite of its

107

destruction is evident from the distribution of tax revenues given in Table 24.[105] As an agricultural district, the region must have depended almost exclusively upon irrigation water lifted from the Tigris, since even in Yāqūt's time some of the land to the

TABLE 24

SITES OF THE ILKHANID (MONGOL) AND LATER PERIODS
IN THE LOWER DIYALA REGION

1. Major settlements, districts, and tax revenues in A.D. 1340 (after Mustawfī [Le Strange, 1919]):

City or Town	District	Revenues in Dinars (1 dinar = 6 dirhems)*
Baghdad	Same	800,000
Barāz-al-Rūz	Same	20,000
(30 villages)	Khālis	73,000
Deir al-ʿAqūl	. . . .	. . . . . .
. . . .	Rādhān and Bayn-al-Nahrayn	50,000
Sāmarrā	Same	. . . .
Baʿqūba		
Bājisrā		
Shahrābān	Tarīq-i-Khurāsān	164,000
Mahrūt		
Tābaq		
(80 villages)†		

2. Late Abbasid sites continuing into, or reoccupied during, the Ilkhanid period (not including those given above):
   Large towns:
   371, Tell Mukherīj (16 ha.); 551, Tell Daimat al-ʿOda (12 ha.).
   Small towns:
   22, 27, 70, 183, 210, 237, 273, 301, 406, 553, 555, 864.
   Twelve sites, approximately 58 hectares of settlement.
   Villages:
   8, 65, 96, 98, 127, 130, 134, 147, 179, 181, 182, 184, 185, 188, 190, 191, 194, 231, 233, 236, 255, 309, 393, 395, 401, 403, 404, 405, 445, 550, 577, 657, 863, 865, 866.
   Thirty-five sites, approximately 61 hectares of settlement.

3. Newly founded sites of the Ilkhanid period:
   Large towns:
   167 (20 ha.).
   Small towns:
   79, Abū Sedere (7.5 ha.).
   Villages:
   10, 103, 106, 164, 172, 187, 226, 242, 314, 322, 362, 474, 503.
   13 sites, approximately 16 hectares of settlement.

In total: Not including the major settlements listed by Mustawfī (about whose size during this period little is known), there are 62 recorded sites aggregating approximately 190 hectares of built-up area.

4. Sites abandoned during or soon after the Ilkhanid period:
   Large towns:
   167, 371, 551.
   Three sites, approximately 48 hectares of settlement.
   Other:
   8, 22, 70, 79, 98, 103, 106, 127, 130, 134, 147, 164, 172, 179, 181, 182, 183, 184, 185, 187, 188, 190, 191, 194, 210, 226, 231, 233, 236, 237, 242, 255, 301, 322, 362, 393, 395, 401, 403, 404, 405, 406, 445, 550, 553, 555, 577, 657, 863, 864, 865, 866.
   Fifty-one sites, approximately 123 hectares of settlement.

In total: Not including the major settlements, 54 sites aggregating 171 hectares of built-up area were abandoned. This was 90 per cent of the recorded area of settlement during the Ilkhanid period.

5. Post-Ilkhanid sites recorded in the archaeological survey:
   Small towns:
   27, 273.
   Villages:
   10, 17, 65, 96, 309, 314, 436, 474, 503, 859.

---

* This equivalence is given by Mustawfī (Le Strange, G. 1919. P. 36).

† The assertion that there were an additional 80 villages in this district seems very unlikely. The context of the passage suggests that it may refer to an earlier period, possibly even the later days of the Sassanians when Shahrābān was founded with 80 subsidiary villages around it (*supra*, p. 80).

108

north of it—through which canals carrying water for Baghdad from the Kātūl al-Kisrawī and the Tāmarrā-Diyala had been conducted during most of the Abbasid period—was described as a waterless plain.[106]

The other zone occupied only the northernmost part of the Diyala basin. It depended upon a network of canals radiating from the foot of the Jebel Hamrīn gorge of the Diyala, similar to those of modern times although the sections then in use were much shorter. The Rūz canal passed through Barāz-al-Rūz and then dwindled away or escaped into the Haur-es-Subaicha south of the town. The Hārūnīya and Shahrābān canals probably disappeared not far to the south of those centers. The Khurāsān canal—or the Jalūlā, if that older name had not yet been replaced—appears to have watered a greater district than any of the others, according to tax receipts; it too, however, came to an end some distance south of Baʿqūba and failed to reach the southern part of the Diyala plains. Finally, the Khālis canal branched from the right bank of the Diyala and watered the land north, northwest, and west of the river, perhaps as far as the present Khālis town (see Fig. 1).

In the absence of a more comprehensive survey of the northern part of the region, a final explanation of the apparent shift in the position of the watercourse known as the Khālis canal cannot be offered, but a plausible sequence can be suggested. In the earlier part of the Abbasid period (and probably earlier as well), the name Khālis was applied to a canal which had its intake below the junction of the Kātūl al-Kisrawī with the Tāmarrā (Diyala)[107] near Baʿqūba and reached the northern outskirts of Baghdad.[108] When the Kātūl-Nahrawān failed in Late Abbasid times, this canal was extended to the northeast along an earlier overflow channel to take its water from the Diyala instead. Such a stopgap substitution would have been within the modest means of the later caliphs, whereas a reopening of the Kātūl itself was not. Moreover, with the reduction of population, the Diyala waters alone now were sufficient without supplementation from the Tigris. Subsequently, the lower part of the canal, i.e., the original canal almost in its entirety, failed during the Ilkhanid period or just before because of inadequate maintenance. As a result, the original name ultimately was applied to a new canal in the region north of the Diyala. This sequence is closely paralleled by the extension of the

Khurāsān canal from its original intake near Baʿqūba to the foot of the Jebel Hamrīn, although in the latter case the older name (Jalūlā) was lost in the process.

Excluding only the continuing concentration of population around Baghdad, it is clear from Table 24 that the population of the Diyala basin had shrunk by the Ilkhanid period back to the level, or below the level, of the Cassite and Old Babylonian periods. As in earlier times, therefore, settlement and cultivation even within main zones of occupance was not continuous but instead was aligned in relatively narrow and vulnerable strips or enclaves along the watercourses. All around these enclaves, we may assume, was the domain of the nomad, whose threat to the settled cultivators waxed as the powers of the central government waned. Still subject to the periodic forays of predatory tax-collectors from Baghdad, and exposed both to the occasional passage of armies bent on the capture of Baghdad and to less dramatic but more continuous nomadic pressure, the lot of the rural cultivator was at best a miserable one. In fact, the balance tipped against farming altogether until the advent of more settled conditions in the nineteenth century. During this long interval, as in the repeated earlier cycles of abandonment, what settlement remained dwindled further. Too little is reported in the final section of Table 24 dealing with post-Ilkhanid sites to permit a useful discussion of their distribution.

Yet in two crucial respects the parallel with earlier phases of abandonment is misleading, and it is appropriate to consider what the differences are. The first is reflected primarily in the changed distribution of the enclaves of settlements that were left as abandonment proceeded. In earlier periods they had been widely scattered over the whole basin, implying a bifurcating and rejoining network of natural streams which retained their courses even when maintenance ceased. Such a regime, as we have indicated, must have been the one under which the bulk of the Diyala alluvium was laid down. Except for the disappearance of the lower Daban and several other Diyala branches just above their junctions with the Tigris, most of the evidence indicates that these conditions of equilibrium survived the particularly severe and prolonged abandonment at the end of the Cassite period. But in the subsequent intensification of settlement, reliance was placed increasingly on artificially extended branch-canal networks, culminating in the construction of the great Nahrawān system. Unfortunately, these later conditions of relatively full, continuous land use do not permit us to see how long the older, "natural" regime might have remained in effect.

The need to extend the Khurāsān-Jalūlā canal from Baʿqūba upstream to the foot of the Jebel Hamrīn, and the decision to construct the new inlet for the Khālis canal at the same place after the demise of the Kātūl-al-Kisrawī feeder, suggests that downcutting had begun at least by the end of the Abbasid period, if not earlier. The paving of the bed of the Diyala suggests a similar interpretation, and was undertaken at roughly the same time (supra, p. 106). But the abandonment of the Mahrūt canal at the end of the Sassanian period, and of some of the tails of the Rūz canal during or soon after the Early Islamic period, may indicate that its real origins were much earlier.

In any case, the result of this change was that the river tended to follow a single incised channel rather than an anastomosing network of aggrading ones. As a result, cultivation came to depend on wholly artificial canals, which by no later than the Late Abbasid period must have required an annually renewed brushwork weir across the Diyala at the foot of the Hamrīn gorge in order to function properly. With declining population and deteriorating political conditions, therefore, the zone of settlement in Late Abbasid and Ilkhanid times receded northward toward the source of its water at the foot of the Hamrīn, for the first time leading to a complete abandonment of settled life in the southern part of the basin except possibly for a fringe along the Tigris.

The processes involved in this massive shift in the regime of the Diyala cannot be finally determined here. The activities of man over a long period surely may have played a part. Thus, deforestation in the headwaters of the Diyala might have led to more rapid runoff and hence to an increased tendency for the river to scour its bed during annual floods. Again, the extensive artificial distribution of silt-laden irrigation water may have altered the natural gradients within the Diyala basin in such a way as to interfere with the regimes of equilibrium which had prevailed earlier. But as has been suggested in Chapter I, a highly credible alternative, or at the very least a supplement, to these explanations is one which in-

109

volves tectonic change. A slow, continuing uplift along the axis of the Jebel Hamrīn would produce virtually all of the physical consequences we have noted.[109]

Whatever its cause, this change appears to have been a cumulative and irreversible one. Contemporary and future irrigators in the Diyala basin face a quite different stream regime than had their predecessors during the great epochs of settlement in the past.

The second major departure from earlier cycles of abandonment is no less important than that involving changing stream patterns and landforms, although it may be stated more simply. We cannot exclude Baghdad and then conclude that conditions of settlement elsewhere in the basin were fairly similar to those during earlier abandonments. Baghdad had become the repository and symbol of a great civilization and tradition, and having survived the lean years until the late nineteenth century it subsequently has served as a powerful stimulant to renewed national growth. However reduced and ineffective at times, Baghdad remained the principal base of all those military and social forces working for pacification and unification of the countryside. Moreover, the needs of its administration and commerce ultimately were among the principal inducements to technological change and external contact.

In short, as was said earlier, the advance in urbanization during the Islamic period was a cumulative, not cyclical, phenomenon. The crucial aspect of the city as a new and very powerful social force was not lost in spite of widespread abandonment during Late Abbasid, Ilkhanid, and later times. Baghdad was, as it remains today, the main embodiment of urbanization as a cumulative historical process.

To recapitulate very briefly, the Islamic period witnessed two somewhat contradictory trends. On the one hand, urbanization was carried to an unprecedented level. Whether we compare Baghdad and Sāmarrā with earlier capitals or with the aggregate of all other contemporary settlement in the Diyala basin, we find a huge imbalance, a qualitative transformation in the character of the city and its institutions. And in spite of six centuries or more of ruin and neglect between the fall of the caliphate and the advent of modern conditions, the effects of this great transformation were never lost.

At the same time, seen from the rural farmstead or provincial town, even the golden age of the caliphate was an age of retrenchment. Wide zones that had been abandoned at the end of the Sassanian period were not reoccupied. Tax receipts never approached those collected under the later Sassanians, and from the mid-ninth century on began to fall precipitately. The pace of town formation slowed, and most settlements (outside the capitals) failed to attain the limits they had reached in the Sassanian period. Beginning early in the tenth century, whole districts were allowed to go out of cultivation, a trend that continued or was accelerated in the Ilkhanid and later periods.

Beneath the apparent contradiction, however, is an underlying unity in these phenomena. The cities were creatures of state policy. Their great size reflects an increasing unconcern with improvement of the rural economy and a preoccupation with the pomp and intrigues of court life. It is no surprise to hear that real rule fell increasingly into the hands of military commanders, while the caliphs amused themselves by building palaces. This was the spirit of an age in which authority at all levels was characteristically shortsighted and corrupt. Under such conditions, the administrative and maintenance responsibilities imposed upon the central government for the successful operation of the great irrigation networks tended increasingly to be poorly executed or ignored, even while programs of monumental building were being pressed. Accordingly, the land and the irrigation works deteriorated, often to the accompaniment of destructive acts by one or another contending party to the ceaseless struggle for power in the capital. Since the requirements for revenue were unending, the consequent shrinkage in agricultural production was met not with attempts to improve conditions in the provinces but with fierce efforts to extract still larger sums from areas still in cultivation. The trained civil service dwindled away, its duties increasingly consigned to the rapacious private tax-farmer.

By the time of the Mongol invasion in the mid-thirteenth century, the effects of this decay were palpable in Baghdad also. After a slight and unavailing resistance, the city was stormed and most of its

110

inhabitants slaughtered, but elsewhere the effects of the invasion appear to have been less disastrous. Even Baghdad quickly resumed its status as a substantial urban center, although remaining much smaller than in Abbasid times until recent decades. Elsewhere in the region, the decline in settlement that had become severe in Late Abbasid times continued through and beyond the Ilkhanid period, leaving in the sixteenth to nineteenth centuries only a few battered towns, a thin strip of small-scale lift-irrigation along the Tigris in the neighborhood of Baghdad, and a fan of canals confined to the northernmost part of the basin, where a few impoverished cultivators fought a generally losing battle with nomads.

9

CONFIGURATIONS OF CHANGE IN IRRIGATION AND SETTLEMENT

THE GREAT depth of time in the ancient Orient and the complexity of its component cultural streams defy any traditional historical treatment that seeks to embrace its whole course. Hence there have arisen the separate domains of the specialized prehistorian, Assyriologist, Byzantinist, and Islamicist, among many others. Except in works of considerable generality and correspondingly reduced analytical penetration, specialists in these fields rarely venture beyond their realms of primary competence. Instead, the task of connected historical treatment spanning successive epochs is left by default to their more philosophically inclined colleagues in other disciplines, who all too frequently approach it with one or another a priori scheme originally worked out for quite different regions or problems. For example, reconstructions assuming a more or less cyclical rise and fall of successive empires sometimes are put forward. Sumerian city-states of the third millennium B.C. and the Islamic state are regarded as organisms whose life processes were very nearly identical. Again, the term ancient Oriental despotism may be applied without distinction to the earliest city-states and to the Sassanian Empire. The immediate advantage of such constructs as these is that they readily permit and even encourage comparison, not only across the span of Mesopotamian history but with other civilizations as well. Their crucial defect is that in the broadest sense they are ahistorical. They may recognize change within the life cycle of a particular creative phase, or they may

disregard even this degree of change and seek to define Near Eastern institutions from a static typological viewpoint. But in either case they tend to assume a basic lack of difference between successive historical epochs, a stasis which then is thought to distinguish the Orient in contrast to the West.

Yet surely the question of cumulative change and growth is as much one for empirical historical study in early Mesopotamia as in industrial western Europe or the United States. If the task is rendered vastly more difficult by gaps in the documentary record, it is nonetheless worthwhile to make a modest beginning wherever the data permit. Herein lies one of the virtues of systematic archaeological reconnaissance, for it sets us face to face with patterns of sequent occupance from which an understanding of at least certain aspects of long-term change may emerge.

The foregoing chapters have not dealt directly with the subject of historical cumulation under Mesopotamian conditions. To a degree, I believe, they have been pertinent to that theme, but they are subject to two important limitations. In the first place, they describe the development of a comparatively small and somewhat arbitrarily defined component of the Mesopotamian alluvium, perhaps even narrowing the geographical field to a point where its prevailing diversity is no longer manifest and where the decisive role of external stimuli is no longer fully apparent. Second, these chapters have sought to identify the underlying features of agricultural subsistence and

112

urban settlement, features which at best are incomplete and indirect reflections of the cultural, political, social, and economic order as a whole. If, nonetheless, we have found evidence for a broad and decisive series of transformations, this suggests that a particularly close and illuminating relationship exists between irrigation and settlement patterns and the basic institutional structure of Mesopotamian society. Perhaps it also points to the usefulness of tracing the development of basic patterns of land-use through an intensive consideration of small but strategic areas. It goes without saying, of course, that such regions as the Diyala plains cannot be assumed to represent fully the larger and more complex cultural or geographical entities within which they occur without a much more extensive study.

If we survey the findings of this study more generally and in their historical order, two major sets of changes emerge which are interdependent and yet separable. The first involves the nature and extent of irrigation, the second is related to population density and distribution.

With regard to irrigation, three successive and contrasting configurations can be identified. The first covers the span from the beginnings of cultivation of the area in the late fifth millennium B.C. or even earlier until its near-abandonment in the early first millennium. This was an epoch in which comparatively little alteration was made in the natural environment. Cultivation was limited to fairly narrow strips or enclaves irrigated through breaches in natural stream levees or by means of small and locally maintained branch canals. Hand-operated lifting devices were known and probably played a minor role, but the aggrading, anastomosing regime of the Diyala network as a whole made flow irrigation relatively simple, adequate, and reliable. The Tigris, with its very large floods and rapid changes of channel, seems to have been avoided as a source of irrigation water, although a string of substantial towns along its banks marked the confluence of Diyala branches and served as ports for what may have been at times a substantial river traffic. Perhaps the most significant aspect of the whole pattern was its durability, for essentially the same network of watercourses is traced at the end of the epoch as at its beginning. Moreover, the culmination reached in the Ur III and Isin-Larsa periods

exceeded only by a fairly slight margin the limits of cultivation that had obtained for a long time.

The second phase may have had its origins in Achaemenid or Neo-Babylonian times, although on present evidence these periods had more in common with their predecessors than with the succeeding phases. At any rate, a reintensification of settlement and irrigation first got underway and during the subsequent Seleucid and Parthian periods rapidly expanded to a level never reached before. By the end of the Parthian period the maximum potential supplies of water available from the Diyala (in the absence of the high storage dams only made possible by modern technology) appear to have been approaching full utilization, and animal-operated water-lifts had been pressed into service along the Tigris as well. Additional cultivation led gradually to an extension of branch-canal networks, in some cases widening the previous enclaves into continuous zones that were served by many branches and substantially altering the regimes of the bifurcating network of natural streams.

The second phase culminated in the Sassanian period, when virtually the entire cultivable area available in the Diyala basin was brought simultaneously under cultivation. Although there is nothing to suggest the introduction of more intensive systems of cultivation than the original (and still prevailing) rotation of alternate years in fallow, the measures taken to extend the zone of cultivation imply that land and not merely water was in short supply. It is with regard to water, however, that the characteristics of this second epoch emerge most clearly. Under the aegis of the state a profound reshaping of the landscape and its water resources was undertaken, not once but repeatedly and in different parts of the region. The best symbol of this new regime was the construction of the gigantic Nahrawān canal in the sixth century A.D., supplementing the now seriously deficient supplies of the Diyala by means of the long feeder presently known as the Kātūl al-Kisrawī. When operating at its full extent, the new regime depended primarily on great artificial canals which crisscrossed a terrain almost continuously occupied with fields and orchards. In consequence, the new regime of land-use was peculiarly dependent on the central government which had undertaken the vast program of canal construction,

113

for the central government alone was capable of administering their operations and maintaining its physical installations.

With the collapse of Sassanian rule we have seen the onset of a slow, irregular, but decisive, process of dissolution in the rural economy, which by Ottoman times may have reduced the area cultivated to a level comparable to that of the Middle Babylonian abandonment twenty-five centuries earlier. Both the deterioration of political control and ecological changes have been adduced as contributing explanations for this catastrophic decline, with the Mongol invasion having been an additional factor that probably in the long run was less important than either of the others. But whatever the causes of the continuing shrinkage of the cultivated zone that ensued, the process of the abandonment appears to differ sharply from that which had gone on after the Isin-Larsa period. In the earlier case, retraction had proceeded fairly slowly and evenly, affecting different parts of the basin more or less equally and leading to a relatively uniform reduction in population density all across the region. But the decline that went on through the Abbasid and Ilkhanid periods was of a different order. Periodically, whole regions were abruptly depopulated, while others remained for a time unaffected. Consistent with the artificially maintained character which the irrigation system had assumed, local acts of destruction or special conditions of local deterioration could lead rapidly to a cessation of all irrigation flow into a wide area, causing a crisis which it was beyond the capacity of the affected population to remedy except by flight or reversion to nomadism. With respect to enforced dependence on central authority, conditions during the later Abbasid and Ilkhanid periods closely resemble the third and most recent irrigation pattern, from which they are separated by several centuries during which cultivation was limited to the peripheries of a few main centers.

The present pattern is an entirely artificial one. Perhaps at least in part as a result of tectonic changes the Diyala is now a single incised channel rather than a network of aggrading ones, and flow is maintained in the network of canals radiating from the foot of the Jebel Hamrīn only with the aid of a weir. In addition, a far larger area is irrigated by lift-fed canals than ever in the past as a result of the introduction of diesel pumps. Other advances that are in prospect also stem from technological innovations that were not available during antiquity; these include a stabilization of Diyala flow throughout the year by means of a high dam at Derbend-i-Khān, the reliance on chemical fertilizers, deep drainage ditches to alleviate salinization, balanced crop rotation systems, and so on. The extent of cultivation is still appreciably less than it was during the Sassanian period, but with the new emphasis on high productivity the total area cultivated may soon become less important than the quality of the land and the intensity of the cultivation methods. State intervention, only having become a requirement in the second epoch for the construction and maintenance of the largest canals, undoubtedly will emerge in this third epoch as a basic factor for control of irrigation, drainage, and cropping practices in the individual fields.

Turning to changing types of settlement, the data that have been presented in detail in the foregoing chapters are summarized in Table 25. As we have seen, of course, the quality and quantity of the available evidence vary tremendously from period to period. Hence the uniformity of the columns in the graph should not be allowed to suggest that the assessments upon which the graph is based are uniformly accurate or unambiguous. There is little doubt, in fact, that the numerical values given in the table are subject to considerable error. They are merely the most reasonable estimates which seem possible with present evidence, and there is every reason to expect that they will be substantially improved upon in the future.

In any case, what is of greatest importance is not the absolute magnitude of the respective levels of population and types of settlement at different periods but their approximate and relative magnitudes. And even if new evidence casts in doubt individual assumptions or interpretations of particular periods, I believe that the general sequence of change illustrated in the table has been shown to rest on a number of converging lines of reasoning and evidence. Its substance, at least, then is likely to remain intact in spite of modification in detail.

During the first and longest epoch of settlement recorded in Table 25, from the fourth or fifth millennium B.C. to the last third of the first millennium, there were several cycles of prosperity and decline or, more accurately, of resettlement and abandonment. Yet even under conditions of relative local autonomy when conditions otherwise were most favorable, the largest communities were towns or very small urban centers covering only around thirty hectares and probably housing not many more than 5,000 inhabitants. To judge from the distribution of towns and smaller villages, regional integration never was carried very far. Even the most important political centers like Eshnunna housed a population which was generally engaged in subsistence agriculture and which exercised at best a loose and sporadic control over surrounding towns and villages. Political supremacy was transitory and led neither to a marked clustering of administrative and service personnel nor to the growth of a wide irrigation network with the political capital of the time at its hub.

Town life virtually ceased throughout the region during the Middle Babylonian period, no doubt largely because of Assyrian, Babylonian, and Elamite contention for its territories. The slow reappearance of towns in the Neo-Babylonian and Achaemenid periods was coincident with the general resumption of

cultivation and settlement, but at least according to the evidence of the survey the second epoch began later and more abruptly—seemingly in large measure as a result of the intensive Hellenistic influence that followed in the wake of Alexander's conquests. For the first time true cities made their appearance, of which Artemita is only the most notable of several early examples.

With the placement of the Parthian and Sassanian capital at Ctesiphon, the Diyala plains became the heart of a great, if loosely knit, empire, and further urban growth was associated with the proliferation of court life and the appearance of a considerable bureaucracy. Political rivalries may have been centered in the cities, but they found their rural reflection in the rapid formation and abandonment of outlying settlements as royal power waxed and waned vis-à-vis the landed nobility. There was also a new emphasis on royally maintained roads as arteries of communications and commerce, on state responsibilities

TABLE 25

POPULATION AND SETTLEMENT TYPES IN THE LOWER DIYALA REGION BY PERIODS

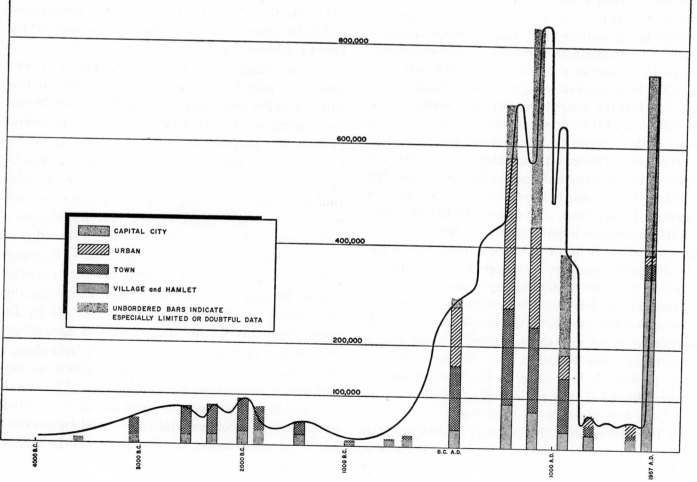

115

for land reclamation and irrigation improvements, and on cadastral surveys, with a dramatic heightening of revenues as a result. A substantial proportion of the new urban residents still may have been farmers, but if so a large part of their production now must have consisted of fruits and vegetables destined for a market patronized by bureaucrats, soldiers, and tradesmen. At least a part of the substantial growth in population of the Diyala region during this epoch, it should be pointed out, can be traced to the relative immunity it enjoyed against the repeated destructive incursions of Roman armies into areas west of the Tigris.

The third epoch of settlement transcended the limits of earlier urbanization by so wide a margin as to justify terming the new centers of Baghdad and Sāmarrā not merely urban but metropolitan. While the rural economy faltered and began to decline, and while stagnation or decline set in also in most of the provincial towns, the capital swelled to house from a minimum of several hundred thousand to a maximum of perhaps a million persons. It is clear from contemporary accounts that the overwhelming bulk of this population aggregate was not engaged directly in agriculture, and that whether occupied instead in administrative, religious, military, entrepreneurial, or service activities the urban inhabitants exhibited little concern for agricultural advancement. Instead, their preoccupation with court intrigues and corruption, and their involvement in sanguinary civil wars, further sapped the resources of the peasantry. Shortsighted attempts to maintain or enlarge tax revenues through corrupt and predatory tax-farming practices under such reduced circumstances further aggravated conditions, and ultimately left Baghdad and its hinterlands impoverished, divided, and virtually defenseless before the Mongol onslaught in the mid-thirteenth century. Yet even the frightful destruction wrought by the Mongols and later waves of nomadic invaders failed to extinguish Baghdad as an urban center, in spite of the near-cessation of cultivation at times and the reversion of most of the surrounding area to nomadism. When conditions again permitted, beginning in the late nineteenth century, Baghdad very rapidly re-emerged as a metropolis in fact as well as in tradition.

In this sense, both the Abbasid period and the present scene can be grouped together as parts of a single configuration of settlement in spite of the many centuries that separate them. Perhaps the most striking difference between these respective patterns of settlement has to do with the greatly increased proportion of the population now living in villages, while, except for Baʿqūba, urban settlements outside the metropolitan complex of the capital have practically disappeared.[1] Several explanations can be adduced for this difference, all of them probably contributing to it in some measure. In the first place, the relative recency and rapidity of the reoccupation of much of the area by settled agriculturalists may not yet have permitted nucleating tendencies outside the capital to proceed very far. Second, such new media of communication as highway networks, radio, and television, all radiating from the capital, exercise a powerful and unprecedented force toward concentration, rather than dispersion, of urban growth. And, finally the resettlement that has taken place during the past century or so has been carried on with an increasing confidence in the essential pacification of the countryside. If this indeed has been a factor conducive to dispersion into villages, it argues that at least a part of the widely acknowledged propensity of the inhabitants of ancient Mesopotamia for living in towns and cities arose from the defensive advantages which larger settlements conferred.

The foregoing résumé, like any brief and schematic summary, may blur or ignore many important features of individual periods and perhaps overstresses the importance of others which are common to several periods. For purposes of summary, however, we are less concerned with the exact delineation of conditions at any given time than with the over-all direction and extent of change implied by the combined record of archaeological survey and documentary testimony. And with respect, at least, to broad patterns of land-use and urban settlement, it seems justified to conclude that several successive epochs can be distinguished, each new epoch witnessing the substantial transformation of the scene left by its predecessor. Recognizing that irrigation agriculture and settlement in towns and cities surely have always been vital components of Mesopotamian economy and society as a whole, we can only ask of historical scholarship in the years to come whether a related succession of developmental epochs and trends cannot be perceived as well in other aspects of the changing institutional fabric.

APPENDIXES

APPENDIXES

APPENDIX A

METHODS OF TOPOGRAPHIC ARCHAEOLOGY

THIS STUDY had its origins in a reconnaissance carried out by Thorkild Jacobsen in the Diyala region during 1936–37. In the context of conditions present on the Mesopotamian plain, that original survey promulgated and succeeded in demonstrating two fundamental principles: (1) that since ancient sites necessarily lay in close proximity to the watercourses upon which they were dependent, the approximate courses of now-vanished streams and canals could be plotted from the positions or ruins adjoining them; and (2) that the periods of occupation of the ancient sites—and thus also of the watercourses connecting them—could be determined from an examination of their surface remains.

The reconnaissance undertaken as part of the Diyala Basin Archaeological Project in 1957–58, while utilizing such newly available data and research aids as aerial photographic mosaics and the results of soil surveys, in its essentials consisted of an application of these principles to the task of systematically reconstructing the sequent patterns of human occupance with more complete data from a larger geographic region. Moreover, the 1957–58 survey was able to draw upon the full records of the earlier reconnaissance, covering 119 sites on the central and northern part of the Diyala plains, graciously made available by Professor Jacobsen.

The procedures followed in the reconnaissance reflect in part the nature and limitations of the research undertaken by the Diyala Basin Archaeological Project as a whole. Only the relatively brief period of a single seven-month field season was available for the survey, and the heavy demands placed upon the available personnel by other activities of the project made it necessary to reduce to a minimum the time necessary for collecting and processing data. While it was obvious that complete and uniform coverage of the region could not be attained, an integrated treatment of past irrigation systems and patterns of settlement with the lower Diyala basin as a regional unit demanded at least a rough and preliminary coverage of an area of approximately 8,000 sq. kms. Moreover, problems of interpretation were magnified by the fact that ancient Mesopotamian settlements in most cases were either continuously occupied or at least periodically reoccupied over very long spans of time. For an understanding not only of factors of change but also of the density of settlement in any given period, it was necessary to determine approximately (from the analysis of surface collections) the history of occupation of all ancient sites that could be located. On the other hand, the objective of formulating merely a broad and provisional synthesis, combined with the generally poor state of preservation of surface remains as a result of brick-robbing and long-continued neglect and erosion, made it inadvisable to deal at length with the physical description of individual ruins.

The reconnaissance methods developed in response to these requirements relied heavily on large-scale maps of the Arabic 1:50,000 series prepared by the Iraq Directorate General of Surveys. These were supplemented by an unpublished contour map (one meter interval) prepared by Sir Murdoch MacDonald and Partners, Ltd., by 1:50,000 Soil Survey sheets compiled for the Development Board of the Iraq

Government by Hunting Aerosurveys, Ltd., and by semi-controlled aerial mosaics also prepared by the latter firm. From these combined sources it was possible not only to identify the major ancient canal levees but also the great majority of ancient sites. Most sites, in fact, were accurately mapped and could be located without consulting the aerial photographs, although some of the more ancient ones apparently escaped the cartographers' attention because of their smooth contours and the absence of dark surface patches of fragmentary baked bricks.

Wherever possible, the survey party advanced by Land Rover along the levee crests, not only because of the greater visibility and better drainage the levees afforded but also because the bulk of the sites to be visited lay close to these old watercourses. Under normal circumstances each site recorded on the maps, detectable as a discoloration on the air photograph or observed as a slight eminence during the reconnaissance, was visited in turn. After its location was confirmed by triangulation with a prismatic compass, the size and salient features of each site were briefly noted and one or more collecting bags were filled with sherds representing all of the periods noted during a systematic search of its surface. Consistent attention was paid during these operations to the possibility of apparent shifts in the area of occupation, e.g., a prolongation of settlement only in a limited part of the site, or the apparent confinement of sherds representing earlier periods to one or another quarter of the later town. Of course, information gained in this fashion on the abandonment of settlements is much more reliable than that on stages in their early growth, but even the latter is not without value. Where sites were small and closely spaced and where communications were easy, as many as twenty sites could be processed daily in this fashion. More often, particularly in cultivated areas or after periods of rain, only a fraction of this number was realized.

The collecting bags were returned to the base camp at Khafājah, where periodically the sherds they contained were noted by type and a provisional dating for each site was assigned. This operation, carried on by the author and Sayyid Fuad Safar in collaboration, not infrequently led to the recognition of new ceramic types or of anomalies in the occupational periods ascribed to a group of apparently related sites, thus leading in turn to further visits and more intensive or specialized collections.

While the initial coverage of an area was uniform and undiscriminating, follow-up studies often retraversed some of the same ground from the point of view of a particular problem. The analysis of the decline of irrigation along the Lower Nahrawān given in Chapter 8, for example, grew out of repeated field surveys aimed at disentangling the succession of canal networks through observation of superimposed levees, brick sizes in subsidiary canal offtakes, and the pottery types seeming to characterize terminal occupational levels in the ruins of adjoining villages and hamlets. These restudies in the field alternated, of course, with attempts at the base camp to map the sequence of changes in the canal system with the aid of air photographs. Specialized follow-up field studies also were undertaken along the original system of branches of the Diyala after its outlines had been established approximately from the initial survey. Observed discontinuities in the pattern of accompanying settlements led to very detailed inspection of the topography along the expected courses, and some additional sites recorded as a result consisted of no more than patches of debris not rising above the level of the surrounding furrows.

The description just given applies to the procedures used in the greater part of the area covered by the survey. Due to the fact that only a single field season was available for the project, however, several fairly small regions on the lower Diyala plains either could not be examined at all or received a more superficial scrutiny. Of those not visited at all during the survey, probably the most important lies along the upper part of the Khālis canal, and it is to be regretted that no conclusion based on archaeological evidence can be reached at present on the developmental history of this watercourse. Most of the other areas in which only a few relatively accessible sites were visited also lay in the northern part of the Basin, at the greatest distance from the particular focus of the project on uncultivated areas in the empty lands of the Nahrawān district. Since they tended to be set aside and left unfinished because of special difficulties with communications, they are less easily and regularly demarcated than the areas that were ignored altogether. An appreciation of the varying intensity of the survey throughout the region may be obtained by closely examining the reconnaissance base map, for this illustrates not only the sites which were visited and recorded but also those which appear on other maps of the area but were not seen.

Still another form of coverage that was more superficial and rapid than what has been described was applied in a few instances to scattered localities where a number of contemporaneous, small, single-period settlements lay at intervals along the branches of a late canal system. No other information was recorded in these cases than the apparent period of occupation as judged from a very rapid surface inspection. While these sites are included in the maps illustrating the distribution of settlements by periods, they are not listed separately in the index of recorded sites (Appendix C) and are identified on the reconnaissance base map only with an accompanying asterisk. In general, it would appear that the survey can be regarded as essentially complete for the southern half or two-thirds of the area, and as seriously incomplete only along the upper reaches of the canals taking off just below the Jebel Hamrīn.

The primary information used for dating the 867 sites dealt with in this study consisted of collections of observations of ceramic "index fossils," easily distinguishable diagnostic features of vessel form, surface treatment, or decorative embellishment. The primary criteria in selecting such features were, first, that they needed to occur in sufficient quantity so that their presence or absence in a collection would assume chronological significance; and second, that their period of use needed to be sufficiently well-established and short-lived to point unambiguously to one of the sixteen major phases into which it has been convenient to divide the history of the region. This later criterion involved, of course, placing a heavy reliance on features which could be identified in and dated by the published record.

In view of the wide scope and brief duration of the project, it was fortunate that there was a relatively full archaeological record from which criteria for dating could be drawn. In spite of lacunae at a few points, a stratigraphically derived framework of archaeological periods already existed, defined in terms of ceramic and other features and provided with numerous historical cross-ties. The earlier part of this record was particularly well-established for the Diyala region itself as the result of the Oriental In-

stitute excavations prior to World War II,[1] and the apparent contemporaneity and close similarity of subsequent changes in ceramics and other artifacts all across the southern Mesopotamian plain made it possible to supplement the Diyala sequence with the results of numerous other excavations. In some cases, of course, it has been possible to supplement published diagnostic features with others from unpublished sources,[2] or with dating criteria which could be established from their regular occurrence in single-period sherd collections made by the survey itself.

Qualities of vessel form and surface treatment which served as dating indicators sometimes were juxtaposed, forming a relatively complex group of elements which together constitute a "type" in New World archaeological terminology. In other cases the diagnostic feature was a simple and relatively minor embellishment or "mode" which may occur on entirely different major classes of contemporary pottery vessels. The approach taken was a frankly pragmatic one, aimed at utilizing the available published material for the purposes at hand. It is freely conceded that substantial refinement is possible, perhaps eventually reaching toward the precision of the twenty-five- or thirty-year periods which recently have been envisioned as attainable in most areas of the world,[3] and that alterations may in time prove to be necessary in the ordering of ceramic traits by chronological periods adopted in this survey. But fortunately the published record of ceramic changes is sufficiently full, so that the essential framework of periodization is likely only to be improved upon without fundamental change.

There are two advantages to the utilization of a relatively limited number of diagnostic features as the basis for assessing periods of occupation at ancient sites. The first is that it permits the trained eye quickly to distinguish significant dating indicators in the usually enormous masses of surface pottery which otherwise could be controlled only through involved and time-consuming sampling procedures. Second, it simplifies the recording of data and permits a relatively clear-cut assessment of the occupational periods present at each site. Since the scope of the reconnaissance demanded the utmost economy in operation, these advantages prevailed.

It should be stressed that there are also certain limitations inherent in this procedure. Since published treatment of Near Eastern pottery generally is based on small numbers of whole vessels rather than on sherds, the full spans of use of particular types or features often are unclear. For purposes of the present study they are assumed to coincide with periods established from historical or architectural criteria, but more commonly the life of a particular vessel form, for example, must have been substantially independent not only of political events but even of changes in other ceramic forms or styles. At best, therefore, "index fossils" only permit dating by approximation, within fairly broad and ill-defined periods whose precise correspondence with historically defined periods is not well-established. Moreover, they do not permit an assessment of the extent of continuity present at a site, since a brief occupation at any time within a period can rarely be distinguished from occupation throughout that period.

To a degree, these limitations can be overcome by a continuing refinement of the types and features selected as dating criteria. An example of this may be seen in the gradual recognition during the course of the reconnaissance of a kind of "decadent" graffito Sāmarrān glazed ware which was not distinguished at first from the "classic" ware (Appendix B, p. 133). As the new type was defined, it became clear that it was associated in surface collections with other types that were later than the Sāmarrān phase of the Islamic period, and that it could serve to differentiate between ruins abandoned in Sāmarrān and post-Sāmarrān times. The definition of that style as a useful "index fossil," in other words, proceeded hand in hand with the reconstruction of changing patterns of settlement. In a number of other cases as well, forms and stylistic elements were noticed in collections, utilized provisionally, and then either retained or discarded according to whether they proved useful in distinguishing between periods or phases that were significant for the history of settlement.

Thus far, this discussion has proceeded on the assumption that most archaeological sites were occupied only briefly, so that surface collections more or less faithfully represent the span of occupation. But of course this is not the case in Mesopotamia; the overwhelming majority of the sites catalogued by the survey were occupied, or repeatedly reoccupied, over long periods. For earlier periods of occupation than the terminal one to be regularly identifiable through the occurrence of their diagnostic features on the sur-

face, it is necessary that the remains of earlier periods somehow be carried upward, fairly continuously and on an extensive scale, through overlying deposits. The fact that this process does occur can be attested to from observed conditions at many hundreds of ancient settlements, although its character remains somewhat obscure.[4] Presumably the most common agencies of disturbance are such activities as well-digging, brick-making, the construction of house foundations, grave-digging, and the like, which serve to churn up earlier levels in a site and to deposit some of their characteristic remains on the surface of later levels. This kind of small-scale activity seldom accomplishes a wholesale inversion of the local stratigraphy, but it does introduce earlier types as minor but recognizable components in collections from the surface of later levels. In addition, larger constructions like city walls or the foundation terraces for monumental buildings can exercise a more profound effect of the same general kind. Further, shifts in the location of a settlement occur frequently, so that often there are areas of early debris in an ancient town which are exposed on the surface even while successively later occupations continue all around; in the Diyala area, the northern part of Tell Asmar (244) serves as a case in point.[5]

Given a comprehensive surface inspection, in other words, it is generally possible to find traces not only of the latest or most widespread levels in a site but of its whole span of occupation. To be sure, progressively greater stress must be placed on the search for "index fossils" representative of earlier levels than the major or final occupation of a site, since they will seldom constitute more than a small fraction of the whole array of sherds visible on the surface.[6]

The availability of data on the surface area of ancient settlements makes possible an archaeological approach, if necessarily a very crude and provisional one, to the problem of estimating population and the degree of land utilization in successive historical periods. The discontinuous—in fact, frequently quite limited—distribution of settlements in many periods implies selective and incomplete utilization not merely of the potentially cultivable lands in the Diyala region but also of the available supplies of Diyala water. But before the limits of cultivation in former periods can be drawn around their respective enclaves of settlement, some estimate must be formu-

122

lated of at least the approximate size of the population to be supported by the crops produced in those enclaves. Such estimates, if they can be arrived at in a uniform fashion for successive periods, then can serve as indices to long-term advance or decline in the gross population of the region and in the degree of urbanization of its component settlements.

The only possible basis for regional population estimates begins with the individual sites that were occupied during a given period, making the reasonable assumption that on the average their individual populations were proportional to the areas they covered. One quantitative assessment of this relationship has been put forward by Henri Frankfort:

> Population figures in ancient sources are so divergent as not to make sense; for Lagash, Entemena gives 3,600 people; Urukagina 36,000; Gudea 216,000. . . . We have computed the population on the basis of extant ruins, a very rough approximation at most, but perhaps not quite valueless. We started with residential quarters at three sites which we know well: Ur, Eshnunna (Tell Asmar), and Khafājah. The latter is eight centuries older than the other two, which can be dated to about 1900 B.c.; but our figures show no significant difference in the densities of their populations. We found about twenty houses per acre with an average area of 200 square meters per house. These are moderately sized houses, and we reckoned that there would be six to ten occupants per house, including children and servants. Considering the number of activities in the East that take place in the streets or public squares and how easily older and distant members of the family become dependents in the house of a well-to-do relative, these figures do not seem excessive. They amount to a density of from 120 to 200 people per acre. We then compared the area and population of two modern Near Eastern cities, Aleppo and Damascus. In both cases we find a density of 160 people per acre—which is precisely the average of our figure.[7]

Frankfort's estimate, of course, is derived from large, densely settled sites, and was intended only to apply to individual examples of the same kind. Its inherent deficiencies are multiplied several times if an attempt is made to apply it to an entire region containing types of settlement whose size and architecture are largely unknown and whose distribution has been incompletely surveyed. But before considering the latter problem, there is reason to question the estimate itself. After all, it has been pointed out in Chapter 3 that a density as high as 160 persons per acre or about 400 persons per hectare occurs in not one of the seventy quarters of the Baghdad old city, nor in a single one of the fifty-five Khuzestan villages for which data are available.

Only a slightly lower estimate than Frankfort's has been given for the population density of Seleucia during the 1st century A.D., based on the excavation of a particularly prosperous residential block near the center of the city. Assuming an average of ten occupants per house, Yeivin initially calculates an average of 80 persons per block of about 2,800 sq. meters, or about 286 persons per hectare. He then raises his estimate to 100 persons per block, or 357 persons per hectare, to take account of what he supposes must have been the large number of retainers and slaves, "always assuming that the buildings in Block B were more than one story high." While recognizing differences between wealthy and impoverished quarters, and between crowded slums and areas devoted to the naval base and public buildings, this figure is then applied as an average to the city as a whole.[8]

The defect in both of these reckonings is that an ideal pattern, the large family with many retainers, is also taken as an average pattern. A recent, comprehensive survey of ancient and medieval populations suggests that even the customary round number of five persons per house or nuclear family is too high for such an average, and that a figure of about 3.5 is more generally accurate.[9] In spite of the rapidly advancing population of the contemporary scene, arising primarily from an abrupt decline in infant mortality and hence being reflected in unprecedentedly large families, evidence has been given in Chapters 2 and 3 that at least in rural areas average family size is still only between five and seven persons. While recognizing many deviations from the norm (generally of a kind which decrease, rather than increase, density), the figure of 150 persons per hectares is used by Russell as a rule-of-thumb for the ancient Near East[10] and seems decidedly nearer the mark than the estimates by Frankfort and Yeivin.

For purposes of calculating what is at best an order of magnitude of the population of an ancient town, the round number of 200 persons per hectare of settlement has been used consistently in this study. In any case, the major importance of such calculations is not their absolute values but their relative values for successive periods, for it is from the latter that a picture can emerge of broad social and economic changes that are all too rarely referred to, much less quantitatively described, in the traditional sources.

As has been indicated, the problem of arriving at a probable figure at a given period for the population of an ancient town whose areal extent at that period is known is made vastly more complex when we seek to extend such an estimate to an entire region. Among the new problems are the following: In the first place, the coverage of the Diyala plains was not exhaustive (especially in the northern part of the region), so that there are a number of ruined sites shown on the base map of the area for whose periods of occupation we have no evidence. Second, with the massive, continuing process of alluviation having deposited perhaps as much as ten meters of silt over parts of the plain since 3000 B.C., it is certain that many abandoned sites have been entirely covered by the rising land surface. The recent, accidental discovery during the construction of a drainage canal of Ras al-ᶜĀmiyah, an ᶜUbaid settlement entirely buried beneath the plain north of Kish, exemplifies this process well.[11] While the density of roughly contemporaneous sites found in some parts of the region makes it highly unlikely (since the same geological processes were operative throughout the basin) that a preponderance of the settlements in any other part escaped detection as a result of these factors, the actual number of settlements during any period (and especially during the earlier ones) undoubtedly exceeded by a considerable margin the number recorded in Appendix C. Probably, however, most of the uncounted settlements were relatively small, so that their effect on a calculation of the aggregate area of settlement, or on an estimate of the total population, would be disproportionately less than that of an equal number of the sites presently known.

Third, in the course of alluviation the level of the land has risen around the sloping margins of former settlements, shrinking their apparent area as it submerges their outskirts. This probably proceeded to the greatest extent in fairly amorphous settlements whose outer limits were not constrained within a thick, high, and long-lasting wall, i.e., in the smaller villages and towns. In the case of the five known large towns whose walls have been more or less surely es-

tablished, the area within the walls is approximately defined by the mound existing today; hence there has been little or no loss in area through alluviation for at least these examples. Without excavation, no basis exists for gauging quantitatively the combined effect of omission in reconnaissance and disappearance or diminution in area through alluviation. There is no doubt, however, that their effect was considerable.

Tending to counteract somewhat these sources of error, however, are other considerations having to do with the calculation of inhabited area and population density at the sites which were included in the survey. First, it has been assumed throughout this study that all towns and villages which were occupied at any time during a given period were occupied simultaneously. This fails to take into account the probability that at least a few sites were occupied sequentially. Second, the figure of 200 persons per hectare makes little allowance for non-residential areas. In addition to public buildings, it is known from excavations that other important areas within the walls were devoted to brick-making, gardens, and the like, or simply left vacant. There is archaeological evidence for at least the latter practice in the Diyala area at Tell Asmar during the Larsa period.[12] As the Epic of Gilgamesh records,

> One *sar* is city, one *sar* orchards,
>   One *sar* margin land; [further] the precinct of
>   the Temple of Ishtar.
> Three *sar* and the precinct comprise Uruk.[13]

A third assumption which has been made throughout this study, and which tends to counterbalance the omission of sites that were not visited or have disappeared, concerns the area of a given multi-period site that was occupied during a particular period. For the closing phase of a site (since debris of this period remains in full evidence as the dominant sherd component upon the surface), and perhaps for its period of greatest areal extent (since, if this is different from the former, its debris still is to be found as the latest that occurs in quantity over the full surface area), the calculation of the area assignable to a particular period is simple enough. However, surface reconnaissance allows no direct check on the area of occupation of a site prior to this maximal or terminal period. The problem of estimating area and population under these circumstances has been met here by considering the maximal area of the site as that which was occupied in all of the historic periods for which the surface collections at that site give evidence, except in instances where there is evidence to the contrary. The assumption that early areas of habitation equaled maximal (or even aggregate) areas of later settlement must tend systematically to increase our estimate of the former, tending to compensate for the greater percentage of loss they have suffered through alluviation.[14]

A fourth factor tending to compensate for the unknown but surely significant number of sites unrecorded in the survey arises from the fact that site areas have been calculated merely by multiplying together their maximum recorded lengths and breadths. Since most or all sites either were roughly circular or oval, or else quite irregular in outline, this procedure has artificially enlarged the listed areas of occupation by perhaps 20 per cent.

The foregoing discussion will have made clear how precarious is the basis for providing estimates of regional population from the data of settlement size alone. To begin with, the population densities within ancient towns have been shown to be subject to considerable uncertainty. Second, only for the terminal or maximal periods of occupation of such ancient towns can their inhabited areas be calculated directly. Third, the data of surface collections generally allow us only to assume that individual towns, or quarters within towns, are occupied contemporaneously and not sequentially within the broad periods of several centuries into which this study is divided. And finally, there are the surely large, although essentially incalculable, losses arising from the process of alluviation and the incompleteness of the survey itself. Against these can be balanced certain assumptions tending to overstate the areas of actual residential construction in the earlier periods at the known sites, but it would be rash to predict with any confidence how well these opposing factors tend to balance each other out.

Calculations of population and area of settlement can be made from present evidence only by assuming provisionally that these factors tend to counterbalance each other. And given the desirability of having at least a relative scale against which to measure the achievements of the successive periods with respect to urbanization, it seems beyond debate that even highly provisional estimates are worth making. Fortunately, there is some further evidence from historical sources, particularly for the Sassanian and Islamic periods, with which they can be at least partially confirmed under the special conditions afforded by the relatively complete utilization of the potentially cultivable land within the region. And in any case, it is hoped that the data and rationale behind the present estimates are given in sufficient detail so that they can be altered if they are found defective.

APPENDIX B

CERAMIC DATING CRITERIA FOR SURFACE RECONNAISSANCE

THE SURFACE reconnaissance of the lower Diyala region utilized four broad classes of evidence for dating the occupation of ancient sites:

1. Ceramic indicators of highly distinctive character and apparently short duration. When sufficiently varied and numerous not to be dismissed as possible "strays," these point unambiguously to an occupation on or near the site at which they were found during a fairly limited and specific period of time. In most cases their span of use can be established from published reports. Particularly for the Sassanian and Islamic periods, however, the paucity of published accounts of ordinary household pottery has made it necessary to supplement the dating criteria which can be established from stratigraphic excavations with others derived from surface observation of numerous single-period assemblages.

2. Less specific ceramic indicators, which either retained their popularity for several of the chronological periods into which the findings are divided or which cannot always be distinguished from other types belonging to earlier or later periods. At least on present evidence these indicators are less reliable for dating; at best, they can only suggest fairly tentatively within what approximate period the occupation of a site may have fallen. On the other hand, at many smaller sites—and particularly those of the Sassanian period—they may constitute all or virtually all of the dating evidence that could be obtained in a brief surface inspection. And, as in the previous category, their span of use in most cases can be documented from published excavation reports.

Both of the above categories can be readily reduced to a brief letter notation which permits rapid analysis and recording. Hence both together form the core of the evidence upon which the spans of occupation for each site given in Appendix C are based, and the examples of both which proved most useful in the survey are illustrated in Figures 11–16. Both categories together, however, obviously include only a small fraction of the potential chronological data which the dense sherd accumulation of Mesopotamian tells can provide.

3. A third category, like the first two, is based on the surface collections that were returned to the base camp for processing. It consists of sherds exhibiting distinctive forms or surface treatments whose chronological range was even less definite, or which were found too rarely to justify the assignment of a special type-letter for them. Except in a very few cases where no diagnostic types of the first two categories could be found, this category played no direct part in the establishment of periods of occupation. It was the residual group that was left in each site-collection after the assignment of more definite types had been completed. Nevertheless, it provided at least a partial and negative check on the possibility of arbitrary and misleading selections of the major type criteria by permitting additional comparisons with dated assemblages elsewhere. Moreover, it was from this category that new types suitable for regular use were first provisionally identified.

4. The final category consists of observations in the field rather than of the collections. For the most

126

part, these have reference only to the final period of occupation at a site, or on a portion of a site. Thus surface pottery at sites abandoned in the Middle Babylonian period or earlier is almost unrelievedly buffware. Seleucid and Parthian sites, on the other hand, have at least a minority of wares with monochrome greenish glaze, Sassanian sites a minority with monochrome bluish glaze, and Islamic sites an increasingly large minority—or even majority—with polychrome glazes of many colors. Again, there were artifacts that were disregarded in the collections although potentially useful for dating. Numerous small copper coins (unfortunately almost all too weathered to be identified), for example, were found to be characteristic of Parthian sites, while Parthian and later sites are increasingly littered with fragments of broken glass. Perhaps most helpful of all are bricks; note was taken of the planoconvex bricks of the Early Dynastic period and of the regularly declining size of Sassanian and Islamic square bricks which were thickly scattered over most sites of those periods.[1] In short, field observations furnish an important check, and supplement to the records of types in the surface collections, and in particular have been the decisive determinant of the most extensive and/or final periods of occupation at each site visited in the survey.

Supplemented by evidence of the latter two categories, the ceramic indicators in the collections that were regarded as definite types are arranged below according to their periods of use. Those which were most unambiguously recognizable, and whose floruit seems most clearly to have been limited in duration, are recorded with capital letters. Less specific or longer-lasting types whose value as chronological indicators is relatively less clear are recorded with small letters at the end of each group of types pertinent to a given period.

1. *ᶜUbaid Period.*
   A. Greenish, overfired clay sickles. Cf. Lloyd, S., and Fuad Safar. 1943. P. 155, Pl. 28 B. (Tell ᶜUqair. *Journal of Near Eastern Studies* 2:131–58).
   B. ᶜUbaid monochrome painted ware. Cf. Lloyd, S., and Fuad Safar. 1943. Pp. 150–54, Pls. 19–21.
   C. Chipped flint celts. Cf. Lloyd, S., and Fuad Safar. 1943. Pl. 29.

2. *Warka and Protoliterate Periods.*
   A. Beveled-rim "votive" bowls. Cf. Delougaz, P. 1952. Pl. 21 (Pottery from the Diyala Region. *Oriental Institute Publications*, 63. Chicago).
   B. Clay nails or cones for architectural mosaics. Cf. Lloyd, S., and Fuad Safar. 1943. Pls. 16, 28 A.
   C. Shallow bowls with characteristic striations suggesting scraping with a flint knive on lower exterior surface. Soft, unslipped buffware, flattened or inward-beveled rims. Cf. Lloyd, S. 1940. P. 19 (Iraq Government soundings at Sinjar. *Iraq* 7: 13–21); Lloyd, S., and Fuad Safar. 1943. P. 153, Pl. 22 A, 4. But note that published examples are deeper and lack flattened rims.
   D. Bent or "drooping" jar spout, with a pronounced taper. Cf. Lloyd, S. 1948. P. 48 (Uruk pottery: a comparative study in relation to recent finds at Eridu. *Sumer* 4:39–51).
   (e) Flattened rim of vessel like type C, broken off short of zone where "flint-scraping" normally appears. May be confused with a much later vessel of similar form (but without striations) which is aid to be a "typical" Larsa dish (Mustafa, M. A. 1949. Soundings at Tell Al Dhibaᶜi. *Sumer* 5:183).
   (f) Flint blade-core, generally small or microlithic in size. Probably spans entire range from pre-ᶜUbaid through Early Dynastic period.
   (g) Denticulated flint sickle blade. Pre-ᶜUbaid through Early Dynastic.
   (h) Plain flint blade, with or without sickle-sheen. Period of primary use, like preceding two types, was probably pre-ᶜUbaid through Early Dynastic periods, but isolated examples also are found (re-used as strike-a-lights ?) on Sassanian and Islamic sites.

3. *Early Dynastic Period.*
   A. Reserve-slip ware. Cf. Delougaz, P. 1952. P. 53, Pl. 39. Begins in the Protoliterate *c* period and terminates soon after Early Dynastic I.
   B. Solid-footed goblets. Cf. Delougaz, P. 1952. Pp. 56–57, Pl. 46. The base, its section taking the form of an irregular truncated cone, is the

sherd ordinarily recognized in surface collections. Apparently confined to the Early Dynastic I period in the Diyala area, although examples in levels IV–II at Warka suggest that the type may begin slightly earlier in the south.

C. Monochrome painted ware. Cf. Delougaz, P. 1952. P. 44, 60–72, Pls. 32, 52–62. The typical surface sherd exhibits geometric designs in thin red, chocolate, or pinkish lines, and does not permit a distinction to be made between the fugitive paint of Early Dynastic "scarletware" and its Protoliterate predecessor. Protoliterate c through Early Dynastic I.

D. Pierced horizontal lug attached to notched ridge forming a gutter below the neck of a large jar, always with incised decoration. Cf. Delougaz, P. 1952. Pl. 41. Confined to the Early Dynastic I period.

E. Deep, irregularly made conical bowl with narrow, flat, string-cut base. Cf. Delougaz, P. 1952. Pp. 34, 58–59, Pls. 20 d, 49 a–d. Begins in Protoliterate c or even earlier and gradually is replaced during Early Dynastic period by type F.

F. More widely flaring conical bowls, characteristic of the latter part of the Early Dynastic period. Cf. Delougaz, P. 1952. Pp. 94–95, Pl. 96 a–e. Note that types E and F form a continuum. Hence a distinction between the two, while useful for chronological purposes, can only be drawn somewhat arbitrarily.

G. "Cutware," decorated with excised triangles or rectangles and sometimes also with parallel notched ridges and incised lines. A variety of shapes are represented, including, stands, "flowerpots," jars, and braziers. Cf. Delougaz, P. 1952. Pp. 55–56, 81, 85, 90–91, and passim.

H. Rim sherds of "fruit stands" and tubular stands. Cf. Delougaz, P. 1952. Pp. 55, 85, 90, and passim.

I. Crosshatched incising, generally in triangular patterns on jar shoulders or in zones on median sections of stands. Cf. Delougaz, P. 1952. Pls. 89, 173, 178–79, 181–82, 191–93.

(j) Stone bowls, various shapes and sizes. While these were made over a long period, it was the experience of the survey that their occurrence in surface collections generally coincided with an early date—Early Dynastic or earlier.

4. *Akkadian Period.*

A. "Ribbed Ware." Horizontal ribs, triangular in profile, either on shoulders of large storage jars or on large ledge-rim bowls. Cf. Delougaz, P. 1952. P. 105, Pl. 115. Andrae, W. 1922. Abb. 3 (Die archaischen Ischtar-Tempel. *Wissenschaftliche Veröffentlichung der Deutschen Orient-Gesellschaft*, 39. Leipzig). Apparently began at the end of Early Dynastic III.

B. Large spouted bowls. Spout has beaded rim and is set immediately below the down-flaring rim of bowl. Cf. Delougaz, P. 1952. P. 111, Pl. 114 c.

(c) Rim sherds of vessels similar to type B, but without spout.

(d) Broad-incised meanders on large bowl and jar sherds, Cf. Delougaz, Pp. 1952. nos. C. jar sherds. Cf. Delougaz, P. 1952. nos. C.365.810c, C.404.350, C.504.370; Andrae, W. 1922. Abb. 33. Probably began in Early Dynastic III.

5. *Ur III and Isin-Larsa Periods.*

A. Low flaring bowl with upright-band rim. Cf. Delougaz, P. 1952. P. 115, Pl. 120 a.

B. Large jars with "column-decorated" rims. Cf. Delougaz, P. 1952. Pl. 127.

C. Globular jar with channel-rim and low horizontal ribs. Cf. Mustafa, M. A. 1949. P. 183, Pl. 3 c.

D. Well-levigated, thin-walled cylindrical cups, usually with vertical or concave sides. Cf. Delougaz, P. 1952. P. 115, Pl. 120.

E. White-filled, incised greyware. Cf. Delougaz, P. 1952. Pp. 119–20, Pls. 124–25.

F. Slightly inset collar and rim of tall cylindrical jar. Cf. Delougaz, P. 1952. Pl. 121 g.

G. Ledge rim (horizontal or down-flaring) of vertical-sided deep bowl or jar with rounded bottom and ring-base, frequently decorated with horizontal grooves. Cf. Delougaz, P. 1952. P. 115, No. C.044.310.

H. Representation on clay plaque of "bull-eared god." Cf. Frankfort, H. 1936. Figs. 69–

70 (Progress of the work of the Oriental Institute in Iraq, 1934/35. *Oriental Institute Communications*, 20. Chicago); Mustafa, M. A. 1949. Pl. 6.

(i) "Sieve" sherds. Cf. Delougaz, P. 1952. P. 115, Pl. 120. Probably these were made in other periods as well, but at least there is a conspicuous concentration in remains of the Larsa period.

(j) String-cut "stump" bases from small jars or cups. Cf. Delougaz, P. 1952. P. 116, no. B.175.720. The same type continued into the Old Babylonian period.

(k) Low, slightly constricted buffware jar necks with a triple horizontal corrugation on the exterior rim.

(l) Flat everted-rim cups or lids. Delougaz, P. 1952. P. 115, no. B.062.210a. This type is said to have been introduced somewhat earlier but is especially characteristic of this period.

6. *Old Babylonian Period.*

   A. Truncated conical base with pedestal for small collared jar. Cf. Reuther, O. 1926. Abb. 9 (Die Innenstadt von Babylon (Merkes). *Wissenschaftliche Veröffentlichung der Deutschen Orient-Gesellschaft*, 47. Leipzig). This type persists into or even through the Cassite period.

   B. Rounded jar with slightly flaring neck, discbase. Cf. Delougaz, P. 1952. Pl. 132. Persists into the Cassite period.

   C. Truncated conical bases for small, rounded, wide-mouthed jars. Cf. Mustafa, M. A. 1949. Pl. 4:2, 6. Probably also persists into the Cassite period.

   D. Medium to large conical base for bell-shaped beaker. Also Cassite.

   E. Slightly flaring large jar rim with exterior channel or groove.

   (f) "Club" or everted-ledge rims for very large cylindrical or rounded storage jars with multiple exterior grooves below rim. This type subsumes a variety of specific shapes, not all of which may be of the same date. Reuther, O. 1926. Abb. 7.

7. *Cassite Period.*

   A. Tall chalice with solid disc-base. Cf. Baqir,

Taha 1945, Pl. 23 (Iraq Government excavations at ᶜAqar Quf 1942–43. *Iraq* (special supplement); Reuther, O. 1926. Taf. 47–48.

   (b) "Hurrian" button-base on small rounded cup or jar. Cf. Speiser, E. A. 1935. Pl. 73, no. 173 (Excavations at Tepe Gawra, vol. 1. Philadelphia); Haller, A. 1954. Tafel 2, ak, an, ap, ax (Die Gräber und Grüfte von Assur. *Wissenschaftliche Veröffentlichung der Deutschen Orient-Gesellschaft*, 65. Berlin-Schöneberg); Reuther, O. 1926. Taf. 52 c3. Possibly continues into Neo-Babylonian times.

8. *Middle Babylonian Period.*

   (a) Large software bowls with flat everted or down-turned rims, usually with several close-spaced grooves near outside of rim or on shoulder. Note that parallels can be assigned only from published reports of later periods, and that typological distinction from Neo-Babylonian types may not always be clear. Cf. Lines, J. 1954. Pl. 38:1 (Late Assyrian pottery from Nimrud. *Iraq* 16:164–67); Haller, A. 1954. Taf. 6: aa–af, ai–al.

   (b) Software jars with vertical or slightly concave necks, rope rims. One or several shallow concentric grooves set off neck from body. Cf. Reuther, O. 1926. Taf. 73:117–18; Haller, A. 1954. Taf. 3, f–m; Lines, J. 1954. Pl. 38:5; 39:1–3.

9. *Neo-Babylonian Period.*

   A. Deep, flaring-sided bowls with short concave or (less frequently) vertical neck above a sharp carination or shoulder. Rim may be rounded or flattened, and many specimens exhibit a thin whitish or greenish glaze which tends to thicken at the rim. Safar, F. 1949. Pl. 3:8 (Soundings at Tell Al-Laham. *Sumer* 5:154–71). Koldewey, R. 1925. Abb. 161 (Das wiedererstehende Babylon. [4th ed., revised] Leipzig); De Genouillac, H. 1924–25. No. 165 (Fouilles française d'el-ᶜAkhmer. Premières recherches archéologiques à Kich. 2 vols. Paris).

   B. Rounded bowls with thickened "rope" rims. Cf. Haller, A. 1954. Taf. 5:ao–ar; 6:bd; Lines, J. 1954. Pl. 37:4–6.

   C. Flaring-sided bowl with "club" rim, thin, greenish-white glaze.

(d) Jars with high vertical or slightly concave necks, rope rims. A characteristic feature is the presence of a sharp, low ridge at the junction of body with neck. With slight variation, this trait apparently persists into Parthian times, although on forms and wares that are distinguishable on other criteria. Cf. Haller, A. 1954. Taf. 3:ai; Koldewey, R. 1925. Abb. 165; Ghirshman, R. 1954b. Pl. 27, G.S.2383; 40, G.S.2342 (Village Perse-Achéménide. *Mémoires de la Mission Archéologique en Iran*, 36. Paris); Madhlum, T. A. 1959. Fig. 6:27 (The excavation at Tell Abū Thar [in Arabic]. *Sumer* 15:85–94).

10. *Achaemenid Period.*

A. Medallion stamps, various shapes and sizes (see Fig. 16). Generally horizontal rows on the necks and shoulders of deep beakers or bowls with rounded, flaring, or ogee profiles. Each stamp impression is placed on an exterior hump or knob formed by a deep fingertip indentation on interior surface. This trait persists through the Seleucid period. Cf. Ettinghausen, R. 1938. P. 651 (Parthian and Sassanian pottery. In "A survey of Persian art" [A. U. Pope, ed.], 1:646–80. New York); Reuther, O. 1926. Taf. 84:191.

B. Same as above, but with stamp showing a vertical palm-leaf impression (see Fig. 16). Cf. Oates, David, and Joan L. Oates. 1958. Pls. 21:20; 22:1–4 (Nimrud 1957. The Hellenistic Settlement. *Iraq* 20:114–57).

C. Horse-and-rider figurines. Cf. Van Buren, E. D. 1930. Fig. 216 (Clay figurines of Babylonia and Assyria. *Yale Oriental Series*, 16. New Haven); Koldewey, R. 1925. Abb. 149–50. These figurines also slightly antedate and postdate the Achaemenid period.

D. "Eggshell ware." Extremely thin, finely levigated deep bowls or beakers in greyish, greenish, or yellowish buff. Cf. Debevoise, N.C. 1934. Figs. 1–3, 5, 172 (Parthian pottery from Seleucia on the Tigris. *University of Michigan Studies*, Humanistic series, vol. 32. Ann Arbor); Rawson, F. S. 1954. Pp. 168 ff. (Palace wares from Nimrud: technical observations on selected examples. *Iraq* 16:168–72); Oates and Oates. 1958. Pl. 24:4, 8–9.

Apparently this ware began in Neo-Babylonian times and continued into the early Parthian period.

E. Vertical or slightly concave jar necks with one or more sharp horizontal ridges around middle or upper exterior. Probably began in Neo-Babylonian times and possibly continued into the Seleucid or Parthian period. Cf. Sarre, F., and E. Herzfeld. 1920. Vol. 4, Taf. 142:3 (Archäologische Reise im Euphrat- und Tigris-Gebiet. Berlin); Haller, A. 1954. Taf. 5:h, k, u, and x. Reuther, O. 1926. Taf. 73.

F. Thin, well-made bowls with rounded profiles and incurving rims. Cf. Madhlum, T. A. 1959. Figs. 4:5, 13. Debevoise, N. C. 1934. Fig. 6. Oates and Oates. 1958. Pl. 23:14–16, 29–31. Note that published examples are apparently Seleucid or Parthian, although our specimens seem to have more affinities with Achaemenid wares and sometimes occur on sites where other Seleucid or Parthian types are not present.

G. Round-bottom bowls or cups in fine, thin clay, with slightly bulging shoulders and high flaring rims. Cf. Lines, J. 1954. Pl. 37:7–9; 38:2–4.

H. Greyware, characteristically with angular profiles and thickened rims suggesting metal prototypes. Cf. Ghirshman, R. 1954b. Pp. 27–28.

(i) Thickened jar necks with flattened rims and multiple exterior horizontal grooves. The prototype, possibly imported, of a long-continuing tradition of utility wares.

(j) "Husking trays," recalling those of the Mesopotamian Early Village horizon. These recur for a brief period in Achaemenid and Parthian times, and are called variously "mortars" and "charcoal-burners," but their function remains obscure. Cf. Ghirschman, R. 1954b. Pp. 23–24, Pl. 30. Harden, D. B. 1934. Fig. 3:2 (Excavations at Kish and Barghuthiat: Pottery. *Iraq* 1:124–36); Debevoise, N. C. 1934. Fig. 344.

11. *Seleucid and Parthian Periods.*

A. Broad-line impressed decoration in sawtooth or chevron pattern beneath thin Parthian-green glaze. Cf. Lane, A. 1947. Pl. 1 (Early Islamic Pottery: Mesopotamia, Egypt, and Persia. London); Debevoise, N. C. 1934. Pl. 3, Fig. 1; Andrae, W., and Lenzen, H. 1933. Taf. 46 h, 491 (Die Partherstadt Assur. *Wissenschaftliche Veröffentlichung der Deutschen Orient-Gesellschaft*, 57. Leipzig); Ettinghausen, R. 1938. Vol. 1, Fig. 219 A; vol. 4, Pl. 182. In Assyria this trait apparently occurs only in Parthian levels; cf. Oates and Oates. 1958. Pl. 21:15.

B. Carved, low-relief decoration, triangular excisions, and appliqued button decoration beneath Parthian-green glaze. Generally combined with chevron decoration; cf. references under previous type.

C. Single or double "twisted rope" handles, generally covered with thin Parthian-green glaze. Cf. Ettinghausen. 1938. Vol. 1, Fig. 219 A and B; vol. 4, Pl. 181 B; Debevoise. 1934. Text Fig. 2; Andrae and Lenzen. 1933. Taf. 46H.

D. Thin, flaring bowls with a slight projecting elbow below simple rim. Probably a continuation of type 9:A, but this type lacks the glaze and sharply contoured profile of the former.

E. Dish or shallow bowl with straight-flaring sides, everted down-flaring or beveled rim. Usually with light greenish glaze. Cf. Madhlum. 1959. Fig. 4:12; Debevoise. 1934. Fig. 194.

F. Outflaring double-rim and vertical neck of jar, with Parthian-green glaze.

G. Vertical neck and thickened rim of jar, with pronounced channels on upper and exterior surface of rim. Jars usually were equipped with double-rope handles and had groups of vertical incisions on neck. Cf. Debevoise. 1934. Pl. A. 5–6; Fig. 183.

H. Punctate decoration, usually consisting of fine comb-tooth impressions in chevrons or intersecting patterns on shoulders of plain jars like those in type G. In many cases, comb-tooth impressions alternate with larger circular impressions possibly produced by hollow bird-bones or reeds. Cf. references under type G. Comb-incised meander deco-

ration also may be present. Cf. Oates and Oates. 1948. Pl. 21:23; 27:4.

I. High inflaring jar neck with rim thickened on inside. Parthian-green glaze characteristically applied to entire inside of vessel and to exterior neck; sometimes it also extends downward a short distance on exterior of globular body.

(j) Globular, neckless jar with close-spaced, concentric grooves below rim on exterior. A crescent-shaped lug sometimes is fixed to shoulder. Reddish clay, with black grit temper.

(k) Square jar rims with multiple exterior grooves. Differs from type 10:i in absence of rim-thickening and in more irregular grooves. Cf. Debevoise. 1934. Fig. 170. Probably continues through the Sassanian period.

(l) Parthian-green glaze.

(m) Plain lids, variable profiles, irregular in thickness. Possibly also served as cups, although unevenly cut bases argue for use primarily with large storage jars. Vessels of this type apparently continued through both the Parthian and Sassanian periods. Cf. Debevoise. 1934. Figs. 20–29; Harden. 1934. Fig. 1:4, 7.

12. *Sassanian Period.*

A. Flaring cup or bowl with thin, whitish-blue glaze and carinated base. Rim is sometimes beaded and usually slightly beveled on inner side. Cf. Harden. 1934. Fig. 2b:2, 4.

B. Sassanian stamp impressions on the bodies of large plainware jars. Horizontal bands of large, widely spaced impressions of rosettes, geometric designs, or animal representations, generally in a rectangular or circular field (see Fig. 16). Cf. Sarre, F. 1925. Pp. 8–11, Taf. 3 (Die Keramik von Samarra. *Die Ausgrabungen von Samarra*, 2. Berlin); Ettinghausen. 1938. 4:186 A.

C. Same as above, but representation is of Sassanian "royal symbol" (see Fig. 16).

D. Same as above, but representation is of "net" or double-x symbol (see Fig. 16).

E. Low ring bases of very large plain jars or bowls with characteristic deep finger indentations widely spaced on exterior surface at junction between base and vessel.

F. Large, coarse jars with slash decoration on low neck and shoulder. Decoration consists of rows of diagonal slashes separated by concentric grooves.

G. Crudely made crescent handle attached to simple rim of very large coarse bowl.

H. Lug in the shape of an inverted "v" attached to shoulder of large, well-made jar with low neck. The lug is always incompletely pierced with depressions on both sides and is usually fixed in a slightly outflaring position. The ware, used only for this type of vessel, is reddish grey, polished, and with large white grit temper.

I. Thickened rim of large bowl, entire interior and exterior rim covered with thin, bluish glaze.

J. Base of thick-sided, flaring bowl, unevenly finished on inside with pronounced spiral corrugations. Low rope-ring base, thickly covered with dark, bluish-green glaze on inside and out.

(k) Truncated base of large "torpedo" storage jar, frequently coated with bitumen on the inside. This form apparently outlasts the Sassanian period, as it is found in quantity at Sāmarrā. Cf. Government of Iraq, Department of Antiquities, 1940. Pl. 12, 14, 20, 29 (Excavations at Samarra 1936–39. Baghdad).

(l) Rope-rim of same storage jar. This is at best a vague chronological indicator since it began at least as early as the Parthian period. Cf. *ibid.*; Debevoise. 1934. Figs. 95–96.

(m) "Honeycomb ware." Body sherds of large globular bowls or jars with a characteristic roughened surface treatment. Apparently antedates the Sassanian period and may also persist somewhat longer. Cf. Andrae and Lenzen. 1933. Taf. 56 h–k, n.

13. *Early Islamic Period.*

A. Large decorated jars of soft buffware, with exteriors covered with greenish glaze. Decoration consists of three principal motifs: broad-line incisions in an "advancing wave" pattern, appliqued wavy lines and dots, and rosettes of smaller appliqued dots. Glaze tends to be uneven in thickness, forming darker concentrations along close-spaced,

horizontal grooves, which suggests that the vessels were built up through a coiling process. This type probably was introduced in the late Sassanian period. Cf. Lane. 1947. Pl. 3; Sarre and Herzfeld. 1920. Vol. 4, Taf. 143; Sarre. 1925. Taf. 6.

B. Rim sherds of previous type, consisting of a low vertical neck with multiple grooves and a flattened ledge-lip. A crescent-lug handle is attached vertically to the body directly alongside neck. Greenish glaze. Cf. Lane, A. 1947. Pl. 3. Sarre, F., and E. Herzfeld. 1920. Vol. 4, Taf. 143. Sarre, F. 1925. Taf. 6.

C. Flaring, slightly rounded bowl with crude, blue-glaze splashes forming a radiating pattern against a white-glazed background on the interior. Cf. Sarre, F. 1925. Abb. 142.

D. Splash-glazed ware in imitation of T'ang imports. Long splashes of green or green and yellow over white slip on a reddish, well-levigated ware, generally form radiating patterns. The most common vessel form is a widely flaring bowl. Cf. Hobson, R. L. 1932. Fig. 13 (A guide to the Islamic pottery of the Near East. London); Sarre, F. 1925. Taf. 32: 4; Government of Iraq, Department of Antiquities. 1940. Pls. 61–64; Pope, A. U. 1938. Vol. 5, Pls. 568 B, 570 ("Ceramic arts in Islamic times: history." 2:1446–1666; 5: Pls. 555–811. In *A Survey of Persian Art* [A. U. Pope, ed.]); Lane, A. 1947. Pl. 7 B.

E. Similar to above but with simple graffito decoration incised through slip under glaze. Loosely drawn curvilinear motifs; carefully arranged patterns are rare and there is no attempt to vary intensity of lines. Cf. Lane, A. 1947. Pl. 6 B; Pope, A. U. 1938. Vol. 5, Pl. 568 A, 569; Government of Iraq, Department of Antiquities, 1940. Pl. 76, 81, 83–85. This type is not always distinguishable from "classic" graffito (type 14:A), and probably overlaps with it in time.

F. Flaring or rounded buffware bowls with all-over white glaze apparently designed in imitation of Chinese celadon. Like their imported prototypes (sherds of which are found very rarely at the larger sites), these vessels often have pronounced vertical ribs or flut-

132

ing. Cf. Sarre 1925. Taf. 23–25; Government of Iraq, Department of Antiquities, 1940. Pls. 99–102; Pope 1938. Vol. 5, Pl. 589A. This type persists at least through the Sāmarrān period.

(g) High-necked jars with horizontal corrugations, flattened rope-rims, and strap handles under light blue glaze.

14. *Sāmarrān Period*.

A. Flaring bowls with fine, complex incisions in "classic" graffito patterns under transparent glaze, including rosettes, floral arrangements, animals, and pseudo-inscriptions. Occasionally combined with earlier splash-glazed technique, but emphasis has shifted to graffito patterns and inner surface is more often left largely white to display them effectively; splashes consist almost exclusively of zones of green or brown dots rather than long radiating stripes. Cf. Sarre 1925. Abb. 161, 165, 168–70; Government of Iraq, Department of Antiquities, 1940. Pls. 77–80, 82, 86–87.

B. Fine *repoussé* decoration on thin-sided vessels of varying shapes, covered with thin, transparent, greenish-yellow glaze. Cf. Lane, A. 1947. Pls. 4, 5A; Hobson, R. L. 1932. Pl. 2, Nos. 2, 5; Koechlin, R. 1928. Pl. 17:132 (Les céramiques musulmanes de Suse au Musée du Louvre. *Délégation en Perse*, Mémoires 19); Government of Iraq, Department of Antiquities, 1940: Pls. 89–91.

C. Fine buff pottery with white lead glaze painted with cobalt blue floral designs. This pigment always diffuses slightly to give a mottled edge. Cf. Hobson, R. L. 1932. Fig. 10; Lane, A. 1947. Pl. 8; Sarre. 1925. Taf. 18; Pope 1938. Vol. 5, Pls. 571–74.

D. Thin buffware bowls with well-executed geometric designs in olive brown or gold luster paint beneath a transparent glaze. Cf. Hobson. 1932. Pl. 4, Fig. 14; Government of Iraq, Department of Antiquities, 1940. Pls. 92–98; Pope. 1938. Vol. 5, Pls. 575–79.

(e) Cooking vessels (?) of soft grey sandstone with flat bottoms, vertical sides, and horizontal ledge-lugs at rim or midside. Narrow, parallel tool-marks are common, giving a characteristic fluted effect.

(f) Small applied knob at the apex of handles of small buffware jars. The knob is usually roughly conical or cylindrical in shape, and perhaps may be regarded as a prototype for later "turbans" applied in the same position (type 15: B). But probably it is also at least partly contemporaneous with the latter. Cf. Pope. 1938. Vol. 5, Pl. 593 A, C, D.

(g) Large, soft buffware dishes and bowls with monochrome, dark, violet-brown glaze on entire inner surface and exterior rim. This type probably continues well into the post-Sāmarrān period.

15. *Late Abbasid Period*.

A. Flaring bowls with black geometric and scroll designs in reserve on white or light buff body under semitransparent blue glaze. Cf. Safar, F. 1945. P. 41, Fig. 19:69 (Wasit: the sixth season's excavations. Cairo); Lane. 1947. Pls. 50–51.

B. Decorated, applied "turbans" on handles of large buffware jars. A variety of slightly different forms (see Fig. 15).

C. "Decadent" graffito designs incised on flaring bowls under transparent glaze with diffused, large splashes of green and reddish-brown. Incised lines are broader, more irregular in width and diffused along their edges than in "classic" graffito, and the slip and glaze are more uneven and tend to flake off. Like other contemporary glazed bowls, the ware tends to be soft, uneven in texture, and buff-colored. This is a type which may be known only in a limited region.

D. Same "decadent" graffito technique under yellowish-brown, green, or blue glaze. Hobson, R. L. 1932. Fig. 19; Hitchcock, E. F. 1956. Fig. 25 (Islamic pottery from the ninth to the fourteenth centuries A.D. London).

E. Large bowls or dishes with soft buff body, entirely covered on inside with turquoise lead glaze which also may be allowed to drip down outside rim. Low ring bases, rounded or flat rims, sometimes with pronounced carination above midside.

(f) Stamp-impressions, generally on shoulders of globular jars. They consist primarily of non-representational designs in a small circular

133

field; cross-hatching, bars-and-dots, stars, radiating wheelspokes, etc. (see Fig. 16). While Islamic motifs in most cases apparently can be distinguished from those of the Sassanian period, no separation of styles by subperiod within the Abbasid and Ilkhanid periods is possible at present. Published examples range from early Abbasid to Ilkhanid date, although the author received the impression during the survey that the use of stamps in general became distinctly more common in the late Abbasid and Ilkhanid periods. Cf. Government of Iraq, Department of Antiquities, 1940. Pl. 31–32; Safar. 1945. Fig. 16: 36–39.

(g) Fine buffware jar rims and necks decorated with multiple grooves and incisions. Cf. Government of Iraq, Department of Antiquities, 1940. Pl. 30, 43–46; Safar. 1945. Fig. 14:3, 8, 9. These began earlier and continued later than the late Abbasid period, but at least the type seems to have reached its greatest popularity at that time.

16. *Ilkhanid Period.*

A. Reserve designs excised from black paint on white slip under white glaze. The most common vessel form is a flaring bowl, and the prevailing motifs are scrolls and geometric designs arranged in panels on the inside and base.

B. Thin flaring bowls with broad-line, blue-and-black designs, frequently including a "horse-shoe" motif, under a thin, poorly applied layer of bluish-white glaze that frequently tends to flake or wear away. Cf. Safar. 1945. Fig. 20: 92.

C. Large, rounded, soft buffware bowls with greyish-white lead glaze that has a curdled or pitted appearance.

D. Large bowls decorated on the interior with black "lightning" or zigzag patterns under a blue or white glaze. According to F. Safar, this is a local ware that he has not encountered elsewhere in Iraq outside the lower Diyala region.

E. Turquoise blue lead glaze on interior of small bowls or the exterior of small jars or pitchers with strap-handles. The junction of handle with body is characteristically fluted with the fingertips, and in addition there are sometimes broad, shallow, excised patterns under the glaze. Cf. Safar. 1945. Figs. 20, 104; Hitchcock. 1956. Fig. 35.

17. *Post-Ilkhanid Period.*

A. A decoration motif applied to soft white buffware bowls, consisting of blue circles surrounded by black dots under a whitish lead glaze. Cf. Safar. 1945. Fig. 18: 61.

B. Radial designs on the inner basal surfaces of bowls, in black and blue under a whitish-lead glaze. Cf. Safar. 1945. Fig. 20: 102.

C. Flat-rimmed dishes with elaborate designs in black and blue (and possibly also green) on white slip beneath a transparent, evenly applied lead glaze. Cf. Safar. 1945. Fig. 20: 99.

(d) Thickened rims of very large bowls with straight-flaring sides. Thick blue or green glaze is applied uniformly on the interior and usually drips over the rim onto the exterior as well. In many cases the outer edge of the rim is decorated with wide-spaced serrations.

(e) Pinkish, very crude cooking pots or jars tempered with large black grits.

134

APPENDIX C

REGISTER OF ARCHAEOLOGICAL SITES IN THE DIYALA REGION

THE FOLLOWING tabulation is keyed to site numbers mentioned in the text and appearing in the figures and reference map of the region. Subject to the reservations on completeness and uniformity of coverage adumbrated in Appendix A, it represents an exhaustive compilation of ancient settlements which have survived the alluviation process and still can be found on the Diyala plains today. Specifically to be mentioned as a limitation is the omission of a number of smaller and less important sites, generally Sassanian and Islamic village settlements clustering uniformly along former canal systems, whose location and date of occupation was noted but for which descriptions otherwise are not available. These sites are shown on the reference map accompanied by an asterisk, and they also appear in the figures recording settlement patterns at different periods.

Sketch maps are given in a few cases, either to simplify a cumbersome verbal description, to correct misleading reconstructions on previous maps (principally the 1:50,000 Arabic series), or because of the intrinsic interest of a site or some of its surface features. It should be understood that these drawings had to be made rapidly under variable field conditions, so that necessarily their accuracy also varies. Hachure is used in certain instances to denote the principal elevation of a mound, while in those cases a solid outline incloses lower areas with surface debris suggesting settlement at approximately the present plain level. All measurements are given in meters, and unless otherwise stated the scale in the drawings is uniformly 1:16,667. Particularly in the lower Nahrawān region, shown at an enlarged scale in Figures 8–9, information on the layout and extent of some of the larger sites is available to supplement these descriptions and sketch maps.

Site descriptions preceded by the date "1937" in parentheses are those which were provided to the author by Thorkild Jacobsen on the basis of his preliminary reconnaissance in that year. There was not sufficient time to re-examine these sites during the 1957–58 survey. It will be noted that data are missing on the height of most of these mounds, and that in some cases, also on sites examined during the later reconnaissance, this or other dimensions were not recorded.

SITE NUMBER

1. 60 NS × 20 × 3.5. Seleucid/Parthian-Sassanian.
2. Tell al-Kawūr. Probably identified by informants in 1937 as Gawri, and identical with ruins of Gaur reported by Keppel (1827. Vol. 1:288. Personal narrative of a journey from India to England . . . London) and of Giaour-Tuppé-sé reported by Buckingham (1830. Vol. 1:38. Travels in Assyria, Media, and Persia. London). Ht. 6 m. Badly quarried for brick. Diagnostic sherds not found and pottery of any description rare. A fort? Probably Sassanian, if an assignment can be made on the basis of mortar and brick size only.

0 _____ 500 METERS

135

3. (1937) 300 × 200 × fairly low. Badly quarried for brick, many bricks and much mortar, no pottery. Probably Sassanian.

4. Tell Ismaᶜil. 240 NW-SE × 110 × 3.5. Immediately E is a tell 100m in diameter surmounted by a modern village, while 300m NE of the latter lie two others of the same size. Small clusters of ruins to NNW, NW, and SW. All of same date: Sassanian.

5. Tell al-Raha. 220 WNW-ESE × 100 × 3. Ruined tower on E end; a small conical mound rises 3 above main part of site. Name derives from water mills, seen there by Keppel (op. cit., p. 288) in ruined condition. The surface collection included few distinctive types but suggested a Sassanian date.

6. (1937) Tell Suleiman saghīr. 80 diam × 2–3; contains a number of shepherds' caves. Parthian.

7. Aq Tepe. 230 diam × 14. Kurdish villages on ESE and SW slopes. A single sherd (2:e) suggests that occupation may have begun already in the Warka/Protoliterate period. The main occupation, apparently continuous, extended from Early Dynastic through Old Babylonian times. Finally, there was a thin but widespread Sassanian occupation.

8. Tell Nabi Ismaᶜil. 220 EW × 110 × 5.5, lower on E end where there are two small Imāms and recent graves. Pottery sparse (Seleucid/Parthian?)–Sassanian, Late Abbasid–Ilkhanid.

9. Tell Shahab. 160 NS × 120 × 6.5. A series of large pits have been cut in a N-S line along crest of tell, exposing bricks 24 × 14 × 6 cms. The full extent of the mound was occupied only during the Early Dynastic period, but a limited occupation may have continued into the Akkadian period. Some Sassanian debris (assumed area, 1 ha.) occurs on the lower slopes.

10. 120 diam × 2. Ilkhanid and later.

11. 110 diam × 2. Surface collection, much corroded by salt, suggested an Achaemenian–Parthian date.

12. Tell Imnethir. 100 NNW-SSE × 60 × 1.5. Exclusively ᶜUbaid pottery was noted, although clay sickles (1:A) were entirely absent.

13. Tell al-Bekhatriya. 100 diam, modern village. (Sassanian?).

14. Both mounds 9.5 m high. Site possibly began in Protoliterate times (one example of 2:e was found) but is mainly Early Dynastic–Akkadian.

14

0 _____ 500 METERS

136

15. Tell al-Hafaᵓir. 900 NNW-SSE × 300. Isolated summits rise to 2.5, but most of site is lower. Large bricks reported as having been quarried from site, accounting for its name. Traces of streets, courtyards, buildings can be detected on surface. Toward SW end of site is a court 100m square with a small high mound at one end of it. Sassanian.

16. Tell Oushaᶜ. 250 diam × 9. Surmounted by a ruined fort or police post. Early Dynastic through Cassite. No definite evidence of an Akkadian occupation.

17. 110 NNW-SSE × 60 × 2. Sassanian, with also a few post-Ilkhanid sherds.

18. 60 diam × 4.5. Akkadian sherds were noted as the dominant surface component, but two sherds (2:e, 3:E) probably indicate an earlier beginning and occupation on some scale apparently continued into the Old Babylonian period.

19. NW mount 2 m, center mound 4.5 m, SE mount 0.5 m high. Approximate area of occupation, 3.7 ha. Seleucid/Parthian–Sassanian.

19

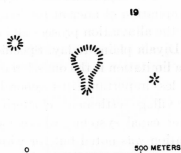

0 _____ 500 METERS

20. Kheit Howās. 190 NW-SE × 100 × about 3. Old–Middle Babylonian, although Cassite chalice bases (7:A) were conspicuously rare.

21. (1937) Tulūl Shokarin. A group of small tells—2 were investigated. Each 80 × 100 × 2–3, uniform pottery. Assumed total area of occupation, 3 ha. Sassanian.

22. (1937) Obara sadrani. 200 diam × 3–4. Late Abbasid–Ilkhanid.

23. Tell Ghasilje. 100 diam × 3. Cassite.

24. Tell Yahūdī. Perhaps originally 200 diam × 4.5, but much dirt removal from NW end, summit, Khanaqin hwy. cuts away some of N side. Early Dynastic through Old Babylonian. 150 m to SE is a tell 50 diam × 1.5, Old Babylonian.

25. Tell Khanjar. 160 diam × 4. Much cut away for hwy. fill. Middle–Neo-Babylonian.

26. Tell Abū Husaiwah. Probably larger than 100 diam × 2, but deep palm garden ditches around edges may exaggerate size. Post-Ilkhanid.

27. Tell Melagādh. Probably 200 diam × about 4, but palm garden ditches may exaggerate size. Mixed with canal banks around sides; uncultivated area on air-

photo shows as 350 NE-SW × 250. From Late Abbasid into post-Ilkhanid times.

28. Kheit Insaysah. 110 NW-SE × 60 × 3.5. Seleucid/Parthian–Sassanian.

29. 40 diam × 1. Neo-Babylonian and Seleucid/Parthian. No evidence was found of an occupation during the intervening Achaemenian period.

30. Tulūl Hmoidhāt. Height of large mounds 4m; others 2m or less. Salty, overgrown with swamp grass, stands in large depression. Assumed occupation area, 8 ha. Seleucid/Parthian.

30

0   500 METERS

31. Tell Jaʿara. 150 NW-SE × 120 × 4.5. Early Dynastic through Old Babylonian.

32. (1937) Ouashad and Tell Balghash. Ouashad is 80 diam × 3.5, sherds rare. Tell Balghash, 100 × 150 × 3.5. Parthian–Sassanian.

33. (1937) Abū Harmal. 200 diam × 5.5 Ur III/Larsa and Old Babylonian.

34. Tell Nither Abdam. 130 diam × 4. Sassanian.

35. N mound 80 diam × 2; SW mound 100 × 60 × 1.5; SE mound 140 × 80 × 3. Approximate total occupied area, 2.3 ha. Sassanian.

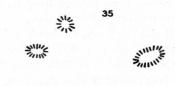

35

0   500 METERS

36. Probably originally 150 diam × 1.5, but now higher and distorted in outline as a result of complete deep-trenching for date cultivation. Neo-Babylonian and Seleucid/Parthian, with the intervening Achaemenian period not well represented.

37. (1937) Imām Sheikh Jabir. 200 × 250 × 4–5. Achaemenian, Sassanian.

38. 120 diam × 2. Sparse, poorly preserved pottery. Probably Seleucid/Parthian–Sassanian.

39. 180 NNW-SSE × 100 × 3. Small summits tail off northward through surrounding depression. Seleucid/Parthian.

40. (1937) 100 × 150 × 1.5. Sassanian.

41. Bint al Emīr, Eski Baghdad (Daskara). See *supra*, p. 92, Sarre and Herzfeld. 1920. Vol. 2:89 (Archäologische Reise im Euphrat- und Tigris-Gebiet. Berlin). Area, 140 ha. From Sassanian through Late Abbasid, although there is a puzzling sparseness of debris inside the great rectangular enclosure wall for an occupation of this length so well attested in documentary sources.

42. Zindān. 550 NNW-SSE (plus large debris-extension or tell at SSE end) × 100 (approximate average width) × 11 (maximum height of debris; lower at N end). Pottery sparse and poor. See Rich. 1836. Vol. 2:253–56 (Narrative of a residence in Koordistan. London; Sarre and Herzfeld (*op. cit.*, pp. 90–91). Sassanian.

43. (1937) Tell Obara. 150 × 200 × 8.5. Early Islamic.

44. (1937) Suboikhi al-saghīr. 200 diam × 3–4. Sassanian.

45. (1937) Tell Qubba. 200 diam × 8.5. Seleucid/Parthian. Possibly pre-Sargonid also.

46. (1937) Tell Mandak. 150 × 320 × 3.5. Ur III/Larsa, Old Babylonian, and Cassite. Possibly pre-Sargonid also.

47. 60 diam × 0.5. Fairly sparse Sassanian surface pottery.

48. 80 diam × 2.5. Sassanian.

49. 80 diam × 5. Many modern graves. Sassanian. Height of tell suggests a longer occupation, but no earlier or later pottery was found.

50. 170 E-W × 90 × 4.5. Sassanian.

51. 90 diam × 2.5. Sassanian.

52. 110 NE-SW × 130 × 2.5 (height around edge). A square fort with large mud brick outer wall to be seen on SE side. Old canal passes NW side, begins at high bluff over Diyala 200 E of site. Opposite bank of Diyala low at this point, and there is no sign of old canal continuing on other side; hence this must be at canal inlet or very near it. Seleucid/Parthian–Sassanian.

53. 600 NNE-SSW × 200 × 6. Major occupation Seleucid/Parthian, with settlement continuing on a much reduced scale (assumed area, 2 ha.) into the Sassanian period.

54. Tell Abū Qubūr. 180 N-S × 80 × 5. Many modern graves. Seleucid/Parthian–Sassanian, with the former better represented in the surface collection.

55. 70 diam × 1. Sassanian.

56. Tell Imm ʿAyyāsh. 180 NNW-SSE × 120 × 4. Early Dynastic through Larsa.

57. 110 WNW-ESE × 60 × 2. Same surface debris occurs on tell 50 diam × 1.5, 400m to ESE. Seleucid/Parthian–Sassanian.

58. (1937). Tell Muhawwile. 90 × 120 × 4. Ur III/Larsa.

137

59. Small tell bisected by railroad track. Originally about 80 diam $\times$ 2, now higher due to spoil from cut. Some debris occurs as outcrops 20–50 diam along old canal bank running SE. Assumed area of occupation, 1 ha. Sassanian.

60. 120 E-W $\times$ 80 $\times$ 2. Surrounded by depression with standing water at time of visit. Sassanian.

61. 240 NE-SW $\times$ 190 $\times$ 5. Seleucid/Parthian.

62. 160 ENE-WSW $\times$ 90 $\times$ 1. Very sparse surface pottery included no diagnostic types. Probably Parthian or Sassanian.

63. 50 diam $\times$ 3. Sparse pottery; Seleucid/Parthian.

64. Small, but so surrounded by rich garden growth and spoil-banks from ditches that size is difficult to estimate. Assumed area of occupation, 1 ha. Sparse pottery (Seleucid/Parthian?).

65. 250 NW-SE $\times$ 150 $\times$ 3. Late Abbasid–post-Ilkhanid.

66. 150 NNE-SSW $\times$ 120 $\times$ 3. Mostly low, with summit near SW end. A small mound of same date 200m SSW. Sassanian.

67. A square ancient fortress, 80 (approx.) along each edge. Rising at points along edges to 3.5. Pottery very sparse, difficult to classify, but probably Parthian or Sassanian.

68. Roughly 100 diam (slightly longer NNW-SSE) $\times$ 4 above plain level, but drops abruptly from E edge for 8 into Kātūl al-Kisrawī. 400m NNW along the Kātūl is another similar mound which may have formed a continuous settlement with the first before the intervening area was eroded away by a deep gully. Early Islamic.

69. A large area is very slightly elevated and out of cultivation, but sparse debris is largely confined to area 200 diam. Seleucid/Parthian.

70. Tell Abū Halāwah. 200 diam $\times$ 3.5. NW edge cut by Baghdad-Kirkuk RR. Post-Sāmarrān through Ilkhanid.

71. Tell al-Dhabab. 250 NNW-SSE $\times$ 200 $\times$ 4. Some very minor recent robber holes. Early Dynastic through Larsa. Two Neo-Babylonian–Achaemenian pots, found together just below surface level, probably indicate a grave of that period.

72. 180 NNW-SSE $\times$ 90 $\times$ 2. Sassanian.

73. 220 E-W $\times$ 160 $\times$ unrecorded height. Sassanian.

74. Karastel. Probably ancient Artemita, as first suggested by Keppel (*op. cit.*, pp. 142–44). Having devoted a day to the examination of the ruins, he was able to identify streets, plazas, gates, and an outer wall with semicircular bastions. Approximate area, 150 ha. Seleucid/Parthian-Sassanian.

75. Height unrecorded. One Seleucid/Parthian sherd hints at occupation during that period, but no other pottery of any description was seen and all brick too fragmentary for measurements to suggest date.

76. (1937) Tell Gurgishāh. 100 $\times$ 160 $\times$ 3.5. Cassite, Achaemenian.

77. Tell Gurgishāh. 150 NNE-SSW $\times$ 70 $\times$ 4. Old canal from which tell is said to take name flows NNE-SSW immediately E of site. Warka/Protoliterate through Old Babylonian. A little later pottery (Middle Babylonian, Neo-Babylonian, and Achaemenid) is confined to so small a portion of the S end of the tell that probably it can be disregarded as a significant settlement.

78. (1937) 90 $\times$ 100 $\times$ 2. Cassite.

79. (1937) Abū Sedere. 250 $\times$ 300 $\times$ 5–6. Ilkhanid.

80. (1937) Merjaniat. A group of natural hills; the name means "the cousins" and refers to two large stones thus called. A single flint flake provides the barest hint of a pre-Sargonid occupation in the vicinity. A Sassanian settlement also occurs, with an occupational area estimated at 0.5 ha.

81. Tell Mājid. 190 NNE-SSW $\times$ 70 $\times$ 4.5. Name is given on U.S. Army $\frac{1}{4}''$ map as Tell Jamid, but this variation comes from fellah with house just below site. A single Cassite chalice base (7:A) may indicate that occupation began in that period. Neo-Babylonian–Achaemenian.

82. Tell Abū Busal. 140 diam $\times$ 3. Achaemenian–Seleucid/Parthian.

83. Two small adjoining tells along old E-W canal. Each about 100 diam $\times$ 2, Sassanian–Early Islamic. 1.7 kms WSW is a third low site ca. 1 ha. in area, Sassanian only.

84. Tell al-Mujēlībah. 220 diam $\times$ 4.5. Entirely composed of fragmentary bricks, with evidence that much more has been robbed from it. Perhaps a fort. Very little pottery, all Sassanian.

85. Tell al-Mujēlībah. Probably a fort, strongly reminiscent of Bismayah (562). Remains of wall 110 N-S $\times$ 70 $\times$ 6.5; inside at little more than plain level. Sassanian; probably also Parthian.

86. Tulūl Abū Qubūr. 240 NE-SW $\times$ 80 $\times$ 2.5. Sassanian through Sāmarrān.

87. Tulūl Abū Qubūr. 120 diam $\times$ 4.5. One Cassite sherd (7:A) seen. The remainder Neo-Babylonian–Achaemenian.

88. Tulūl Abū Qubūr. 80 diam $\times$ 1.5. Again, only one Cassite sherd. The main occupation Neo-Babylonian through Parthian.

75

0 _____ 500 METERS

138

89. NE tell 180 diam $\times$ 4. SW tell 110 diam $\times$ 1.5. Seleucid/Parthian, the surface collection including a coin of Pacorus II (A.D. 78–115).

90. 230 diam $\times$ 3.5. Early Islamic.

91. 200 N-S $\times$ 110 $\times$ 3.5. Sassanian.

92. 150 N-S $\times$ 60 $\times$ 1.5. Seleucid/Parthian.

93. WSW tell 70 diam $\times$ 1. ENE tell 30m away, 60 diam $\times$ 1.5. Sassanian.

94. (1937) Tell Ahmar. 50 $\times$ 150 $\times$ 2–3. Seleucid/Parthian.

95. (1937). Tell Hor. 90 $\times$ 120 $\times$ 2–3. Sassanian.

96. Imām Abū Idrīs. Modern cemetery surrounds a large ruined imām. A rough guess of the size of the original site (now hidden by canals, graves, grass) about 100 diam $\times$ 0.5. Late Abbasid, Ilkhanid, and later.

97. Moderately thick surface debris and pottery within an area 150 diam at surface level. Old Babylonian–Cassite.

98. Tulūl Abū Sekhūl. 80 diam $\times$ 3. Late Abbasid–Ilkhanid.

99. Tulūl Abū Sekhūl. 90 diam $\times$ 2. Neo-Babylonian, with traces of a possible antecedent Cassite–Middle Babylonian occupation.

100. Tulūl Abū Sekhūl. Probably still 180 diam, but mostly low. A conical summit at W end is 60 diam $\times$ 3, and shows red and black discoloration from old brick-kiln which may have consumed much of original mound. Akkadian through Old Babylonian.

101. Largest tell about 100 NW-SE $\times$ 70 $\times$ 1.5; another very slightly smaller $\times$ 2.5. Other small outcrops include two to ENE that are 150m apart N-S and less than half the area of the main tells. Finally there are three still smaller outcrops to E and SE. Assumed area 2 ha., about 4 villages (?). Sassanian.

102. Abū Hilāl. Small SW mound (80 $\times$ 40 $\times$ 1.5) Early Dynastic; NW mound (160 $\times$ 70 $\times$ 2.5) Early Dynastic—Akkadian; main mound (280 $\times$ 250 $\times$ 6) and SE outlier Akkadian through Cassite.

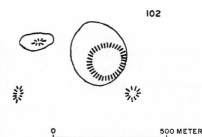

103. Imām Sheikh Tamīn. 160 NNE-SSW $\times$ 60 $\times$ 2.5. Ilkhanid.

104. 120 EW $\times$ 80 $\times$ 1.5. Whole E half deeply trenched for date garden; same at foot of W end. Small outcrops S and WSW. Pottery very sparse, but probably all Sassanian.

105. Tell Shejeir. 150 diam $\times$ 3.5. 50 SE lies another tell of same periods 120 NW-SE $\times$ 50 $\times$ 1.5. Two other very small outcrops S of main tell. Early Dynastic, Akkadian not noted; Ur III/Larsa through Cassite.

106. Tell Abū Hilāl. Name actually applies mainly to 102, but is said locally to be used also for this one. Ht. 5m. Approximately 1.6 ha. area. Ilkhanid.

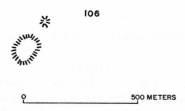

107. 70 N-S $\times$ 40 $\times$ 2. Mainly Neo-Babylonian. The few Seleucid/Parthian sherds noted (including a worn female figurine perhaps showing Hellenistic influence) probably can be disregarded as strays from nearby 108.

108. Largest mound 4m, others 2.5m or less in height. Main occupation Seleucid/Parthian, with an area of approx. 4 ha.; a small Sassanian occupation (assumed to be 0.5 ha.) was largely confined to the westernmost mound.

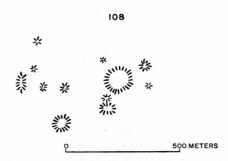

109. Abū Rāsain. As measured on the ground, 280 diam $\times$ 5.5, with a central ridge forming two equal summits on NW-SE line. On the other hand, the discoloration of its outline scales off air photo—with a clear and regular pattern suggesting a defensive wall—as 450 NW-SE $\times$ 300. Early Dynastic, with no trace of earlier periods found in the surface pottery in spite of a prolonged search. Yet there were greater quantities of worked flint of all kinds than have ever been encountered by the author on an alluvial site.

110. Tell Afwah. 120 diam $\times$ 2. Very salty surface, making pottery difficult to distinguish and badly corroded. Probably mainly Sassanian.

111. Tell Abū Ijmalah. 200 NNE-SSW $\times$ 120 $\times$ 4. Seleucid/Parthian–Sassanian.

112. Avg. height 3m. In addition to the mounds shown, scattered clusters of debris along old canal levee to SSE

suggest an occupation aggregating about 5 ha. Seleucid/Parthian–Sassanian.

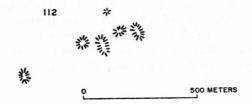

113. (1937) Abū Salabikh. 250 × 250 × less than 1. Many large unworked stone blocks give site its name, "father of stones." Early Dynastic.

114. 180 E-W × 120 × 3.5. Small outcrops to E, N, and SW. A much smaller tell adjoins old canal 1.1 km. NE. Total area, 2.2 ha. Seleucid/Parthian; possibly an earlier Achaemenian occupation also.

115. Tell Saʿad. 180 N-S × 100 × 3. Note possibility that former watercourse flowed between this site and 116. Old Babylonian–Cassite.

116. Tell Saʿad. 350 × 220 × 8. Appears to have been continuously occupied from the Akkadian through the Parthian period except for a probable hiatus during Middle and Neo-Babylonian times.

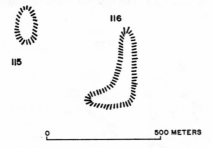

117. S tell 80 diam × 1.5, has recently abandoned village on top. N tell also 80 diam, but has a small conical summit rising to 4.5. Sparse Seleucid/Parthian pottery.

118. E tell 120 N-S × 30 × 2 (reaching this height only at S end). W tell 30 diam × 1.5. Total area about 0.5 ha. Mainly Neo-Babylonian, with a few Cassite sherds on the E tell suggesting that the occupation may have begun in that period.

119. Tell i-Blāl. 80 diam × 2. Mainly Seleucid/Parthian, with rare "push-out" stamps (10:A) indicating a probable beginning in the Achaemenian period.

120. Two mounds about 70 diam × 2. Another smaller mound SW of the western one. Neo-Babylonian, Seleucid/Parthian; no evidence for an intervening Achaemenian occupation was found.

121. Hachure in sketch denotes sherd-strewn 1.5m summits; other areas within outline are low with sparse pottery. Total area 3.5 ha. Neo-Babylonian through Parthian, with the former occurring not only on the

E tell but also as the dominant surface component on the NW summit of the main tell.

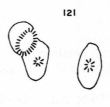

122. 110 N-S × 30 × 2.5. Early Dynastic through **Larsa** periods.

123. 100 diam × 4. Ur III/Larsa through Cassite.

124. Tulūl al-Jifjāf. Two cigar-shaped N-S parallel tells along old canal banks. E bank 250 × 110 × 3; W bank smaller and lower. 3.5 ha. area. Early Islamic–Sāmarrān.

125. Tulūl al-Jifjāf. Main mound 3m, others 2m or less in height. Approx. area 6 ha. Seleucid/Parthian–Sassanian.

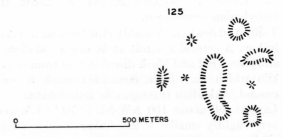

126. Tulūl al-Jifjāf. NW mound 2 m, others 1m in height. Approx. area of Sassanian occupation, 2 ha. A few Neo-Babylonian sherds suggest an occupation, probably smaller, during that period also.

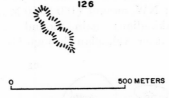

127. 120 diam × 2.5. Early Islamic through Ilkhanid.

128. Tell al-Shetēt. 140 NW-SE × 60 × 4. Much dug-up by brick-robbers and badly eroded away by floods. Seleucid/Parthian–Sassanian.

129. Tell al-Debaichah. 300 N-S × 250 × 3. Sassanian.

130. Tell Abū Fayyādh. 130 diam × 3.5. Modern graves on E end. 200 NNE stands Imām of same name in modern village. Rare sherds suggest a small, underlying Sassanian–Early Islamic occupation, but the bulk of the mound is Late Abbasid and Ilkhanid.

131. 90 diam × 1.5, covered with village debris. Inspection limited by dogs, but sparse Sassanian pottery was observed.

SITE
NUMBER

132. Height 1.5m. Sassanian.

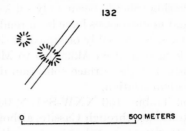

133. 80 diam × 2. Old Babylonian through Neo-Babylonian.

134. 60 diam × 1.5. Late Abbasid–Ilkhanid.

135. Abū Hasan. Low mounds, height 1m. Area approx. 1.5. ha. Sassanian.

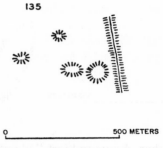

136. Tell Abū Halāwa. 180 N-S × 120 × 3, with low tail to SSE. Tell to SW is 70 diam × 3. 2.9 ha. area. Sassanian.

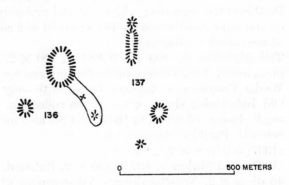

137. Tell Abū Halāwa. Main tell at N 220 N-S × 50 × 3.5. Middle tell 80 diam × 3.5. Approx. area 1.7 ha. While a few sherds suggest that a small settlement may have existed here in Cassite and Middle Babylonian times, the major occupation occurred only in the Neo-Babylonian and Achaemenian periods.

138. 100 diam × 1.5. One Cassite chalice base (7:A) seen. Sassanian.

139. 60 diam × 1. Overgrown with camelthorn. Neo-Babylonian–Achaemenian.

140. Tell Abū Khazaf al-Gharbi. Main mound 190 × 100 × 3.5. Canal between two summits is recently

SITE
NUMBER

abandoned, with high spoil-banks. 1.9 ha. area. Neo-Babylonian–Achaemenian.

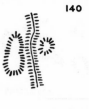

141. 90 diam × 2.5, with low tail extending 80m farther S. Approx. 1 ha. area assumed. Seleucid/Parthian–Sassanian.

142. Abū Khazaf. Mounds do not exceed 2m in height. Site surrounded by old canal banks, and in fact appears as such on Arabic 1:50,000 map. Assuming that the existing summits once were parts of a continuous settlement, its area would have been about 4.4 ha. Old Babylonian–Cassite.

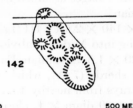

143. Abū Aglain. 240 N-S × 100 × 3 (at S end; N end lower). Bricks have been mined from site on small scale: 33 × 33 cms. Mainly Sassanian, but with traces of an underlying Neo-Babylonian settlement.

144. 170 diam × 4. Seleucid/Parthian–Sassanian.

145. Smaller summit lies immediately N of Mandali Road, is 100 E-W × 80 × 6.5. Neo-Babylonian–Achaemenian, continuing into the Parthian period on a smaller scale. Immediately S of road, in fact with N edge of site cut away by road, is tell 180 diam × 2.5. Seleucid/Parthian–Sassanian.

146. Height 2.5m. Neo-Babylonian–Seleucid/Parthian. Absence of diagnostic Achaemenian types noted.

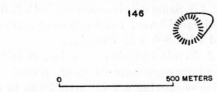

147. Tell Abū Jāwan. Height 3m. Late Abbasid–Ilkhanid.

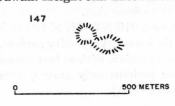

141

148. Largest mound 1.5m high. Sparse surface pottery. Sassanian, continuing into the Early Islamic period.

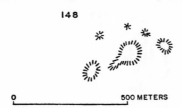

149. (1937) Tell Hant. 100 × 400 × 7. Cassite, Achaemenian.

150. Two tells 150 apart NE-SW. Each about 80 diam × 0.5. Sassanian.

151. Because of irrigation, only one small mound in middle of this long N-S chain could be visited. Most of the mounds are small and include canal spoil-banks, but height near north end reaches 3–3.5. Tells shown on map as extending for 3 kms NNE-SSW, but I believe total area of occupation does not exceed 16 ha. at most; 6 separate villages assumed from clusterings of debris. Sassanian.

152. 200 NW-SE × 140 × 2.5 Ur III/Larsa–Cassite, possibly continuing into Middle Babylonian.

153. 140 N-S × 120 × 1.5. Sassanian–Early Islamic, with a few Cassite sherds (7:A), which probably can be regarded as strays from nearby 152.

154. Two tells about 60 diam × 1, closely adjoining one another along a former NE-SW branch canal. Sassanian–Early Islamic.

155. Tell al-Bidwiyyah. Main mound 200 × 50 × 2. Approx. total area 3 ha. Seleucid/Parthian–Sassanian.

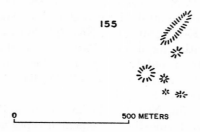

156. 160 diam × 4.5. Same debris continues both NW and SE along old canal levee. Total extent of settlement must exceed 4 ha. Seleucid/Parthian.

157. 60 diam × 2. Neo-Babylonian–Parthian. W and NW of this mound are numerous others of approximately the same size occupying a total area 750m in diam which was perhaps ½ continuously settled. Seleucid/Parthian–Sassanian.

158. Tell Lämlūm. 210 NW-SE × 120 × 5 (but southern half mostly lower). Very salty surface. Early Dynastic–Old Babylonian, with at best a small Cassite occupation (or perhaps only graves) suggested by rare chalice bases (7:A).

159. An area 180 diam is slightly elevated and hence out of cultivation. Sherds occur only on scattered hummocks and in most cases have been rendered unrecognizable by salt. Probably occupied at some time during the long span from Akkadian to Middle Babylonian times, but the surface collection did not permit a closer identification.

160. Tell Abū Tibbin. 150 NNW-SSE × 90 × 2.5. Warka/Protoliterate through Cassite, although the rarity of the latter suggests only a very small settlement or cemetery.

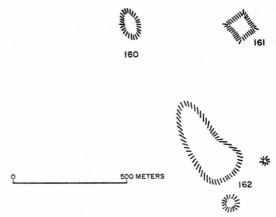

161. Tell Minther. A square "fort," about 120 × 120, rising to 2.5 around outer walls; interior 1.5 lower. Extensive pits and trenches for agricultural storage (?). Most of the observed surface pottery is Seleucid/Parthian; the remaining, older material probably indicates only that the nearby 162 was used as a source of mud-brick for the walls.

162. Tell Abū Tibbin. 400 NNW-SSE × 200 × 2. Approx. area 7.5 ha. Pottery badly decomposed by salt. Warka/Protoliterate through Larsa, with only one Old Babylonian sherd (6:C) in the collection. The small clusters of debris to the S and SE also include Seleucid/Parthian–Sassanian material.

163. (1937) 50 diam × 2.5. Cassite.

164. (1937) Abū Mujarish. 100 × 130 × 2. Ilkhanid.

165. 40 diam × 2. Neo-Babylonian–Achaemenian with a few sherds suggesting an earlier (Larsa–Middle Babylonian) occupation as well. 100m NNE lies a Seleucid/Parthian–Sassanian mound of approx. the same size.

166. 140 diam × 4, with a small outcrop 100m E. Possibly Ur III/Larsa. Certainly Old Babylonian and Cassite.

167. A low, rectangular site 800m E-W × 250 × 1.5 high around edges (lower in center). The large size and low height would seem to argue against this having been a fort, but at least the remains do suggest the existence of some sort of enclosing wall. Sassanian–Early Islamic and (after an apparent period of abandonment) Ilkhanid.

168. 120 diam × 2. Sassanian–Early Islamic.

169. Tell al-Ḥalfayah. 230 N-S × 140 × 7. Debris at plain level extends the site southward for an additional 90m. Approx. area 4.5 ha. Warka/Protoliterate through Old Babylonian.

170. 90 diam × 1. Neo-Babylonian–Achaemenian. A Seleucid/Parthian mound of approx. the same size lies about 400m NW.

171. 120 N-S × 60 × 2. Neo-Babylonian–Achaemenian. A very broad low levee extends N with scattered Parthian pottery along it for about 500m.

172. 90 diam × 1. Ilkhanid.

173. 100 diam × 1. Lies just SE of an ancient canal bed below plain level. Across canal to NW is a low bank with sparse sherds of same date. Sassanian–Early Islamic. One km to NE is a low mound about 100m diam of Sassanian date.

174. 110 NNE-SSW × 70 × 1.5. A disused road cuts through W part of site. Four very small mounds of same date lies to SSW. Approx. total area 2.5 ha. Sassanian.

175. Tulūl al-Shimlāsiyah. 80 NNE-SSW × 40 × 1.5. Across old canal from 174, but apparently somewhat earlier in date; 11:A is plentiful here and 13:A extremely rare, while the opposite is true on 174. (Parthian-) Sassanian.

176. Tell al-Haurah. 170 NW-SE × 80 × 2.5. Early Dynastic, perhaps continuing on a reduced scale into the Akkadian period.

177. 80 diam × 1.5. 300m to NNE is a still smaller mound, 30 diam × 1. Both are Sassanian.

178. 60 diam × 1. Sparse Sassanian pottery.

179. Bier ᶜAun. An old brick-lined well adjoining a very small, low mound. Well said to have been permanently dry until about 1946–48; now it has a permanent brackish water. Depth of water in April, 1958, about 6.5m, or about 4.5 below plain level, since both well and tell are situated on old, wide canal levee. Approx. area of site, 0.5 ha. Sāmarrān–Ilkhanid.

180. Two small settlements 50m apart N-S just E of high Nahrawān bank. Each about 50 diam × 1. Sassanian.

181. Tell Mussbagha. 100 diam × 4. 200m to S lies a high old canal bank running SE that still is locally called Jalūlā, the apparent name of the proto-Khurāsān canal in Abbasid sources. Sāmarrān–Ilkhanid and perhaps later.

182. Tell Ghadīr Hassnah. 120 diam × 3.5. Sāmarrān–Ilkhanid.

183. Tell Abū Ghazaf al-khabir. 200 diam × 4. Sāmarrān–Ilkhanid.

184. Tell Abū Ghazaf al-saghīr. 150 diam × 3 (but mostly less than 2). A detached extension to the SE of 183. Sāmarrān–Ilkhanid.

185. (1937) Medawar wastani. 80 × 130 × 3. Sāmarrān–Ilkhanid.

186. Tell Abū Qubūr. 250 EW × 80 × occasionally as much as 2 ht. Pottery sparse, and site blends with very old canal underneath it at either end, making original extent difficult to estimate. Neo-Babylonian–Achaemenian.

187. Tell Saleh. 100 diam × 3. Ilkhanid.

188. (1937) Efreiji. 150 diam × 3.5. Sāmarrān–Ilkhanid.

189. (1937) Abū Barabich. 200 × 300 × 4-5. Cassite.

190. (1937) Abū Thaᶜalib. 100 × 200 × 5. Sassanian, Late Abassid–Ilkhanid.

191. (1937) Tell Imām al-Abyadh. 100 × 300 × 2. Late Abbasid–Ilkhanid.

192. (1937) Bdeir. 200 × 250 × ht. not recorded. Ur III/Larsa–Cassite. Flint blades (2:g, h) suggest a possible pre-Sargonid occupation also.

193. (1937) Ageir. A series of mounds running from NW to SE. Surface collection made at the largest, a Cassite (and possibly earlier) mound 150 × 200 × 7. Remainder of series (assumed area, 4 ha.) Sassanian.

194. (1937) Haji Beid. 140 × 150 × (?). Seleucid/Parthian–Sassanian and Late Abbasid–Ilkhanid.

195. (1937) Haji Beid. 60 × 90 × (?). Cassite–Achaemenian.

196. (1937) Bahrzawi. 150 diam × 1. Pottery scarce, not distinctive. Probably Sassanian–Early Islamic.

197. Tell Itwaim. NW tell 90 diam × 3; SE tell 80 diam × 2. Old Babylonian–Neo-Babylonian.

198. Tell Abū Idragh. Large SE tell 4m, others 2.5m ht. Seleucid/Parthian, perhaps beginning in the Achaemenian period.

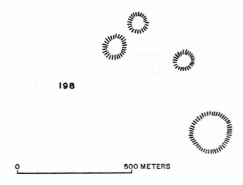

198

0   500 METERS

199. 90 diam × 1.5. Covered with pits and straw, pottery very sparse. Another smaller summit lies 150 NE. Sassanian.

200. 70 diam × 2. Collection indicated that site was mainly Sassanian, but there was also a limited Early Islamic occupation.

201. Probably 100 diam × 2, but so surrounded by old and new canal banks that real size is impossible to determine. Sassanian.

SITE
NUMBER

202. (1937) Tulūl Khirr Kushad. 100 × 180 × 1. Early Islamic–Sāmarrān.

203. Tell Shelef. 180 NW-SE × 70 × 2. Old Babylonian–Middle Babylonian and Seleucid/Parthian–Sassanian.

204. Tell Aswad. 140 diam × 2. Three very small outcrops lie to W. Sāmarrān.

205. Tell Abū Khanazīr. 130 diam × 2.5, with a long tail southeastward along old canal. Sassanian.

206. NW tell 3m, SE tell 2.5m ht. In addition to the mounds shown in sketch, a site 100 diam × 2 lies 1.5 km E. All are Sassanian.

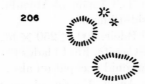

0 _____ 500 METERS

207. Tell al-Rōf. Most of site has been deeply trenched for melon cultivation. Sassanian. 2.2 kms SW along old canal is a small (about 1 ha.) site with Sāmarrān and Late Abbasid pottery.

208. Tell al-Murādiyah. 250 diam × 2. W end of mound cut off by road. 300m WNW is small tell 90 diam × 2. Both are Sassanian.

209. A small mound of indefinite size and height, surmounted by a brickkiln, is all that remains of what is shown on older maps as a large tell. Remains 700m farther E consist mainly of canal spoil-banks, with very sparse pottery. Possibly mainly of Sassanian date; very few identifiable sherds seen. (Assumed area, 0.5 ha.?).

210. 200 diam × 2. Surface pottery observed to be mainly Late Abbasid–Ilkhanid with only traces of Sassanian–Sāmarrān. Assumed area: later period, 4 ha.; earlier, 0.5 ha.

211. Tell Sakhar. Probably a khan or fort; rises to 3m around edges, low in center. Brick and mortar wall may have extended completely around it. Pottery extremely sparse. Several small mounds 250m N are also without pottery but with many brick and mortar fragments. Each of the latter is about 60 diam × 2.5. Approx. total area, 3.9 ha. Probably Sassanian.

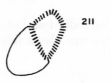

0 _____ 500 METERS

SITE
NUMBER

212. 120 diam × 2.5. Ur III/Larsa–Old Babylonian.

213. Tell Helib. 90 diam × 2.5., with outcrop to SE. Akkadian–Ur III/Larsa.

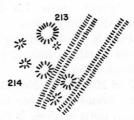

0 _____ 500 METERS

214. Tell Helib. Both major mounds are about 70 diam × 4. Warka/Protoliterate–Old Babylonian; small, low mounds to W and S are Seleucid/Parthian.

215. Tell at N end of group 200 diam × 4.5. One Achaemenian sherd (10:A), but site is mainly Seleucid/Parthian. For 500m S from this tell extend low ruins interspersed with canal banks, but debris is sparse and occupied area must have been small. S of this area is another irregular occupational cluster, about 150 diam × 2, which appeared to be slightly earlier although also continuing into Parthian times. Neo-Babylonian–Parthian. Assumed area of occupation in the Neo-Babylonian and Achaemenian periods: 1 ha.; in the Seleucid/Parthian period: 7 ha.

216. 110 NNE-SSW × 50 × 2 (at S end; N end low). Sparse, not distinctive pottery of the Seleucid/Parthian or Sassanian periods.

217. Tell Dhiliᶜ. 140 NNE-SSW × 90 × 4, but the N end is low and with only sparse sherds and debris. Traces of a large buttressed building of mud brick can be seen on the surface at the S end. Akkadian–Old Babylonian.

218. 300 NE-SW × 200. Mostly very low, but a mound of about 40 diam near NE end rises to 3. Here there are very clear mud brick walls forming a large square building with concentric walls and ornamental buttresses. 600 WNW is another large area of debris belonging to the same period (200 diam × 2.5). Seleucid/Parthian.

219. Irregular scatter of low (1–2m) Sassanian tells along an old branch canal, representing at least 400 × 400 of continuous settlement.

220. Tulūl Khattāb. 150 NW-SE × 100 × 6. One sherd (2:e) suggests a Warka/Protoliterate occupation. Site is mainly Ur III/Larsa through Cassite. The latter period is particularly well represented.

221. Tulūl Khattāb. 100 diam × 4. Bulk of surface material Warka/Protoliterate through Akkadian. What little Ur III/Larsa and Old Babylonian material there was may come only from graves. Probably this tell

144

can be regarded as the forerunner of the later and larger settlement of 220 and 222. Together all three form a contiguous unit in the northern part of this very large, long-lived, and important complex of mounds.

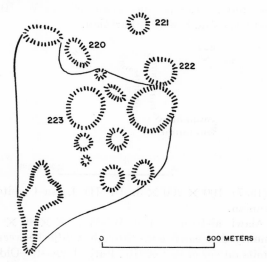

222. Tulūl Khaṭṭāb. 140 diam × 7. Akkadian–Neo-Baby-lonian.
223. Tulūl Khaṭṭāb. Thirteen mounds of 4–6m elevation covering area of at least 750 × 750. The Neo-Baby-lonian and Achaemenian surface remains are limited to tell in the extreme SE of group. Remainder is main-ly Seleucid/Parthian. Neo-Babylonian–Achaemenian assumed area 2 ha.; Seleucid/Parthian, 56 ha.; Sas-sanian, approx. 20 ha.
224. 90 diam × 1.5. Pottery sparse. Sassanian.
225. TellᶜAtash. Ht. 4m. Early Dynastic–Larsa. Many sherds of Sassanian storage jars, including one partly exposed with child burial unaccompanied by objects. Perhaps the Sassanian component represents only a cemetery, but in that case it would be a large one.

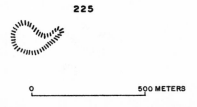

226. 180 NE-SW × 120 × 1. Sassanian, Ilkhanid.
227. TellᶜAtash. Main tell 100 diam × 5, with a ruined police post on top. To SE is a tell of same period 60 diam × 1.5. Seleucid/Parthian.
228. Tell at end of old canal branch is 160 NW-SE × 90 × 2; surface inspection suggested it continued from Sas-sanian times into the Late Abbasid period with one sherd (10:A) suggesting a possible underlying Achae-menian occupation. Higher up the branch to the NW is tell 70 diam × 1.5; apparently Late Abbasid, but

composed mostly of brick and with sparse pottery. Farther NW near the inlet of branch is large tell in-termingled with canal bank; sparse Sassanian sherds.
229. Tell Halāwa. 330 NW-SE × 220 × 2.5. Warka/ Pro-toliterate–Old Babylonian.
230. 200 E-W × 80 × 1. Sassanian.
231. (1937) Tell Dhahab. 150 × 200 × 2–3. Sāmarrān–Ilkhanid.
232. 120 diam × 3.5. Two Neo-Babylonian sherds (9:A) suggest an occupation of this date. Mainly Seleucid/ Parthian–Sassanian.
233. Tell al-Baghi. 110 diam × 3. Mainly Late Abbasid–Ilkhanid, but with a possible Sassanian–Sāmarrān occupation as well.
234. Tell al-Tayyān. Mounds 280 × 120 × 3 and 120 diam × 2.5. Seleucid/Parthian, possibly continuing into the Sassanian period.

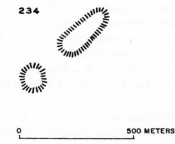

235. Tell al-Madār. Three small tells forming a triangle with its apex at N. Two are less than 100 diam × 1, at N end elev. of 1.5 is reached. Sassanian.
236. Tell al-Madār. 60 diam × 1. Sāmarrān–Ilkhanid.
237. Tell Zuᶜaytir. 200 diam × 2.5. Village on N end of tell. Sassanian–Ilkhanid.
238. 70 diam × 2.5. A brickkiln of indeterminate date stands on top. Neo-Babylonian–Achaemenian.
239. Tell Muhesin. 60 diam × 1.5. Another tell of same date, 30 diam × 1.5, lies 100 WNW. Achaemenian–Parthian.
240. (1937) Three small mounds in row; largest 80 diam × 1–2. Seleucid/Parthian.
241. 100 diam × 1.5. Sassanian.
242. (1937) 100 × 150 × 2. Seleucid/Parthian–Sassanian. There also appears to have been a small Ilkhanid occupation.
243. (1937) 100 diam × 2–3. Seleucid/Parthian.
244. Tell Asmar–ancient Eshnunna. From a beginning, in the Warka/Protoliterate period (or probably even earlier), Tell Asmar maintained what seems to have been a virtually continuous sequence of occupation until its abandonment at the end of the Ur III/Larsa period. Serving at times as the prosperous political capital of the region, at other times large areas within its walls were in ruins. For site map and sequence of occupation see Delougaz, P. 1952. Pl. 201 and Table

145

III. (Pottery from the Diyala Region. *Oriental Institute Publications*, No. 63. Chicago).

245. (1937) Two small mounds, assumed area 1 ha., Sassanian.

246. Tell Amlah. 400 diam $\times$ 2.5, with small outcrops occurring to the S of main tell. Seleucid/Parthian–Sassanian.

247. Tell al-Wān. 280 NW-SE $\times$ 160 $\times$ 5. Mainly Ur III/Larsa–Cassite with what appears to have been a thin Sassanian occupation over most of its surface.

248. 100 EW $\times$ 60 $\times$ 2.5. Tell was concluded from visit to be mainly Sassanian with very little Early Islamic. To N are several dozen small (10–50 diam $\times$ 1–1.5m) summits of Sassanian date only. Total area about 4 ha.

249. (1937) A very small settlement (assumed area .2 ha.) adjoining old canal bank. Sassanian pottery observed.

250. Eight major 1.5–2.5m summits within area 500m sq. All fairly irregular in outline, many outcrops. Same debris occurs on a small area (1.5 ha.) 2 kms W and on a larger area (400 $\times$ 700, but less than half occupied) 1–2 kms WSW. Regarded as one 25 ha. town, one 12 ha. town, one 1.5 ha. village. All Sassanian.

251. An area 110 diam has low 1.5m mounds around edge, but debris at center is at plain level; possibly a former fort. Seleucid/Parthian.

252. Tell Abū Jaʿarī. 300 $\times$ 350 $\times$ 8. Figures reflect only the central mounds and do not include a long extension to S and a large, low area to NW. Based on air photos and reconnaissance, this sprawling settlement covered at least 1.5 sq. kms. It is unique in its extensions outward from the central core along numerous waterways, and in the great hub of ancient canals which it seems to form. Islamic pottery very sparse; settlement essentially confined to the Sassanian period.

253. 250 N-S $\times$ 100; N summit 3, S summit 3.5. N end is entirely Ur III/Larsa–Cassite, S end is Akkadian–Old Babylonian with only Cassite graves. Baked bricks 30 $\times$ 20 $\times$ 9 cms. Debris extends at plain level N to an additional summit 140 N-S $\times$ 30 $\times$ 2. Three more very small summits of same date occur 300 NNW of latter, and low debris extends at least 300 farther NNW before finally disappearing. 20 E of the N end of the main tell occurs another little outcrop of the same period. Although not very wide, this settlement thus ran fairly continuously for at least 1.3 kms along a NNW-SSE line. Early Dynastic–Cassite.

254. Scatter of 14 small Sassanian–Early Islamic tells within 1500 NNW-SSE $\times$ 600 $\times$ 1.5–2. Average size about 50 diam. Approx. 4 clusters or villages.

255. (1937) Imām Hmoid. 60 $\times$ 180 $\times$ 1. Late Abbasid–Ilkhanid.

256. 250 WNW-ESE $\times$ 90 $\times$ 1.5. Ur III/Larsa–Old Babylonian.

257. Tulūl Derbanji. Same name and dating applies to scattered outcrops and small tells to W. Ht. near center, 3.5m. Seleucid/Parthian.

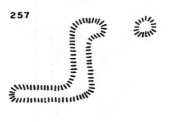

257

0   500 METERS

258. (1937) 100 $\times$ 200 $\times$ 3. Ur III/Larsa–Cassite, Sassanian.

259. ʿAlawi al-Humir. 150 WNW-ESE $\times$ 80 $\times$ 1.5. A newly dug canal cuts through saddle between summits on either end of site. Early Dynastic–Old Babylonian. Short distance to the NW is a small tell (assumed 1 ha.) with a Sassanian occupation.

260. Tell Sebʿe. 4 small tells in NW-SE line, each about 100 $\times$ 130 $\times$ 2. Older periods apparently on SE mounds, younger on other two. Ur III/Larsa–Cassite, Sassanian.

261. 100 N-S $\times$ 70 $\times$ 2. Early Dynastic–Larsa.

262. 80 diam $\times$ 1.5. Site mainly Seleucid/Parthain—difficulty in finding early sherds may indicate that apparent earlier occupation was not a significant one. Early Dynastic, Cassite, Seleucid/Parthian.

263. Tell Umm Jirin rises to 2.5 only at center. Sassanian–Early Islamic. A small (.5 ha.) Sassanian site lies 1 km N. Apparently a glass kiln site; at any rate, great quantities of molten glass refuse were noted.

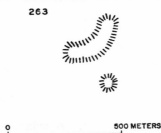

263

0   500 METERS

264. (1937) Tulūl Dhibaʿi (C). 150 $\times$ 300 $\times$ 5, not including a long narrow spur toward SW. Early Dynastic, Old Babylonian–Cassite.

265. (1937) Tulūl Dhibaʿi (D). 60 $\times$ 120 $\times$ 2. Early Dynastic, Sassanian.

266. (1937) Tulūl Dhibaʿi (E). 60 $\times$ 70 $\times$ 2–3. Sassanian.

267. (1937) Tulūl Dhibaʿi (B). 200 $\times$ 250 $\times$ 4. ʿUbaid–Early Dynastic.

SITE
NUMBER

268. (1937). Tulūl Dhiba⁽ (A). 200 × 250 × 4.5. Early Islamic–Sāmarrān.

269. Tell Abū Chīt. Main tell 200 diam × 5, but debris is sparse around edges. Debris runs off fairly continuously ENE for 500–700m, with three minor summits. Scattered houses on W and SW slopes. Cassite bases (7:A) noted as present but not numerous; mainly Seleucid/Parthian–Sassanian.

270. Tell Gergur. 70 E-W × 40 × 2. Early Dynastic.

271. Tulūl Garagir. Main mound 160 × 100 × 1.5; others same ht. Mainly Sassanian; Islamic pottery confined to SW tell.

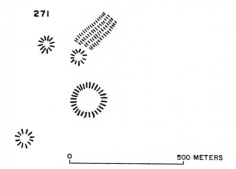

272. 50 diam × 1.5. Sassanian.

273. Tell Zengalīk. Main tell 160 diam × 3, with scattered small summits and debris on all sides suggesting settlement greater than 200 diam. Early Islamic–Sāmarrān sherds noted as very rare on surface. Mainly Late Abbasid–post-Ilkhanid.

274. Old Babylonian sherds found only on middle tell (160 × 140 × 2.5), and very sparse there; apparently a very small occupation of that date. On top of SE tell (300 × 180 × 3) there is a low outer wall 80m sq. that may represent a fort. This and other mounds are mainly or entirely Sassanian.

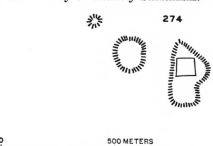

275. Tell al-Dīmī. Ht. of main mound 4 m. Predominantly Seleucid/Parthian, continuing into the Sassanian period.

276. (1937) Tīamūr. Measurements not recorded. Early Dynastic.

277. Tell Abū Halfayah. 100 diam × 2. Seven much smaller summits to E and SE. Early Islamic–Late Abbasid.

278. At least 18 summits within 1 sq. km; settlements clus-

SITE
NUMBER

tered in NE and SW quadrants. Mounds all 1–3m high, sparsely covered with debris. Assumed total area 10 ha., mainly Sassanian. Sparse traces of Early Dynastic (3:E).

279. 110 diam × 1.5. Sparse Sassanian pottery.

280. (1937) Tell Abū Mishmish. 100 × 200 × (?) (estimate, not measured). Early Islamic–Late Abbasid.

281. Abū Derwīsh. 160 diam × 5. Several summits, modern graves, a few pits. Sassanian pottery observed— also on scattered group of tells to SE.

282. (1937) Tell Abū Samada. 100 × 200 × (?). Nondescript surface pottery assigned an Early Islamic date at time of visit.

283. 80 diam × 2.5. Old Babylonian–Cassite.

284. 100 diam × 2.5. Old Babylonian–Cassite.

285. 60 diam × 2.5. Old Babylonian–Cassite.

286. Tell Borākhān. 150 diam × 6. Mainly Seleucid/Parthian pottery noted at site, although several Cassite bases (7:A; possibly only strays from 283–85) were seen.

287. Tell Borākhān al-saghīr. About 1 km N-S × 200 (avg.) × up to 3m. Many summits. Seleucid/Parthian–Early Islamic.

288. 160 NW-SE × 90 × 5.5. Old Babylonian–Neo-Babylonian, with a very minor Early Islamic–Sāmarrān surface component. From N foot of this high mound a lower Sassanian tell runs 300m NE-SW × 120 × 1–2 ht.

289. Main mound 80 diam × 6.5, Old Babylonian–Middle Babylonian. On summit there is a later building, possibly a Sassanian fort.

290. 600 N-S along old canal × 40–120 (avg. about 80) × up to 2. Sparse Sassanian debris mixed with canal banks.

291. 200 ENE-WSW × 60 × 2.5. Old Babylonian–Middle Babylonian.

292. Tell Abū Dhaba⁽. One of a practically continuous line of tells and debris. 250 NNE-SSW × 120 × 4. Approx. total area 5 ha. Seleucid/Parthian–Sassanian.

293. 80 diam × 1.5. Old Babylonian–Middle Babylonian.

294. Irregular scatter of tells for about 1.5 kms along old ENE-WSW watercourse. Largest summit 100 diam × 2.5. Total area 1.5–2.0 ha. Cassite, Seleucid/Parthian.

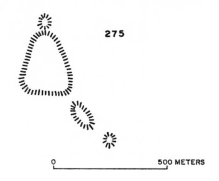

147

295. 180 diam $\times$ 3, also a smaller summit to S. Both are Old Babylonian–Cassite. Remainder of group mainly Sassanian but includes a small Seleucid/Parthian settlement (approx. total area 8 ha.).

296. 80 diam $\times$ 3. Old Babylonian–Cassite.

297. 110 E-W $\times$ 60 $\times$ 2.5. Akkadian–Cassite, with one sherd (3:E) suggesting a possible Early Dynastic occupation.

298. 90 diam (slightly longer N-S) $\times$ 2 (?). Heavy saline crust. Early Dynastic–Old Babylonian.

299. Approx. area 1 ha. Low tells difficult to distinguish from accompanying canal bank. Small, irregular areas of debris and sparse sherds. Much recent disturbance by bulldozers and silt-mining for brick-kiln immediately to N. Early Islamic sherds noted to very few in number; probably only strays. Sassanian.

300. A continuation to the S of 299 but with denser debris, higher tells. Still impossible to separate occupational debris from canal banks. Total area about 500 $\times$ 500 $\times$ up to 3—although probably only $\frac{1}{2}$ of this is continuous settlement. It may be significant that the distinction between this site as mostly Seleucid/Parthian (with some Sassanian) and 299 as Sassanian emerged from study of the collections and was not apparent at the time they were made. Approx. total area 12 ha.

301. Tell Sudairah. 300 $\times$ 250 $\times$ 4. Active excavation of mound underway at time of visit for nearby brick factory. Early Islamic–Ilkhanid.

301

0   500 METERS

302. 100 NW-SE $\times$ 70 $\times$ 2. Akkadian (possibly continuing into the Ur III/Larsa period).

303. Tulūl Wuldayah. 90 diam $\times$ 4. Cassite–Neo-Babylonian.

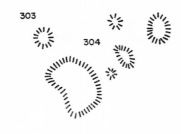

303

304

0   500 METERS

304. Tulūl Wuldayah. The diagnostic pottery here is clearly Seleucid/Parthian, but there are plainware affinities with nearby 303 which may suggest continuity between them. Maximum ht. 6m.

305. Tell Munaisif. 80 diam $\times$ 4. Akkadian–Cassite.

306. 60 diam $\times$ 1. All but central part has been trenched for cultivation (Ur III/Larsa) Old Babylonian–Cassite.

307. 100 diam $\times$ 3. Akkadian–Old Babylonian.

308. Tell Isheiri, formerly called Sifwah, both names denoting "stone" or "rock" and deriving from the many fragments of baked bricks which cover it. The mound is divided by the Nahrawān into a small western and a large eastern mound, the western mound being cut on its W side by the Diyala. The cut exposes several brick wells or drains. The occupation layer seemed shallow, about 2m. Surviving mound is 250 N-S $\times$ 100, but a broken continuation farther S appears on air photos. Approx. original area, 5 ha.(?). Sassanian–Sāmarrān. See account of town in text, pp. 91–92.

309. Tell Isheiri, or Sifwah. Approx. area of mound E of Nahrawān Canal 20 ha. (Max. dimensions 850 $\times$ 350). Sassanian–post-Ilkhanid.

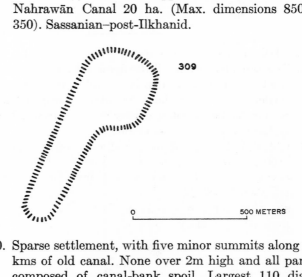

309

0   500 METERS

310. Sparse settlement, with five minor summits along 1.2 kms of old canal. None over 2m high and all partly composed of canal-bank spoil. Largest 110 diam. Approx. total area, 3 ha. Mainly Sassanian; same date applies to very small tell 1.8 kms W.

311. N tell in group is 70 diam $\times$ 2. Main cluster centers 500m farther S along old canal, consists of seven small tells mostly about 40 diam $\times$ 1.5 but reaching 90 diam $\times$ 2 on E end. Seleucid/Parthian–Sassanian.

312. Seven distinguishable (although only partially disjoined) tells, averaging 50 diam $\times$ 1.5. Sassanian.

313. 100 diam $\times$ 3. Sassanian–Late Abbasid. On S Nahrawān bank and 100m downstream is a Sassanian settlement 150m long with sparse pottery. Farther downstream the Nahrawān opens out abruptly into a much wider pool recalling that below the Qantara weir. In addition, the very high and numerous canal banks taking off both sides of the Nahrawān above

this point strikingly recall the Qantara weir. In short, this may be "Upper Weir" of the Arabic sources, with the weir itself having been destroyed almost completely by brick-robbers.

314. Imām Abū ᶜArrūj. 300m NNW-SSE × 70. Debris of settlement rises 1.5 over ht. of underlying canal bank. A recent cemetery lies around the undistinguished Imām building. Ilkhanid–post-Ilkhanid.

315. 120 diam × 3. Concluded from visit that Sassanian–Early Islamic apparently was terminal level in SE part of site, while smaller Sāmarrān and Late Abbasid was confined to NW and center of tell.

316. (1937) 100 diam × 2–3. Seleucid/Parthian–Sassanian.

317. (1937) Tell Meyah khabir. Relatively small, assumed area, 1 ha. Sassanian.

318. (1937) Tell Meyah saghīr. A group of 3 small mounds, each 100 × 150 × 2. Early Islamic–Late Abbasid.

319. Irregular outcrops of small debris occur to N of tell that is shown. 1–1.5m high. Approx. total area, 3.8 ha. Sassanian.

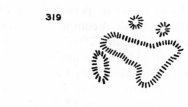

319

0 _____ 500 METERS

320. 550 NNW-SSE along old canal bank in six clusters 50–100 diam × 1.5–2.0. Many low canal banks confuse site area. Approx. area 3.6 ha. Sassanian–Early Islamic, with a single Cassite sherd (7:A).

321. 100 diam × 1.5. Lies on old canal bank. Mainly Neo-Babylonian–Achaemenid, with three sherds (6:D) suggesting a possible Old Babylonian occupation.

322. Seven small summits of about 10–20 diam avg. × 1–1.5m, forming an irregular NNE-SSW chain for 500m. These are all Sassanian, but at N end, abutting old canal branch, the Sassanian occupation is overlaid by an Ilkhanid level on a tell 60 diam × 1. N of this, just across old canal, is a tell 70 diam × 2; 40m farther N is another of same area. Both of latter are Sassanian only.

323. Irregular cluster of mounds comprising a scattered settlement of about 2 ha., max. ht. 2–2.5. Mainly Seleucid/Parthian with a smaller Sassanian settlement.

324. Twelve summits of 10–20 diam × 1.5, plus scattered surface debris. Fairly continuous settlement within area 250 in diam. Sassanian.

325. (1937) 300m along old canal levee; width and ht. not noted. Assumed area, 2 ha. Sassanian.

326. Tell al-Mujardam. 130 diam (slightly longer axis

E-W) × 3. Achaemenian, probably continuing on a smaller scale into the Seleucid/Parthian period.

327. Tell on E end of group 140 diam × 3. Irregular scatter of small low summits continues W and WNW for 500m. Perhaps a total area of 4 ha. Seleucid/Parthian.

328. 900 NS along old canal × 50–80 × 1. 600m S of southern end is another small accumulation of debris of about .2 ha. Sassanian.

329. Tulūl Umm al-Tarish. A great, irregular, horseshoe-shape with many outlying small tells. Following around the horseshoe, one must have almost 1.5 kms of length × 100–150 width, up to 3m ht. Approx. total area, 18 ha. Seleucid/Parthian-Sassanian.

330. 190 diam × 2. Sparse pottery, Sassanian.

331. Tulūl Umm al-Tarish. 120 E-W × 80 × 3. Achaemenian.

332. Tulūl Umm al-Tarish. 500 NW-SE × 100–180 × 3. Dimensions may include some canal banks, but surface debris is uniformly thick. Sassanian.

333. 120 E-W × 80 × 2.5. Seleucid/Parthian–Sassanian.

334. 140 NNE-SSW × 70 × 2.5. Sassanian.

335. 600 E-W × 100 × 3, with small outlying tells to NE, NNW, S. Possibly Seleucid/Parthian in part, but mainly Sassanian.

336. 180 N-S × 110 × 2.5. Sassanian.

337. ᶜAlāwi Bismār. Main tell 240 NNW-SSE × 90 or less × 2.5, but low debris stretches off indefinitely to SE. Another tell about 90 diam × 2 lies W and slightly S of main summit. Sassanian.

338. Tell Jimᶜah. Very large, irregular shape, with two tails projecting SE, one tail SW. Main tell in N central part rises 5m. From apex of triangle on N to end of SE tails is 1 km; from apex to end of SW tail is at least 1.5 kms. Something approaching 1 sq. km of settlement must have existed here during the Sassanian period. Sparser Seleucid/Parthian debris suggests an earlier settlement of roughly a fourth that size.

339. 90 diam × 1.5. Possibly Middle Babylonian. Certainly Neo-Babylonian–Achaemenid.

340. 100 diam × 1. Questionable Akkadian sherds (4:d). Ur III/Larsa.

341. Main mound 100 NW-SE × 60 × 1.5. Another 70 NW-SE × 60 × 1, lies 70m E across low intervening area of debris. Early Dynastic, Ur III/Larsa–Cassite. Assumed area, 1.0 ha.

342. (1937) Tell Khuweish. A group of seven small hillocks, the biggest 100 × 150 × (?). Seleucid/Parthian. Two flint blades (2:h) may suggest a small pre-Sargonid occupation.

343. 60 diam × 1. Short distance to WNW is an area at plain level 150 diam covered with pottery of same date: Akkadian–Old Babylonian.

149

344. SE mound 80 NW-SE $\times$ 30 $\times$ 1. NW mound 50 diam $\times$ 1, lies 40m away. Latter is mainly Ur III/Larsa–Old Babylonian to judge from surface inspection, while former had one ᶜUbaid sherd (1:A) and a predominantly Early Dynastic–Larsa occupation. Just E of the S mound is some minor Sassanian settlement not represented in the collection.

345. (1937) 100 $\times$ 200 $\times$ (?). Sassanian, with two isolated finds (2:h; 5:j) hinting at a small earlier settlement.

346. 170 NW-SE $\times$ 120 $\times$ 2.5, with a low extension to NE from middle of tell. Sassanian.

347. (1937) Umoyl. The junction of three ancient canal heads, with traces of an adjoining small settlement. Assumed area, .5 ha. Early Islamic–Late Abbasid.

348. Tell Abū Sukheir. 200m ENE-WSW $\times$ 100 $\times$ 5.5. Much broken brick, very sparse pottery. Sassanian.

349. 120 N-S $\times$ 50 $\times$ 1.5. Seleucid/Parthian.

350. 40 diam $\times$ 2.5. Early Dynastic–Larsa. Three lower tells of equal area to NNW, ENE, and E are all of Sassanian date.

351. E tell 140 NNW-SSE $\times$ 50 $\times$ 3. Center tell (across old canal from former) 50 diam $\times$ 2. W tell still smaller. Early Islamic–Sāmarrān.

352. Irregular area with perhaps 10 small summits, all 40m or less diam $\times$ 1–1.5 ht. Approx. total area 1.2 ha. Sassanian.

353. Close-spaced cluster of three tells in form of triangle, each 50–100 diam $\times$ 2. Area 1.5 ha. Seleucid/Parthian–Sassanian.

354. Tulūl Shilbiyāt. 150 NW-SE $\times$ 80 $\times$ 1.5. Main occupation Early Dynastic–Larsa, with the latter especially well represented. One sherd (2:e) hints at a Protoliterate occupation.

355. Tulūl Shilbiyāt. Elevated area is only 70 diam $\times$ 3, but debris extends for 150 NE, 350 NW of its foot. Main occupation Early Dynastic–Akkadian, although continuing into Ur III/Larsa. Approx. area, 3 ha.

355

0   500 METERS

356. 230 NW-SE $\times$ 130 $\times$ 2.5. Mainly Early Islamic, but continuing into the Sāmarrān and Late Abbasid periods on a smaller scale.

357. 70 NW-SE $\times$ 40 $\times$ 1.5. Early Dynastic–Larsa. A larger, lower mound of Sassanian debris lies immediately adjoining to the W (.5 ha.).

358. Tell Salāmah. A large, complex group of tells stretch-

ing 1.2 kms NNE-SSW. Main concentration is in N, where group is 600 wide $\times$ 4. Less dense elsewhere, but debris is everywhere fairly continuous. Small outcrop 600m E. Assumed area, 20 ha. Seleucid/Parthian–Sassanian.

359. Debris at plain level within approx. 200 diam. Early Dynastic. 800m to the SW is a tell 100 diam $\times$ 3.5. Seleucid/Parthian–Sassanian. 300m NE is a small tell with irregular outline where only Sassanian pottery was observed.

360. (1937) Abū Khusan khabir. 250 diam $\times$ 2. Early Islamic–Sāmarrān.

361. Several small tells closely grouped for 400m along N-S line. Of irregular size, but none exceeding 2 high $\times$ perhaps 80 diam. Assumed area, 3.2 ha. Sassanian–Early Islamic.

362. 130 NW-SE $\times$ 100 $\times$ 1.5. Traces on summit of mound of a large, multiroomed mud brick building. Late Islamic pottery observed to be widespread on site but thin everywhere. Quantities of solid-foot goblets (3:B) suggest that site was abandoned early in Early Dynastic period. Early Dynastic, Ilkhanid.

363. Tulūl Rughāth. A complex group of 20 major summits occupying an area 700 diam. Fairly continuous settlement, to judge from profuse debris on plain between tells. Concluded from visit that while Early Islamic was widespread, Sassanian was the dominant component. Assumed area 49 ha. Sassanian; 20 ha. Early Islamic.

364. Tulūl Rughāth. Two tells each 70 diam $\times$ 3, 40m apart on a N-S line. Warka–Old Babylonian.

365. (1937) Tulūl Rad. Three small mounds, each about 100 diam Early Islamic.

366. Tell Sebᶜe. 300 diam $\times$ 5. Site is crescent-shaped, with a big bay cut into S side. This reduces area considerably (perhaps $\frac{1}{2}$), if rising plain here does not merely conceal a lower-lying section of settlement. Early Dynastic–Larsa.

367. (1937) Group of low mounds, each about 100 diam. Sassanian, assumed area, 3 ha.

368. (1937) 100 diam $\times$ 4. Considerable chipped flint (2:f, g, h) suggests a pre-Sargonid occupation. Mainly Ur III/Larsa, Sassanian–Early Islamic.

369. 120 diam $\times$ 2. Early Islamic–Late Abbasid.

370. 300 diam $\times$ 1. A small, low site for so long a span of occupation. Traces of the Early Dynastic (3:E) and Cassite (7:B) periods. Akkadian through Old Babylonian.

371. Tell Mukherīj. An irregular group of mounds at an old canal nexus. Low remains of a brick-and-mortar tower near the middle of complex are of 37 $\times$ 37 $\times$ 7 cm. (Sassanian) brick. Possibly these are re-used, or else the one Sassanian sherd in collection signifies a minor earlier occupation. Total area hard to com-

pute, since canal banks and tells merge. Perhaps the main tell is 400 × 200, with an equal area in scattered summits around it, none over 2 high. Sassanian–Ilkhanid.

372. Tell Mukherīj. A group composed of seven little summits, averaging less than 100 diam, of which only the highest reaches 3 m. Assumed area, 4.0 ha. Two in SE are Early Dynastic–Akkadian, possibly with Islamic graves only. Others are Early Islamic–Sāmarrān.

373. Tell Mukherīj. N mound within former enclosure wall (?) 4m high, elsewhere only 2m high. Early Islamic.

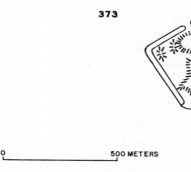

0   500 METERS

374. 140 N-S × 90 × 1. Sassanian.

375. 90 diam × 2.5. Another summit 140 N-S × 90 × 2. Five or six other much smaller surrounding summits. Approx. area, 3 ha. One Cassite "stray" (7:A). Seleucid/Parthian–Sassanian.

376. 100 diam × 3. Sassanian.

377. About 500 NE-SW × 100 max. (mostly less) × 1–2.5 high. Ill-defined, spread along old canal bank. Assumed area, 3 ha. Early Islamic.

378. (1937) 100 × 200 × (?). Early Islamic.

379. Main tell roughly 200 diam (but irregular outline) × 4. Estimated total area of settlement 7 ha. Sassanian–Early Islamic.

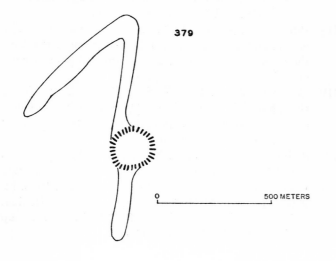

0   500 METERS

380. NW tell (150 × 110 × 1) Old Babylonian. SE tell (180 × 70 × 1.5) Akkadian–Larsa. One sherd (2:e) hints at a Warka/Protoliterate occupation.

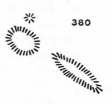

0   500 METERS

381. Low tell mixed with later canal bank. About 100 diam × 0.5 ht. Early Dynastic–Larsa; two sherds (6:C, E) suggest that a limited occupation may have continued into the Old Babylonian period.

382. Central mound is 140 E-W × 80 × 2.5, with two very small outlying tells to N and E. Early Islamic–Sāmarrān.

383. 130 diam × 1.5. Early Islamic.

384. Abū Zambīl. Surface pottery not plentiful and boundaries of mound hard to define. About 450m diam. Rises in NW corner abruptly to a high, sharp ridge 9 high and 90 long × 30 wide. One ᶜUbaid sherd (1:B) found here. Remainder of site much lower, 2–3 high. A little Sassanian–Early Islamic debris and pottery, especially on small outlying mounds to SW and SE. Old Babylonian sparse and perhaps represents only graves. Site is primarily ᶜUbaid–Larsa, and an important one for this long period.

385. Scattered small tells 1–2m high. Approx 2 ha. total area. Sassanian–Sāmarrān.

386. 200 N-S × 140 × 3.5. Early Islamic–Late Abbasid.

387. 80 diam × 1.5. Sassanian.

388. 100 diam × 2, with debris tailing off indefinitely N along old canal. Sassanian.

389. 150 diam at plane level; sherds moderately thick. Old Babylonian–Middle Babylonian.

390. A thin scatter of sherds for 120 NE-SW × 60 × 0.2 ht. along old, low levee. Old Babylonian–Middle Babylonian.

391. Tell Abū Dhabiᶜ. 170 NE-SW × 80 × 2.5. Early Islamic.

392. 150 diam at plain level, sherds moderately thick. Old Babylonian–Middle Babylonian.

393. 100 diam × 1.5. Another mound to NE is lower, about 80 diam. Uniform debris on both and on intervening plain. Early Islamic–Ilkhanid, with the later pottery being particularly fine in spite of the small size of the site.

394. Two tells on NE-SW line, each 70 diam × 1. Mainly Sassanian, with a smaller Sāmarrān—Late Abbasid occupation. One Cassite "stray" (7:A).

SITE
NUMBER

395. Tell al-ʿArīdh al-khabir. 170 diam, with a low tail to the SE along old canal. Sāmarrān–Ilkhanid.

396. Tell al-ʿArīdh. 210 E-W × 140 × 2. One ʿUbaid celt (1:C), Early Dynastic, Ur III/Larsa–Cassite.

397. Tulūl Abū Yiwālik. About 350 diam, but E-W dimension is slightly the larger. W summit 2.5, E summit 3, with a saddle between; E summit again divided into a N and S summit. Much evidence of mud-brick architecture, probably including one or more temples (there is even a fairly convincing little "altar" in one), streets, and houses. Mainly ʿUbaid–Larsa; Old Babylonian–Cassite material occurs only on extreme E end. An important site deserving further attention.

398. Tulūl Abū Yiwālik. Main tell is 320 N-S × 200 × 3.5. Highest near N end, very low at S. Akkadian–Larsa. A small (about 1 ha.) Sassanian tell lies alongside.

399. Tulūl Abū Yiwālik. 160 diam × 5. Old Babylonian–Cassite.

400. Five small summits, all about 50 diam × 1–1.5. To the SW are three small, semidetached summits of about 50 diam × 1. Approx. total area, 1.5 ha. Old Babylonian–Cassite.

401. 120 diam × 1. Sāmarrān–Ilkhanid.

402. 120 diam × 1. Sāmarrān–Late Abbasid.

403. Tell Imām Bajli. NW of the Imām is a tell 110 diam × 2.5, about 250 away. Imām stands on NW end of a low tell strewn with brick fallen from tower; no pottery seen here. At SE end of group is a tell 100 diam × 3, covered with graves. Mound to NW is Early Islamic–Sāmarrān; mound to SE is Late Abbasid–Ilkhanid. The Imām tower is in precarious condition, but still largely intact. Constructed of 22 × 22 cm bricks, replaced in some places with rectangular ones half as wide as long.

404. Tell Abū Sijlah. N mound in group is 40 diam × 4, with low, larger outliers to N and E. Early Islamic–Sāmarrān. Middle tell 140 N-S × 80 × 2. S tell 100 diam × 3.5. Latter include some Sāmarrān, but apparently are mainly Late Abbasid–Ilkhanid.

405. 120 diam × 2. Sāmarrān–Late Abbasid.

406. NW tell 200 diam × 4. A smaller tell adjoins it to S. SE tell 250 N-S × 150 × 4. Sāmarrān–Ilkhanid.

407. Nine low summits (max. 2 high) occupying perhaps half their total enclosed area of 500 × 500. Sassanian.

408. Two small tells deep in leached depression (haur), 70–90 diam × 1.5–2.0 high. Sassanian.

409. Tell al-Imdēfir. Rectangular mound 140 × 60 × 5. Extensions at lower height to N and SE. Composed mainly of 34 × 34 cm bricks and mortar, with traces of inner rooms and a large court to be seen on top as depressions. Pottery very rare. Sassanian.

SITE
NUMBER

410. Main mound (ht. 2.5 m) Old Babylonian–Cassite; others, Seleucid/Parthian.

410

0   500 METERS

411. Tell al-Dhibaʿi. Cf. Mustafa, M. A. 1949. Pp. 173–99. (Soundings at Tell Al-Dhibaʿi. Sumer 5). Akkadian–Cassite. Area 4.5 ha. Attained full size only in Ur III/Larsa period. Apparently burned and partly abandoned at end of that period.

412. Tell Fadhilīya. 85 diam × 4–5. Old Babylonian–Cassite.

413. Tell Abū Harmal—ancient Shaduppum. Cf. Baqir, T. 1946. Pp. 22–30. (Tell Harmal: a preliminary report. Sumer 2.) Akkadian–Cassite. Area. 1.8 ha. Wall constructed only in Ur III/Larsa period. Destroyed by fire at time of rise of First Dynasty of Babylon and thereafter abandoned for a time.

414. Tell Mohammad. Area given by Herzfeld (Sarre, F., and E. Herzfeld. 1920. 2:95. Archäologische Reise im Euphrat- und Tigris-Gebiet. Berlin.) as 80 ha., but no trace exists of the "Stadtgebiet" he identified to N and NW of mound. Mound itself is 400 × 600. Dating is highly uncertain. To judge from higher sites along same watercourse, it is probably Akkadian through Ur III/Larsa or Old Babylonian with a continuing occupation or re-occupation in Cassite and later times (cf. p. 50).

415. (1937) Dadawie. 80 diam × 3–4. Seleucid/Parthian.

416. 40 diam × 1. Sassanian.

417. Now entirely plowed-over, but visible as a low rise with salt-encrusted soil and surface pottery 30 diam × 0.5. Old Babylonian–Cassite.

418. 180 NW-SE × 80 × 1. Old Bablonian–Cassite. A few Sassanian sherds also noted, but they are so few that they may represent only graves and not a proper occupation.

419. ʿAlwat Khatītah. 350 NW-SE × 100 × up to 2.5 (although mostly lower). Early Dynastic–Old Babylonian, with sparse Cassite perhaps representing no more than graves of that period.

420. String of small tells in a NNW-SSE line. The largest is 120 × 80 × 1. Approx. total area, 3 ha. Sassanian.

421. Khafājah—ancient Tutub. Cf. Delougaz, P. 1952. Pl. 200 and Table III (Pottery from the Diyala Region. Oriental Institute Publication, 63. Chicago) for map of site and general stratigraphy.

152

SITE
NUMBER

422. 15 diam $\times$ 0.5. Pottery sparse. Akkadian–Old Babylonian.

423. 80 diam $\times$ 1.5. Early Islamic.

424. 200 NNW-SSE $\times$ 100 $\times$ 2–3. To the SW is a lower area 300 $\times$ 100 $\times$ 1. Sassanian.

425. (1937) Tell Abū Ghazaf. Two fairly high mounds, surrounded by a very considerable area of flat ground covered with potsherds. No measurements taken. Search trench on top of two high mounds revealed remains of Hammurabi period, directly beneath shallow late remains. Ur III/Larsa–Old Babylonian, Sassanian.

426. Abū Gali. Small, area approx. 1 ha., measurements not recorded. Seleucid/Parthian.

427. 30 diam $\times$ 1. Cut on sides to a depth of 0.5 by the 1954 Diyala flood. Old Babylonian–Neo-Babylonian.

428. 100 diam, low. Sassanian.

429. Only scattered hummocks remain above plain level within an area 150 diam. Highest 0.5. Early Dynastic, Ur III/Larsa–Neo-Babylonian all represented, but Old Babylonian–Cassite were believed to be preponderant phase at time of collection.

430. 50 diam $\times$ 1. Old Babylonian.

431. A thin scatter of sherds over an area 100 diam. Old Babylonian–Cassite.

432. Three small (0.5–1.5) tells in a row; center tell is largest with a diam of 90. Approx. total area, 1.6 ha. Sassanian–Late Abbasid.

433. 180 N-S $\times$ 100 $\times$ 1. A small detached outcrop of the same date occurs just S of the main tell. Warka/Protoliterate–Old Babylonian. To the N this mound blends off into another, approx. 1 ha. in area, of Sassanian–Early Islamic date.

434. Settlement adjoining old canal, approx. area 1 ha. Sassanian.

435. Low, ill-defined; about 150 diam $\times$ 0.5. A possible Ur III/Larsa–Cassite occupation. Mainly Neo-Babylonian–Parthian.

436. Small, no measurements. Approx. area, .5 ha. Post-Ilkhanid.

437. Jozia. A very small, undated site on right bank of Nahrawān. Fragments of baked bricks but no sherds.

438. Two adjoining mounds which seem to have been given over mainly to brickkilns. Few sherds, at best a very minor occupation. 1 km to NE is a small low occupational site associated with same old canal. Probably all were Sassanian, although few sherds observed that were useful for dating purposes.

439. 80 diam $\times$ 2.5. Akkadian–Old Babylonian.

440. 130 diam $\times$ 2.5. Seleucid/Parthian.

441. 120 diam $\times$ 2. Warka/Protoliterate–Old Babylonian.

442. Ishchali. Ancient Nēribtum. Cf. Frankfort, H. 1936. Fig. 58. (Progress of the Work of the Oriental Institute in Iraq, 1934/35. Oriental Institute Communications,

SITE
NUMBER

20. Chicago); Delougaz, P. 1952. Pl. 203 and Table III for maps and general stratigraphic sequence. Surface collection indicates that occupation may have begun in Akkadian times. It continued into the Old Babylonian period. Area about 23 ha.

443. Tell al-Tewaim. N tell 100 diam $\times$ 3, with minor pits. S tell (separated only by modern canal) 70 diam $\times$ 2.5. A small amount of late pottery probably represents only graves, and modern graves occur on S tell. Both heavily salt-encrusted. Akkadian–Cassite.

444. Three small tells aggregating 1 ha. area $\times$ 1. Sassanian–Early Islamic.

445. Approx. area 1 ha., low (no measurements). Late Abbasid–Ilkhanid.

446. Abū ʿObayyah al-saghīr. 200 diam $\times$ 1.5. Warka–Old Babylonian; a few Cassite sherds are probably strays from 447.

447. Abū ʿObayyah al-khabir. SE of 446. 100 diam $\times$ 4. Old Babylonian–Neo-Babylonian.

448. 100 diam, low. Early Islamic.

449. At best a very small settlement (possibly a single building) at headworks of branch canal. Early Islamic pottery, although 22 cms sq. bricks suggest also Late Abbasid repairs to sluices (?).

450. Main mound 450 NNW-SSE $\times$ 250 $\times$ 2.5. Mainly Sassanian except in the NE quadrant where Neo-Babylonian–Parthian is common. Traces, but no more, of Early Dynastic–Cassite. Other mounds in group are Sassanian, average 100 diam $\times$ 1.0–1.5 high.

451. 300 WNW-ESE $\times$ 100, low. Sassanian.

452. (1937) 80 diam; ht. not recorded. Probably Early Islamic.

453. (1937) Two extremely small Early Islamic mounds. Dimensions not recorded.

454. Tel al-Yahūdīyah. About 200 diam; ht. not recorded. Many fragments of brick. Early Islamic.

455. Tell Abū Qubūr al-saghīr. 180 EW $\times$ 100 $\times$ 4.5. One sherd (2:C) suggests that occupation may have begun in the Warka period. Mainly Akkadian (or earlier) into the Old Babylonian period. In spite of a careful search, only one Cassite base (7:A) was seen. This suggests that the Cassite occupation was at best extremely small and may have consisted only of graves.

456. Tell Ibrāz. 140 diam $\times$ 5. Seleucid/Parthian.

457. 160 NW-SE $\times$ 100 $\times$ 2. A big recent canal has apparently destroyed a small outcrop of the same tell that lay a short distance to the SW. Neo-Babylonian–Parthian.

458. Tell Midār Ihmūd. Warka/Protoliterate–Cassite; although the latter is absent on S tell (150 diam $\times$ 4) it is heavily represented on the others (largest 120 diam $\times$ 3).

153

459. 90 diam $\times$ 2. Seleucid/Parthian.

460. Tulūl Midr Mehaisin. Five large tells; three in N form a close-spaced equilateral triangle, each of about 130 diam, one rising to 5.5 high. S across recent canal branch is another tell of same size, rising 6. SE of latter is a tell 250 NW-SE $\times$ 120 $\times$ 2.5. Total area, 9.8 ha. Seleucid/Parthian.

461. Tulūl Midr Mehaisin. 140 diam $\times$ 4. Another tell to NW is 110 diam $\times$ 2.5. Both are Seleucid/Parthian.

462. Main tell is 200 NW-SE $\times$ 150 $\times$ 4. Two semidetached rises to N and E are each 100 diam $\times$ 2.5. All have old, superficial pits. Early Dynastic–Cassite with the latter confined to NE end of complex. A low, irregular scatter of Early Islamic mounds begins a few hundred meters to the SW.

463. Tell Midr Daᶜud. 80 diam $\times$ 4. Warka/Protoliterate–Larsa, with a very limited Sassanian occupation on NW end.

464. 90 diam $\times$ 2. Seleucid/Parthian. A very small Islamic tell, with sparse and not distinctive pottery, and hence of uncertain date, lies immediately SE.

465. 120 diam $\times$ 3. Warka/Protoliterate–Cassite. An Achaemenian occupation apparently confined to W end.

466. 40 diam $\times$ 1.5. Old Babylonian–Cassite.

467. A low tell and debris at plain level occupying an area of 500 diam. Sassanian–Early Islamic.

468. Abū Qubūr khabir. 200 diam $\times$ 8. Many fragments of baked bricks (apparently 36 $\times$ 36 $\times$ 8 cms), brick-robbers' trenches, sparse pottery. Sassanian.

469. Irregular chain of tells extending N-S for 700m. Most are less than 100 diam $\times$ 2; debris sparse. Approx. total area, 3.5 ha. Sassanian.

470. Tell Abū Khanzīrah. 80 diam $\times$ 2, small outlying hummocks to NW, SW, and SE. One very doubtful Cassite sherd noted; otherwise Achaemenian.

471. 40 diam $\times$ 1, with a still smaller outlying mound to SE. Cassite–Middle Babylonian.

472. Fleye. Five major summits grouped in area 500 NW-SE $\times$ 350; continuous debris within this area. Sassanian.

473. Tell Bier Zambūr. 120 NW-SE $\times$ 80 $\times$ 3. Sassanian.

474. A small mound (est. area, .5 ha); measurements not noted. Ilkhanid–post-Ilkhanid.

475. Eight small summits in an area 450 EW $\times$ 300. Largest has irregular outline of about 120 diam, none more than 2 high. Approx. total area, 3 ha. Sassanian.

476. ᶜAlwat Husaichah. Central mound 190 WNW-ESE $\times$ 90 $\times$ 4. Small outlier to N separated from main tell by old canal. An even smaller outlier is immediately to S. Seleucid/Parthian.

477. ᶜAlwat al-Hamra. Stretches for 1.2 kms WNW-ESE along old canal, mainly 1–1.5m in ht. and rising to 2 only at W end. Width exceed 100 only at a few

points and is mainly around 50, but within this narrow strip the debris is fairly continuous. Approx. total area of settlement, 6 ha. Sassanian.

478. Tell Abū Tuyūr. 350 NNW-SSE $\times$ 150 $\times$ 6.5. Seleucid/Parthian–Sassanian.

479. 40 diam $\times$ 1.5. Neo-Babylonian–Achaemenian.

480. Tell Abū Chit. Area of debris that suggests continuous settlement is 750 NNW-SSE $\times$ 250, although part of this is at plain level only. Sassanian.

481. Surface debris only within 100 diam. Mainly Old Babylonian–Cassite with one Ur III/Larsa (5:C) and one possible Middle Babylonian (8:b) sherd seen.

482. 150 diam; ht. not recorded. Early Islamic–Sāmarrān.

483. (1937) 190 diam $\times$ 2–3. Sparse pottery suggestive of an Early Islamic–Sāmarrān date.

484. Small low mound, approx. area 0.5 ha. Seleucid/Parthian sherd types noted with coin of Vologases III (A.D. 148–91) or more probably IV (A.D. 191–207).

485. Approx. area 0.5 ha.; about 4–5 high. Many brick fragments. Early Islamic–Late Abbasid.

486. 200 $\times$ 150 $\times$ 1–2. Pottery in collection all Sassanian, although 32 $\times$ 32 cm bricks suggest later construction also.

487. 160 diam, low. E half almost exclusively Old Babylonian; W half Seleucid/Parthian.

488. 50 diam $\times$ 1–2. Sassanian.

489. Zuᶜaytir. A very small mound detached just to the SW of 490. 30 diam $\times$ 2, probably reduced in size substantially by an Islamic kiln on top of it. Early Dynastic–Cassite.

490. Zuᶜaytir. 400 WNW-ESE $\times$ 200; ht. not noted. Sāmarrān–Late Abbasid.

491. 150 diam $\times$ 2. Sassanian.

492. Medar. 600 EW $\times$ 450 $\times$ 5. Collection suggests a smaller Seleucid/Parthian site followed by a major Sassanian occupation.

493. ᶜAlwat Hami. About 300 diam; occupies bed of old canal of this name and so is probably later than abandonment of canal. Early Islamic–Sāmarrān.

494. Small tell about 100 diam; ht. not noted. Seleucid/Parthian.

495. ᶜAlwat Hunayt. 150 NW-SE $\times$ 50 $\times$ 2.5. Neo-Babylonian–Parthian.

496. 130 NW-SE $\times$ 70 $\times$ 1, with small outcrops over a somewhat larger area. Boundary of site to S particularly ill-defined; probably there is secondary disturbance there by a later Sassanian canal. Ur III/Larsa–Cassite.

497. Abū Jilāj. Continuous debris with an area 1,100 $\times$ 500. Major mounds shown in sketch reach 3–4m. Seleucid/Parthian–Sassanian.

498. 120 NW-SE $\times$ 70 $\times$ 1. Ur III/Larsa. Cassite.

499. Lamāle. Main mound 300 NW-SE $\times$ 200 $\times$ unrecorded ht. Small outliers to NE and SW add perhaps

1 ha. of settlement area. Traces of a possible Old Babylonian/Cassite occupation (6:C, 7:A); Seleucid/Parthian–Sassanian.

497

0   500 METERS

500. 250 diam × 2–3. Sassanian.

501. 150 diam × ht. not recorded. Sassanian.

502. Sirtab. 130 diam × 3–4. Sparse, not distinctive sherds suggest a possible Seleucid/Parthian, primarily Sassanian occupation.

503. Approx. area, 1 ha.; ht. unrecorded. Ilkhanid–post-Ilkhanid.

504. Tell Jāfūf. 160 diam × 2, slightly elongated E-W. Sassanian.

505. Two closely adjoining tells, one 100 diam, one less; both 1.5 ht. Immediately E of 504. Sassanian.

506. 170 diam × 1. Sassanian.

507. 100 diam × 1. Seleucid/Parthian–Sassanian.

508. ᶜAlwat al-Badᶜīya. 200 diam × 3–4. Old Babylonian–Achaemenian.

509. Two very small, low tells of same date, one 200m SW of the other, approx. total area 0.2 ha. A single Cassite "stray" (7:A). Neo-Babylonian–Achaemanian.

510. 200 diam × 2. Seleucid/Parthian–Sassanian.

511. Three tells averaging perhaps 80 diam × 1.5. One Cassite "stray" (7:A). Possible Sassanian surface sherds, but recorded collection was solely Early Islamic.

512. Tell Mugtaᶜ. Somewhat irregular shape, but about 110 diam × 1.5. Akkadian–Old Babylonian; Sassanian occupation confined to NW end.

513. (1937) Small, low, no measurements recorded. Seleucid/Parthian–Sassanian.

514. Tell Jaᶜara. Fairly continuous but not dense former settlement along Nahrawān for 1+ km × 500m × up to 1.5 high. Early Islamic–Sāmarrān.

515. Tell Agrab. Apparently founded in the ᶜUbaid period, it was almost wholly abandoned late in the Early Dynastic period and then temporarily and partially reoccupied during the Ur III/Larsa period. Cf. Delougaz, P. 1952. Pl. 202 and Table III for map and stratigraphic sequence.

516. 90 diam × 1.5. Sassanian–Early Islamic.

517. Tell Abū Kubeir. 160 diam × 7. ᶜUbaid–Early Dynastic.

518. (1937) three small tells in a cluster, the largest measuring 100 × 80 × 2–3. Total area approx. 1.5 ha. Early Islamic.

519. Seven low summits, none over 1.5 high. Six averaging 40 diam or less. Other is 170 long NW-SE × 70. Total area 2.4 ha. Sassanian.

520. (1937) 200 × 300 × 3-4. Primarily Early Dynastic; Ur III/Larsa pottery occurs only within a very circumscribed area, perhaps representing no more than a single house.

521. 200 diam; ht. not recorded. Two flint blades suggest a possible pre-Sargonid occupation. Early Islamic(?).

522. 120 diam; ht. not recorded. Probably Ur III/Larsa, Old Babylonian.

523. Closely spaced tells each about 100 diam, rising in ht. from 1.5 (NW) to 2.5 (SE). Sparse collection suggests probably dating between the Sassanian and Sāmarrān periods but cannot be more precisely defined.

524. Tell ᶜUlaywat al-Yatama. 120 diam × 3. Occupies bed of a large Sassanian canal; yet somehow the same canal clearly continued in use in Islamic period. 100m NNW is a contemporary low settlement 200 diam. Early Islamic–Sāmarrān.

525. Two adjoining mounds 100 diam × 2.5. 400m E lies another, 90 diam × 2.0. Sassanian.

526. S Mound is 80 diam × 1.5. To N lie two summits 150m apart in NW-SE line, 50 diam × 2 and 120 × 60 × 1.5. Sassanian.

527. Two small mounds each 80 diam × 1 and 1.5 high, 100m apart in a NW-SE line. Sassanian.

528. Four sparse and irregular clusters of brick with little pottery. All 30–50 diam × 1. Sassanian.

529. 200m NW-SE × 80 × 1.5. Sassanian.

530. Abū Rāsain. 190 diam × 5, two closely spaced summits in N-S line. ᶜUbaid–Old Babylonian. Cassite very sparse; may represent graves only.

531. 90 diam × 3, tailing off imperceptibly to SE. Central summit noted as containing ᶜUbaid–Early Dynastic pottery, while Akkadian–Old Babylonian material was on the flanks only. There was only one possible Cassite sherd (7:A[?]) seen.

532. 120 diam × 1.5. Sassanian–Early Islamic.

533. Low, irregularly outlined and spaced mounds with sparse debris occupying about 0.9 ha. from mound shown on map almost to 531. Largest mounds 200 NE-SW × 90 × 2 and 110 diam × 2. Sassanian–Early Islamic.

534. 90 diam × 1.5. ᶜUbaid–Early Dynastic, apparent absence of Akkadian noted during collection, Ur III/Larsa–Old Babylonian.

535. 80 diam × 2. ᶜUbaid, Akkadian–Ur III/Larsa.

536. Three small mounds in NW-SE line, 3.0, 2.0, and 1.5 high in that order, all about 120 diam. Akkadian–Old Babylonian. To NE are two smaller Early Islamic–Sāmarrān mounds.

537. 130 diam × 2. Sassanian. On the other hand, irrigation here apparently continued later. A sluice gate leading here from main canal is of Late Abbasid (22 × 22 cms) brick.

538. A widely scattered group of small mounds rising to 2.5m. Largest cluster to SE (700 × 500), but even here settlement was discontinuous. For NW one km of site there is only a shallow, discontinuous occupation along canal bank. Bricks 32 × 32 cm. Total area approx. 14 ha. Sassanian.

539. Seven semidetached summits, largest 200 diam × 2.5; other lower, smaller. Approx. total area, 7 ha. Early Islamic–Sāmarrān.

540. Five closely grouped tells averaging less than 100 diam. Total area 3.5 ha.; max ht. 3. Sassanian.

541. Abū Rāsain al-Gharbi. 90 diam × 2. Akkadian–Old Babylonian. The very few Cassite sherds (7:A) seen may not denote a real occupation.

542. Three closely spaced summits 100 diam × 1. Mainly Sassanian, continuing on a smaller scale into the Early Islamic period.

543. Seven minor tells strung out along an EW distance of 1.4 km. Up to 2m high. A central area of about 350 EW × 200 is relatively continuously built up, but outliers add only about 1 ha. of area. Sassanian.

544. Perhaps 14 distinguishable low mounds, 1.5–2.5 high, within area of one sq. km. Probably it represents no more than $\frac{1}{4}$ this amount of continuous settlement. Sassanian–Early Islamic.

545. 100 diam × 1.5. Ur III/Larsa–Old Babylonian.

546. 140 diam × 1.5. Sassanian.

547. Tell al-ᶜAbid. 110 diam × 3. Another larger tell of same period, but with sparse sherds and of lower height, lies just to NE. Total area, 3 ha. Early Islamic–Late Abbasid.

548. 150 diam × 2. Early Islamic–Late Abbasid.

549. Two summits 300m apart in E-W line. W tell 90 diam × 1.5, with a low western extension. E tell 120 diam × 1. Sassanian–Early Islamic.

550. Main tell 110 diam × 3. Adjoining to SE is another 70 diam × 1. Sāmarrān–Ilkhanid.

551. Tell Daimat al-ᶜOda. Pair of central mounds are at N, each about 300 × 150 × 4. Scattered areas of debris are connected with three smaller summits. Early Islamic–Ilkhanid, with the late Abbasid and later debris mainly in N part of site.

552. Tell al-ᶜOda. 140 diam × 5. Very small outlying clusters of debris to E, W, and S. Early Islamic–Late Abbasid.

553. Uneven N-S line of tells, consisting of six distinguishable summits 100–120 diam × 2. Early Islamic–Ilkhanid, with southernmost tell mainly (or even entirely) abandoned after the Sāmarrān period.

554. 80 diam × 2.5. Three very small, low tells of same period lie within 1 km N from this site along old canal. Early Islamic–Sāmarrān.

555. Tell Imhamūd. Main mound 200 N-S × 110 × 4.5 (N end only). Early Islamic–Ilkhanid; later pottery particularly at N end. To E and NE is a low, irregular mound, perhaps as large but with only Early Islamic–Sāmarrān pottery.

556. Tell al-Rashshād. 140 diam × 7.5. Top covered with modern graves. Salt-encrusted. Warka–Cassite, although latter period is very sparsely represented.

557. Tell Khatlah. 110 N-S × 70 × 4. Seleucid/Parthian or Sassanian; sparse and not distinctive surface pottery.

558. Tell Rishād. 300 diam, rising near N end to 8m ht. Heavily salt-encrusted. Early Dynastic–Old Babylonian, with one sherd (2:e) suggesting a still earlier origin.

559. (1937) Tell Hamman. 100 × 120; ht. unrecorded. Dating uncertain, probably falling between the Sassanian and the Sāmarrān periods.

560. Uncultivated area is 300 NNW-SSE × 150 × 2, but most of this area is low and with only sparse sherds. Salt-encrusted. Seleucid/Parthian.

561. Well-defined low tell (about 1 ha. area) adjoining old canal, but with scarcely any surface pottery. Possibly Seleucid/Parthian.

562. Bismayah. Approx. rectangular, 320 × 180 × 8. Clear traces of a surrounding wall built of mud brick 39 × 39 × 10 cms. Sassanian. A few Old Babylonian sherds probably are strays from 563.

563. An L-shaped ring of debris around the Sassanian Bismayah enclosure, covering the NW, W, SW, and S approaches to that site. Three clusters of debris are most evident—but there is a fairly continuous distribution of debris between these clusters as well. Some of the early material probably is secondarily deposited here (as canal spoil-banks?), but most is not. Warka–Old Babylonian. The early material is overlain by small amounts of Sassanian pottery. Cassite traces noted to be sparse.

564. 80 diam × 3. Many large 34 × 34 cm bricks, and surface contours suggest that tell consists only of one large building. Almost no pottery to be found on surface. Probably Sassanian.

565. 120 E-W × 60 × 1. Canal passes immediately N of site, then to N of canal is a further area of occupation perhaps $\frac{2}{3}$ as large. Sassanian–Sāmarrān.

566. Tulūl Abū Thailah. 90 diam × 4. Old Babylonian–Parthian.

SITE
NUMBER

567. 500 WNW-ESE × 100 or less × 2.0–2.5—a line of low tells. Short distance to SW is a tell 80 diam × 5; to W is another 140 E-W × 80 × 3. Area assumed, 5 ha. Seleucid/Parthian–Sassanian.

568. 250 diam × 7. Warka/Protoliterate–Old Babylonian.

569. Tell Gabr al-Faras. 120 NE-SW × 80 × 3. A few Cassite "strays" (7:A); otherwise Seleucid/Parthian.

570. 40 diam × 1. Sassanian.

571. Tell Seraij. Four or more major summits, several minor ones, covering 500 N-S × 150 × up to 4. Complex hooks E at S end. Approx. area, 7.5 ha. Seleucid/Parthian–Sassanian.

572. Two tells: 140 diam × 2; other to WNW, 120 × 80 × 2. Sassanian.

573. Tell al-Gurziyah. L-shaped: E-W leg 500 × 2.5; N-S leg 200 × 2.5. 7 ha. Early Islamic.

574. Tell al-Gelāb. 80 diam × 1.5. Sassanian.

575. 500 NW-SE × 100 × 2. Old Babylonian–Cassite.

576. 20 diam × 0.2—just a hummock above the plain is left of this tell. Warka/Protoliterate–Akkadian.

577. (1937) 100 × 200 × 3. ᶜUbaid, Old Babylonian–Cassite. Late Abbasid–Ilkhanid.

578. Tell Gubebah. Three tells in rough E-W line, each about 120 diam × 1.0–1.5. Sassanian, with a few worn Cassite "strays." A small conical mound surrounded by debris at plain level extending over several hundred meters square lies 500m WNW from site of collection. Sassanian–Early Islamic.

579. Tulūl Midr Sālmah. 200 E-W × 80 × 3.5. 150 NNE is a mound $\frac{1}{3}$ as large × 3, of same date. Warka/Protoliterate–Old Babylonian.

580. Tulūl Midr Sālmah. Two tells about 100 diam, one nearby of 150 diam. One of the smaller tells rises steeply to 6.5, but others are low. Seleucid/Parthian.

581. 60 diam × 1.5. Early Dynastic–Ur III/Larsa. Perhaps a vestigial Old Babylonian occupation (one sherd, 6:A).

582. Main tell 220 NNW-SSE × 120 × 3. Small, low outliers to N and NE. Five small tells just E of this site with same surface pottery, all less than 100 diam × 2. Total area, 5 ha. Seleucid/Parthian.

583. (1937) 100 diam × 1–2. Sassanian–Early Islamic.

584. Tell Muwailih. 300 NE-SW × 170 × 6. Major occupation was Seleucid/Parthian with a possible minor continuation into the Sassanian–Early Islamic periods.

585. 120 diam × 1.5. Early Islamic–Sāmarrān.

586. Irregular E-W string of four tells, all less than 100 diam. Westernmost tell alone reaches 3. Sassanian–Early Islamic.

587. 200 N-S × 80 × 4.5 (only reaching this height in a small conical summit). Several other small tells of same period scattered nearby, all considerably distorted by modern canal digging. Sassanian.

SITE
NUMBER

588. Tulūl Mujailiᶜ. Hollow ring (suggesting a fortification) 300 diam × 3.5, with an extension to the NNW. Achaemenid–Parthian pottery noted as terminal in the S underlying small area of Sassanian pottery in N.

589. 90 diam × 1.5. Same period represented on four other smaller summits, three lying 500 SW, one lying 750 ESE. Sassanian.

590. Tulūl Mujailiᶜ. 500 NNW-SSE × 200 × 6.5 (at N end). Main surface material Cassite through Neo-Babylonian, but Early Dynastic–Old Babylonian also represented. A long sequence and possibly an important site.

591. 90 diam × 2. Sassanian.

592. 500 NW-SE × 200 × 2.5. Early Islamic.

593. 200 diam × 2. Sassanian.

594. Approx. area 1 ha.; ht. 2–3m. Sassanian–Early Islamic.

595. Tell Abū Shauk. 150 diam × 3–4. Seleucid/Parthian.

596. Abū Yebīsa. 300 NNW-SSE × 200 × 4–5. Seleucid/Parthian.

597. Abū Jāwan. 250 E-W × 100; ht. not recorded. Sassanian–Sāmarrān.

598. Three tells in a rough WNW-ESE line. Largest on E end is 110 diam × 2. Others one-half these dimensions. Sassanian.

599. A continuous E-W ridge with saddle in middle, 200 × 90 × 3. Warka/Protoliterate–Ur III/Larsa.

600. 300 E-W × 150 × 1. Early Islamic.

601. Continuous settlement extending over an area 500 E-W × 300; elevation of debris up to 2. Sassanian. Collection included sherd types 12:A, G, H, I, and two silver coins of Chosroes II (A.D. 590–628) minted at Maibud in Kerman.

602. Three tells forming triangle. Those at S and SE are 80 diam × 1.5, separated only by an old canal running between them. N tell is smaller. Total area approx. 1.6 ha. Early Islamic.

603. Tulūl Midr Beᶜayir. 180 diam × 4. Seleucid/Parthian–Sassanian.

604. Tulūl Midr Beᶜayir. 120 NW-SE × 70 × 3; saddle separates summits at ends. Neo-Babylonian–Parthian.

605. Tulūl Midr Beᶜayir. 250 diam × 4. Seleucid/Parthian–Sassanian. Low, semidetached mounds to SE, S, SW, and W are mainly Sassanian.

606. 250 NW-SE × 150 × 2.5, with a further extension to the NW at plain level. Many 21 × 21 cms bricks noted. Early Islamic–Late Abbasid.

607. Tulūl Midr Rumaili. 900 WNW-ESE, 400m wide at ESE end, boundaries converging to form apex of triangle at WNW. Max. ht. 3. Seleucid/Parthian.

608. Abū Sūqa. Main tell 500 N-S × 150 (N end)–250 (S end) × 5–6. Some brick fragments. Seleucid/Parthian–Sassanian.

609. 500 NW-SE $\times$ 120 $\times$ 1.0–1.5. NW end semidetached. A few Cassite "strays" (7:A) on SE end; otherwise Sassanian.

610. Tell al-Hewaish. 300 E-W $\times$ 150 $\times$ 3.5 (along S edge). A pronounced escarpment on S, and high also on E and W sides (sloping down toward N). There is no equivalent wall on N end, and center is low. Ur III/Larsa–Cassite and Seleucid/Parthian. Perhaps a fort of Seleucid/Parthian date, heaped up out of debris from an earlier tell.

611. Two tells 100 diam $\times$ 1.5. Sassanian.

612. 80 diam $\times$ 1. Seleucid/Parthian.

613. Tell Abū Fahadah. 500 N-S $\times$ 200 $\times$ 2.5. Sassanian–Early Islamic.

614. 140 NW-SE $\times$ 60 $\times$ 0.5. 31 $\times$ 31 cms bricks, yet no Islamic pottery was seen. Sassanian.

615. 110 diam $\times$ 2. Early Islamic–Sāmarrān.

616. 200 E-W $\times$ 130 $\times$ 3. Early Islamic.

617. Tell Abū Dāl. 230 diam $\times$ 5.5. Seleucid/Parthian.

618. A very irregular scatter of small hummocks left after apparent rise of plain level. Extends approx. 400 NW-SE $\times$ 250 $\times$ 1.5. Seleucid/Parthian.

619. Extends 500m along Nahrawān bank, but width not more than 150; 4 high. Rare Cassite "strays." Sassanian–Early Islamic.

620. ᶜAbertā. Size, scaled off air photo, approx. 2 km/E-W along Nahrawān, 750 wide. See account of town in text, p. 95, and Fig. 8. Estimated total areas of settlement by periods: Sassanian, 150 ha.; Early Islamic–Sāmarrān, 100 ha.; Late Abbasid–Ilkhanid, 4 ha.

621. 150 $\times$ 100 $\times$ 4. Early Islamic–Sāmarrān.

622. 25 NW-SE $\times$ 15 $\times$ 1.5. Possibly only the surviving summit of a larger settlement now nearly submerged. Old Babylonian–Cassite.

623. Low mound consisting only of a mud brick building 16m sq. with possible niches on exterior. (These are perhaps no more than missing bricks from outer wall.) Debris spreads out to 25 diam. Seleucid/Parthian.

624. Only 50m E of 623, but distinct from it. 110 $\times$ 40 $\times$ slightly more than 2. Another contemporary small summit 150m ENE. Several more too small to record on map WNW. If these are surviving vestiges of a single site, it may have been quite large. Old Babylonian–Cassite.

625. Scattered mounds 300 diam $\times$ up to 2.5. Sassanian.

626. Tell Gulat ᶜAzīz. 300 along Nahrawān bank $\times$ 180 $\times$ 3. Sassanian–Late Abbasid.

627. Tell Tabl. 1,100 along S bank of Nahrawān $\times$ 400 $\times$ up to 7, tailing off farther to SE. Approximate area, 44 ha. Seleucid/Parthian–Sāmarrān.

628. Khashin Wāwi. 250 diam $\times$ 4. Only one early sherd (1:A) noted in intensive search. Akkadian–Old Babylonian. A few Seleucid/Parthian graves. In a test-

core obtained on SE edge of mound sherds were still encountered at maximum depth reached, 6.7m below plain level.

629. Abū Jezewāt (name of adjoining old canal-head). Secondarily redeposited pottery on spoil-bank adjoining Nahrawān canal over area of 20–30m sq. Neo-Babylonian–Achaemenian. Faint traces of a probable old canal observed to run SE from this point, with widely scattered Old Babylonian–Achaemenian sherds along its course.

630. A thin scatter of sherds on plain over 120m diam. Sassanian.

631. 200 diam $\times$ 4.5. Seleucid/Parthian types 11:A, B, F, G, occurring together in collection with three coins of Vologases V (A.D. 207–22).

632. Tell Jubayl. 400 NW-SE $\times$ 250 $\times$ 4. Traces of a small Sassanian occupation, but mainly Early Islamic–Late Abbasid.

633. 220 NNE-SSW $\times$ 80, rising gently to 2.5 near N end while S end is low. Another contemporary mound lies 300m SE, 80 diam $\times$ 2. Additional outcroppings occur between the mounds and to S. Approximate area, 2.4 ha. Early Dynastic, Cassite, Seleucid/Parthian–Sassanian.

634. Elevated mound is 120 NW-SE $\times$ 80 $\times$ 2; on the other hand, discoloration on air photo suggests somewhat larger dimensions of 150 $\times$ 100. ᶜUbaid–Early Dynastic.

635. 150 NE-SW $\times$ 100 $\times$ 2. A single classic graffito sherd (14:A) found. Otherwise Early Islamic.

636. 180 NW-SE $\times$ 90 $\times$ 1; another, to S, 80 diam $\times$ 1. Early Islamic.

637. 90 diam $\times$ 2. Early Dynastic, Ur III/Larsa–Cassite.

638. Abū Traychīyah al-Shemāli. Ill-defined toward S and SW, tailing off into scattered debris at plain level. Rises in abrupt escarpment on NE to 4m. A number of Cassite bases (7:A) may represent a small settlement, or merely "strays" from nearby 639. At any

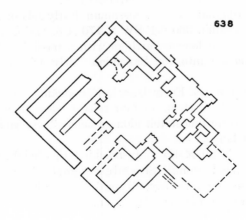

638

158

rate, settlement is primarily Achaemenian, covering an area of about 3 ha. Presumably the clear traces of temple (?) architecture that are shown in accompanying sketch plan date to that period. Walls shown at present take the form of very shallow depressions in room debris, possibly suggesting later brick-robbing. The dotted extension on SE end (where brick impressions suggest that normal size was 34 or 35 cm sq.) may represent either the bricking-up of entrance or stairway to entrance. Sparse overlying Sassanian sherds probably come from a small tell (about 0.5 ha.) of this date SE of mound.

639. Abū Traychīyah al-Jenūbi. Main summit is in the NE. The settlement appears to have been partly submerged by rising plain to the W and S, leaving only low, scattered hummocks in these directions. 200m to E is a low area 150 diam with same surface pottery. Approx. total area, assumed 6 ha. Ur III/Larsa–Cassite.

640. 250 N-S × 70 × 1.5. Crescent-shaped, opening to the W. Small contemporary tell 40 diam × 1.5 noted 2.3 kms E with same surface pottery. Early Islamic.

641. Tell Zuhra (Medina). Extends 1,000m along E bank of Nahrawān × about 400 × 5. Early Islamic–Samarrān.

642. Tell Mirhij. 700 along W bank of the Nahrawān × 300 × 3. Early Islamic–Late Abbasid.

643. 170 diam × 2. Contemporary tell 1 km SSW, 120 diam × 2; another 2.5 kms SSW at junction of canal branches, about .5 ha. area. Early Islamic.

644. A group of contemporary tells dependent on same canal branch. Largest, 170 diam × 4.5, another 300m NNW of it, 120 diam × 2. Four others to W, NNW, and SE as shown on map. Total area, approx. 7.9 ha. Sāmarrān–Late Abbasid.

645. 120 diam × 2.5. 1.1 kms E is another, 140 NE-SW × 90 × 2. Early Islamic–Sāmarrān.

646. 100 diam × 1. Old Babylonian–Cassite.

647. Scattered occupation for 300m NNW-SSE along canal × 150 × 1.5. Sassanian, with one Cassite "stray."

648. Abū Rāsain al-Sharqī. 170 diam, 2 summits of 5. Ubaid, Early Dynastic–Ur III/Larsa; questionable traces of Old Babylonian.

649. Irregular occupied area falling with NE-SW rectangle 700 × 400. Seven summits 1.5–2.0. Probably represents less than ½ this area of continuous occupation. Early Islamic.

650. Mazrur Rukhaimah. Central mound is an inverted T, with both EW and N-S arms 250 × 100 × 4. Early Islamic–Late Abbasid.

651. 150 NW-SE × 40 × 1.5. Early Islamic–Late Abbasid.

652. 90 diam × 1.5. Early Islamic–Late Abbasid.

653. 170 NW-SE × 120 × 4. SE of this a short distance are two small tells 80 and 110 in diam × 1, at junction of small branch canals. 1.2 kms WNW is a small site of the same period. Approx. total area, 4.3 ha. Early Islamic–Sāmarrān.

654. Two tells, each approx. 130 diam × 1.5. E one apparently is composed mainly of slag or cinders. Early Islamic–Sāmarrān.

655. Tell Mujassas. Settlement almost continuos for 2 kms along old canal. Rises to 4 at points, but mostly less than 2. Average width is not over 150 m. Distinct mound occurs only at N where diam is 250. Early Islamic–Sāmarrān.

656. Tell Umm Killaghana. 200 N-S × 90 × 3.5. Early Islamic–Sāmarrān.

657. Etlēl Idhlaᶜ. 90 diam × 1. Late Abbasid–Ilkhanid.

658. Tell Mughaisil. 280 diam × 5. Sassanian–Early Islamic.

659. Tell al-Dhahab. 200 N-S × 70 × 3. Salt-encrusted surface. Sassanian–Early Islamic.

660. Tell Muhaishich. 250 N-S × 140 × 3.5. Sassanian–Sāmarrān.

661. 100 diam × 6. Covered with modern graves. Two smaller contemporary tells 50 diam × 2.5 to W and SW. Approximate area, 1.5 ha. Seleucid/Parthian–Sassanian.

662. 250 × 180 × 5.5 (W part is very low). Seleucid/Parthian types 11:A, B, C, D, F occur together with coin assignable to either Gotarzes II (A.D. 38–51) or Volagases I (A.D. 51–78).

663. Tulūl Bāwi. 750 NE-SW × 200 × 7. Seleucid/Parthian–Sassanian.

664. Tulūl Bāwi. 900 NNE-SSW × 150–250 × 4. Seleucid/Parthian–Sassanian.

665. 300 E-W × 110 × 1. Surface dissected with many shallow trenches. Early Islamic.

666. Salmān Pāk, Taq-i-Kesrā, ancient Ctesiphon. Cf. supra, pp. 62–63, 73; Christensen, A. 1944. Pp. 383 ff. (L'Iran sous les Sassanides. 2d ed. [rev. and enl.] Copenhagen.) Reuther, O. 1929. P. 438. (The German excavations at Ctesiphon. Antiquity 3.) Kuhnel, E. 1933. Map. (Die Ausgrabungen der zweiten Ktesiphon-Expedition. Islamische Kunstabteilung der Staatlichen Museen, Berlin.) Seleucid/Parthian area (assumed), 100 ha.; 540 ha. max. in the Sassanian period, then rapidly declining.

667. Tell Thahab. Still regarded locally as the palace of Chosroes. 200 diam × 8. Seleucid/Parthian–Sassanian.

668. Tulūl al-Mijdādi. N tell: 180 NE-SW × 60 × 3.5; S tell: 120 NE-SW × 60 × 3.5. Both composed mainly of brick and mortar fragments, extensively dug into for bricks, almost no sherds. Each probably consists of one building only. Seleucid/Parthian or Sassanian.

159

669. 140 diam $\times$ 2.5. Seleucid/Parthian–Sassanian.

670. Five tells 50–120 diam $\times$ up to 4. Many smaller outcrops, forming at most a discontinuous settlement. Seleucid/Parthian–Sassanian. Only the latter period is represented at six additional small sites farther down the same old canal branch.

671. Tell Abū Shbaybah. 350 NNW-SSE $\times$ 200 $\times$ 5.5. Minor outliers to S, SE, W, and E do not increase area appreciably. Seleucid/Parthian.

672. 300 N-S $\times$ 250 $\times$ 3. Seleucid/Parthian–Sassanian. To S is a tell 130 diam $\times$ 1.5, mainly Seleucid/Parthian and earlier. Sherd types 11:A, C, D with coin assignable to either Orodes II (57–37 B.C.) or Phraates IV (37–2 B.C.).

673. Tell Jumaidat Ihsain. 250 NE-SW $\times$ 140 $\times$ 3. Seleucid/Parthian–Early Islamic, with latter limited to N end of tell and sparse even there.

674. Tell Abū Tatwah. 170 NW-SE $\times$ 130 $\times$ 5. Sassanian–Sāmarrān.

675. Tell al-Drāzi. NE tell 150 diam $\times$ 2. Tells running to SW from there are practically continuous, cover an area 750 $\times$ 750m, rise at center to 4. Early Islamic–Sāmarrān, Sassanian occupation limited to a small (about 1 ha.) separate settlement at extreme W end of site.

676. 250 diam $\times$ 3.5. There are two smaller contemporary sites 3–4 kms E along old canal levee, Sassanian.

677. 120 diam $\times$ 1.5. Early Islamic–Sāmarrān.

678. 220 diam $\times$ 2.5. To SW is another, 120 diam $\times$ 4, with a very low extension to E. A slight rise extending N for a long distance with sparse pottery may qualify as a third component. Approx. area, 7 ha. Seleucid/Parthian.

679. Tell al-Huwaish. 120 diam rising in NW-SE ridge to 3.5 near SE end. To NW about 100m is a very low, small subsidiary mound and pottery continues thick at plain level for 500m to NW. Approx. total area, 2.5 ha. Seleucid/Parthian.

680. 120 E-W $\times$ 80 $\times$ 5.5. Seleucid/Parthian.

681. 220 diam $\times$ 3.5. Early Islamic.

682. Tulūl Abū Jāwan. 500 N-S $\times$ 350 $\times$ up to 6. Three summits, the two main ones adjoining in the N part of site. Seleucid/Parthian–Sassanian, with rare Achaemenian sherds (10:A, j) suggesting a possible smaller underlying settlement.

683. Tulūl Abū Jāwan. 500 NW-SE $\times$ 150 $\times$ 4. Early Islamic–Sāmarrān.

684. Tulūl Abū Jāwan. 180 diam $\times$ 1.5. Seleucid/Parthian.

685. Tulūl Abū Jāwan. Solid line in sketch map denotes area of sherd concentration; portions of original settlement remaining elevated above present plain surface much smaller. Max. ht. 4 at WNW end, 2.5 at E end, with a low saddle between. If 687 is part of same

site, as seems likely, original settlement may have been about 900 WNW-ESE $\times$ 350. ᶜUbaid–Old Babylonian, with the latter period relatively sparse and surely representing a reduction in area and/or duration of settlement. Very small old excavations on S side of main mound said to have been the source of a large number of tablets twenty years or more ago. An important site, deserving further investigation.

686. 250 diam $\times$ 2. Early Islamic–Late Abbasid.

687. Tulūl Abū Jāwan. Center tell 140 diam $\times$ 2, NW tell 40 diam $\times$ 1, SSE tell 60 $\times$ 2. Earlier pottery occurs mainly on SSE tell. Akkadian–Old Babylonian, Neo-Babylonian–Achaemenian.

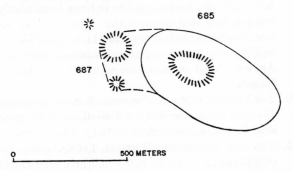

688. 150 E-W $\times$ 120 $\times$ 1.5. Early Islamic–Sāmarrān.

689. Scattered small summits within area of 700 diam $\times$ 3.5. Probable total settlement area 20 ha. Sassanian–Early Islamic.

690. 180 ENE-WSW $\times$ 80 $\times$ 2. Early Islamic.

691. 190 NE-SW $\times$ up to 100 $\times$ 3. Really three semidetached tells in a line with the indicated width and height being reached only in the center tell. Early Islamic–Late Abbasid.

692. Tell Dahhān. 150 diam $\times$ 6.5. Early Islamic–Sāmarrān.

693. W tell about 170 diam $\times$ 4; E tell, 250 E-W $\times$ 120 $\times$ 1.5. One sherd (10:A) suggests a small Achaemenian occupation. Mainly Seleucid/Parthian.

694. Tell Umm Minjal. 150 diam $\times$ 2.5. Early Islamic–Late Abbasid.

695. 80 diam $\times$ 3. Small, low outliers to S and E. Early Islamic–Late Abbasid.

696. 80 diam $\times$ 2. Early Islamic–Late Abbasid.

697. 100 diam $\times$ 2. Small contemporary sites 1 km SW and 2 km SE. Total area, 2 ha. or less. Sāmarrān–Late Abbasid.

698. Main tell 180 diam $\times$ 2.5. Two much smaller tells closely spaced to S reach 3 ht. Approx. total area, 4 ha. Achaemenian–Seleucid/Parthian.

699. Two small brick-covered tells, each 80 diam $\times$ 1.5–2.0. Sāmarrān–Late Abbasid.

700. 900 NW-SE $\times$ 400, with low, narrow tongue of debris extending 500m out from SW side. Rises to 4m. Approx. area, 40 ha. Sassanian–Sāmarrān.

160

SITE
NUMBER

701. 100 N-S $\times$ 80 $\times$ 4. Sassanian.

702. 140 diam $\times$ 2. Early Islamic–Sāmarrān.

703. String of small tells along old canal. Northernmost is 350 N-S $\times$ 100 $\times$ 2.5. Other four are less than 100 diam $\times$ 2. Early Islamic–Sāmarrān.

704. Tell Abū Khansīrah. Main mound about 400 diam $\times$ 4.5; others much smaller, not over 2 high. Sassanian–Late Abbasid, with the outlying mounds all terminal Sassanian. Probable total area of Sassanian settlement, 25 ha.; of Islamic settlement, 16 ha.

705. About 1,000 NE-SW $\times$ 100–300 $\times$ 2.5. Sassanian–Early Islamic.

706. Ill-defined group of low mounds, perhaps 6 major ones 50–100 diam $\times$ up to 2. Approx. area, 3.5 ha. Early Islamic–Sāmarrān.

707. Small amorphous settlement, no elevated mound but useful as dating reference for adjoining old, low canal. Area, 0.1 ha. Sassanian. Bricks 31 $\times$ 31 cms and 33 $\times$ 33 cms.

708. Tell Shaᶜlān. Scattered mound group, 300 diam $\times$ 3. Also 3m mound on SW bank of Nahrawān, just opposite. Sassanian–Sāmarrān.

709. 60 diam, no elevation above plain. Early Islamic–Sāmarrān.

710. Tell Maᶜbūd. Runs 600 along W Nahrawān bank $\times$ 200. Five recognizable summits rising to 3. Early Islamic–Late Abbasid.

711. Tell Zuhra al-Sharqī. Mounds extending perhaps 500m along NE Nahrawān bank $\times$ 200 $\times$ 6. Seleucid/Parthian–Sassanian, with a continuing Early Islamic–Sāmarrān settlement confined to the NW end.

712. Abū Yiwālik. 700 $\times$ 100 $\times$ up to 5-6. Sassanian–Early Islamic.

713. 200 NE-SW $\times$ 100 $\times$ 2.5. Two small, low subsidiary mounds to SW, scattered debris to SE along Nahrawān bank. Approx. area, 2.5 ha. Early Islamic–Late Abbasid.

714. Small mound 1 high and amorphous brick-clusters to NW along Nahrawān right bank represent settlement of perhaps 300 N-S $\times$ 100 aggregate area. Early Islamic–Sāmarrān.

715. Settlement debris and spoil banks along canal branch for perhaps 300 $\times$ 80 $\times$ 2. Two probable Old Babylonian sherds (6:C) may indicate a small early settlement. Mainly Sassanian.

716. Perhaps settlement was originally 150 diam. Now only 0.2 high at most—only small hummocks protruding from a more recent plain surface. Bricks 33–34 cms sq. Sassanian.

717. 300 diam $\times$ 2.5. Size possibly reduced by flood action along N and on E. Many particularly fine examples of classic graffito ware (14:A). Sassanian–Sāmarrān.

718. Al-Qantara. Environs of the weir at Qantara (Figs. 18–19). Sherds from top of weir abutments and from

SITE
NUMBER

mound just upstream on W bank, about 200 $\times$ 100 $\times$ up to 3. Early Islamic–Sāmarrān.

719. 140 N-S $\times$ 80 $\times$ 1 (max. width only near S end). Another contemporary mound 1 km away, slightly W of S, 70 diam $\times$ 1. Early Islamic–Sāmarrān.

720. Two mounds at offtake of large branch canal flowing W: one 200m N of junction, 190 diam $\times$ 1.5; one on E bank of offtake, 70 diam $\times$ 1.5. Early Islamic–Sāmarrān.

721. 200 NW-SE $\times$ 80 $\times$ 1.5. Early Islamic–Sāmarrān.

722. W tell 120 diam $\times$ 2, E tell 300 $\times$ 120 $\times$ 2.5. Sassanian–Early Islamic.

723. Two mounds 200 apart, each about 150 diam $\times$ 1.5. Sāmarrān–Late Abbasid.

724. 450 NNE-SSW $\times$ 200 (but narrowing toward SSW) $\times$ 2.5. Approx. area 7 ha. Sassanian–Early Islamic.

725. Two small mounds, each 100 diam $\times$ 1.5-2.0. Sassanian–Early Islamic.

726. 180 diam $\times$ 3. Sāmarrān–Late Abbasid.

727. Tell Shāhin. WNW mound 100 diam $\times$ 3.5. The other, Tell Shāhin proper, (see sketch) lies 1 km ESE and rises near SE end to 3. Traces of a Sassanian occupation. Mainly Early Islamic–Late Abbasid.

727

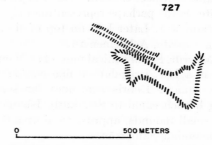

0   500 METERS

728. Umm Zifrāyah. 320 NW-SE $\times$ 180 $\times$ 2.5. 100m ESE is another, 180 N-S $\times$ 110 $\times$ 1. Ur III/Larsa–Cassite. Two early Islamic–Sāmarrān tells, each 1.5-2.0 high $\times$ 80–100 diam lie immediately to N.

729. 200 N-S $\times$ 160 $\times$ 2.5. Early Islamic–Sāmarrān.

730. 150 diam $\times$ 1.5. Ur III/Larsa–Cassite.

731. 80 diam $\times$ 1.5. Early Islamic–Late Abbasid.

732. Two small settlements each less than 30 diam $\times$ 2, on opposite banks of old, eroded canal levee branching E from Nahrawān below Qantara weir. Very little distinctive pottery, probably Sassanian.

733. Tell Imhamūd. Main mound is a building, perhaps a khān or fort, with walls 5 bricks thick (about 160 cms), oriented approximately to cardinal points, of size approx. 50m sq. Large central court, flanked by rooms on all sides. Rises to 2.5–3.0. Early Islamic–Sāmarrān.

734. Sumaka, ancient Uskāf banī Junayd. Cf. pp. 95–96, Figs. 8–9, for estimated outlines of settlement during Islamic period. Max. area, about 400 ha., must have been attained first during Sassanian period. Based on

161

extreme paucity of Achaemenian and Seleucid/Parthian sherds, and their localization only in the central part of the sprawling later city, only a small fraction of the Sassanian area must have been occupied during those periods.

735. Sparse debris within about 120 diam $\times$ 1. Sassanian.

736. Tell al-Khārim. 300 NE-SW $\times$ 200 $\times$ 4. There is an additional low extension to SE for 150m. Early Islamic–Late Abbasid.

737. 120 diam $\times$ 1. Sassanian–Sāmarrān.

738. Ill-defined, spread E-W along old canal for more than 1 km, 2.5–3.0 high. A few widely scattered Cassite sherds may—or may not—indicate a settlement. Seleucid/Parthian–Sāmarrān, with max. area of occupation (about 5 ha.) apparently having been reached during the Sassanian period.

739. Small scattered summits (approx. total area 3.5 ha, up to 3 ht.) along old canal. Two Cassite bases (7:A) probably not signifying a significant settlement. Early Islamic.

740. A number of small scattered summits up to 3 high. Area, 2 ha. Sassanian–Sāmarrān.

741. 100 diam $\times$ 0.5. A thick litter of sherds suggests considerable surface erosion. Old Babylonian, sparse Cassite sherds perhaps representing only graves.

742. 100 diam $\times$ 1. Later kiln on top of site. Old Babylonian–Cassite, Achaemenian.

743. Tell Mazrūr. Small conical mound at N end rises to 8. Rest is a low, irregular outline contained within a 250m square. Debris continues for some distance along branch canal to SE. Early Islamic–Sāmarrān.

744. Two small mounds, approx. total area 0.4 ha., 2.5m ht. Sassanian–Sāmarrān.

745. Two small mounds, both less than 50 diam. N is 1.5, S is 2.5 ht. Seleucid/Parthian–Early Islamic.

746. Group of three tells: southernmost, 120 diam $\times$ 1, probably Sassanian. The two to the N are both about 120 diam $\times$ 2.5; one is Early Islamic, one Early Islamic–Sāmarrān.

747. 50 diam $\times$ 1.5. Additional contemporary small tells occur at intervals along adjoining old canal levee, as shown in Fig. 8. Total area, about 1 ha. Sassanian–Early Islamic.

748. 300 $\times$ 80 $\times$ 2.5. Early Islamic–Sāmarrān.

749. String of small tells 80–100 diam $\times$ 2.5–3.0 high along old canal branch. Continuous debris along canal bank between them. Approx. area of settlement 3.0 ha. Early Islamic–Sāmarrān.

750. 300 E-W $\times$ 200 $\times$ 2.5. Early Islamic–Sāmarrān.

751. 140 E-W $\times$ 80 $\times$ 1.5. Ur III/Larsa–Cassite.

752. 40 diam $\times$ 1. Early Islamic–Sāmarrān, possibly continuing into the Late Abbasid period.

753. 60 diam $\times$ 2. Early Islamic–Sāmarrān, possibly continuing into the Late Abbasid period.

754. 120 E-W $\times$ 80 $\times$ 2. Early Islamic–Late Abbasid.

755. 200 E-W $\times$ 150 $\times$ 2, with a low, small extension to W. Early Islamic–Late Abbasid.

756. Six small mounds up to 3 high falling in area 900 NE-SW $\times$ 250 but probably representing less than half that area of continuous settlement. Seleucid/Parthian and Early Islamic. A small Sassanian–Early Islamic mound 1.5 km. SW.

757. 60 diam $\times$ 2. Early Islamic–Sāmarrān.

758. About 100 diam $\times$ 3. Sāmarrān–Late Abbasid.

759. 400 E-W $\times$ 200 $\times$ 6.5. Sāmarrān–Late Abbasid.

760. Four small mounds 1.5 high. (Approx. total area 3.5 ha.; dimensions not noted). Three extended in an E-W line for about 400m; one lies off to S of this line near E end. Sāmarrān–Late Abbasid.

761. Tell Jeriat al-Wastaniyah. Crescent-shaped, open only to the NE. Enclosed area, 250 diam $\times$ 4.5. Sāmarrān–Late Abbasid.

762. 200 diam $\times$ 3. Early Islamic–Sāmarrān.

763. 250 NW-SE $\times$ 100 $\times$ 2. A lower but equal area is slightly detached to S. Bricks 34 $\times$ 34 cms. Approx. area, 5 ha. Seleucid/Parthian–Sassanian.

764. Tell Sumāka al-Sharqī. About 300 diam $\times$ 7, flat-topped or even with slight depression in center. Low spur projects S, adds little to total area. Bricks 35 $\times$ 35 cms. Seleucid/Parthian–Sassanian.

765. Debris extends 300 along E-W canal, but only 100 wide $\times$ 1.5–2.0 high. Early Islamic–Sāmarrān.

766. Tell Muᶜalam Bardi. 200 diam $\times$ 2; a hollow ring of small tells with the center at about plain level. Early Islamic–Sāmarrān.

767. Irregular group of low mounds extending over an area at least 250 diam $\times$ up to 1.5. Seleucid/Parthian–Sassanian.

768. 150 diam $\times$ 4. Early Islamic, possibly continuing into Sāmarrān–Late Abbasid.

769. Four adjoining tells, all about 100 diam $\times$ 2.5. Early Islamic–Late Abbasid.

770. About 1 km NE-SW averaging 150m wide $\times$ 2–3. Seleucid/Parthian.

771. Extends along what is shown as canal bank for 500m $\times$ avg. 150 $\times$ 2 (rising in one small summit to 4). Sassanian–Late Abbasid.

772. 200 NW-SE $\times$ 80 $\times$ 2. Seleucid/Parthian, as are also seven small tells to E (one 4m ht.) and debris at plain level to NW. Total area 4 ha. Many badly worn Cassite bases (7:A) seen. Possibly strays from 773—or possibly a settlement.

773. 220 ENE-WSW $\times$ 80 $\times$ 1; W end slightly detached. Old Babylonian–Cassite.

774. Extends 300m along E-W canal $\times$ 120 $\times$ 4. One Cassite "stray," Early Islamic.

775. A later continuation to the SW of 776. Main mound 180 diam $\times$ 3.5, is in the southern part of the com-

plex and is apparently a huge Sassanian pottery kiln composed almost entirely of pots and kiln-wasters, including the whole range of utility wares. N and NW of this are lower-lying but more extensive mounds that are also mainly Sassanian kilns. S along the canal at W of site Sassanian occupation continues as a narrow strip, with still more kilns. One Cassite "stray," otherwise Sassanian.

776. Scattered ruins extending fairly continuously over an area of 1,000m × 500 × up to 2.5. Two early "strays" (6:D, 7:A), rare Achaemenian sherds, predominantly Seleucid/Parthian.

777. N tell 100 diam × 1.5, but pottery at plain level suggests original area of settlement was 200m in diam, with extension to E. A kiln of indeterminate date is on top of this mound. Sassanian–Late Abbasid. S mound much smaller, entirely Sassanian.

778. Tell Jariat al-Sharqīyah. 220 diam × 4. Many 20–23 cm sq. bricks. Sāmarrān–Late Abbasid.

779. 300 NW-SE × 180 × 3, with that height reached only at SE end. Seleucid/Parthian.

780. 140 diam × 3. Early Islamic–Late Abassid.

781. Tel al-Mukarram al-Gharbi. 250 N-S × 140 × 4. Sāmarrān–Late Abbasid.

782. 80 diam × 2. Sassanian–Early Islamic.

783. Tell al-Mukarram al-Sharqī. 140 E-W × 110 × 4.5. Late Abbasid.

784. 40 diam × 1.5. Early Islamic–Late Abbasid.

785. Three little mounds forming an equilateral triangle 100m on side. N tell is the largest, reaches 2m high. Approx. total area, 0.5 ha. Early Islamic–Late Abbasid.

786. 40 diam × 2, with a smaller, lower adjunct immediately to the NW. Early Islamic–Late Abbasid.

787. 200 N-S × 110 × 3. Early Islamic–Late Abbasid.

788. 110 × 60 × 2.5. Sassanian–Sāmarrān.

789. 140 N-S × 60 × 3. Early Islamic–Late Abbasid.

790. Thin scatter of sherds along 200m of old canal levee at a junction. A similar sparse settlement of same date occurs at next major confluence of canal branches to the S. Probable total area of occupation, 1 ha. or less. Sassanian.

791. Tell al-Deir, ancient Deir al-Āqūl. Cf. *supra*, p. 91. Max. occupation (about 1 sq. km) seems to have occurred in the Sassanian period, but surface examination and sherd collection indicate that the Seleucid/Parthian (probably only Parthian, to judge from location in relation to changing Tigris course) town also must have been a substantial settlement (assumed, 50 ha.). Islamic occupation was largely confined to the large L-shaped SE mound (which alone reaches 7m ht.), probably occupying a reduced total area of only about 20 ha.

792. Main tell 90 diam × 2. Two smaller tells form a line

to SSE. Approx. total area, 1 ha. Early Islamic–Sāmarrān, with only a half-dozen sherds (15:B, C) to suggest a briefly continuing later settlement.

793. 90 NW-SE × 50 × 1. Sassanian–Early Islamic.

794. 120 diam × 4. Early Islamic–Late Abbasid.

795. 190 NW-SE × 90 × 2.0. One Neo-Babylonian sherd (9:A) hints at a minor occupation. Mainly Achaemenian–Seleucid/Parthian.

796. 110 diam × 1.5. Doubtful traces of Seleucid/Parthian, mainly Sassanian.

797. 50 diam × 2.5. 250m to ESE is a group of 3 tells forming essentially a 200m N-S ridge × 40 × 1.5. Sassanian–Sāmarrān.

798. 50 diam × 3. Salt-encrusted. Seleucid/Parthian–Sassanian.

799. Jamdat Shahrazād. Two mounds on left bank of the Nahrawān, 6 on right. Debris on surrounding plain in about the same proportions. About 700m along W bank, 200 along E bank, extending back 200m from both banks. Up to 3m high in small summits, mostly low. Approx. area 18 ha. Seleucid/Parthian–Sāmarrān.

800. N tell 120 diam × 2.5. 20–23 cm sq. common bricks, Early Islamic–Late Abbasid. S tell 100 diam × 2. Early Islamic only.

801. 200 or more along Nahrawān bank × 80 × 1.5. Seleucid/Parthian–Sassanian.

802. 550 N-S × 250 × as much as 2 high only in a few places. 30–32 cm sq. bricks common. Seleucid/Parthian–Sassanian.

803. S tell 130 diam × 1.5, N tell smaller. Approx. area, 2.5 ha. Sassanian.

804. Tell Mayyāh al-Sharqī. Main tell 800 NW-SE × 200 (irregular) × 4. Smaller, lower mounds to N. Approx. area, 19 ha. Early Islamic–Late Abbasid.

805. 240 diam × 4.5. Bricks, 29–30 cm sq. and 20–23 cm sq. seen. Early Islamic–Late Abbasid.

806. Central mound 110 diam × 3. S mound 60 diam ×

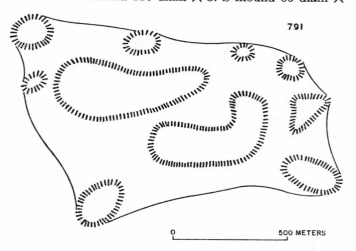

1.5. NNW mound 80 × 2. Early Islamic–Late Abbasid.

807. Group of mounds extending along roughly 750 of E-W canal, scattered debris area 200 in width, but probably not representing settlement continuously over more than half of this. Heights up to 3. Many 20–23 cm sq. bricks. Sāmarrān–Late Abbasid.

808. 200 along E-W canal bank, but debris is sparse and width does not exceed 50. Height of 2 probably includes mostly canal spoil-banks. Early Islamic.

809. WSW tell 60 diam × 2.5; center tell 80 diam × 1.5; ENE tell 80 diam × 2; all closely spaced. 20–23 cm sq. bricks common, but 31 cm sq. bricks also present. Early Islamic–Late Abbasid.

810. Tell al-Lāmi (al-Sharqī). 350 NW-SE × 150 × 3.5. Early Dynastic–Larsa only on S end of site, Old Babylonian–Cassite only on N end. Across old canal directly to W of site are four very small Seleucid/ Parthian–Sassanian tells (approx. total area, 0.5 ha.) with much early material as well.

811. Two small adjoining tells 50 or less diam × 2. Seleucid/Parthian.

812. 180 NE-SW × 60 × 3. Seleucid/Parthian.

813. Tulūl al-Lawami. 140 diam × 4.5. Ur III/Larsa–Cassite.

814. Tulūl al-Lawami. Begins immediately S of 813 and forms with it an almost continuous N-S line. 450 N-S × 200 × 6.5 (max. ht. reached immediately S of 813; elsewhere mostly a flat-topped plateau of 4). Area to NE, E, SE, and S is covered almost continuously with Seleucid/Parthian debris and smaller tells. Max. area approx. 1 sq. km. Seleucid/Parthian.

815. 120 diam × 1.5, with westward extension along old canal levee. Early Islamic–Late Abbasid. 1 km NNW is a small (about .5 ha) Sassanian site.

816. String of small tells up to 50 diam × 1.5, along an old canal levee. Approx. total area, 1 ha. Sassanian–Early Islamic, possibly continuing into the Late Abbasid period.

817. Settlement along old canal for 1 km, but mostly less than 100 in width and 2.5 high. Approx. total area, 8 ha. Seleucid/Parthian.

818. NE tell 140 diam × 2.5, ᶜUbaid through Ur III/Larsa. SW tell 120 diam × 1.5, mainly Old Babylonian–Cassite. Separated only by a later canal passing between them.

819. Extends 250 round rt. angle bend in old canal levee. Average width 80, ht. 2.5. Sāmarrān–Late Abbasid.

820. 180 E-N × 100 × 2.5. Early Islamic.

821. A NW-SE string of very small tells. At NW end is one 40 diam × 1, mainly Old Babylonian–Cassite. Next is 30 diam × 1, mainly Akkadian through Ur III/ Larsa and with traces of a large mud brick building showing on surface; small outcrops suggest that most

of this tell has been submerged by rising plain. Next to SE is a tell 40 diam × 1, mostly Old Babylonian–Cassite. At the SE end are two Sassanian tells of similar size.

822. Perhaps 8 major summits averaging 60 diam × 2.0–2.5, representing semicontinuous settlement within an area 600 E-W × 250. Many small outcrops of debris. Sassanian–Late Abbasid.

823. Relatively continuous low mounds cover 350 NW-SE × 200 × up to 2.5. Early Islamic–Sāmarrān.

824. 350 NW-SE × 100 × 2. NW end mainly Seleucid/ Parthian, with diagnostic types 11:C, E, F, G occurring together with a Parthian coin (representation of goddess Tyche crowned with fortress; undatable). A few scattered Cassite sherds, probably strays from nearby sites, also occur there. SE end of site is Akkadian, and a diffuse scatter of debris of this period extends for 500m farther S.

825. 150 diam × 1.5. Akkadian, Old Babylonian.

826. Tulūl al-Shuᶜailah, probably the classical Scaphae and Arabic Lower Uskāf. 2.5 kms along E bank of Nahrawān × 300–500m width × up to 4 is scattered summits. Represents fairly continuous settlement of approx. this maximum size (i.e., approaching 1 sq. km) in Seleucid/Parthian–Sassanian times. Islamic settlement covers only the S third of the site, and Islamic surface debris becomes progressively later and thicker toward S end. Sāmarrān settlement estimated to cover one-fifth of max. area, Late Abbasid settlement barely one-tenth.

827. 80 diam × 1. Early Islamic.

828. Tulūl al-Shuᶜailah. 250 diam × 3 (4.5 above Nahrawān bed, dropping in steep escarpment). Sassanian–Late Abbasid.

829. 120 diam × 3.5. Low spur extends SE. Seleucid/ Parthian.

830. A triangular-shaped mound 120 to a side bounded by two converging old canal levees. 3m high. Approx. area, 0.8 ha. Early Islamic–Late Abbasid.

831. SE tell 120 diam × 3.5, cut on NE end by old RR track bed. NW tell smaller, 2 high. Approx. area, 2.4 ha. Sassanian–Early Islamic.

832. 200 NW-SE × 110 × 3.5. One sherd (9:A) suggests a Neo-Babylonian occupation. Mainly Achaemenian–Seleucid/Parthian.

833. Tell al-Mlaich. 750 NW-SE × 500 × 6.5. These dimensions include outcrops as well; the central tell rising to the indicated ht. is only 350 in diam. Total area of settlement about 18 ha., probably reaching this maximum only in the Seleucid/Parthian period. Occupation continued during the Sassanian period and then terminated, except at extreme W end of site where Early Islamic pottery was observed on a small mound.

164

SITE
NUMBER

834. Main tell in group of contemporary flat-topped mounds, 400 E-W $\times$ 200 $\times$ 2.5 Early Islamic–Late Abbasid.

835. 40 diam $\times$ 1. Early Dynastic–Old Babylonian. Rare Cassite sherds probably do not reflect a significant occupation. A later (probably Parthian) kiln stands on mound.

836. 500 NE-SW $\times$ 200 $\times$ 2.5—fairly continuous low tells within these dimensions. Seleucid/Parthian–Sassanian.

837. 60 diam $\times$ 1. Salt-encrusted. Old Babylonian.

838. Main tell 100 diam $\times$ 3. A very low, small adjunct lies immediately to SSW across an old canal. Old Babylonian–Cassite.

839. Tell Abū Tuyūr al-Sharqī. Two semidetached summits on W form a continuous area 180 diam $\times$ 4. To the E lies a tell of the same area $\times$ 3.5. Approx. total area, 6.4 ha. Sassanian–Early Islamic.

840. 250 NW-SE $\times$ 70 $\times$ 2.5. Early Islamic.

841. 140 diam $\times$ 1.5. 31 cm sq. and 27 cm sq. bricks noted. Sassanian–Early Islamic.

842. Tell Abū Dibis. A high, photogenic mound, reminiscent of Tell Agrab (515) and perhaps as important an ancient town. 340 NE-SW $\times$ 300 $\times$ 9. Rises in two peaks with a saddle between, but W summit is only 6.5. Near NW foot of site traces were noted of a thick mud brick wall which appeared to be part of the town's defenses. ᶜUbaid–Old Babylonian.

843. 600 NNE-SSW $\times$ 100–250 $\times$ 8. Bisected by new ᶜAzīzīya–Kūt hwy. Another large detached tell and a very large area of low ruins lie to the NW. Many small outcrops to the E and N. Major occupation appears to have been Seleucid/Parthian (about 10 ha.), with the terminal Sassanian settlement probably extending over no more than one-fifth of this area.

844. Tulūl Hadba. Two parallel scattered lines of tells; largest 200 $\times$ 100 $\times$ 5. Estimated total area, 3 ha. Seleucid/Parthian–Sāmarrān, possibly continuing into the Late Abbasid period.

845. 180 diam $\times$ 1.5. Early Islamic.

846. 50 diam $\times$ 2. Akkadian–Cassite, Sassanian debris in small quantities occurs along old canal levee immediately to N.

847. 90 diam $\times$ 1.5. Early Islamic–Sāmarrān.

848. Main tell iin NNW part of complex, irregular but roughly equivalent to 150 diam $\times$ 4. Other tells much smaller. Approx. total area, 3 ha. Sassanian.

849. Very small settlement adjoining clear, wide traces of old watercourse. Sherds are confined to the area of spoil-banks only. Since the canal levee is of Seleucid/Parthian date, it seems reasonable to conclude that the sherds were thrown up as a secondary deposit during cleaning of the canal and do not represent a primary settlement. Ur III/Larsa–Old Babylonian.

SITE
NUMBER

850. Tell Kammāz. About 300 diam $\times$ 9, with a long spur extending N. Highest point near S end. In spite of great height of debris. this site apparently is exclusively Seleucid/Parthian. Several hundred meters E is an Early Islamic tell, 120 diam $\times$ 2, with surrounding low area of debris.

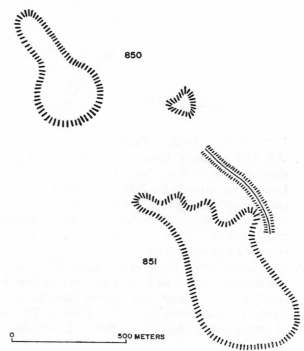

851. Possibly ancient Diniktum. Site is mostly low, largely submerged by rising plain, hard to define. An area at least 600m diam is raised and out of cultivation, and hence must represent a zone of continuous settlement. Sherds and debris, however, are mainly concentrated on numerous small outcrops that rise to 2.5–3.0. ᶜUbaid–Cassite. Identification based on objects brought to the Iraq Museum by a local resident in Spring, 1960, and said to come from this site. These included six Ur III/Larsa cylinder seals, one with an inscription giving the name of the god Ninib, and a baked well- or cistern-brick with the following inscription:

ᵈSin - ga - mi - il	Sin-gamil
ra - be - an	
MAR -TU	the great leader of Martu
Ša Di - ni - ik - tim^{ki}	of the city Diniktum
dumu ᵈSin - še - mi	son of Sin-šemi

852. 160 diam $\times$ 2.5. To the NW is an area perhaps 150 diam of low, closely spaced outcrops. 2 kms SE is another small tell of same date. Early Islamic–Sāmarrān.

853. 110 diam $\times$ 2. Early Islamic.

854. Four closely spaced tells in a diamond pattern, averaging 80 diam $\times$ 2. Sassanian–Early Islamic.

165

855. Ht. 2.5–3.0m. Early Islamic–Late Abbasid. Same dating applies also to small sites 1.5 kms NW and 2.2 kms N, each approx. 0.5 ha.

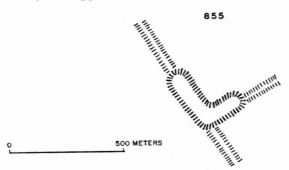

855

0   500 METERS

856. 120 NW-SE × 80 × 2. Early Islamic–Sāmarrān.

857. Tell Abū Ghuraib. Low, ill-defined, but fairly continuous ruins within about 160 diam × up to 2.5. Low debris extends for 500m or more to NE along canal branch, and is found on tell 4.5 kms to NE down this branch. While the latter tell is small, debris extends upstream from it for 300–400m. Total area of occupation about 4.5 ha., all Late Abbasid.

858. Low, sparse debris along wide old canal levee 1.5 kms NNW-SSE. Impossible to separate occupational from canal debris. Certainly not large or high; just a relatively continuous small strip of settlement. Total area of settlement, perhaps 1 ha. Seleucid/Parthian–Sassanian.

859. Tell al-Muᶜalam. Central tell is irregular in shape but averages 100 diam × 2. W across old canal is tell 150 × 60 × 2.5. To the E of the central tell is a small outcrop. Late Abbasid, possibly with a resumption of occupation in post-Ilkhanid times.

For location of the following sites, see Figure 7:

860. Tell Nazūz. 60 diam × 3 (height may include a submerged natural hillock). Sparse pottery suggests a date in the Akkadian–Ur III/Larsa range.

861. Tell al-Siwwān. Site is 120 diam × 4, but this elevation may partly be accounted for by a natural rise beneath it. Surface has been at least 50 per cent pitted, but only in small round pits that do not exceed 1.5m in depth. Located on top of vertical conglomerate bluff just N of Tigris bend (and offtake of Kātūl al-Kisrawī), with only available cultivation based on dry

agriculture in depressions immediately behind it. On the other hand, the Tigris may not have flowed at immediate foot of the bluff at the time of occupation, leaving a flood plain for cultivation by irrigation. The major component of the surface collection at this site can be assigned to the (prehistoric, not Islamic) Sāmarrān period. A large collection included elaborate stands, jars, bowls, etc., in the fully developed, Sāmarrān painted tradition, together with a non-microlithic flake-blade, chipped-stone industry, alabaster bowls, limestone mortars and rubbing stones. In addition there were several sherds of Hassuna incised ware and a few Halaf sherds, but the bulk of the pottery clearly falls within the Sāmarrān tradition. Thus it appears that the Sāmarrān occupation was the maximal one, overlying, and perhaps extending beyond, the Halaf and Hassuna (and possibly earlier) settlements on all parts of the mound. A small Old-Babylonian–Cassite settlement is confined to the SW quadrant of the site. Excavations were begun on this site in 1964 by the Directorate General of Antiquities.

862. 80 diam × 4. Sassanian–Early Islamic.

863. Tell al-Khirbah. 160 diam × 5.5. Late Abbasid–Ilkhanid.

864. Tell Aswad. 220 diam × 5.5. 21 cm sq. and 24 cm sq. bricks in profusion, very extensively robbed for bricks. Late Abbasid–Ilkhanid.

865. 150 diam × 1.5. Sparse pottery, site partly eroded away. Late Abbasid–Ilkhanid.

866. Extends for 150m along N Kātūl al-Kisrawī bank × 100 × 1.5. Late Abbasid–Ilkhanid.

867. Tell al-Dhuluᶜiyyah. Cf. Jones, J. F. 1857a. Pp. 130–32, map. (Narrative of a journey, undertaken, in April, 1848, by Commander James Felix Jones, I.N., for the purpose of determining the tract of the ancient Nahrawān Canal. *Selections from the Records of the Bombay Government* [n.s.], 43.) Conclusion during present survey was that Jones's description errs in its implication that this was a large and populous community. Instead it seems quite modest in size, although strung out and accompanied by many great canal banks and numerous former brickkilns. These banks and kilns give the impression of extensive and continuous occupational debris, but on closer inspection this is lacking. Estimated total area of settlement, about 6 ha. Sassanian–Early Islamic.

166

REFERENCES AND NOTES

PREFACE

Notes:

1. Jacobsen, T. 1958a. Salinity and irrigation agriculture in antiquity. Diyala Basin Archaelogical Project, report on essential results June 1, 1957, to June 1, 1958 (mimeographed). Baghdad.

Jacobsen, T. 1958b. Summary of a report by the Diyala Basin Archaeological Project, June 1, 1957, to June 1, 1958. *Sumer* 14:79–89.

2. Cf. especially Tolstov, S. P. 1953. Auf den Spuren der Altchoresmischen Kultur. *Sowjetwissenschaft*, Beiheft 14. Berlin. Ghirshman, R. 1953. S. P. Tolstov, Drevniy Choresm (La Chorasmie antique). *Artibus Asiae* 16:209–37, 292–319.

3. Willey, G. R. 1953. Prehistoric Settlement Patterns in the Virú Valley, Perú. Bureau of American Ethnology, *Bulletin* 155. Washington, D.C.

4. Government in Iraq, Development Board, 1956. Z.A.D. irrigation projects: Nahrawān, ᶜAdheim, and Ishaqī areas. 2 vols. London: Binnie, Deacon, and Gourley.

Government of Iraq, Development Board, 1958. Lower Diyala Development: soils, agriculture, irrigation, and drainage. Diyala and Middle Tigris Projects, Report no. 2. London: Sir M. MacDonald and Partners, Ltd.

CHAPTER 1

General References:

Al-Barazi, Nuri K. 1961. The geography of agriculture in irrigated areas of the middle Euphrates Valley. Vol. 1. College of Arts, Baghdad University, Baghdad.

Buringh, P. 1960. Soils and soil conditions in Iraq. Republic of Iraq, Directorate General of Agricultural Research and Projects. Baghdad.

Great Britain, Naval Intelligence Division 1944. Iraq and the Persian Gulf. *Geography Handbook Series*, B.R. 524. London.

Mitchell, C. W. 1959. Investigations into the soils and agriculture of the lower Diyala area of eastern Iraq. *Geographical Journal* 125:390–97.

Neumann, H. 1953. Die physisch-geographischen Grundlagen der kunstlichen Bewasserung des Iran und Irak. Deutsches Institut für Länderkunde, *Wissenschaftliche Veröffentlichungen* (N.F.) 12:4–46.

Vaumas, E. de 1962. Introduction géographique à l'étude de Bagdâd. *Arabica* 9:229–46.

Notes:

1. E. Unger has shown that the ancient Babylonian system of orientation was inclined forty-five degrees, following the directions of the prevailing winds rather than the cardinal points. (Unger, E. 1935. Ancient Babylonian maps and plans. *Antiquity* 9:311–22.) Professor Landsberger informs me that the *shamal* was the iltānu, the cooling wind of the Babylonians, while the *sharqī* was the shadū, the mountain wind.

2. Government of Iraq, Development Board, 1958. Lower Diyala Development: soils, agriculture, irrigation, and drainage. Diyala and Middle Tigris Projects, Report no. 2. London: Sir M. MacDonald and Partners, Ltd. Sect. 2, pp. 4–5.

3. *Ibid.*, Sect. 3, pp. 206–7.

4. Russel, J. C. 1957. Tillage practices in Iraq. Iraq College of Agriculture, Abū Ghraib (mimeographed). P. 20.

5. Government of Iraq, Development Board, 1958. Sect. 3, p. 207.

6. *Ibid.*, Sect. 3, pp. 9–11.

7. An indication of the relatively dense, if low, cover of vegetation which this region could support, at least along its Tigris River margin to the south, is provided by Robert Mignan in his account of a journey in 1827: "November 3. I cannot say whether we missed any antiquities on our road this day or not, as our path lay through an almost impenetrable forest of brushwood, which extended into the Desert as far as the eye could see" (Mignan, Robert 1829. Travels in Chaldaea, including a journey from Bussorah to Baghdad, Hillah and Babylon, performed on foot in 1827. . . . London).

8. Government of Iraq, Development Board, 1956. Z.A.D. irrigation projects: Nahrawān, ᶜAdheim, and

Ishaqī areas. 2:25–37. London: Sir M. MacDonald and Partners, Ltd.

Professor Landsberger informs me that *shauk* probably is to be identified with the *ashāgu* of the cuneiform sources. It shares its ideogram with *eddetu*, at one time identified as *Alhagi maurorum* but now thought to be the boxthorn *Lycium barbatum*.

9. Cf. Government of Iraq, Irrigation Development Commission, 1951. Report on the control of the rivers of Iraq and the utilization of their waters. Baghdad. P. 38. el-Kholy, F. H. 1952. Hydrology of the River Tigris. Government of Iraq, Directorate General of Irrigation. Baghdad. P. 145.

10. *Ibid.*, p. 146.

11. Government of Iraq, Irrigation Development Commission. 1951. P. 26.

12. Ionides, M. G. 1937. The Regime of the Rivers Euphrates and Tigris, London. P. 255.

13. Government of Iraq, Irrigation Development Commission. 1951. P. 25.

14. Great Britain, Naval Intelligence Division, 1944. Iraq and the Persian Gulf. Geography Handbook Series, B. R. 524. London. P. 83.

15. The Jebel Hamrīn has been identified as the mountain Abih (later Ebih) of the cuneiform sources. Cf. discussion, and references to earlier literature: Gelb, I. J. 1938. Studies in the topography of western Asia. *American Journal of Semitic Languages and Literatures* 55:67–68.

16. el-Kholy. 1952. P. 148.

17. de Vaumas, E. 1962. Introduction géographique à l'étude de Bagdâd. *Arabica* 9:238–41.

18. Russel, R. J. 1939. Louisiana Stream Patterns. *Bulletin American Association of Petroleum Geologists* 23: 1199–1227 and *passim*.

19. Russel, R. J. 1954. Alluvial Morphology of Anatolian Rivers. Association of American Geographers, *Annals* 94:365, 390.

20. Government of Iraq, Development Board, 1956. 2: 81–82.

21. Buringh, P. 1957. Living conditions in the Lower Mesopotamian Plain in Ancient Times. *Sumer* 13:38–39.

22. *Ibid.*, p. 41. Government of Iraq, Development Board, 1956. 2:30–31.

23. Russel, R. J. 1939. Pp. 1210–11.

24. Cf. Koldewey, R. 1925. Das wiedererstehende Babylon. (4th ed., revised) Leipzig. P. 18.

25. Russel, R. J. 1939. P. 1210.

26. Mitchell, R. C. 1958. Instability of the Mesopotamian Plains. *Bull. Société de Géographie d'Égypte* 31:129.

27. Lobeck, A. K. 1939. Geomorphology: An Introduction to the Study of Landscapes. New York. P. 225.

28. *Ibid.*, pp. 224–28.

29. Phillips, P., J. A. Ford, and J. B. Griffin. 1951. Archaeological Survey in the Lower Mississippi Alluvial Valley, 1940–47. Peabody Museum of Harvard University, *Papers* 25:7.

30. Russel, R. J. 1939. Pp. 1205–6.

31. Lobeck, A. K. 1939. Pp. 227.

32. Matthes, G. H. 1941. Basic aspects of stream-meanders. National Research Council, Amer. Geophysical Union. *Transactions*, Part III, p. 635.

33. Phillips, Ford, Griffin 1951. P. 8.

34. Chawner, W. D. 1936. Geology of Catahoula and Concordia parishes, Louisiana. Louisiana Geology Survey, *Bulletin* 9, Department of Conservation. Pp. 23–24. Cited in Phillips, Ford, Griffin, 1951. P. 8.

35. Chesney, R. A. 1850. The expedition for the survey of the rivers Euphrates and Tigris, carried on by order of the British Government, in the years 1835, 1836, and 1837. 2 vols. London.

36. Ionides, M. G. 1937. P. 176.

37. Russel, R. J. 1954. P. 366.

38. Lees, G. M., and N. L. Falcon. 1952. The geographical history of the Mesopotamian plains. *Geographical Journal* 118:24–39.

39. Mitchell, R. C. 1957. Recent tectonic movement in the Mesopotamian plains. *Geographical Journal* 123:569–71.

40. Government of Iraq, Development Board, 1958. Sect. 1, pp. 11–12.

41. Mitchell, R. C. 1958. P. 137: "A rate of sedimentation of 20 cms/century, a rate of erosion of 0.54 cms/century, a eustatic rise of sea level of 7 cms/century, an upward isostatic movement of about 0.35 mm/century, tectonic positive movements within the plain of 0.305 to 100 cms/century and negative movements of the order of 60 cms/century, seismic movements within the plains of perhaps 20 cms/century—such can be *estimated* from known data as occurring within the tectonic basin comprising the Mesopotamian plains and Persian Gulf. No individual estimate aims at precision, nor can it be treated singly. The interaction of sedimentation, erosion, eustatism, recoil, tectonic disturbance, seismic dislocation are all so intricately interwoven in time and space that precise analysis of movements defy understanding."

42. Government of Iraq, Development Board, 1958. Sect. 2, p. 6. On the other hand, Professor Hans Bobek has pointed out to the author (personal communication) that the foregoing analysis is based on the assumption that the entire Diyala plain below the Jebel Hamrīn can be regarded purely as a consequence of alluvial levee formation. Quite possibly, he argues, the steeper, upper portion of the Diyala's course may have been laid down to a degree by processes of true fan formation under semi-arid conditions. So long as the predominant activity was aggradational, this would lead the river continuously to shift its course as it blocked its own channel with new deposits of sediment. If loads decreased, on the other hand, it would begin to incise its channel into the fan laid down previously. At least at times, such conditions may have applied not only along the river's course above the Jebel Hamrīn but for a short distance below it. If so, artificial means (temporary weirs,

168

dredging of channels) may have been employed virtually since the beginnings of agriculture in the area in order to maintain the flow of water to existing settlements and to forestall sudden, disastrous shifts. Moreover, this should permit us to explain the recently incised character of the Diyala's bed across the upper portion of the plain without reference to the possible uplift of the plain itself.

Unfortunately, the region around the Diyala's outlet from the Jebel Hamrīn was not fully covered during the survey because of lack of time. Probably only a joint archaeological and geomorphological investigation could determine whether fan formation or alluvium formation was the primary contributing agency along the upper edges of the Diyala plains. The relatively uniform, fine-textured character of the deposits argues for the latter.

CHAPTER 2

General References:

Al-Barazi, Nuri K. 1963. The geography of agriculture in irrigated areas of the middle Euphrates valley. Vol. 2. College of Arts, Baghdad University, Baghdad.

Buringh, P. 1960. Soils and soil conditions in Iraq. Republic of Iraq, Ministry of Agriculture, Directorate General of Agricultural Research and Projects. Baghdad.

Davies, D. H. 1957. Observations on land use in Iraq. *Economic Geography* 33:122–34.

Great Britain, Naval Intelligence Division, 1944. Iraq and the Persian Gulf. *Geography Handbook Series*, B.R. 524. London.

Millon, René. 1962. Variations in social responses to the practice of irrigation and agriculture. In "Civilizations in desert lands" (R. B. Woodbury, ed.), pp. 56–88. University of Utah, *Anthropological Papers*, 62.

Mitchell, C. W. 1959. Investigations into the soils and agriculture of the lower Diyala area of eastern Iraq. *Geographical Journal* 125:390–97.

Poyck, A. P. G. 1962. Farm studies in Iraq (an agroeconomic study of the agriculture in the Hilla-Diwaniya area in Iraq). *Mededelingen van de Landbouwhogeschool te Wageningen, Nederland*, 62 (1).

United Nations, Food and Agricultural Organization, 1959. FAO Mediterranean Development Project, Iraq Country Report. Rome.

Wirth, Eugen. 1962. Agrargeographie des Irak. Institut für Geographie und Wirtschaftsgeographie der Universität Hamburg, *Hamburger geographische Studien*, 13.

Notes:

1. Jacobsen, T. 1958b. Summary of a report by the Diyala Basin Archaeological Project, June 1, 1957, to June 1, 1958. *Sumer* 14:79–89.

2. A reduction of less than 10 per cent in grain yield is reported to occur after a single early grazing of barley (Government of Iraq, Development Board, 1958. Lower Diyala Development: soils, agriculture, irrigation, and drainage. Diyala and Middle Tigris Projects, Report no. 2.

London: Sir M. MacDonald and Partners, Ltd.). On the other hand, the importance attached to this early grazing seems to be locally variable, and in some areas barley has begun to be treated virtually as a fodder crop. "In Kanᶜan Nāhiya, the majority of the holders sold their young growing crops for grazing to pastoralists from other Liwas who fed their flocks of sheep and goats on these lands until the grazings were exhausted. It is estimated that between 40 and 60 thousand were pastured in this way from other districts. The holders later flooded the fields and obtained a second crop which they harvested themselves for the grain. Yields from this second crop as might be expected were small" (Government of Iraq, Principal Bureau of Statistics, 1954. Report on the agriculture and livestock census of Iraq, 1952–53. Baghdad).

3. *Ibid.*, Sect. 3, pp. 15, 114.

4. The 1952–53 agricultural and livestock census groups men, women, and boys as the agricultural labor force. For the Baghdad, Diyala, and Kūt *liwās*, into parts of which the entire lower Diyala basin falls, the gross area of landholding (cultivated and fallow) per agricultural worker was 3.4, 4.5, and 4.5 hectares, respectively (Government of Iraq, Principal Bureau of Statistics, 1954).

5. Government of Iraq, Development Board, 1956. Z.A.D. irrigation projects: Nahrawān, ᶜAdheim, and Ishaqī areas. 1:101. London: Binnie, Deacon, and Gourley.

6. Government of Iraq, Development Board, 1958. Sect. 3, p. 113.

7. Poyck, A. P. G. 1962. Pp. 55–58. Without denying the oppressive schedule of crop-shares charged against tenant farmers, from Poyck's data emerges the surprising conclusion that they enjoy a higher standard of income and caloric intake. They lose about half of the proceeds of cultivation of an area twice as large, but the really significant factor appears to be that they are able to dispose of much larger areas of fallow land suitable for grazing (p. 75).

8. Government of Iraq, Principal Bureau of Statistics, 1954.

9. Poyck, A. P. G. 1962. P. 57.

10. *Ibid.*, p. 35.

11. It is interesting to compare the present agricultural calendar with the calendar which can be reconstructed from Sumerian and Akkadian sources (Landsberger, B. 1949. Jahreszeiten im Sumerisch-Akkadischen. *Journal of Near Eastern Studies* 8:248–97). The principal differences appear to be that sowing formerly was spread over a fourmonth period instead of three months, beginning in September rather than October, and that considerable attention was given during the late spring and summer months to preparatory treatment of moist lands recently covered with flood waters. In other essential features, however, the calendars are very similar.

12. Government of Iraq, Principal Bureau of Statistics, 1954. P. 114.

13. Government of Iraq, Development Board, 1958. Sect. 3, pp. 218–19.

14. *Ibid.*, Sect. 3, p. 184. These figures are contradicted by Hardan's informants in Khān Banī Saʿad, who reported to him that they customarily used 100 to 120 kg. of barley and 60 to 80 kg. of wheat per hectare as seed.

15. *Ibid.*, Sect. 3, p. 218.

16. *Ibid.*, Sect. 1, pp. 6–7.

17. *Ibid.*, Sect. 3, p. 76.

18. We are concerned here only with the traditional agricultural system, not with the more intensive system now being introduced to replace it. An integral part of the latter is the construction of a large and expensive system of deep outfall drains in order to prevent the disastrous rise in the water table which otherwise would quickly follow the utilization of Derbendi Khān dam for large-scale summer irrigation.

19. Government of Iraq, Development Board, 1958. Sect. 3, p. 182.

20. *Ibid.*, Sect. 3, p. 189.

21. *Ibid.*, Sect. 3, p. 182.

22. Data are not available on the proportions of fruit trees within the lower Diyala plains as a separate region, but their approximate distribution is suggested by a breakdown into the three *liwās* in parts of which the entire region falls (Government of Iraq, Principal Bureau of Statistics, 1954).

	Baghdad	Diyala	Kūt
Proportion in Orchards (in per cent)	2.5	2.2	0.6
Number of fruit-bearing trees:			
Date	1,311,691	2,198,022	489,668
Orange	513,038	575,961	36,139
Pomegranate	282,657	804,079	65,452
Apple	444,025	110,885	43,878
Apricot	191,874	126,349	39,092
Sweet lemon	155,704	118,635	7,203

23. Hardan reports that date orchards and vegetable crops in the Baʿqūba area must be irrigated every ten days during the summer.

24. Government of Iraq, Development Board, 1958. Sect. 3, pp. 70–71.

25. *Ibid.*, Sect. 3, pp. 70–71.

26. Government of Iraq, Development Board, 1956. 1:47.

27. Davies, D. H. 1957. Pp. 127–28.

CHAPTER 3

General References:

Adams, Doris G. 1958. Iraq's people and resources. Berkeley.

Longrigg, S. H. 1925. Four centuries of modern Iraq. Oxford.

Longrigg, S. H. 1953. ʿIraq, 1900 to 1950; a political, social, and economic history. London.

Mantran, R. 1962. Bagdâd à l'époque Ottomane. *Arabica* 9:311–24.

Poyck, A. P. G. 1962. Farm studies in Iraq (an agroeconomic study of the agriculture in the Hilla-Diwaniya area in Iraq). *Mededelingen van de Landbouwhogeschool te Wageningen, Nederland*, 62 (1).

Sousa, Ahmed. 1953. Atlas of Iraq. Baghdad.

Notes:

1. It is significant that 1952–53 figures, based on the Agricultural and Livestock Census and information supplied by the authorities responsible for the anti-malarial campaign, substantially increased the number of villages reported in 1947. In Baʿqūba, Kanʿan, Balad Rūz, Khān Banī Saʿad, Mansūrīya, Khālis, Abū Saʿda, and Miqdadīya Nāhiyas, the 1947 figures given in Table 3 record a total of 443 villages, while the total for the same Nāhiyas was 683 in 1952–53 (Government of Iraq, Development Board, 1958. Sect. 2, p. 9). In so short a period only a minor part of this difference can reflect the formation of new villages. The rest must have been overlooked in the 1947 census.

2. Al-Barazi, Nuri K. 1961–63. The geography of agriculture in irrigated areas of the middle Euphrates valley. 2 vols. College of Arts, Baghdad University, Baghdad. 2: 137–40, 228–30.

3. Deimel, A. 1931. Sumerische Tempelwirtschaft zur Zeit Urukaginas und seiner Vorgänger. *Analecta Orientalia*, 2. Rome. Pp. 78–79.

4. Certain minor corrections are necessary in Sousa's table as it is given on p. 9 (Sousa, Ahmed. 1953); in computing these figures use has been made of the map of quarter boundaries on p. 8. Old quarters within Karkh, the portion of the city on the west bank, are included in the calculations.

5. Gremliza, F. G. L. 1962. Ecology of endemic diseases in the Dez irrigation pilot area. A report to the Khuzestan Water and Power Authority and Plan Organization, Government of Iran. New York: Development and Resources Corporation.

6. *Ibid.*, pp. 77–78.

7. Cf. Longrigg, S. H. 1925. Longrigg, S. H. 1953.

8. He later reports glimpsing Persian towns at a distance to the left when in reality they must have lain to the right (above the Jebel Hamrīn?), but the general line of march from Baghdad to Tauq is clear enough.

9. Rauwolff, Leonhart. 1582. Beschriebung der Reysz Leonhardi Rauwolffen . . . in die Morgenländer. . . . Frankfurt; Part 2, pp. 102–3.

10. Valle, Pietro della. 1681. 2:7. Viaggi di Pietro della Valle il Pellegrino, descritti da lui medesimo in lettere familiari. 4 vols. Venice.

11. Olivier, G. A. 1800–1807. Voyage dans l'Empire Ottoman, l'Égypte et la Perse fait par ordre du gouverne-

ment, pendant les six premières années de la République. With atlas. 6 vols. Paris. 4:307.

12. Kinneir, John MacDonald. 1818. Journey through Asia Minor, Armenia, and Koordistan, in the years 1813 and 1814. London. P. 474.

13. Rich, Claudius James. 1836. Narrative of a residence in Koordistan and on the site of ancient Nineveh; with a journal of a voyage down the Tigris to Baghdad and an account of a visit to Shirauz and Persepolis. 2 vols. (ed. by his widow) London. 2:156.

14. Lynch, H. B. 1839. Note on a part of the River Tigris between Baghdad and Samarrah. *Journal of the Royal Geographic Society.* London. 9:471–72.

15. Southgate, Horatio. 1840. Narrative of a tour through Armenia, Koordistan, Persia, Mesopotamia. . . . 2 vols. New York. 2:198–99.

16. Jones, J. 1857a. P. 73 (Narrative of a journey, undertaken, in April 1848, by Commander James Felix Jones, I.N., for the purpose of determining the tract of the ancient Nahrawān Canal. *Selections from the Records of the Bombay Government,* n.s. 43, pp. 34–134).

17. *Ibid.,* p. 77.

18. Jones, J. 1857b. P. 138 (Narrative of a journey to the frontier of Turkey and Persia. *Selections from the Records of the Bombay Government,* n.s. 43, pp. 136–213).

19. Geary, Grattan. 1878. Through Asiatic Turkey. 2 vols. London. 1:300.

20. Černik Expedition. 1875. Technische studien-expedition durch die Gebiete des Euphrat und Tigris. 2 vols. *Petermanns geographische Mitteilungen.* Erganzungsheft no. 44–45. 1:36.

The comparable population of the area today, excluding Baghdad in both instances, can be calculated from the 1957 census, grouping together the entire reported population of Khālis and Banī Saᶜad *nāhiyas* of Diyala *liwāᵓ* and the "rural" population of Adhamīya and Karrāda *nāhiyas* of Baghdad *liwāᵓ*. It is 187,793 persons, roughly 19 times as large as 90 years ago.

21. *Ibid.,* p. 32.

22. Geary, Grattan. 1878. 1:333.

23. Great Britain, Admiralty War Staff, Intelligence Division, 1916–17. A Handbook of Mesopotamia, 4 vols. London. 2:101.

24. *Ibid.,* p. 93.

25. *Ibid.,* 3:196.

26. *Ibid.,* p. 20.

27. *Ibid.,* 2:93–94.

28. Longrigg, S. H. 1953. P. 213.

29. Ionides, M. G. 1937. The Regime of the Rivers Euphrates and Tigris, London. Pp. 163 ff.

30. Great Britain, 1916–17. 3:185, *passim.*

31. Herzfeld, E. 1907. Eine Reise durch Luristan, Arabistan und Fars. *Petermanns Mitteilungen* 1907. P. 50.

32. Great Britain, 1916–17. 2:95.

33. M.E.F. Survey Party, 1918. Tribes of the Baghdad Wilāyat (map). Scale: 1 inch to 4 miles.

CHAPTER 4

General References:

Beek, M. A. 1962. Atlas of Mesopotamia (tr. by D. R. Welsh; ed. by H. H. Rowley). London and Edinburgh.

Childe, V. G. 1952. New light on the most ancient East. London.

Falkenstein, A. 1954. La cité-temple sumérienne. *Cahiers d'histoire mondiale* 1:784–814.

Jacobsen, T. 1957. Early political development in Mesopotamia. *Zeitschrift für Assyriologie* 52:91–140.

Jacobsen, T. 1958a. Salinity and irrigation agriculture in antiquity. Diyala Basin Archaeological Project, report on essential results June 1, 1957, to June 1, 1958 (mimeographed). Baghdad.

Kraeling, C. H., and R. M. Adams (eds.) 1960. City invincible: an Oriental Institute symposium. Chicago.

Kramer, S. N. 1963. The Sumerians: their history, culture, and character. Chicago.

Perkins, A. L. 1949. The comparative archaeology of early Mesopotamia. *Studies in Ancient Oriental Civilization,* 25. Chicago.

von Soden, W. 1961. Sumer, Babylon und Hethiter bis zur Mitte des Zweite Jahrtausends v. Chr. In "Propyläen Weltgeschichte" 1:523–609. Frankfurt.

Notes:

1. Braidwood, Robert J., and Bruce Howe. 1960. Prehistoric investigations in Iraqi Kurdistan. *Studies in Ancient Oriental Civilizations,* 31. Chicago.

2. Braidwood, Robert J., Bruce Howe, and C. A. Reed. 1960. The Iranian prehistoric project. *Science* 133:2008–10.

3. Hole, Frank. 1962. Archeological survey and excavation in Iran, 1961. *Science* 137:524–26.

4. Adams, Robert M. 1963. The origins of agriculture. In "Horizons of Anthropology" (Sol Tax, ed.), pp. 120–31. Chicago.

5. Tell al-Siwwān (site no. 861 in the survey) represents perhaps the southernmost outlier of the Assyrian prehistoric village tradition. Its surface collection, characterized by traces of Halaf and Hassuna wares and a rather elaborate Sāmarrān assemblage, revealed no trace of prehistoric wares identified with the alluvium.

6. Adams, Robert M. 1960:26. Factors influencing the rise of civilization in the alluvium: illustrated by Mesopotamia. In C. H. Kraeling and R. M. Adams, eds., pp. 23–34.

7. Stronach, David 1961. The excavations at Ras al ᶜĀmiya. *Iraq* 23:95–137.

8. Lloyd, S., and Fuad Safar. 1943. Tell ᶜUqair. *Journal of Near Eastern Studies* 2:131–58.

9. Delougaz, P. 1952. Pottery from the Diyala Region. *Oriental Institute Publications,* 63. Chicago P. 29, Pl. 17 a–c.

10. Cf. Fig. 2 and Adams, Robert M. 1958. Survey of

171

ancient water courses and settlements in central Iraq. *Sumer* 14: Fig. 1.

11. This follows the conclusion of the excavator that Ras al-ᶜĀmiya was occupied only contemporaneously with Eridu XI, just after the end of the Haji Mohammed period (Stronach, D. 1961:121). Of course the finding of Ras al-ᶜAmiya itself underlines how limited the present evidence is for early periods of occupation in the alluvium—and hence how tenuous any generalization must be.

12. Delougaz, P. 1952. P. 29.

13. Frankfort, H. 1934. Iraq excavations of the Oriental Institute 1932/33. *Oriental Institute Communications*, 17. Chicago. Delougaz, P. 1940. The temple oval at Khafājah. *Oriental Institute Publications*, 53. Chicago. Delougaz, P., and S. Lloyd. 1942. Pre-Sargonid temples in the Diyala Region. *Oriental Institute Publications*, 58, Chicago.

14. Delougaz, P. 1952.

15. Possibly ancient Diniktum. For details of a recent inscription supporting this identification see Appendix C.

16. Cf. Jacobsen, T. 1957.

17. Delougaz, P. 1940. Delougaz, P., and S. Lloyd. 1942.

18. Langdon, S. 1924. Excavations at Kish, vol. 1. Paris. MacKay, E. 1929. A Sumerian palace and the "A" Cemetery at Kish, Mesopotamia. Field Museum of National History, *Anthropology Mem.*, vol. 1, no. 2. Chicago.

19. Safar, F. 1950. Eridu: A preliminary report on the third season's excavations, 1948–49. *Sumer* 6:27 ff.

20. Heinrich, E. 1931. Fara. Ergebnisse der Ausgrabungen der Deutschen Orient-Gesellschaft in Fara und Abu Hatab 1902/03. Berlin. Pp. 12–15.

21. Frankfort, H. 1934. Pp. 23–39. Delougaz, P. 1952. P. 105.

22. Gelb, I. J. 1955. Old Akkadian inscriptions in the Chicago Natural History Museum. *Fieldiana: Anthropology* 44, no. 2:181. Chicago.

23. Baqir, Taha. 1946. Tell Harmal: a preliminary report. *Sumer* 2:22, map.

24. Fernea, Robert A. 1959. Irrigation and social organization among the El Shabana: a group of tribal cultivators in southern Iraq. Unpublished Ph.D. dissertation, Department of Anthropology, University of Chicago. Pp. 139–48.

Summarized in Millon, René. 1962. Variations in social responses to the practice of irrigation agriculture. In "Civilizations in desert lands" (R. B. Woodbury, ed.), pp. 68–74. University of Utah, *Anthropological Papers*, 62.

25. Cf. Wittfogel, K. A. 1957. Oriental despotism: a comparative study of total power. New Haven.

26. An Old Babylonian reference to "cinq cents barques amarrées au quai de Diniktum" clearly suggests, as Dossin observes, that the town was located on the Tigris rather than merely on the Diyala (Dossin, Georges. 1956. Une lettre de Iarîm-Lim, roi d'Alep, a Iasub-Iahad, roi de Dîr. *Syria* 33:67).

27. A recent estimate of "maximum practical usage from the Diyala waters" is 4,250 sq. kms. (B. M. U. Bennel,

cited in Jacobsen, T. 1958a. P. 73), but this includes waters withdrawn for irrigation above the Jebel Hamrīn.

28. Finkelstein, J. J. 1963. P. 464. Mesopotamian historiography. American Philosophical Society, *Proceedings*, vol. 107, no. 6, pp. 461–72.

29. Cf. Kraus, F. R. 1955. Pp. 65–66. Provinzen des neusumerischen Reiches von Ur. *Zeitschrift für Assyriologie* 51:45–75.

30. Jacobsen, T. 1957. P. 137.

31. Widely divergent views continue to be held on ethnic identifications, and on the significance of self-conscious ethnic interaction, in early Mesopotamian history. Cf., e.g., Jacobsen, T. 1939b. The assumed conflict between Sumerians and Semites in early Mesopotamian history. *Journal of the American Oriental Society* 59:485–95; and Gelb, I. J. 1960. Sumerians and Akkadians in their ethno-linguistic relationship. *Genava* (n.s.) 8:258–71. However, it is not within the competence of the author to contribute to the question, and it has seemed satisfactory for the present study to skirt the question of ethnic identifications entirely.

32. Edzard, D. O. 1957. Die "Zweite Zwischenzeit" Babyloniens. Wiesbaden. P. 165.

33. Jacobsen, T. 1939c. The Sumerian king list. Oriental Institute, *Assyriological Studies*, 11. Chicago. P. 115.

34. I am indebted to Professor Landsberger for this observation.

35. Frankfort. 1934. Pp. 1–22. Delougaz and Lloyd. 1942. P. 203. Delougaz, P. 1952. Pp. 109–13.

36. Delougaz, P. 1952. Pl. 200.

37. Several hundred tablets from the excavations in Akkadian levels at these sites, mostly from Tell Asmar, have been published in transliteration. (Gelb, I. J. 1952. Sargonic texts from the Diyala region. *Materials for the Assyrian Dictionary*, 1. Chicago.) An additional group of around fifty Old Akkadian tablets, unfortunately from an unknown provenience within the Diyala area, has been published with translation and commentary (Gelb, I. J. 1955).

38. Baqir, Taha. 1946. P. 25.

39. Mustafa, M. A. 1949. Soundings at Tell Al Dhibaᶜi. *Sumer* 5:183.

40. Baqir, Taha. 1946. P. 25. Mustafa, M. A. 1949. Figs. 1 and 2.

41. Frankfort. 1934. Pp. 23, 26.

42. Professor Landsberger informs me that he is doubtful, on grounds quite different from those adduced here, that later Sumerian sources are historically accurate in the destructiveness they attribute to the Gutians. He notes that even Dūr-Rimush, the fort established by Rimush in the Diyala area, continued its existence until a later period. He suggests that the unique "Provinzliste" of Ur-nammu (Kraus, F. R. 1955. Provinzen des neusumerischen Reiches von Ur. *Zeitschrift für Assyriologie* 51:45–75), which delineates administrative districts adjacent to the Diyala region but across the Tigris from it, implies that these

districts were fully functioning almost at the outset of the Third Dynasty of Ur. If so, it would hardly appear that they had been seriously disrupted by any prolonged period of invasion. Finally, of course, this was the period of the extraordinary flourishing of Lagash under Gudea. Thus he concludes that perhaps the basic effect of the Gutian conquest was temporarily to detach the Diyala region from the remainder of the alluvial plain, without necessarily campaigning very hard to do so. "The 'dragon of the mountains' preferred to sit in his mountains and collect fat tribute."

CHAPTER 5

General References:

Beek, M. A. 1962. Atlas of Mesopotamia (tr. by D. R. Welsh; ed. by H. H. Rowley). London and Edinburgh.

Edzard, D. O. 1957. Die "Zweite Zwischenzeit" Babyloniens. Wiesbaden.

Kraeling, C. H., and R. M. Adams (eds.) 1960. City invincible: an Oriental Institute symposium. Chicago.

Kramer, S. N. 1963. The Sumerians: their history, culture, and character. Chicago.

von Soden, W. 1962. Der Nahe Oste im Altertum. In "Propyläen Weltgeschichte," 2:41–133. Frankfurt.

Notes:

1. The especially rich archival sources for the period, stemming from a half-dozen towns in the district, are summarized by Harris, R. 1955. Pp. 34–35 (The archive of the Sin Temple in Khafājah [Tutub]. *Journal of Cuneiform Studies* 9:31–88). To that listing now must be added the more recent publication of additional texts from Tell Harmal and other sites (Simmons, S. D. 1959–61. Early Old Babylonian tablets from Harmal and elsewhere. *Journal of Cuneiform Studies* 13:71–93, 105–19; 14:23–32, 49–55, 75–87, 117–25; 15:49–58, 81–83).

2. Cf. especially Jacobsen, T. 1940 (pp. 116–200, in Frankfort, H., S. Lloyd, and T. Jacobsen, The Gimilsin Temple and the Palace of the Rulers at Tell Asmar. *Oriental Institute Publications*, 43. Chicago) and Edzard, D. O. 1957.

3. Delougaz, P. 1952. Pottery from the Diyala Region. *Oriental Institute Publications*, 63. Chicago. P. 113.

4. Mustafa, M. A. 1949. Soundings at Tell Al Dhibaᵓi. *Sumer* 5:174–75, 183.

5. Delougaz, P. 1952. P. 114.

6. Mustafa, M. A. 1949. Pp. 176 ff.

7. Baqir, Taha. 1946. Tell Harmal: a preliminary report. *Sumer* 2:25.

8. Since no excavations were carried into pre-Isin–Larsa levels, this conclusion is based on surface collection. The presence of Early Dynastic seals (Frankfort, H. 1936. Progress of the work of the Oriental Institute in Iraq, 1934/35. *Oriental Institute Communications*, 20. Chicago. Fig. 66) may indicate an earlier settlement.

9. *Ibid.*, pp. 74 ff.

10. Jacobsen, T. 1958a. Salinity and irrigation agriculture in antiquity. Diyala Basin Archaeological Project, report on essential results June 1, 1957, to June 1, 1958 (mimeographed). Baghdad. P. 69.

11. Jones, J. F. 1857a. Narrative of a journey, undertaken, in April 1848, by Commander James Felix Jones, I.N., for the purpose of determining the tract of the ancient Nahrawān Canal. Selections from the Records of the Bombay Government (n.s.) 43:74, 100.

12. Jacobsen, T. 1939a. The inscription of Takil-ili-su of Malgium. *Archiv für Orientforschung* 12:363.

Goetze, A. 1950. Sin-iddinam of Larsa: new tablets from his reign. *Journal of Cuneiform Studies* 4:94.

Edzard, D. O. 1957. Pp. 100, 159 ff.

Falkenstein, A. 1963. Zu den Inschriftenfunden der Grabung in Uruk-Warka, 1960–61. Deutsches Archaologisches Institut, *Baghdader Mitteilungen* 2:39–40.

13. Frankfort, Lloyd, and Jacobsen. 1940. 200.

14. Frankfort, H., T. Jacobsen, and C. Preusser. 1932. Tell Asmar and Khafājah: the first season's work in Eshnunna, 1930/31. *Oriental Institute Communications*, 13. Chicago. P. 37.

15. Ungnad, A. 1933. Datenlisten. In "Reallexikon der Assyriologie," 2:184. Berlin and Leipzig.

16. Baqir, Taha. 1946. P. 25.

17. Mustafa. 1949. P. 176.

18. Delougaz, P., and S. Lloyd. 1942. P. 219. Pre-Sargonid temples in the Diyala region. *Oriental Institute Publications*, 58. Chicago; Delougaz, P. 1952. Table 3.

But note that a few purchased seals said to have come from the site have been described as Old Babylonian in style (Frankfort. 1955. Pl. 92).

19. Delougaz, P. 1952. P. 150.

20. One of the towns which must have been affected by this destruction is Akshak, generally assigned a location on the opposite bank of the Tigris from the lower Diyala or ᶜAdheim region and at the confluence of the Tigris River with one of its tributaries. For example, a reference to Upi, surely in the immediate vicinity of Akshak, speaks of the sale of a slave in Upi with the document sworn to in the house of one of its witnesses "on the bank of the Dūr-ul [Diyala]" (Schollmeyer, A. F. 1928–29. Urkunden aus der Zeit der III. Dynastie von Ur, der I. Dynastie von Isin und der Amurru-Dynastie. In "Altorientalische Studien: Bruno Meissner zum sechzigsten Geburtstag." *Mitteilungen der Altorientalischen Gesellschaft* 4:188, 190, corrected by I. J. Gelb).

While the author is not competent to enter into the long debate over the exact position of Akshak-Upi-Opis on the basis of the classical and cuneiform sources (comprehensively summarized, if hardly settled, in Barnett, R. D. 1963. Xenophon and the wall of Media. *Journal of Hellenic Studies* 83:1–26), several topographic points bearing on this debate perhaps are worth noting:

(*a*) Discussions over the position of Akshak, Upi, and Opis henceforward must take cognizance of the apparent shift in the courses of both the Tigris and Diyala rivers for which these surveys provide evidence.

(b) Absolutely no evidence of an early occupation was observed by the author in the area of Ctesiphon, nor at Seleucia in a careful examination of that site by the author and Dr. V. E. Crawford in 1957. In our experience, some evidence would survive in the form of at least scattered early sherds on the surface if there were any significant early occupation. Both this negative finding and the positive evidence for an alternative Tigris course seem to preclude Seleucia and Ctesiphon from consideration as the immediate locations for Akshak and Upi, if not necessarily for Opis.

(c) Survey along the presumed ancient courses of the Tigris, as defined by sites at the mouths of channels of the Diyala system of watercourses, was especially careful and complete. Certainly no large mounds were overlooked from Baghdad downstream to at least the modern town of ᶜAzīzīya.

(d) It follows that the most probable location for Akshak in the area covered by the Diyala Basin Archaeological Project is one of the six sites representing the confluence of the early Tigris course with minor tributary watercourses: Tell Mohammad, 414; Tell Rishād, 558; 568; Tulūl Mujailiᵓ, 590; Tell Abū Jāwan, 685; 851.

(e) From the evidence of archaeological reconnaissance, Tell Mohammad seems less likely than the others in that the channel along which it lies does not antedate the Akkadian period, whereas Akshak was of more than local importance in pre-Sargonid times.

(f) The large unnamed site (851) at the mouth of what has been tentatively identified as the River Daban probably may be ruled out as either Akshak or Upi on the grounds that any later settlement in its vicinity would have been too far to the east to represent a reasonable terminus for Nebuchadnezzar's Median Wall. In any case, as has been indicated earlier, this site now has been tentatively identified as Diniktum.

(g) Of the remaining sites, Abū Jāwan (685) is apparently the largest and most strategically located, and hence perhaps most important. Possibly also to be considered in connection with the Akshak-Upi-Opis problem—although much less likely—is a large early site underlying the northern part of the great Sassanian and Islamic city of ᶜUkbarā, adjoining the old bed of the Tigris 5.5 kms. west of the present course at 33°47′30″ N. lat. These ruins are outside the area covered by the Diyala Basin Archaeological Project, and will be discussed in a forthcoming publication on the findings of the Oriental Institute Iraq Surface Survey in ancient Akkad.

21. Baqir, Taha. 1946. P. 25.

22. Mustafa. 1949. P. 184.

23. Ungnad, A. 1933. P. 181. A unique date-formula, probably to be assigned to a period 75 or so years earlier, speaks of the "Year when [the course of] the Diyala River was changed" (Harris, R. 1955. P. 65). While Eshnunna

continued to flourish after this change, conceivably it may have had to depend on an artificial canal leading to the town from the now more distant river (cf. Frankfort, Lloyd, and Jacobsen. 1940. P. 193, DF 118). Such a canal in turn would have been more vulnerable to destruction through subsequent flooding than a natural watercourse.

24. Thureau-Dangin, M. F. 1942. Pp. 15–19 (La chronologie de la première dynastie Babylonienne. Mémoires de l'Académie d'Inscriptions et Belles-Lettres 43: 2. Paris); Frankfort, Lloyd, and Jacobsen. 1940. P. 200.

25. Ugnad, A. 1933. P. 185.

26. Jones, J. F. 1857a. P. 78. The account is not clear as to whether Jones himself initiated the excavations or merely examined objects deriving from them.

27. Layard, A. H. 1853. Discoveries in the ruins of Nineveh and Babylon. London. P. 477.

28. Sarre, F., and E. Herzfeld. 1920 (Archäologische Reise im Euphrat- und Tigris-Gebiet. Berlin). 2:95–96.

29. Harris, R. 1955. P. 31. Professor Landsberger informs me that, since Hammurabi had no other palace outside of Babylon, these objects must have been brought to Tell Mohammad as booty at some time subsequent to his reign.

30. A small-scale plan is provided in Frankfort, H. 1955. Pl. 93. For brief preliminary reports on the conduct of the excavations see Bulletin of the American Schools of Oriental Research 67:2–6; 68:12–13 (1937); 70:7–10; and 71:18–20 (1938).

31. Mustafa, M. A. 1949. P. 184.

32. E.g., into central Akkad, where a very substantial increase in settlement has been noted at about this time (Adams, Robert M. 1958. Survey of ancient watercourses and settlements in central Iraq. Sumer 14:101–3).

33. al-Wailly, F. 1953. The political history of the Cassite period in Babylonia. Unpublished Ph.D. dissertation, University of Chicago, Department of Oriental Languages and Literatures. P. 91, passim.

34. Baqir. 1946. P. 25.

35. Mustafa, M. A. 1949. P. 183.

36. Rawlinson, H. 1884. The cuneiform inscriptions of Western Asia. Vol. 5:33 i:33–37. London. Tr. in al-Wailly, F. 1953. P. 69.

37. Luckenbill, D. D. 1926. Ancient records of Assyria and Babylonia. 2 vols. Chicago: University of Chicago Press. 1:49 ff.

38. al-Wailly, F. 1953. Pp. 112 f.

39. Weidner, E. F. 1933. Die Feldzüge Šamši-Adads V gegen Babylonien. Archiv für Orientforschung 9:89–104.

40. What appears at first to be a somewhat different picture, suggesting a fairly dense population and sufficient prosperity to ensure considerable booty, is provided by the annals of ninth-century Assyrian campaigns. In his fourth campaign, for example, Shamshiadad V speaks of crossing the Turnat or Diyala and destroying Karnê, a "royal city," together with 200 cities in its environs. Continuing further, "the cities of Datêbir [and] Izduia, which are situated at

the side of the city of Gananati, together with 200 cities of their environs, I captured, 330 of them I smote" (Luckenbill, D. D. 1926. 1:258). Niqqu, another "strong, walled city" of the land of Tupliash (Luckenbill, D. D. 1926. 1: 235), vaguely identified with the Diyala region, is alternately described as having been deserted and smitten with weapons.

However, these accounts remain terribly elusive. The major "cities" themselves have not been located, and it is not unlikely that most or all of them are to be found not on the Diyala plains at all but to the north of the Jebel Hamrīn. As to booty, the grouping of different regions with a common total makes it virtually impossible to determine what part may have come from the Diyala watershed in the most inclusive sense. Furthermore, references to hundreds of "cities" obviously involve a large element of exaggeration. For all these reasons, the contrast between the Assyrian accounts of the region and the one given here is more apparent than real.

CHAPTER 6

General References:

Bikerman, E. 1938. Les institutions des Séleucides. Paris.

Cary, M. 1951. History of the Greek world from 323 to 146 B.C. 2d ed. London.

Debevoise, N. C. 1938. A political history of Parthia. Chicago.

Ghirshman, R. 1954a. Iran, from the earliest times to the Islamic conquest. *Pelican Book* A 239. Harmondsworth.

Jones, A. H. M. 1940. The Greek city from Alexander to Justinian. Oxford.

Olmstead, A. T. 1948. History of the Persian Empire. Chicago.

Pigulevskaya, N. 1963. Les villes de l'état Iranien aux époques Parthe et Sassanide. École Pratique des Hautes Études, Sorbonne, VI Section, *Documents et Recherches*, 6. Paris, The Hague.

Streck, M. 1917. Seleucia und Ktesiphon. *Der Alte Orient*, 16, 3–4. Leipzig.

Tarn, W. W. 1952. Hellenistic Civilization. 3d ed. (rev. by W. W. Tarn and G. T. Griffith). New York.

Notes:

1. Layard, A. H. 1853. Discoveries in the ruins of Nineveh and Babylon. London.

2. At least the central part of the Diyala region, the district around Eshnunna, is to be equated at this time with the land of Tupliash in the Assyrian annals (Hommel, F. 1926. Ethnologie und Geographie des alten Orients, *Handbuch der Altertumswissenschaft*, 3 Abt., 1 Teil, 1 bd. Munich. P. 296). Tiglath-Pileser III (744–727 B.C.) is the apparent exception to the generally predatory policies of his line with respect to the area. After sacking the city of Niqqu of the land Tupliash in his ninth regnal year, he claims to have rebuilt and resettled it with prisoners from other conquered lands (Luckenbill, D. D. 1926. Ancient records of Assyria and Babylonia. 2 vols. Chicago: University of Chicago Press. I, 278).

3. Adams, R. M. 1962. Agriculture and urban life in early southwestern Iran. *Science*, 136:109–22. It is interesting to contrast this apparent absence of a pronounced emphasis on hydraulic agriculture on the western flanks of the Achaemenian realm with Tolstov's observation that the great networks of irrigation canals in Choresm first were constructed during approximately the same period (Tolstov, S. P. 1953. Auf den Spuren der Altchoresmischen Kultur. Berlin. P. 112; Ghirshman, R. 1953. S. P. Tolstov, Drevniy Choresm (La Chorasmie antique). *Artibus Asiae* 16:215). Perhaps this suggests that the immediate stimulus to, and expert knowledge necessary for, large-scale canal construction in Choresm came from the east rather than from southwestern Asia.

4. Hagen, O. E. 1894. Keilschrifturkunden zur Geschichte des Königs Cyrus. *Beiträge zur Assyriologie und vergleichenden semitischen Sprachwissenschaft* 2:213.

5. Pausanias in Joanne Malalas, VIII, 203, cited in Streck, M. 1917. P. 6, n. 4.

6. Ammian, XXIII, 6, 4.

7. There is wide divergence in estimates of Seleucia's population. Pliny (N. H. vi, 122) puts it at 600,000, while at the time of its sack by Avidius Cassius, a century later, it is given by Dio Cassius (lxxi) as 300,000. As Yeivin observes (in Waterman, Leroy, *et al.* 1933. P. 39. Second preliminary report upon the excavations at Tel Umar, Iraq. Ann Arbor), this admitted reduction may tend to confirm the economic decline which can be deduced from purely archaeological evidence. Yeivin's own estimate, which assumes a residential area of about 200 blocks with an average population of 100 persons each (see Appendix A) and large areas of the site which at any time were devoted to public buildings or other non-residential uses, is that Seleucia had only 20,000 inhabitants. The surface area of the site, about 4 sq. kms., would suggest a population of about 80,000 persons if we apply the standards of population density used in the Diyala survey.

8. Strabo 16 I. 16.

9. Debevoise, N. C. 1938. P. 160, n. 65.

10. Keppel, G. 1827. Pp. 142 ff. Personal narrative of a journey from India to England . . . 1824. London.

11. Herzfeld, E. 1948. Geschichte der Stadt Samarra. *Die Ausgrabungen von Samarra*, 6. Hamburg. P. 55.

12. Hoffman, G. 1883. Nachtrag zu H. Kieperts karte der Runinenfelder von Babylon. *Zeitschr. der Gesellschaft für Erdkunde zu Berlin* 18:444.

13. Schoff, W. H. (ed.). 1914. Parthian Stations, by Isidore of Charax. Philadelphia.

14. Streck, M. 1917. P. 15; Debevoise, N. C. 1938. P. 14; Herzfeld, E. 1948. Pp. 36 f.

15. Debevoise, N. C. 1938. Pp. 24 f.

16. Cf. bibliography in Christensen, A. 1944. Pp. 383 ff.

175

L'Iran sous les Sassanides. 2d ed. (rev. and enl.). Copenhagen.

17. Streck, M. 1917. P. 15.

18. Ammianus Marcellinus, XXIII, 6, 23.

19. Strabo 16 I. 16.

20. Debevoise, N. C. 1934. Parthian pottery from Seleucia on the Tigris. *University of Michigan Studies*, Humanistic series, 23. Ann Arbor.

21. Madhlum, T. A. 1959. The excavation at Tel Abu Thar [in Arabic]. *Sumer* 15:85–94.

22. A similar and roughly contemporary trend has been observed in Egypt. Karl Butzer cites classical, medieval, and early modern sources to suggest that the population of Egypt during Graeco-Roman times was not rivaled again until after 1882. He indicates that at times during this long interval it may have been as low as one-fourth of the approximately 8,000,000 inhabitants present during the time of Flavius Josephus. "The archaeological evidence supports this supposition very strongly, for the settlement remains and cemeteries of the Hellenistic period preserved on the edge of the desert are simply unlimited and outweigh the sum total of older and younger remains by a total of several to one" (Butzer, K. W. 1960. Remarks on the geography of settlement in the Nile Valley during Hellenistic times. *Bulletin Société de Géographie d'Égypte* 33:7–8). Of course the post-Hellenistic developments in the two countries differ, but in the contrast between Hellenistic times and earlier antiquity they are strikingly similar in this respect.

23. Christensen, A. 1944. P. 383.

24. The aggregate area of the questionable sites in Table 18 is only about 15 hectares.

25. The following Parthian coins were identified by Sayyid Fuad Safar. All were collected from mounds which were regarded—prior to the identification of the coins—as having terminated in the Parthian period on the basis of ceramic surface collections:

Site Number	Coin Identification
89	Pacorus II (A.D. 78–115)
484	Vologases III or IV (A.D. 148–207)
631	Vologases V (A.D. 207–222)
662	Gotarzes II or Vologases I (A.D. 38–78)
672	Orodes II or Phraates IV (57–2 B.C.)

26. Rostovtsev, M. I. 1932. Seleucid Babylonia: Bullae and seals of clay with Greek inscriptions. *Yale Classical Studies* 3, 1. Pp. 90–91.

27. Altheim, F., and R. Stiehl. 1954. Ein asiatischer Staat: Feudalismus unter den Sasaniden und ihren Nachbarn 1:11. Wiesbaden.

28. Laessøe, J. 1953. Reflections on modern and ancient Oriental waterworks. *Journal of Cuneiform Studies* 7:5–26.

29. Pliny VI, xxi. 131.

30. A full discussion of sites along this older course, and of evidence for changes in the meander pattern, is planned for a forthcoming publication on the results of the Iraq Surface Survey in Akkad.

31. Reuther, O. 1929. The German excavations at Ctesiphon. *Antiquity* 3:439.

32. Le Strange, G. 1895. P. 41. Description of Mesopotamia and Baghdad, written about the year A.D. 900 by Ibn Serapion. *Journal Royal Asiatic Society*.

33. Cf. Obermeyer, J. 1929. Die Landschaft Babyloniens im Zeitalter des Talmuds und des Gaonats. *Schriften der Gesellschaft zur Forderung der Wissenschaft des Judentums*, 30. Frankfurt. Pp. 186–87.

34. Sarre, F., and E. Herzfeld. 1920. Vol. 2, Abb. 179.

35. Government of Iraq, Development Board, 1958. Sect. 2, p. 15. Lower Diyala Development: soils, agriculture, irrigation, and drainage. Diyala and Middle Tigris Projects, Report no. 2. London: Sir M. MacDonald and Partners, Ltd.

CHAPTER 7

General References:

Altheim, F., and R. Stiehl. 1954. Ein asiatischer Staat: Feudalismus unter den Sasaniden und ihren Nachbarn, vol. 1. Wiesbaden.

Christensen, A. 1944. L'Iran sous les Sassanides. 2d ed. (rev. and enl.). Copenhagen.

Ghirshman, R. 1954a. Iran, from the earliest times to the Islamic conquest. *Pelican Book* A 239. Harmondsworth.

Nöldeke, T. 1879. Geschichte der Perser und Araber zur Zeit der Sasaniden, aus der arabischen Chronik des Tabarī. Leiden.

Obermeyer, J. 1929. Die Landschaft Babyloniens im Zeitalter des Talmuds und des Gaonats. *Schriften der Gesellschaft zur Forderung der Wissenschaft des Judentums*, 30. Frankfurt.

Pigulevskaya, N. 1963. Les villes de l'état Iranien aux époques Parthe et Sassanide. École Pratique des Hautes Études, Sorbonne, VI Section, *Documents et Recherches*, 6. Paris, The Hague.

Notes:

1. Frye, R. N. 1956. Notes on the early Sassanian church and state. In "Studi orientalistici in onore di Giorgio Levi Della Vida," 1:319, 324. *Pubblicazioni dell'Istituto per l'Oriente*, 52. Rome.

2. Altheim, F., and R. Stiehl. 1954. Pp. 12 ff.

3. Adams, Robert M. 1962. Agriculture and urban life in early southwestern Iran. *Science* 136:109–22.

4. Nöldeke, T. 1879. Pp. 32 f.; Christensen, A. 1944. Pp. 220 ff.

5. Baynes, N. H. 1926. The successors of Justinian. In "Cambridge Medieval History" (H. M. Gwatkin, J. P. Whitney, eds.), 2:298.

6. On its location cf. Fig. 6. The ruins are now west of the Tigris but lay on the river's east bank until the thirteenth century.

176

7. Herzfeld, E. 1948. P. 64 (Geschichte der Stadt Samarra. *Die Ausgrabungen von Samarra*, 6. Hamburg); Pigulevskaya, N. 1963. P. 127.

8. Nöldeke, T. 1879. P. 57.

9. *Ibid.*, p. 165. The location of this city is unclear. Procopius (II, 14) places it one day's journey distant from Ctesiphon. Nöldeke (1879. P. 16, n. 4) assumes that it is identical with ruins still known as Rumīyā, noted by Chesney in 1836 (1850. The expedition for the survey of the rivers Euphrates and Tigris, carried on by order of the British Government, in the years 1835, 1836, and 1837. 2 vols. London), probably about 5 kms. northeast of the modern town of Suweira. These are not shown on more recent maps, and the area was not visited by the author during the reconnaissance. However, that location raises virtually insurmountable problems in that it cannot be linked into the remaining network of irrigation canals in the lower Diyala basin with which the site clearly belongs. Moreover, the Abbasid city of Rumīyā is described by Yaᶜqūbī (Wiet, G., tr.). 1937. Les Pays. *Publications de l'Inst. Français d'Archéologie Orientale, Textes et traductions d'auteurs orientaux*, 1. Cairo. P. 163) as about two or three miles from Asfānabr, which in turn underlies the modern town of Salmān Pāk. Hence Le Strange (1905. The Lands of the Eastern Caliphate. Cambridge. Pp. 33–34) properly regards the new Antioch-of-Chosroes as a "suburb" of Ctesiphon, rather than as a site 25–30 kms. downstream where it is placed by Nöldeke. According to O. Reuther (1938. Sāssānian architecture, History. In "A survey of Persian art" [A. U. Pope, ed.], 1:574. New York) and M. Bachmann (Christensen, A. 1944:386), the city may have occupied an area now known as al-Bustān-i-Kesrā, a short distance southeast of Ctesiphon, of which only a rectangular corner of an apparent city wall has survived the erosive action of the Tigris. Still another possibility is the apparent group of fairly extensive ruins that can be observed on air photographs in the next succeeding loop of the Tigris below Ctesiphon (4 kms. south-southeast of site 669 on the reference map of the area), but that were not visited during the survey.

10. Ammianus Marcellinus, XXIV, 3, 10.

11. *Ibid.*, XXIV, 6, 1.

12. *Ibid.*, XXIV, 4, 1; XXIV, 7, 2, *passim*.

13. Streck, M. 1917. Seleucia and Ktesiphon Der Alte Orient, p. 24. Leipzig.

14. Nöldeke, T. 1879. Pp. 15–16.

15. Ammianus Marcellinus, XXIV, 5, 3.

16. This finding will be discussed in a forthcoming publication of the results of the Oriental Institute Iraq Surface Survey. It is interesting to note that an exactly corresponding process seems to occur in Choresm at the same period. The left bank of the Amu Darya, long fought over with the Sassanians, saw an increasingly decadent trend of cultural development and, ultimately, the abandonment of numerous settlements and major irrigated areas. Meanwhile, on the right bank, the Afrīghid-Hephthalites continued to flourish (Ghirshman, R. 1953. S. P. Tolstov, Drevniy Choresm (La Chorasmie antique), p. 230. *Artibus Asiae* 16:209–37,292–319).

17. Tabarī, ann. I, 897–98. Cited in Altheim, F., and R. Stiehl. 1954. Pp. 133–34; Christensen, A. 1944. Pp. 365–66.

18. Altheim, F., and R. Stiehl. 1954. P. 41. The conversion to contemporary currency is a frankly hazardous one, and is intended to convey the order of magnitude of the tax receipts rather than their equivalence in purchasing power. Nöldeke (1879:355) favors an equation of 600 million dirhems with 294 million Marks (or over 360 million Francs) of that period. In turn this may be equated with $69,972,000 in 1879. Price inflation since then has raised this figure about 2.95 times (G. F. Warren and F. A. Pearson. 1935, "Gold and Prices," Table 1, New York; for years since 1913 cf. Bureau of Labor Statistics, Retail Price Index), or to more than $204,000,000 in maximum annual tax receipts by Chosroes II from all of his realm. For Kavadh, then, the taxes from the Sawād alone would have yielded 214,000,000 × 204,000,000/600,000,000, or around $73,000,000.

By way of comparison, it may be noted that tax revenues during the period 1951–57 from the whole of Iraq and from all sources other than oil averaged I.D. 37,139,000 (United Nations, Food and Agricultural Organization 1959. FAO Mediterranean Development Project, Iraq Country Report. Rome. Table II/20). This is 42 per cent more than Kavadh obtained from the Sawād alone, but less than Chosroes II Parvez ultimately collected there in annual revenue.

19. Cited in Altheim, F., and R. Stiehl. 1954. P. 46.

20. Sarre, F., and E. Herzfeld. 1920. 2:58 ff. (Archäologische Reise im Euphrat- und Tigris-Gebiet. Berlin); Reuther, O. 1929 (The German excavations at Ctesiphon. *Antiquity* 3:434–51); Reuther, O. 1938; Kuhnel, E. 1933 (Die Ausgrabungen der zweiten Ktesiphon-Expedition. Islamische Kunstabteilung der Staatlichen Museum, Berlin).

21. Cf. Reuther, O. 1938; Watelin. L. C. 1938 (The Sassanian buildings near Kish. In "A survey of Persian art" [A. U. Pope, ed.] 1:584–92. New York).

22. Ettinghausen, R. 1938. (Parthian and Sassanian pottery. In "A survey of Persian art" [A. U. Pope, ed.] 1:664–65. New York). Cf. Kuhnel, E. 1933. P. 28.

23. Ghirshman, R. 1954a. P. 289.

24. Reuther, O. 1929. P. 437.

25. In part, this trend may be a consequence of the survey's inability to record several known Sassanian towns (cf. Table 19, note). But since some of these might be classifiable as cities in terms of the present classification if they were known, and since at least one city also is missing in the tabulation (Weh-Antiokh-i-Khosrau), it seems likely that the contrast with the Parthian period still would remain if they were taken into account.

26. Wiet, G. (tr.) 1937. Yaᶜkubi, Les Pays. *Publications*

de l'Inst. Français d'Archéologie Orientale, Textes et traductions d'auteurs orientaux, 1. Cairo. P. 163.

27. On Weh-Antiokh-i-Khosrau cf. supra, p. 70, note 9. On Sābāt, Shekunsib and Humānīya see Obermeyer, J. 1929: 184 ff. Jarjarāyā does not occur in Obermeyer's Talmudic sources, and apparently was regarded by him only as an Islamic settlement. However, since Yaᶜqūbī reports that the town was inhabited by the descendants of Persian nobility (Wiet, G., tr.) 1955. Ibn Rusteh, Les atours précieux. Pub. de la Soc. de Gèog. d'Égypte. Cairo), its origin during the Sassanian period, if not earlier, probably can be assumed. Of these cities and towns, Ctesiphon (with its sister city of Asfānabr), Weh-Antiokh-i-Khosrau, and Shekunsib lay on the eastern bank of the river, within the lower Diyala basin of the time.

28. Study of aerial photographs indicates that one or more branches of the Diyala once flowed substantially farther north than the present position of the river adjacent to Jalūlā and Saᶜadīya (Qizil Rubāt). Several imposing tells now on the right bank of the river thus were once along its left or eastern bank. They could not be visited, however, and their periods of occupation are unknown.

29. Quite possibly supporting villages also were part of the comprehensive plan, but since the western half of this network lay at or beyond the limits of the survey their remains were not studied.

30. Nöldeke, T. 1879. P. 57.

31. Geog. Dict. VII, 181, tr. in Jacobsen, T. 1958a. Salinity and irrigation agriculture in antiquity. Diyala Basin Archaeological Project, report on essential results June 1, 1957 to June 1, 1958 (mimeographed). Baghdad. P. 78.

32. Ethe, H. (tr.). 1868. Zakarijaben Muhammed ben Mahmūd el-Kazwīni's Kosmographie, Leipzig. P. 374.

33. Nöldeke, T. 1879. P. 239.

34. Ibid., p. 274.

35. Jones, J. F. 1857a (Narrative of a journey, undertaken, in April, 1848, by Commander James Felix Jones, I.N., for the purpose of determining the tract of the ancient Nahrawān Canal. Selections from the records of the Bombay Government, n.s. 43, 33–134); Herzfeld, E. 1948.

36. Le Strange, G. 1895. Description of Mesopotamia and Baghdad, written about A.D. 900 by Ibn Seraphion. Journal Royal Asiatic Society. 1895. Pp. 265–70. Herzfeld's topographic studies make it clear, however, that Ibn Serapion's account errs on a number of specific details (Sarre, F., and E. Herzfeld. 1920. 1:53–64; Herzfeld, E. 1948. Pp. 71–76).

37. Le Strange, G. 1895. P. 272, n. 2.

38. But cf. Herzfeld's reconstruction: "Der Qātūl al-kisrawī ist nicht nur seines Namens wegen ein Kanal der Sasanidenzeit. Der Qātūl abu l-djund ist ein Werk des Rashīd, und der Name al-Maʾmūnī weist den andren Qātūl dem Maʾmūn zu, auch wenn das nicht besonders erwännt wird. Als al-Muᶜtasim nach einem Ort suchte, eine Stadt zu bauen, fand er diese Kanäle vor. Daher fand er das Gelände von al-Qātūl 'zu eng.' Die Vergrösserung des Qātūl al-kisrawī ist das Werk des Mutawakkil und blieb unvollendet. Dazu gehört auch die Kanalisation des ᶜAdaim und der Staudamm, wo dieser Fluss den Hamrīn durchbricht, der Band i ᶜAdaim" (Herzfeld, E. 1948. P. 76).

39. B. M. U. Bennell, in Jacobsen, T. 1958a. P. 79.

40. Government of Iraq, Development Board, 1958. Sect. 2, pp. 15 ff. Lower Diyala Development: soils, agriculture, irrigation and drainage. Diyala and Middle Tigris Projects, Report no. 2. London: Sir M. MacDonald and Partners, Ltd.

41. Jones, J. F. 1857a. P. 121.

A Persian geographic treatise written in A.D. 982 speaks of a river called the Sās (Sābus?) which "rises in the Armenian mountains and is utilized in the fields; when it reaches the town ᶜUkbarā [spelled ᶜAkbura] nothing remains of it" (Minorsky, V. 1937. Hudūd al-ᶜĀlam, "The regions of the world," a Persian geography 372 A.H.-A.D. 982. E. J. W. Gibb Memorial [n.s.] 11. London. P. 76). Minorsky notes that the Nahr Sābus "seems to correspond to the ᶜAdheim, though the latter rises, not in Armenia but near Kirkūk, in southern Kurdistan" (Minorsky, V. 1937. P. 218). The problem here is that, just as in the case of the available accounts of the Kātūl's course across the lower ᶜAdheim, this description contains no reference to the crossing of the Kātūl.

42. Herzfeld, E. 1948. Pp. 76 ff.

43. Jones, J. F. 1857a. P. 121. It is now called the Wadī Shtait, and is closely paralleled by the main Baghdad-Kirkūk road.

44. In the early nineteenth century, it was still said that "the superfluous waters [flood waters?] of the Azemia [ᶜAdheim] also discharge themselves into [the Diyala] at Tchubook" (Rich, Claudius James. 1836. Narrative of a residence in Koordistan and on the site of ancient Nineveh; with a journal of a voyage down the Tigris to Baghdad and an account of a visit to Shirauz and Persepolis. 2 vols. [ed. by his widow]. London. 2:288), presumably via this branch.

45. Le Strange, G. 1895. Pp. 271, 273, n. 4.

46. Ibid., p. 266.

47. The curious "goosenecks" on the Nahrawān, not far above Al-Qantara, are not to be interpreted as a localized, highly developed meander but rather as a design feature. It will be noted that many of the major branch canals elsewhere as well have their offtakes at sharply defined bends in the main canal. This may be explained in terms of contemporary design procedures: "In order to restrict entry of sediment into the canals it is normal practice to site the headworks on the outside of a bend, at which point the slower moving water carrying sand and gravel gravitates to the inside of the bend and the canal takes off comparatively clear water" (Government of Iraq, Development Board, 1958. Sect. 2, p. 106). The importance of reducing silt-loads from the viewpoint of the designers of the Nahrawān system perhaps can be better explained by noting that

178

the spoil-banks removed from the head reaches of such canals during ancient de-silting operations still constitute by far the most impressive monuments to man's former occupation of the now-empty regions along the middle and lower Nahrawān.

48. Rawlinson, H. C. 1841. Pp. 92–98 (Notes on a Journey from Tabriz, through Persian Kurdistan, to the ruins of Takhti-Soleiman, and from thence by Zenjan and Tarom, to Gilan, in October and November, 1838: with a Memoir on the Site of the Atropatenian Ecbatana. *Journal of the Royal Geographical Society of London* 10:1–158); Streck, M. 1917. P. 33 (Seleucia und Ktesiphon. *Der Alte Orient*, 16, 3–4. Leipzig).

49. Le Strange, G. 1905. P. 60.

50 Sarre, F., and E. Herzfeld, 1920. 2:88.

51. Jacobsen, T. 1958a. P. 76; cf. Herzfeld, E. 1948. Pp. 56 f.

52. Sarre, F., and E. Herzfeld. 1920. 2:78.

53. Hamzā of Isfahan, "die beste Quelle," attributes its founding to Hormizd I, 272–73 (Herzfeld, E. 1948. P. 44). The somewhat obscure Sassanian references to this site and its surroundings are summarized in Marquart, J. 1931. Pp. 59–60 (A catalogue of the provincial capitals of Eranshahr [G. Messina, ed.]. *Analecta Orientalia*, 3. Rome) and Pigulevskaya, N. 1963. Pp. 150–53, the latter also providing an interesting discussion of the shifting meaning of the term from a plot of land worked by a slave to a fortified rural estate or castle.

54. Le Strange, G. 1905. P. 62.

55. Ghirshman, R. 1954a. P. 308; Christensen, A. 1944. Pp. 501, *passim*.

56. Obermeyer, J. 1929. P. 81.

57. Le Strange, G. 1895. P. 298.

58. Lees, G. M., and N. L. Falcon. 1952. The geographical history of the Mesopotamian plains. *Geographical Journal* 118:24–39.

59. Wiet, G. (tr.) 1955. Ibn Rusteh, Les atours précieux. *Pub. de la Soc. de Géog. d'Égypte*. Cairo. P. 106.

60. Obermeyer, J. 1929. P. 126.

61. This may be instead merely another Jokha, recorded by Ibn Rusta (Le Strange, G. 1895. P. 301) as being in the Wāsit district.

62. With regard to the local impact of the invading Arab forces, it is instructive to consider the course of events at some representative towns in the Diyala region. As reported in al-Bilādhurī's Book of Conquests, a raiding party sent out by the Arab general Khālid ibn-al-Walīd received, or perhaps extracted, gifts from the inhabitants of ʿUkbarā, but passed through otherwise without incident (Hitti, P. K. [ed.] 1916. The origins of the Islamic State. *Columbia University, Studies in History, Economics and Public Law*, 68, New York. P. 399). When the Islamic forces entered Rumīyā during their advance on Ctesiphon, a choice was given to the populace either to leave or to remain. Those who followed the latter course were directed merely to pay homage, to continue their traditional obligations as to the kharāj (land tax), to act as guides if necessary, and to show no treachery (Hitti, P. K. 1916. P. 419). At Daskara we are told that the local dikhān was put to death because of treachery, but at nearby Mahrūdh the dikhān was able to retain his position simply by coming to terms and making a payment (*Ibid.*, p. 421). There is no suggestion in any of these reports of extensive destruction of civilian life or property, or of popular unrest, in connection with the Arab conquest of the region.

CHAPTER 8

General References:

Bagdâd 1962. Volume spécial publié à l'occasion du mille deux centième anniversaire de la fondation. *Arabica*, 9, no. 3. Leiden.

Brockelmann, C. 1949. History of the Islamic peoples (J. Carmichael and M. Perlmann, trs.). London.

Herzfeld, E. 1948. Geschichte der Stadt Samarra. *Die Ausgrabungen von Samarra*, 6. Hamburg.

Le Strange, G. 1905. The lands of the eastern caliphate. Cambridge.

Levy, R. 1962. The social structure of Islam. Cambridge.

Mez, Adam. 1922. Die Renaissance des Islâms. Heidelberg.

Spuler, B. 1952–53. Geschichte der Islamischen Länder. *Handbuch der Orientalistik*, 6, nos. 1–2. Leiden.

von Grünebaum, G. E. 1955. The Muslim town and the Hellenistic town. *Scientia* 90:364–70.

Notes:

1. E.g. von Kremer, A. 1875 (Culturgeschichte des Orients. 2 vols. Vienna); Mez, Adam. 1922; Løkkegaard, Frede. 1950 (Islamic taxation, with special reference to circumstances in Iraq. Copenhagen).

2. de Goeje, M. J. 1889. P. 11. Kitâb al-Masâlik waʾl-Mamâlik, auctore Abuʾl-Kâsim Obaidallah ibn Abdallah Ibn Khordâdhbeh. Accedunt excerpta e Kitâb al-Kharâdj, auctore Kodâma ibn Djaʿfar. *Bibliotheca Geographorum Arabicorum*, 6. Leiden.

3. von Kremer, A. 1875. 1:258–60.

4. de Goeje, M. J. 1889. P. 11.

5. "Sicher ist es, dass der finanzielle Verfall mit Omar II. begann, den dieser bigotte Chalife brachte durch seine verkehrten Regierungsanordnungen die Finanzen in die grösste Unordnung, so dass Provinzen, die früher immer activ gewesen waren, nun plötzlich nichts mehr an die Centralkasse abfuhrten, ja sogar von dieser bedeutende Summen beanspruchten" (von Kremer, A. 1875. 1:262). However, a more recent and favorable view of the financial policies of Omar II is suggested by Gibb's analysis of his fiscal rescript (Gibb, H. A. R. 1955. The fiscal rescript of ʿUmar II. *Arabica* 2:1–16).

6. de Goeje, M. J. 1889. Pp. 180–81.

7. *Ibid.*, pp. 6–10.

The usually accepted figure of 78,000,000 dirhems seems too low. Accepting de Goeje's equivalences of 1 khurr wheat = 545 dirhems and 1 khurr barley = 355 dirhems (de Goeje, M. J. 1889. P. 9), the tabulated total of collections in kind by districts reaches this amount. But in addition it is stated that 9,350,000 dirhems were collected in silver.

8. Mez, A. 1922. P. 123.

9. von Kremer, A. 1888. P. 287 (Über das Einnahmbudget des Abbasiden-Reiches vom Jahre 306 H (918–919). *Denkschriften der Kaiserlichen Akademie der Wissenschaften, Vienna. Phil.-hist. Classe*, vol. 36).

10. von Kremer, A. 1888. P. 312.

11. Mez. A. 1922. P. 123.

12. Le Strange, G. 1919. P. 36 (The geographical part of the Muzhat-al-Qulūb composed by Hamd-Allāh Mustawfī of Qazwīn in 740 (A.D. 1340). *E. J. W. Gibb Memorial Series*, vol. 23, 2. Leiden).

13. von Kremer, A. 1888. Pp. 323–24.

14. Margoliouth, D. S. (tr.). 1921. 4:347–49. The eclipse of the Abbasid caliphate: original chronicles of the fourth Islamic century. Vols. 4–5, Miskawaihi, The experiences of the nations. London.

15. *Ibid.*, pp. 439–40.

16. *Ibid.*, 5:99.

17. *Ibid.*, p. 177.

18. Løkkegaard, Frede. 1950. P. 161.

19. Yāqūt I, 252; tr. in Jacobsen, T. 1958a. P. 82. Salinity and irrigation agriculture in antiquity. Diyala Basin Archaeological Project, report on essential results June 1, 1957, to June 1, 1958 (mimeographed). Baghdad.

20. Margoliouth (tr.). 1921. 5:100–5.

21. Le Strange, G. 1900. Baghdad during the Abbasid Caliphate. Oxford.

For references to more recently published source materials as well as to differences of interpretation which they engender cf. especially Makdisi (Makdisi, G. 1959. The topography of eleventh-century Bagdâd: materials and notes. *Arabica* 6:178–97, 281–309), Bagdâd 1962, and Lassner (Lassner, J. 1963a. Notes on the topography of Baghdad: the systematic description of the city and the Khatīb al-Baghdâd. *Journal of the American Oriental Society* 83: Pp. 458–69). As Lassner notes, scholars of the generation of Le Strange on the whole failed to deal critically with the ages of component elements in the systematic descriptions of the city, so that a picture of changing topographic details today would be drawn much more cautiously.

22. Following the correction in the attribution and metrical equivalency of these figures suggested by Lassner (Lassner, J. 1963b. P. 228. The habl of Baghdad and the dimensions of the city: a metrological note. *Journal of the Economic and Social History of the Orient*, 6).

23. Makdisi, G. 1959. P. 282.

24. In Bagdâd 1962. P. 295.

25. Broadhurst, R. J. C. (tr. and ed.). 1952. Pp. 234–38. The travels of Ibn Jubayr. London.

26. Longrigg, S. H. 1925. Four centuries of modern Iraq. Oxford.

27. Herzfeld, E. 1948. P. 137.

But cf. the more cautious statements of Russell (1958. Late ancient and medieval populations. *American Phil. Society, Transactions*, 48, 3), whose point of departure is a widely based comparative view of the medieval demographic evidence. Taking the occupied area of Baghdad as about 3,000 hectares, he comments that, "Since it contained many public buildings as well as palaces and great dwellings it cannot have been densely populated. . . . Much of the 3,000 hectares apparently consisted of gardens and small holdings. Under these conditions it seems very unlikely that the average density was more than 100 to the hectare, or about 300,000. This still would have made it larger than Constantinople, but would have been about right for an empire of 20 million inhabitants" (Russell, J. C. 1958. P. 89).

In light of the much larger contemporary estimates of the size of Baghdad cited above, which seemingly are both careful and reliable, Russell's use of 3,000 ha. for the size of the city no longer can be accepted. And while non-residential structures and gardens undoubtedly occupied considerable areas, there is much eye-witness testimony to the density of housing elsewhere within the city. What this suggests, as indeed this chapter seeks to demonstrate with different data, is that perhaps the size of the capital was *not* "about right for an empire of 20 million inhabitants."

28. Wiet, G. (tr.) 1937. Pp. 44–63. Yaᶜkūbī, Les Pays, *Publications de l'Inst. Français d'Archéologie Orientale, Textes et traductions d'auteurs orientaux*, 1. Cairo.

29. Herzfeld, E. 1948.

30. Sousa. Ahmed. 1948. The irrigation system of Sāmarrā during the Abbasid Caliphate. Vol. 1 (in Arabic). Baghdad.

31. Musil, A. 1927. P. 139. The Middle Euphrates: a topographical itinerary. *American Geographical Society, Oriental Explorations and Studies*, 3. New York.

32. This is one of several estimates which Adler finds "apparently exaggerated," whereas in earlier stages of his itinerary "the Traveller has always appeared to underestimate the Jewish population" (Adler, M. N. [ed. and tr.]. 1907. P. 35. The itinerary of Benjamin of Tudela. London). Adler concludes that Benjamin must have proceeded directly from Isfahan to Egypt, basing his exaggerated statements on hearsay information. The fact that ᶜUkbarā is said to be a two days' journey from Baghdad, about twice its actual distance, may tend to substantiate the view that Benjamin never undertook the journey.

33. Herzfeld, E. 1948. P. 69; Canard, M. 1953. P. 151 (Histoire de la dynastie de H'amdanides de Jazīra et de Syrie, vol. 1. *Publications de la Faculté des Lettres d'Alger*, 21. Paris).

34. Wiet, G. (tr.). 1937. Pp. 162–63.

35. Le Strange 1905. Pp. 34–38.

36. Wiet, G. (tr.). 1955. P. 214. Ibn Rusteh, Les atours précieux. *Pub. de la Soc. de Géog. d'Égypte.* Cairo.

37. Rashīd al-Dīn Tabīb 1836. P. 267. Histoire des Mongols de la Perse (M. Quatrmère, tr.). Paris.

38. Le Strange, G. 1919. P. 52.

39. Le Strange, G. 1905. P. 35.

40. Obermeyer, J. 1929. P. 186. Die Landschaft Babyloniens im Zeitalter des Talmuds und des Gaonats. *Schriften der Gesellschaft zur Forderung der Wissenschaft des Judentums,* 30. Frankfurt.

41. Wiet, G. (tr.). 1955. P. 215.

42. Obermeyer, J. 1929. P. 186.

43. Le Strange, G. 1919. P. 48.

44. Obermeyer, J. 1929. P. 192.

45. Jones, J. F. 1857a. Pp. 71, 72, 74 (Narrative of a journey, undertaken, in April, 1848, by Commander James Felix Jones, I.N., for the purpose of determining the tract of the ancient Nahrawān Canal. *Selections from the Records of the Bombay Government* [n.s.] 43: 34–134).

46. Jones, J. F. 1857b. P. 147 (Narrative of a journey to the frontier of Turkey and Persia. *Selections from the Records of the Bombay Government* [n.s.] 43: 136–213); Kiepert, A. 1883: map (Zur Karte der Ruinenfelder von Babylon. *Zeitschrift der Gesellschaft für Erdkunde zu Berlin,* 18).

47. Wiet, G. (tr.). 1937. P. 164.

48. Le Strange, G. 1905. P. 37.

49. Wiet, G. (tr.) 1955. Pp. 189–90.

50. Obermeyer, J. 1929. P. 146.

51. Le Strange, G. 1905. P. 61.

52. Sarre, F., and E. Herzfeld. 1920. 2:82 (Archäologische Reise im Euphrat- und Tigris-Gebiet. 4 vols. Berlin).

53. Le Strange, G. 1919. P. 53.

54. Le Strange, G. 1905. P. 62.

55. Sarre, F., and E. Herzfeld. 1920. 2:82.

56. *Ibid.,* p. 86.

57. Le Strange, G. 1919. P. 162.

58. della Valle, Pietro. 1681. 2:7. Viaggi di Pietro della Valle il Pellegrino, descritti da lui medesimo in lettere familiari. 4 vols. Venice.

59. Otter, Jean. 1781–89. 1:167. Johann Otters . . . reisen in die Türkey und nach Persien. Nürnberg.

60. Olivier, G. A. 1801–1807. 5:6. Voyages dans l'Empire Ottoman, l'Égypte et la Perse fait par ordre du gouvernement, pendant les six premières années de la République. With atlas. 6 vols. Paris.

Cf. Dupré, Adrien. 1819. 1:221–22. Voyages en Perse fait dans les années 1807, 1808 et 1809 en traversant la Natolie et la Mésopotamie. 2 vols. Paris.

61. Ker Porter, R. 1821–22. 2:237–38. Travels in Georgia, Persia, ancient Babylonia, etc. 2 vols. London.

62. Buckingham, J. S. 1830. 1:19–20. Travels in Assyria, Media, and Persia. 2 vols. London.

63. Keppel, G. 1827. Pp. 145–46, 148. Personal narrative of a journey from India to England . . . 1824. London.

64. Jones, J. F. 1857b. Pp. 140–41.

65. Petermann, Julius Heinrich. 1865. 2:275. Reisen im Orient. 2 vols. Leipzig. Somewhat contradicting Jones's and Petermann's reports is that of a French officer posted to the Persian army, J. P. Ferrier (1856. Caravan journeys and wanderings in Persia, Afghanistan, Turkistan, and Beloochistan [translated from the unpublished manuscript by William Jesse]. London). Passing through Shahrābān with a caravan in 1845, he noted cursorily (p. 6) that there were from two hundred and fifty to three hundred houses, many crowned with up to five or six nests of storks. The closer knowledge of the region, as well as the more detailed observations, of Jones and Petermann suggest that this estimate—at least insofar as it applies to *inhabited* buildings—was probably excessive.

66. Valle, Pietro della. 1681. 2:7.

67. Petermann, J. H. 1865. 2:276.

68. Le Strange, G. 1905. P. 61. Yāqūt I, 534–35.

69. Le Strange, G. 1919. P. 45.

70. Otter, J. 1781–89. 2:23.

71. Jones, J. F. 1857b. Map facing p. 136.

72. Wüstenfeld, F. 1864. Jâcût's Reisen, aus seinem geographischen Wörterbuche beschreiben. *Zeitschrift der Deutschen Morgenländischen Gesellschaft,* 18:439.

73. Le Strange, G. 1919. P. 49; Sarre, F., and E. Herzfeld. 1920. 2:82, n. 2.

74. Olivier, A. G. 1807. 5:5–6; cf. Dupré, A. 1819. 1:221.

75. Rousseau, Jean Baptiste Louis Jacques. 1809. Pp. 80–81. Description du Pachalik de Bagdad. Paris. There is no evidence in his account that Rousseau ever visited the town; inaccuracies in the location he gives for it also suggest that he may have been poorly informed.

76. Buckingham, J. S. 1830. 1:15.

77. Keppel, G. 1827. Pp. 139–40.

78. Fraser, J. B. 1840. 2:171. Travels in Koordistan, Mesopotamia, etc. 2 vols. London.

79. Ferrier, J. P. 1856. P. 3. As noted earlier (*supra,* n. 65), Ferrier's estimate may include houses in ruins as well as occupied houses and hence may be excessive as an index to population. To the usually precise eye of Felix Jones, only a year later, Baʿqūba could only boast "of some good gardens, and a few wretched houses embosomed in a date-grove, watered by a cut from the Kharasan or Jelluleh canal" (Jones, J. F. 1857b. P. 139).

80. Černik-Expedition, 1875–76. Technische studienexpedition durch die Gebiete des Euphrat und Tigris. 2 vols. *Petermanns geographische Mitteilungen.* Ergänzungsheft nos. 44–45, 1:34.

81. Herzfeld, E. 1907. P. 50. Eine Reise durch Luristan, Arabistan und Fars. *Petermanns Mitteilungen,* 1907.

82. Yāqūt III, 604.

83. Yāqūt I, 252; Le Strange, G. 1905. P. 59.

84. Sarre, F. 1925 (Die Keramik von Samarra. *Die Aus-*

grabungen von Samarra, 2. Berlin); Government of Iraq, Department of Antiquities, 1940 (Excavations at Sāmarrā, 1936–39. Baghdad).

85. Safar, F. 1945. Wāsit, the Sixth's Season's excavations. Cairo.

86. Altheim, F., and R. Stiehl (1954. Ein asiatischer Staat: Feudalismus unter den Sasaniden und ihren Nachbarn. 1:41. Wiesbaden) point out that at the time of Qudāma the entire Sawād produced only about 2/5 of the tax revenues of the Abbasid caliphate.

87. Le Strange, G. 1895:266. Description of Mesopotamia and Baghdad, written about the year 900 A.D. by Ibn Serapion. Journal Royal Asiatic Society. 1895:33–76, 255–315.

88. The silt-carrying capacity of a watercourse is proportional both to its slope and its cross-sectional area. The latter is sharply reduced in the case of a branch-canal offtake from a larger canal, leading to the rapid deposition of silt. Cf. p. 178, note 47.

89. Sarre, F., and E. Herzfeld. 1920. 2:84–85. Possibly a part of the district of the "two Dhibs" also lay outside the lower basin, since Herzfeld equates one of them with the present Khālis canal and one with the Abi-i-Shirwān. The latter flows into the Diyala from the north just *above* the Jebel Hamrīn.

90. Le Strange, G. 1905. P. 35.

91. The conversion of 1 Jarīb = 1592 sq. m. is given by Lassner (1963. P. 228). It is implicit in Ibn Khurradādhbah's summary of the results of ᶜUmar's cadastral survey that the tax was levied both on fields in crop and those in fallow. For example, the indicated tax base for the Sawād is an area of 36,000,000 Jarībs or 5,731,200 hectares —somewhat larger than what is presently regarded as the total cultivable area in the same region. Yet unless this entire area were taxed at the given rates the revenues accounted for could not have been raised. The taxing of land in fallow under ᶜUmar's edict is explicitly affirmed by Tabarī (Nöldeke, T. 1879. P. 246. Geschichte der Perser und Araber zur Zeit der Sasaniden, aus der arabischen Chronik des Tabarī. Leiden).

92. Ibn Khurradādhbah, in de Goeje. 1889. P. 11.

93. Mustawfī, in Le Strange, G. 1919. P. 35.

94. In the case of Chosroes I Anōsharwān, whose graduated head-tax almost certainly was used as a model by ᶜUmar, Nöldeke comments that "Natürlich war der geringste Satz weitaus der allgemeinste. . . ." In fact, a Chinese traveler, Hsüan Tsang, merely describes each family in the Persian kingdom as paying the lowest of the annual rates given by Tabarī (Nöldeke, T. 1879. P. 246, n. 2).

95. As noted in Chapter 2, there is a considerable discrepancy between actual and officially recorded crop yields. Since present land rents are based on crop percentages, it is probable that peasants tend to keep official yields low in order to reduce their payments. Hence actual yields have been used here instead, for with a fixed tax per unit area the farmer would naturally seek to maximize his output. Under such conditions, it is interesting to note that there would have been less inducement to use the growing barley crop as a source of forage. But no data are available from which it might be determined whether herds of livestock in fact were correspondingly smaller then than they are at present.

96. Since these rates are based on calculations of modern gross yields from standing crops without regard for any loss during the harvesting process, they are somewhat lower than the actual rates that must have been enforced by tax-collectors. Tabarī describes the larger tax on wheat than barley as a special surcharge for the support of the army. He states that the additional surtax amounts to one- or two-tenths of the crop (Nöldeke, T. 1879. Pp. 246–47), which is consistent with the calculations given here. Citing Māwardī's Ahkām as-Sultānīya, Lambton concludes that "The rates imposed appear to have been half the produce on unirrigated land, one-third on land irrigated by dālīeh, and a quarter on land irrigated by dūlāb [also a type of water wheel]" (Lambton, A. K. S. 1953. Landlord and peasant in Persia. London. P. 33). Given the inevitable differences between legal theories and actual collections, these rates also are consistent with our calculations.

97. Le Strange, G. 1895. P. 270.

98. Harris, S. A. 1958. The Gilgaied and bad-structured soils of Central Iraq. Journal of Soil Science 9:169–85.

99. Sarre, F., and E. Herzfeld. 1920. 2:86.

100. Le Strange, G. 1905. P. 60.

101. Although this study is concerned only with the Diyala region, it is perhaps worth noting that the prevailing pattern of deterioration observed there cannot be assumed to represent the Islamic world generally during the two or three centuries preceding the Mongol conquest. Professor Hodgson informs me, for example, that numerous towns, with a flourishing intellectual as well as commercial life, still were to be found in the Jazīra (upper Mesopotamia) during the eleventh and twelfth centuries. It is not unlikely, however, that conditions in the Sawād as a whole were essentially similar to those on the Diyala plains.

102. Cf. Howorth, H. H. 1888. 3:123 ff. History of the Mongols, from the ninth to the nineteenth century. Vol. 3, The Mongols in Persia. London.

103. *Ibid.*, p. 132.

104. *Ibid.*, p. 127.

105. This pre-eminence was, of course, relative to the generally reduced state of the country. Sixty years after the Mongol conquest not a tenth part of the Abbasid city remained (*Ibid.*, p. 132).

106. Le Strange, G. 1905. P. 58.

107. Le Strange, G. 1895. Pp. 265, 271, 273; Salmon, Georges 1904. P. 144 (L'Introduction topographique à l'histoire de Bagdâdh d'Abou Bakr Ahmad ibn Thabit al-Khatib al-Bagdâdhî [323–463 H. = 1002–1071 J.-C.]. Bibliothèque de l'École des Hautes Études, 148. Paris).

108. There was a later tradition that the original course of the Khālis was laid out by ᶜAli, who set its course by dragging a spear point along the ground behind his horse (Petermann, J. H. 1865. 1:311).

109. Stuart A. Harris suggests (personal communication) that a careful program of leveling at measured intervals along ancient canals whose approximate date has been determined by this study would provide a means for testing this hypothesis.

CHAPTER 9

Notes:

1. Urban centers, as defined in the map of Islamic settlements (Fig. 6), exceed 30 hectares in size. At a density of 200 persons per ha., the minimal "urban" population under modern conditions would be about 6,000 persons. This equivalency is the basis for the comparison that is given.

APPENDIX A

Notes:

1. Delougaz, P. 1952. Pottery from the Diyala Region. *Oriental Institute Publications*, 63. Chicago.

2. The unpublished ceramics from Nippur, deriving from eight seasons of excavations since World War II, were of exceptional importance as a source of securely dated diagnostic features. The author is indebted to Richard Carl Haines, field director of the expedition to Nippur, for copies of preliminary drawings of the entire body of Nippur pottery. The Nippur sequence is, in fact, basic to the sequence of surface types worked out by the Diyala Basin Archaelogical Project for the entire span of time from the beginning of the Early Dynastic period into the Parthian period.

3. Rowe, John H. 1959. Archaeological dating and cultural process. *Southwestern Journal of Anthropology* 15: 317–24.

4. Harris, S. A., and R. M. Adams. 1957. A note on canal and marsh stratigraphy near Zubediya. *Sumer* 13: 157–63.

5. Frankfort, H. 1933. Tell Asmar, Khafaje and Khorsabad: second preliminary report of the Iraq Expedition. *Oriental Institute Communications*, 16. Chicago.

6. Alcock, Leslie. 1951. A technique for surface collecting. *Antiquity* 25:75–76.

7. Frankfort, H. 1948. Kingship and the gods. Chicago: University of Chicago Press. P. 396, n. 23.

8. Waterman, Leroy, *et al.* 1933. P. 39. Second preliminary report upon the excavations at Tel Umar, Iraq. Ann Arbor.

9. Russell, J. C. 1958. Late ancient and medieval populations. American Phil. Society, *Transactions* 48, 3. P. 12.

10. Russell, J. C. 1958. Pp. 49, 81, *passim.*

11. Stronach, David. 1961. The excavations at Ras al-ᶜAmiya. *Iraq* 23:95–137.

12. Frankfort, H. 1933. P. 55.

13. Pritchard, J. B. (ed.) 1950. Ancient Near Eastern Texts relating to the Old Testament. Princeton. P. 97.

14. To give concrete examples from the Diyala region, the available data on excavations at Tell Agrab and Khafājah indicate that the area of Early Dynastic settlement approximately coincided with that of later periods. At Tell Asmar, however, the town wall built in the Larsa period was found to enclose a considerably larger area than had been settled earlier. While the outline of the Early Dynastic town at Tell Asmar cannot be determined at present, the limited known segment of its wall suggests that it may have been only a small town rather than the regional capital it later became (Delougaz, P. 1952. Pl. 201). In this and similar instances, the area of earlier settlement must have been significantly less than the figures we are constrained to assume from later periods.

APPENDIX B

Notes:

1. The following sequence of brick sizes was worked out independently by the author from observations during the surface reconnaissance and by Mohammed Ali Mustafa during excavations at Sumaka and El-Qantara:

Period	Approximate range in sizes
Sassanian	34–38 cm. sq.
Early Islamic	29–32 cm. sq.
Sāmarrān	25–28 cm. sq.
Late Abbasid	21–23 cm. sq.

INDEX

Ghuzz, Turkish tribal grouping, 92

Girsu (Bau temple), 23–24

Ground water: artificial drainage of, 17; lateral movement of, 18; rise of, 17–18, 81; salinity of, 9, 17

Gutian invasion, 44–45, 49

Gyndes, 25, 60. See also Diyala River

Hammurabi: king of Babylon (1792–1750 B.C.), 47, 48, 49, 50, 52; palace of, 50

Hārūn-al-Rashīd, Abbasid caliph (A.D. 786–809), 77, 89, 97, 102

Hārūn ibn Gharīb, 85–86

Hārūnīya: canal, 19, 108; town, 92, 94

Haur es-Subaicha (seasonal swamp), 19, 35, 51, 57, 79, 81, 108

Heraclius, Byzantine emperor (A.D. 610–641), 69, 70, 79, 80, 81

Herodotus, 25, 60

Herzfeld, Ernst, 28, 78, 90

Hilla, 16, 107

Hulagu, Mongol khan (Baghdad, A.D. 1258–1265), 90, 91, 106–7

Humānīya, 74, 91, 107

Ibn Fadl, 85

Ibn Hauqal, 85, 92

Ibn Jubayr, 90

Ibn Khurradādhbah, 97, 100–103

Ibn Rāʾiq, emir in Baghdad (A.D. 936–942), 86, 103

Ibn Rusta, 82, 91–92, 94, 99, 106

Ibn Serapion, 77, 78, 79, 100, 102

Ibn Sherzād, 86

Ibn Yāqūt, 86

Ilkhanid period, 106–11

Indo-Europeans, 55

Irrigation, lift. See Irrigation system: pump-fed; Shādūf; Sharrad

Irrigation canals: design and capacity of, 77; levees, 6, 8–9, 66, 120; silting up of, 81, 104–5. See also Nahr

Irrigation system: contemporary layout of 19; extension of, 26, 28, 35–36, 40–41, 42, 44, 65–66, 68, 76, 82–83; maintenance of, 19, 40–41, 66; political requirements for, 41, 69, 80, 82, 113, 114; pump-fed, 19, 27–28

Ischali (ancient Neribtum), 43, 46, 47, 48, 51

Jalūlā, 92

Jalūltā, 92

Jarjarāyā, 11, 74, 91

Jebel Hamrīn, 6–7, 12, 75

Jerboah (Arab tribe), 27

Jones, James Felix, 27, 50, 78, 91, 94

Julian, Roman emperor (A.D. 361–363), 62, 70

Kanʿan, 5

Kashtiliashu IV, Cassite king (1242–1235 B.C.), 55

Kātūl al-Kisrawī, 76–78, 80, 81, 90, 99, 108, 113

Kavadh, Sassanian king (A.D. 499–531), 70, 71

Keppel, George, 61

Kermanshāh, 94

Khafājah (ancient Tutub), 9, 34, 35, 37, 38, 41, 43, 45, 46, 47, 49, 50, 51, 52, 120, 123

Khālis: canal, 19, 26, 67, 78, 102, 108, 120; town, 5, 15

Khān Banī Saʿad, 7, 16, 27

Kharnābāt, 95

Khurāsān (Jalūlā) canal, 19, 80, 81, 106, 108, 109

Khuzestan, 24–25, 60, 69. See also Elam; Susa

Kish, 39, 71

Kūfa, 91, 107

Kūt al-ʿAmāra, 28, 79, 82, 102

Land use patterns, as reflection of institutional structure, 112–13

Later Abbasid (post-Sāmarrān) period, 102–6

Luristan bronzes, 55

Lynch, H. B., 26

Mahdī, Abbasid caliph (A.D. 775–785), 89

Mahrūt (Gukha?) canal, 19, 28, 80, 81, 99, 100, 109

Malgium, 48

Malikshāh, Saljūk sultan (A.D. 1072–1092), 92

Maʾmūn, Abbasid caliph (A.D. 813–833), 89

Mansūr, Abbasid caliph (A.D. 754–775), 89, 91, 98

Mansūr Rashīd, Abbasid caliph (A.D. 1135–1136), 90

Masʿudī, 71

Mazdakite movement, 70, 75

Medar, 67

Mercenaries, Turkish and Dailemite, 86, 87–89

Meturnu, 60

Middle Babylonian period, 55–57

Miskawaih, 85–89

Mithradates I, Parthian king (171–138 B.C.), 62

Mohammad, Saljūk sultan (A.D. 1105–1118), 90

Molon (Seleucid satrap), 62

Mosul, 90

Muʿāwiya, Omayyad caliph (A.D. 661–680), 84

Muʿizz al-Daulah, Būyid emir in Baghdad (A.D. 945–967), 87–88

Muqaddasī, 90, 91, 92

Muqtadir, Abbasid caliph (A.D. 908–932), 86

Muradīya canal, 67

Mustaʿin, Abbasid caliph (A.D. 862–866), 89

Mustawfī, 91, 92, 94, 107

Muʿtadid, Abbasid caliph (A.D. 892–902), 94

Nahr Abū-l-Jund, 77, 102

Nahr al-Mālik (Yūsifiyah canal), 66, 70, 74

Nahr al-Māmūnī, 77

Nahr al-Rāsāsi, 76

Nahr al-Yahūdī, 77

Nahrawān: canal, 3, 9, 67, 76, 77, 81, 86, 87, 95, 100, 103, 104–5, 106, 113, 120; lower weir, see Al-Qantara; outfall into Tigris, 79; town (Sifwah), 74, 78–79, 81, 82, 91–92; upper weir, 79

Najaf, 107

Nāsir, Abbasid caliph (A.D. 1180–1225), 85

Neo-Babylonian period, 58–59

Nobility, landed, 69, 70, 73, 81

Nomads, 25, 27, 28, 42, 52, 92, 99, 109, 114

Oriental history, cumulative changes in, 112, 116

Pacorus I, Parthian prince (d. 38 B.C.), 62

Population, modern distribution by settlement size, 21–23

Population density: ancient, 41, 122–25; effects of land tenure system on, 15, 25; modern rural, 15, 23, 24–25, 29; modern urban, 24

Population "pressure" on land, water resources, 42, 63–65, 74–75

Qanāt, 75

Qasr-i-Shīrīn, 71

Qazwīnī, 76

Qudāma, 85

Radī, Abbasid caliph (A.D. 934–940), 85–86

Rapiku, 47

Ras al-ʿĀmiyah, 34, 124

Reconnaissance data, completeness of, 120–21

Rich, Claudius J., 26

Rimush, Akkadian king (2278–2270 B.C.), 43

Road: Khurāsān, 86, 92, 94, 105; royal Achaemenian, 61

Roman and Byzantine campaigns, 61–62, 70, 116

Rūz canal, 19, 81, 106, 108, 109

Sābāt, 74

Salinity, effects on cultivation and settlement, 18, 48, 99

Saljūks, Turkish sultans in Baghdad (A.D. 1118–1157), 87, 89, 105

Salmān Pāk. See Ctesiphon

Sāmarrā, 76, 77, 89, 90, 96, 97, 98–99, 116

Samsuiluna, king of Babylon (1749–1712 B.C.), 49

Sargon I, Akkadian king (2334–2279 B.C.), 43

Sassanian period, 69–83

Sawād: economic decline of, 84–85, 87–89; taxes from, 71, 84–85, 97, 102

Scaphae (lower Uskāf), 61, 66–67, 80

Sediment-carrying capacity, 8, 105

186

INDEX

ILLUSTRATIONS

Maps

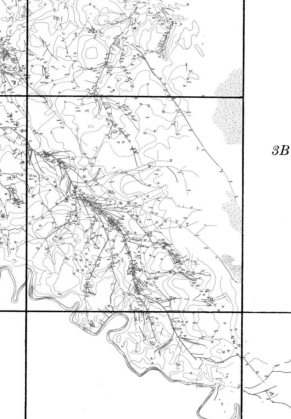

1B

2B

3B

4A

4B

THE DIYALA PLAINS
Remains of Ancient Settlements and Watercourses

The following eight pages illustrate the modern topography of the Diyala plains. Features which are only of contemporary or recent importance have not been shown, and major emphasis is placed on the vestiges of former occupations. Thus, in a sense, the purpose of these maps is to summarize the cumulative, visible effects of six millennia of irrigation and human settlement on the contemporary Diyala landscape.

While the maps of individual historical phases (Figs. 1–6) depict the whole area, here the intent is to illustrate the existing topography on as large a scale as possible. Hence the map has been divided into eight sections, proceeding in order from north to south across the whole length of the alluvial fan of the Diyala. To facilitate reference to a particular site or district, these sections slightly overlap one another. For an explanation of the cartographic sources used for this map, and of the procedures and limitations of the archaeological survey for which it served as a basis, see Appendix A.

LEGEND

Contour interval, 1 meter

●∙ 446   Site of former settlement, generally a mound or group of mounds. For description refer adjoining number to corresponding entry in Appendix C

Spoil-banks or depressed bed of former watercourse

Depression without external drainage

Seasonal marsh

Sand dunes

34° 15'

34° 00'

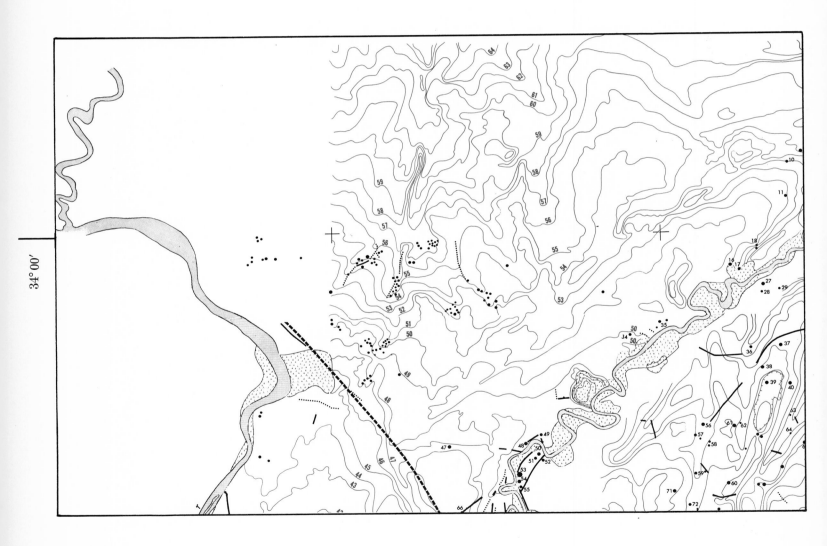

SECTION 1A

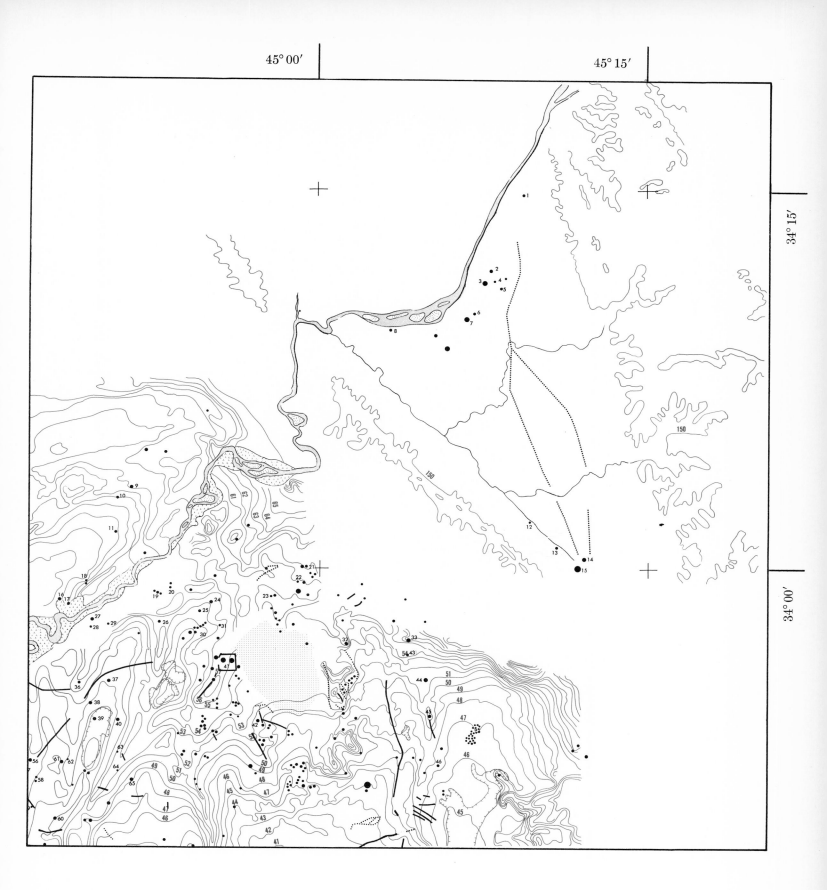

SECTION 1B

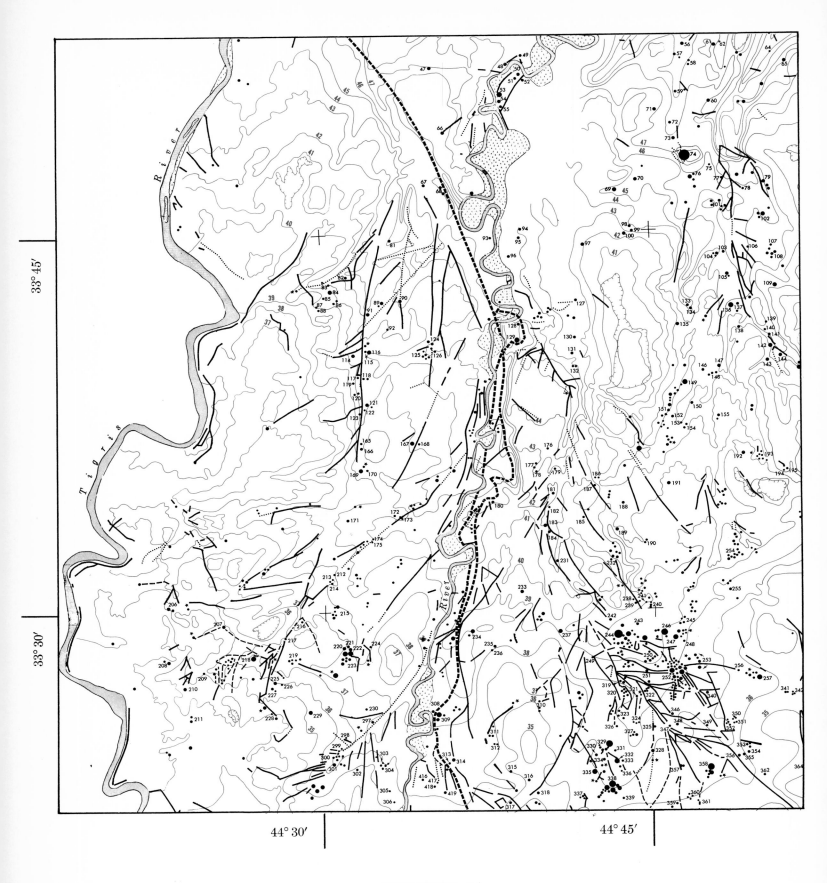

SECTION 2A

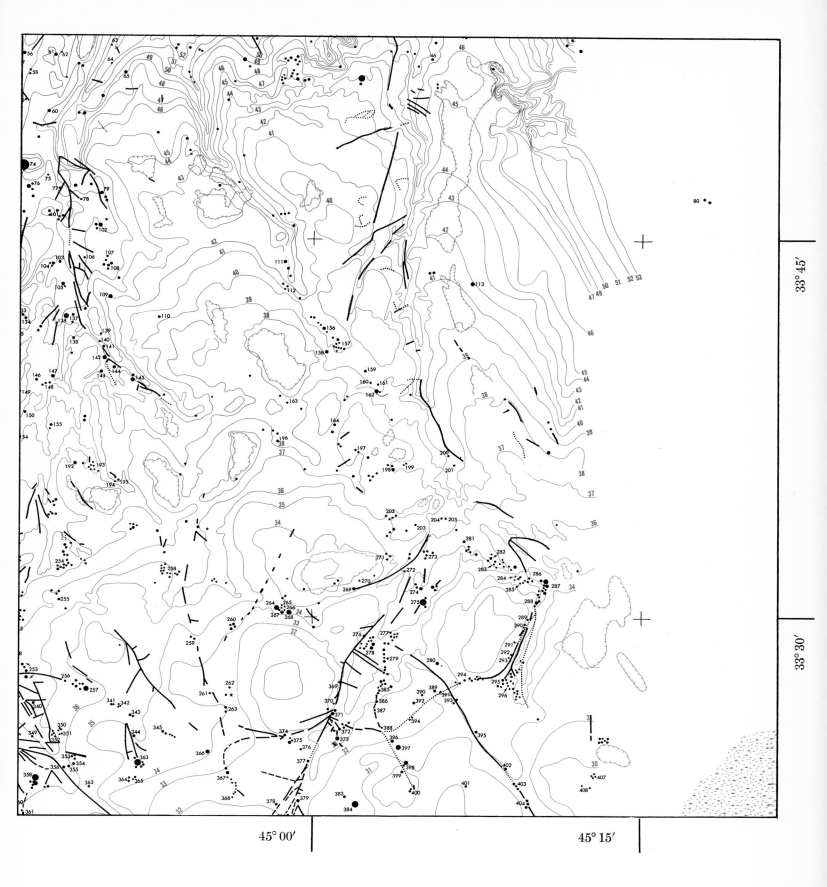

SECTION 2B

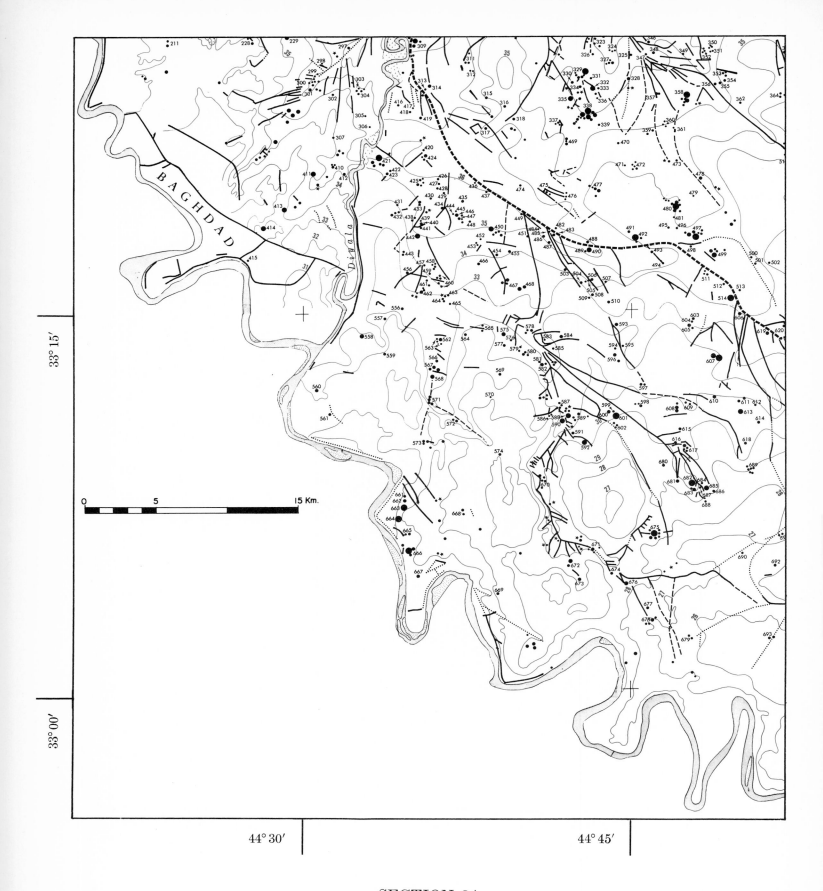

SECTION 3A

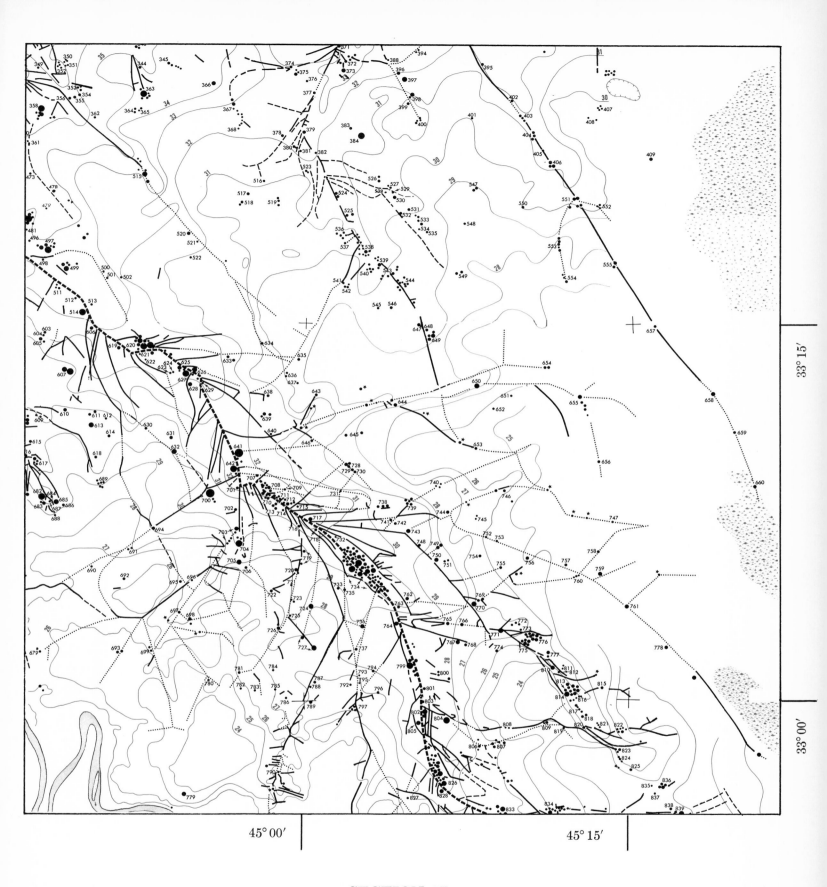

SECTION 3B

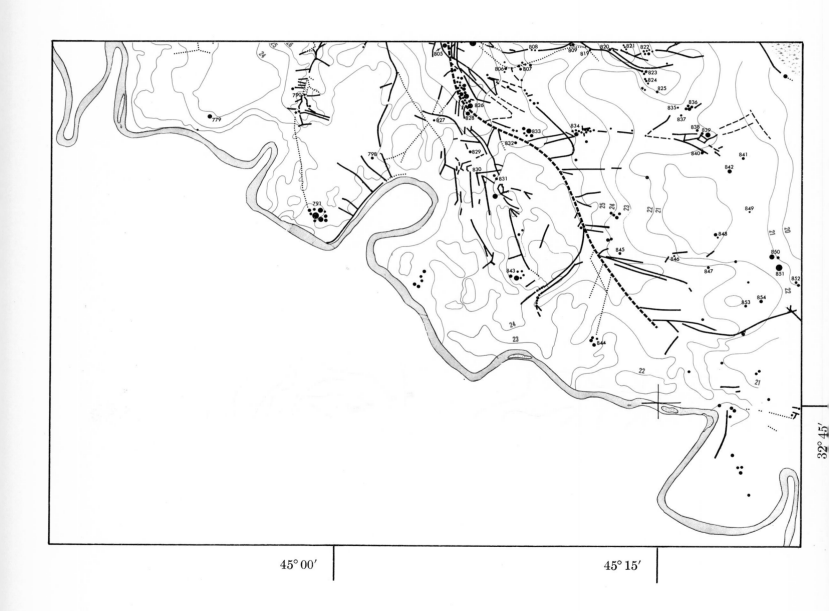

45° 00'   45° 15'

SECTION 4A

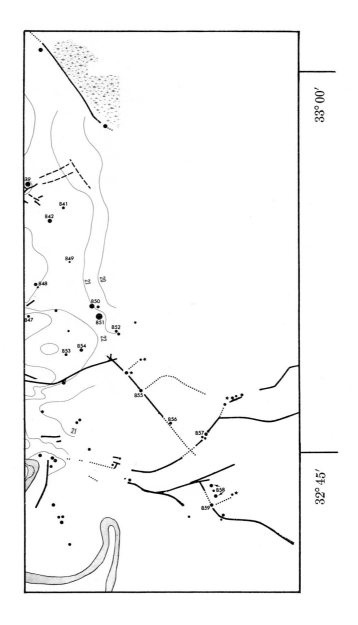

SECTION 4B

FIGURE 1

Modern zones of cultivation, canals, and major settlements on the lower Diyala plain

 Approximate limits of cultivation, 1872 (source: Černik-Expedition 1875–76, Taf. 3)

 Approximate limits of cultivation, 1918 (source: M.E.F. Map Compilation Section, T.C. Series 1:63,360 maps)

 Limits of cultivation, 1954 (source: Hunting Aerosurveys, Ltd., semi-controlled 1:50,000 aerial mosaics, and Government of Iraq, Development Board 1956, land use maps)

Illustrated canal network ca. 1941 (source: simplified from U.S. Army Map Service, Quarter Inch [1:253,440] series maps)

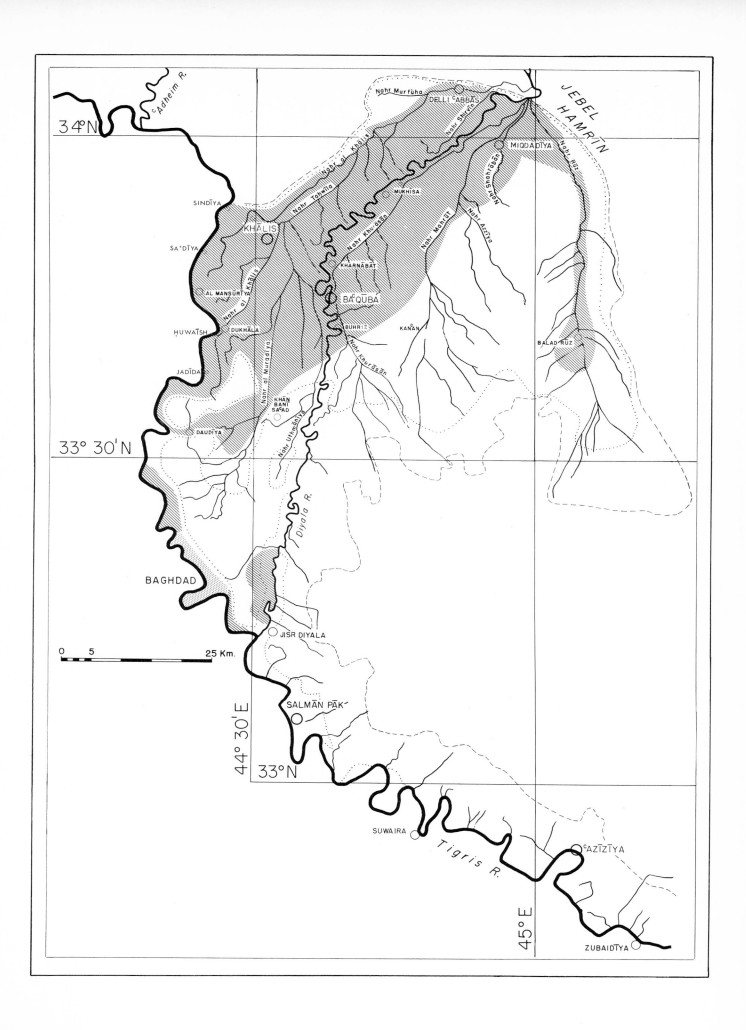

FIGURE 2

Settlements and watercourses on the lower Diyala plains: ᶜUbaid-Gutian Periods (ca. 4000–2100 B.C.)

○   Dating provisional, settlement probably small

·   Village or hamlet ruins, less than 4 ha.

•   Small town, more than 4 and less than 10 ha.

⬤   Large town, more than 10 ha.

Black numbers indicate occupational periods:

1. ᶜUbaid (ca. 4000–3500 B.C.)

2. Warka and Protoliterate (ca. 3500–3000 B.C.)

3. Early Dynastic (ca. 3000–2300 B.C.)

4. Akkad and Guti (ca. 2300–2100 B.C.)

Red numbers are those assigned to individual sites in Appendix C.

Reconstructed watercourses dating from prehistoric periods

Reconstructed watercourses dating from Akkadian period

Unoccupied or lightly occupied reach of watercourse, reconstructed from better known upstream and downstream reaches

Land without permanent settlement and presumably beyond limits of contemporary irrigation

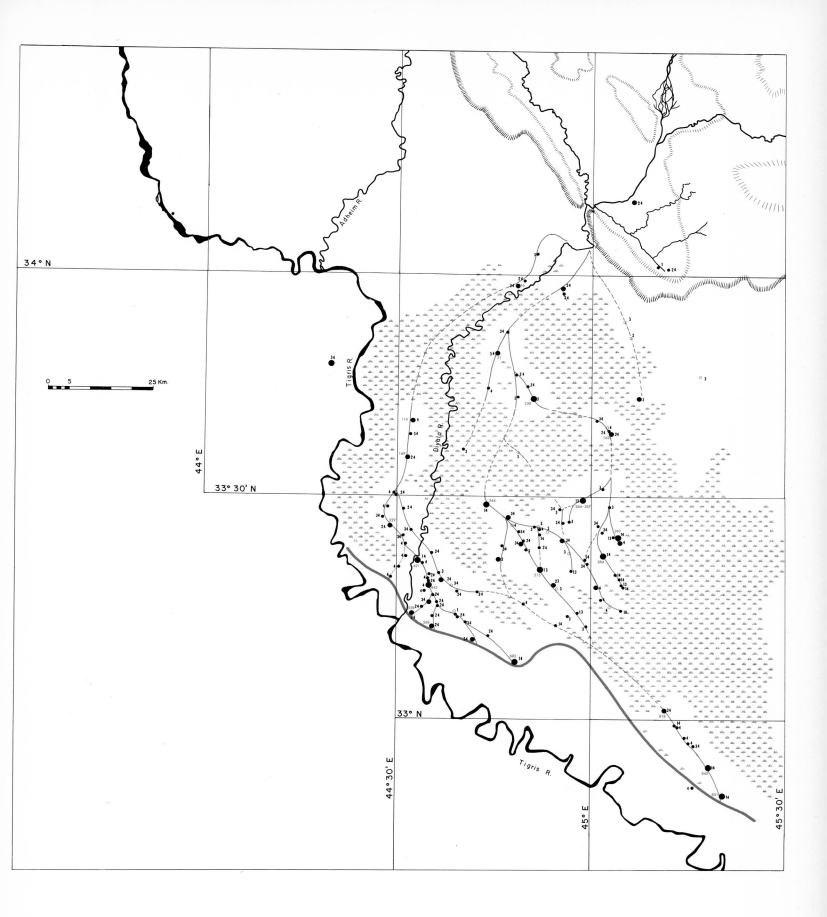

FIGURE 3

Settlements and watercourses on the lower Diyala plains: Ur III–Middle Babylonian periods (ca. 2100–625 B.C.)

- ○   Dating provisional, settlement probably small

- ·   Village or hamlet ruins, less than 4 ha.

- •   Small town, more than 4 and less than 10 ha.

- ●   Large town, more than 10 ha.

Black numbers indicate occupational periods:

4. Akkad and Guti (ca. 2300–2100 B.C.), shown only where occupation continued into period of this map

5. Ur III–Isin–Larsa (ca. 2100–1800 B.C.)

6. Old Babylonian (ca. 1800–1600 B.C.)

7. Cassite (ca. 1600–1100 B.C.)

8. Middle Babylonian (ca. 1100–625 B.C.)

9. Neo-Babylonian (ca. 625–537 B.C.), shown only where occupation began during period of this map

Red numbers are those assigned to individual sites in Appendix C.

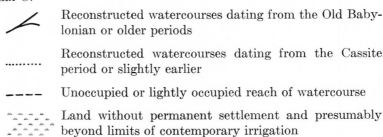

Reconstructed watercourses dating from the Old Babylonian or older periods

Reconstructed watercourses dating from the Cassite period or slightly earlier

Unoccupied or lightly occupied reach of watercourse

Land without permanent settlement and presumably beyond limits of contemporary irrigation

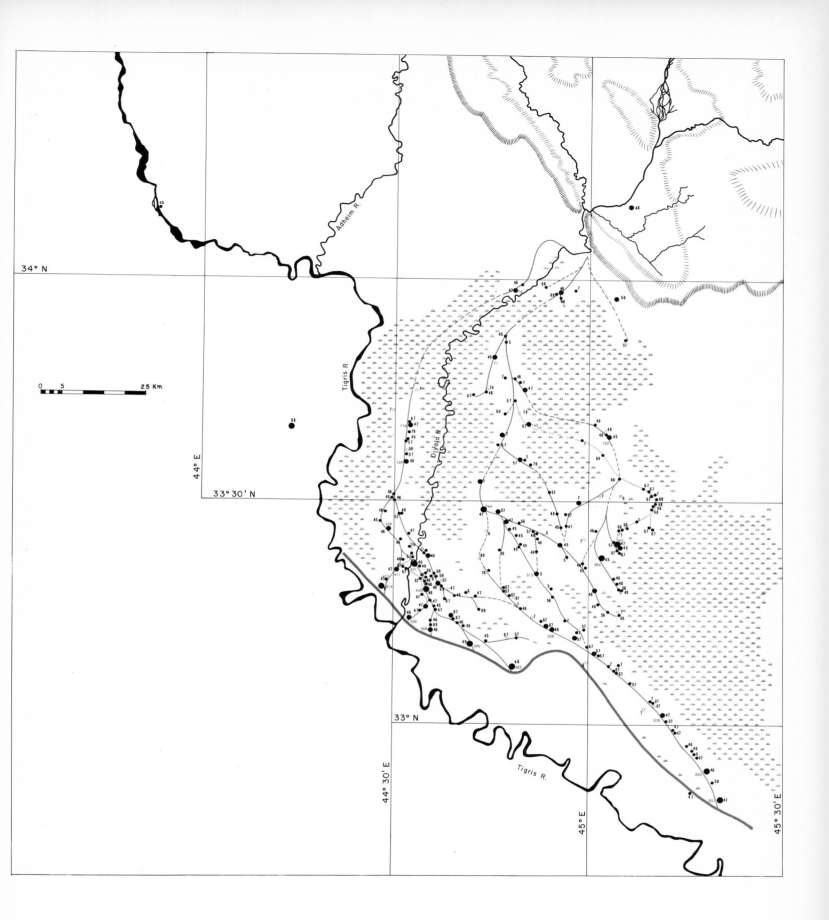

FIGURE 4

Settlements and watercourses on the lower Diyala plains: Neo-Babylonian–Parthian periods (625 B.C.–A.D. 226)

- ○   Dating provisional, surface collections difficult to obtain
- ·   Village or hamlet ruins, less than 4 ha.
- •   Town, more than 4 and less than 30 ha.
- ●   Small urban center, more than 30 and less than 100 ha. (1 sq. km.)
- ●   City, more than 1 sq. km.
- ▨   Capital city

Black numbers indicate occupational periods:

1. Neo-Babylonian (ca. 625–537 B.C.)
2. Achaemenian (ca. 537–311 B.C.)
3. Seleucid-Parthian (ca. 311 B.C.–A.D. 226)
4. Sassanian (ca. A.D. 226–637), also shown in following map (Fig. 5)

Red numbers are those assigned to individual sites in Appendix C.

Relatively well-attested watercourses; levees and adjoining settlements both present

Unoccupied or lightly occupied reaches of watercourses

Land without permanent settlement and presumably beyond limits of contemporary irrigation

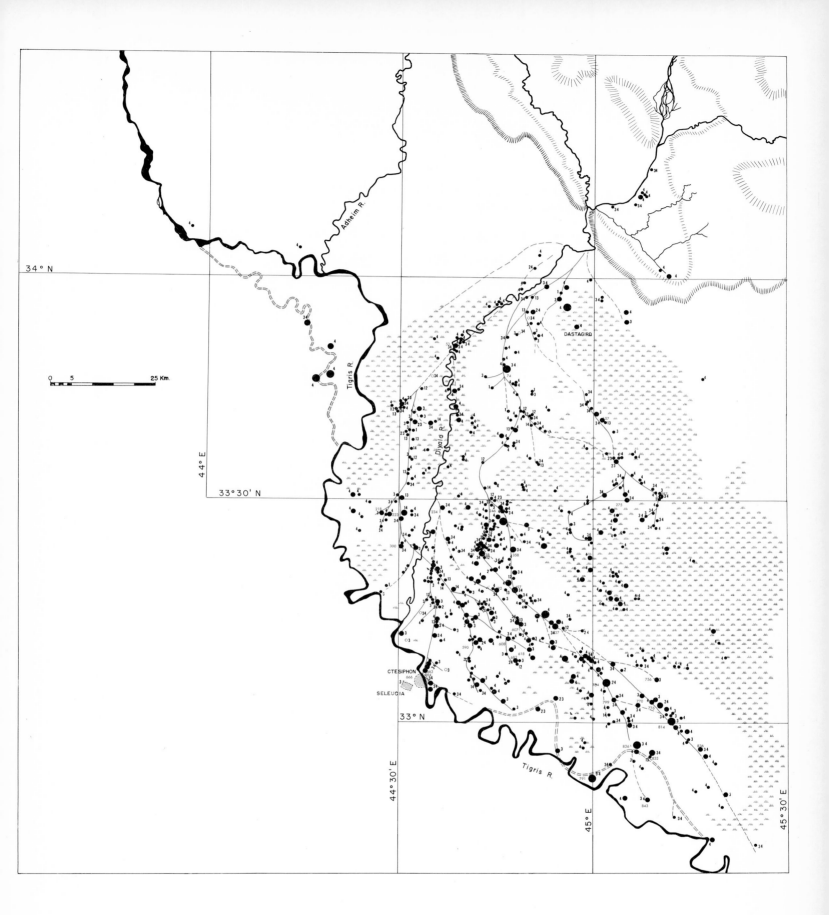

FIGURE 5

Settlements and watercourses on the lower Diyala plains: Sassanian period (ca. A.D. 226–637)

- ○   Dating provisional, surface collections difficult to obtain

- ·   Village or hamlet ruins, less than 4 ha.

- •   Town, more than 4 and less than 30 ha.

- ●   Small urban center, more than 30 and less than 100 ha. (1 sq. km.)

- ⬤   City, more than 1 sq. km.

- ▨   Capital city

Black numbers indicate occupational periods:

     1–3. Neo-Babylonian–Parthian (ca. 625 B.C.–A.D. 226), same as in preceding map (Fig. 4)

     4. Sassanian (ca. A.D. 226–637), also shown in preceding map

Red numbers are those assigned to individual sites in Appendix C.

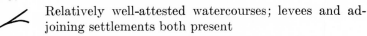

Relatively well-attested watercourses; levees and adjoining settlements both present

- - - -   Unoccupied or lightly occupied reaches of watercourses

Land without permanent settlement and presumably beyond limits of contemporary irrigation

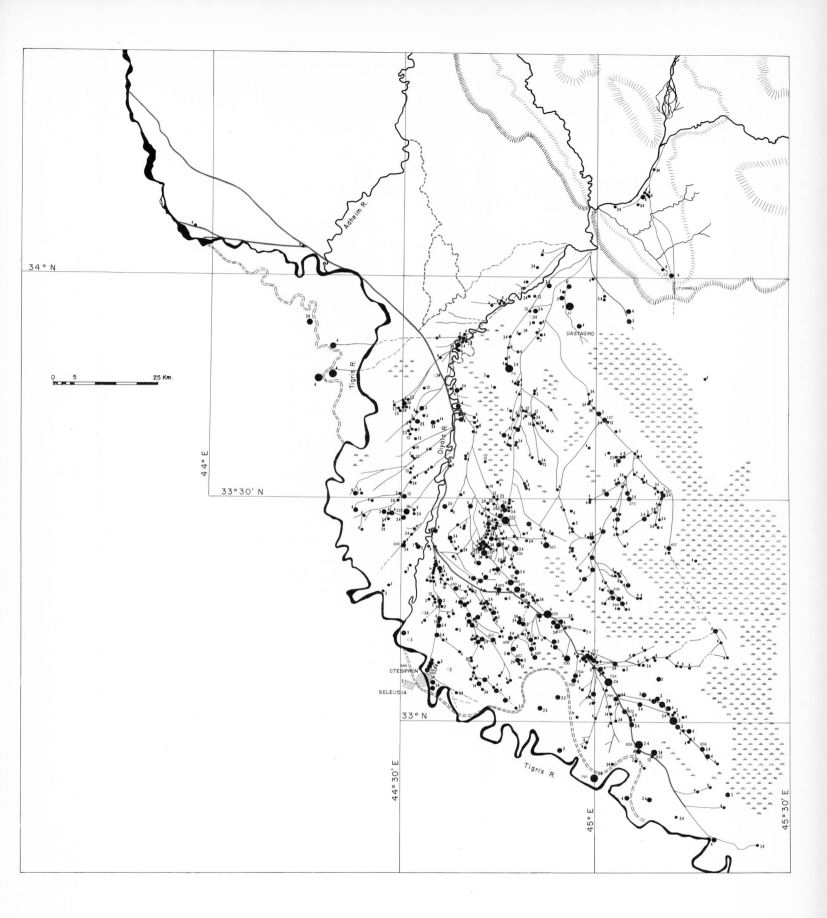

FIGURE 6

Settlements and watercourses on the lower Diyala plains: Islamic period (ca. A.D. 637–1500)

- ○   Historically attested town, either not visited or covered by modern settlement

- ·   Village or hamlet ruins, less than 4 ha.

- •   Town, more than 4 and less than 30 ha.

- ●   Small urban center, more than 30 and less than 100 ha. (1 sq. km.)

- ●   City, more than 1 sq. km.

 Capital city

Black numbers indicate occupational periods:

4. Sassanian (ca. A.D. 226–637), shown only where occupation continued into period of this map

5. Early Islamic–Sāmarrān (ca A.D. 637–883)

6. Post-Sāmarrān Abbasid (ca. A.D. 883–1258)

7. Ilkhanid and later (ca. A.D. 1258–1500)

Red numbers are those assigned to individual sites in Appendix C.

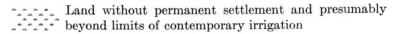 Relatively well-attested watercourses; levees (frequently including canal banks) and adjoining settlements both present

 Land without permanent settlement and presumably beyond limits of contemporary irrigation

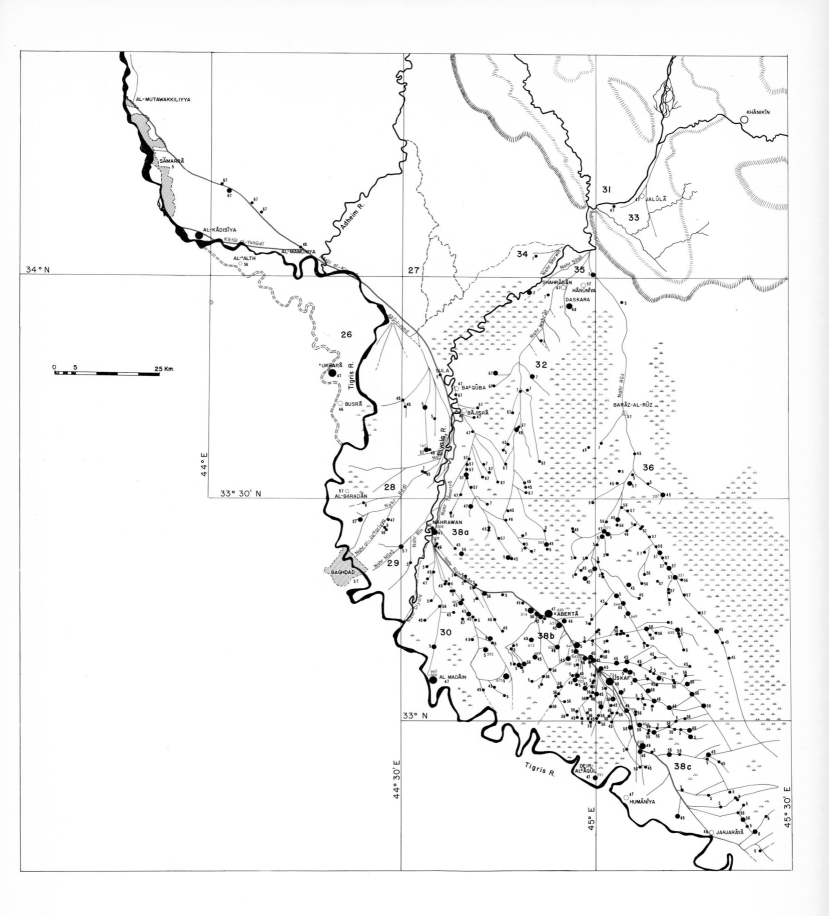

FIGURE 7

Inlets to the Kātūl-al-Kisrawī in the vicinity of Sāmarrā.

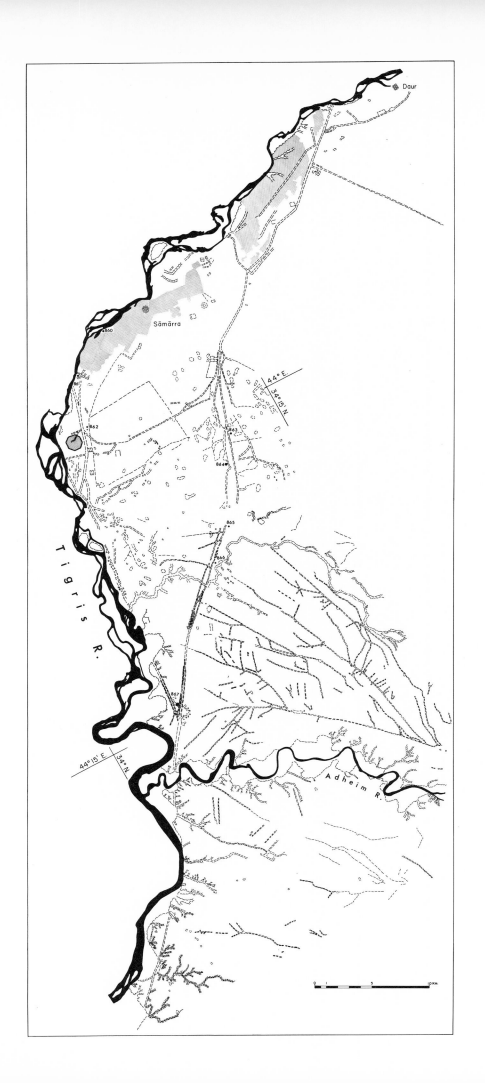

Daur

Sāmārra

860

861

862

863

864

865

866

867

Tigris R.

Adheim R.

44° E.

34° 15' N

44° 15' E.

34° N

0   1   5   10 Km.

FIGURE 8

Settlements and irrigation canals in the lower Nahrawān region:
Early Islamic–Sāmarrān periods (ca. A.D. 637–883)

- Hamlet, less than 1 ha.

- Village, more than 1 and less than 4 ha.

- Town, more than 4 and less than 30 ha.

Urban area, more than 30 ha., shown by outline of ruins

Site not visited, shown approximately to scale

Site abandoned or virtually abandoned prior to Sāmarrān period

Numbers adjoining site symbols are those assigned to individual sites in Appendix C.

The canal network shown is approximately that in use during the Early Islamic period. Its replacement by the network shown in following map (Fig. 9) was a gradual and irregular one extending over several centuries, so that not all parts of it may have been in use simultaneously.

Canal courses antedating the network shown. Mainly Sassanian, but some may have continued in use for part of the Early Islamic period.

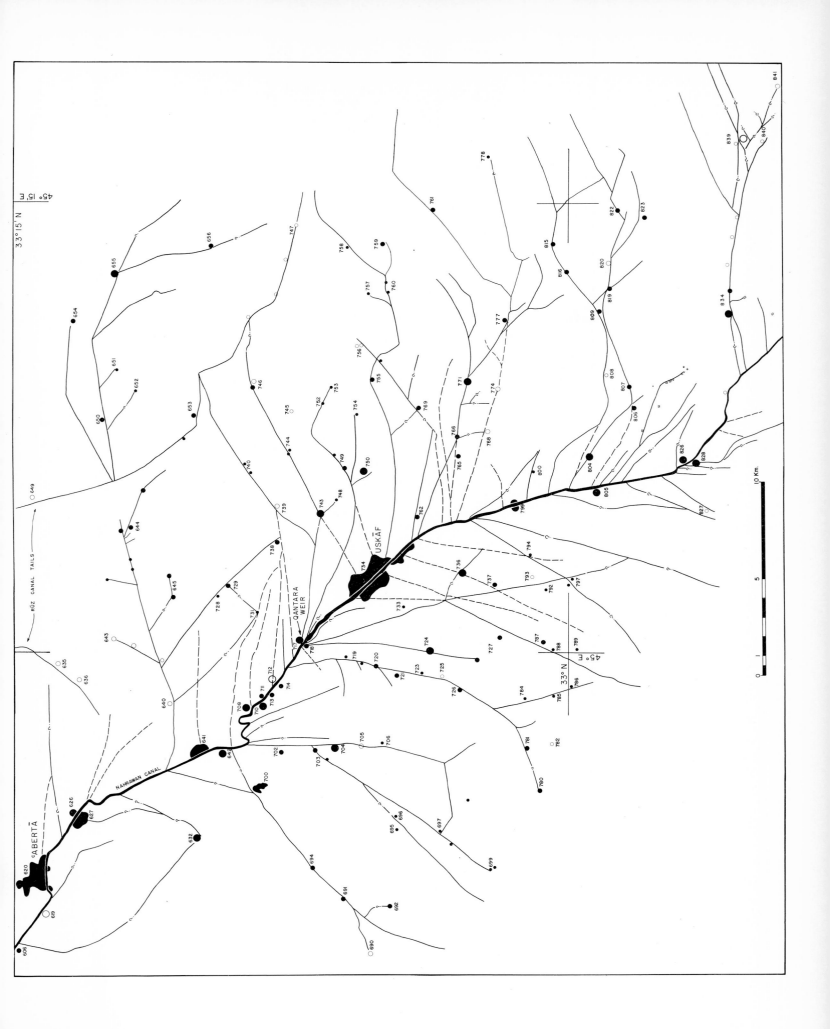

FIGURE 9

Settlements and irrigation canals in the lower Nahrawān region: Post-Sāmarrān Abbasid Period (ca. A.D. 883–1150)

- Hamlet, less than 1 ha.
- Village, more than 1 and less than 4 ha.
- Town, more than 4 and less than 30 ha.

 Site not visited, shown approximately to scale

Numbers adjoining site symbols are those assigned to individual sites in Appendix C.

The canal network shown is approximately that in use at termination of permanent settlement in most of the lower Nahrawān region (ca. A.D. 1150).

Soil classification (slightly generalized):

 Seriously leached solonetzic soils associated with gilgai depressions

Less seriously leached solonetzic soils

Non-saline or moderately saline soils

Absence of soil symbols indicates solonchak soils of the desert, including both saline and moderately saline facies.

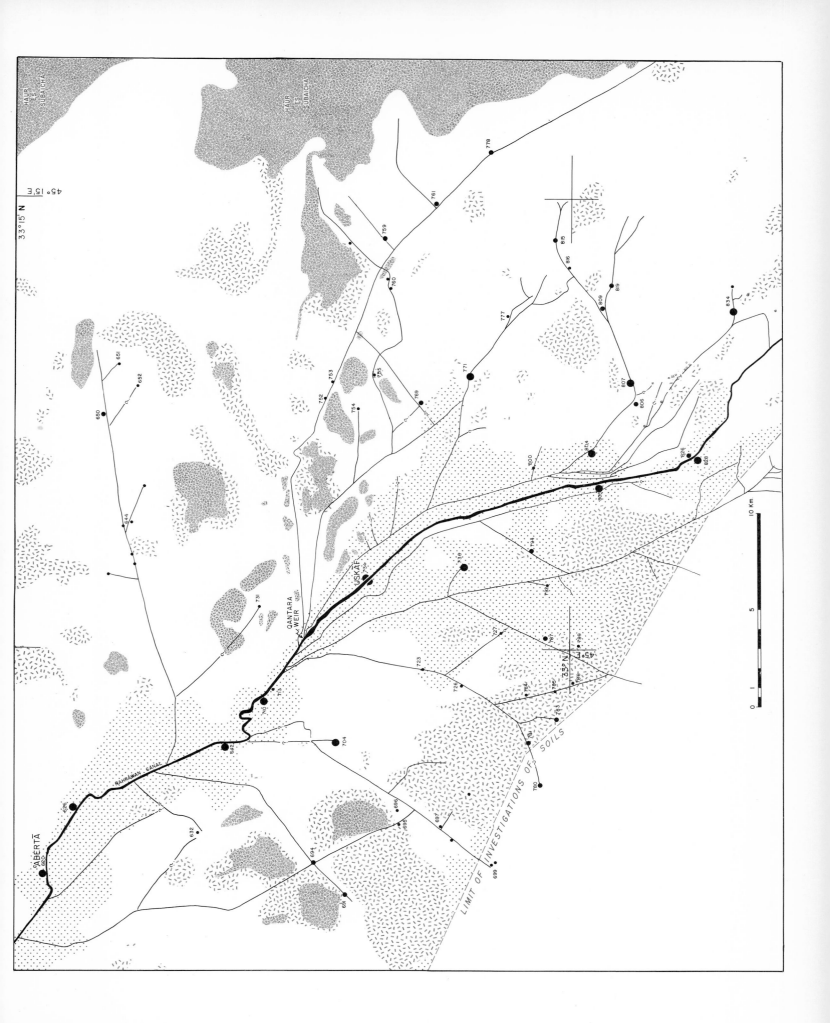

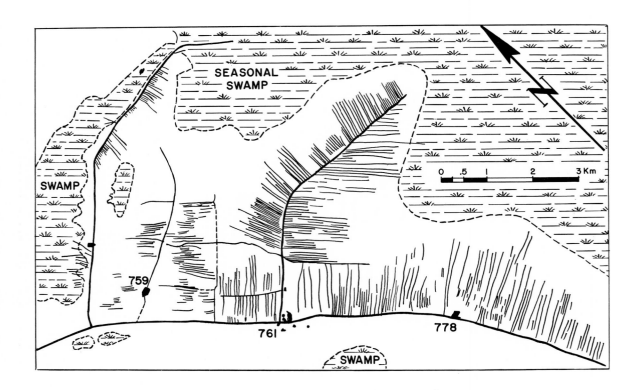

FIGURE 10

Example of field canal layout in the lower Nahrawān region:
post-Sāmarrān period

Pottery

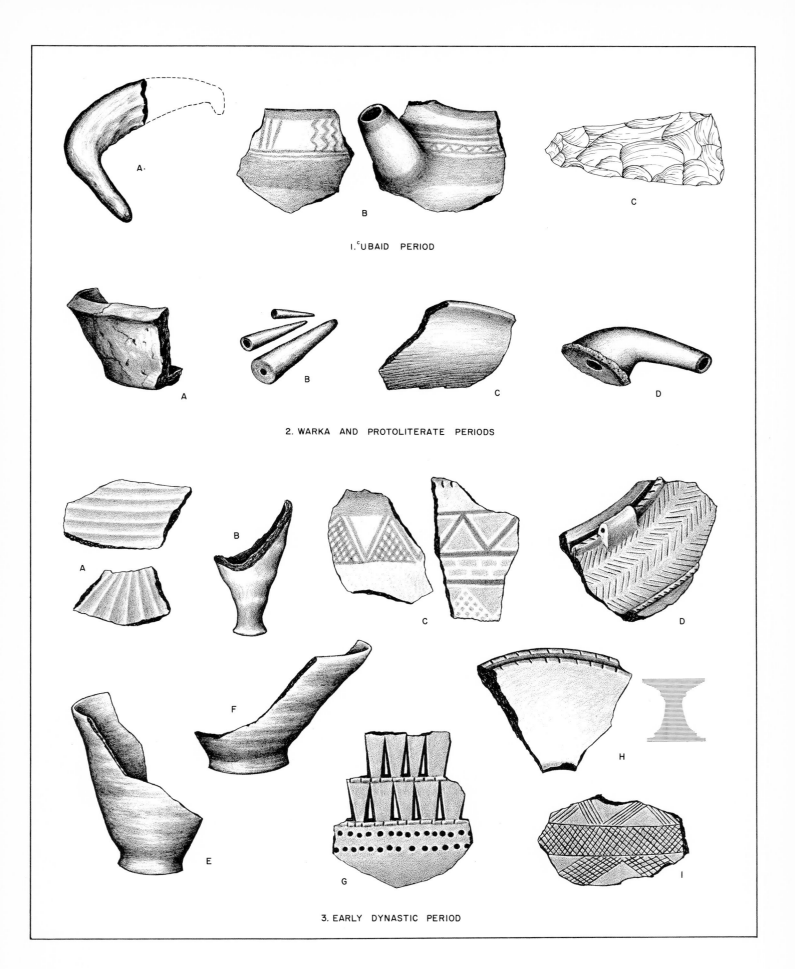

1. ᶜUBAID PERIOD

2. WARKA AND PROTOLITERATE PERIODS

3. EARLY DYNASTIC PERIOD

FIGURE 11

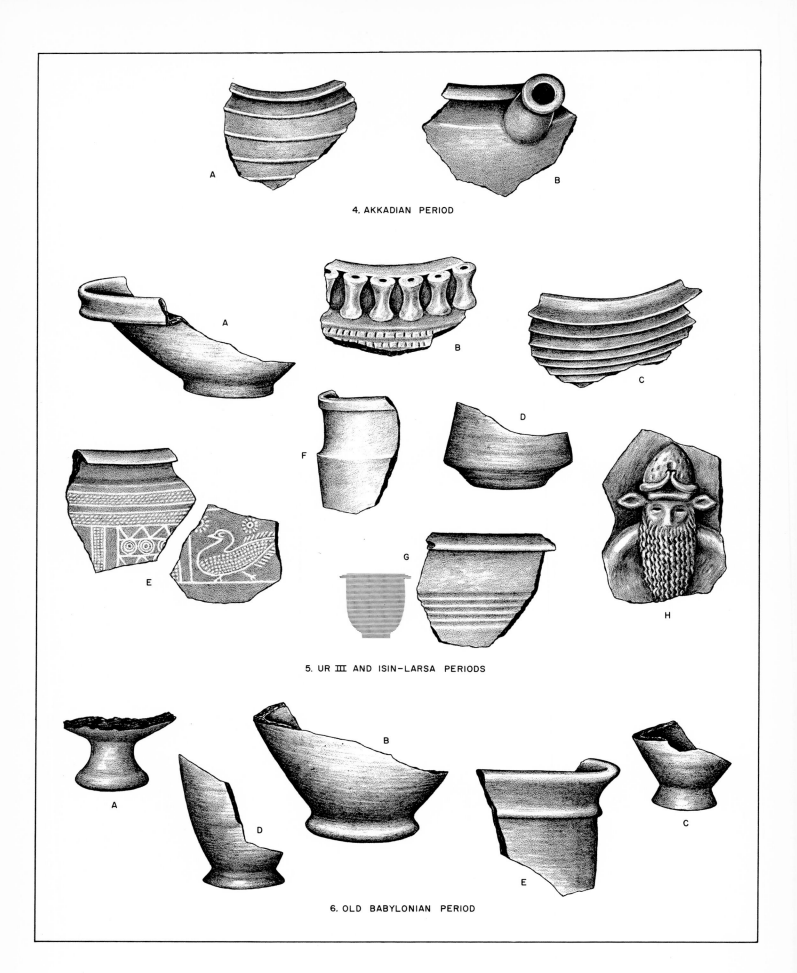

4. AKKADIAN PERIOD

5. UR III AND ISIN—LARSA PERIODS

6. OLD BABYLONIAN PERIOD

FIGURE 12

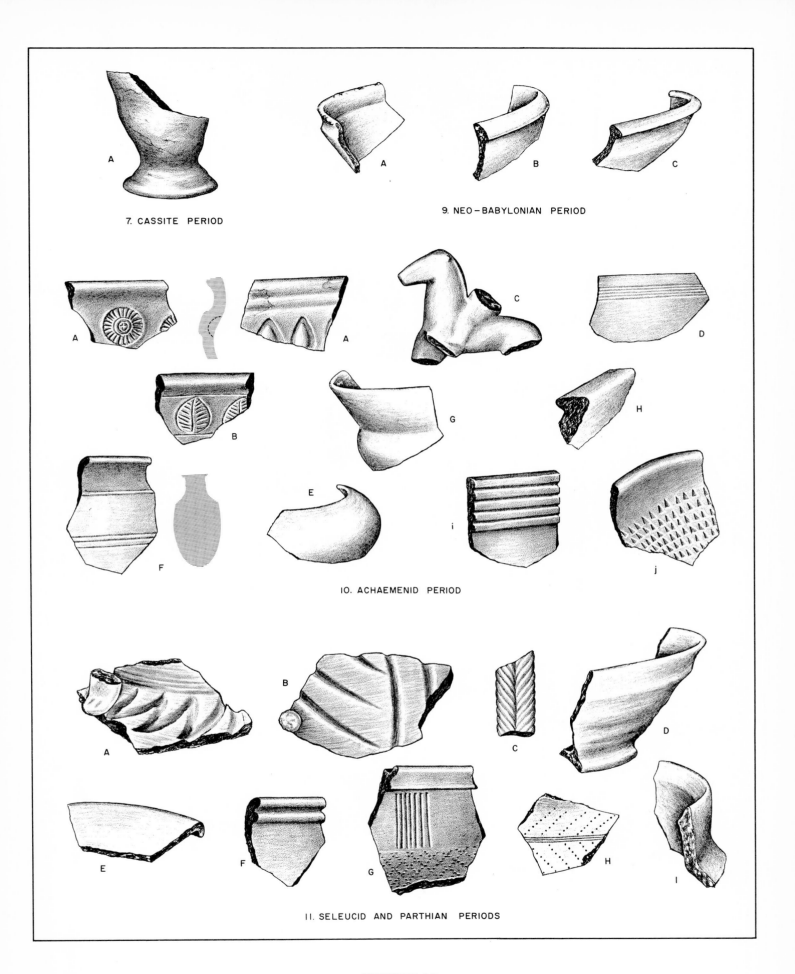

7. CASSITE PERIOD

9. NEO−BABYLONIAN PERIOD

10. ACHAEMENID PERIOD

11. SELEUCID AND PARTHIAN PERIODS

FIGURE 13

12. SASSANIAN PERIOD

13. EARLY ISLAMIC PERIOD

FIGURE 14

14. SÂMARRÂN PERIOD

15. LATE ABBASID PERIOD

17. POST—ILKHANID PERIOD

FIGURE 15

A   B

10. ACHAEMENID PERIOD

B

C   D

12. SASSANIAN PERIOD

f

15. LATE ABBASID PERIOD

FIGURE 16

Ancient Irrigation Works

Section and Plans

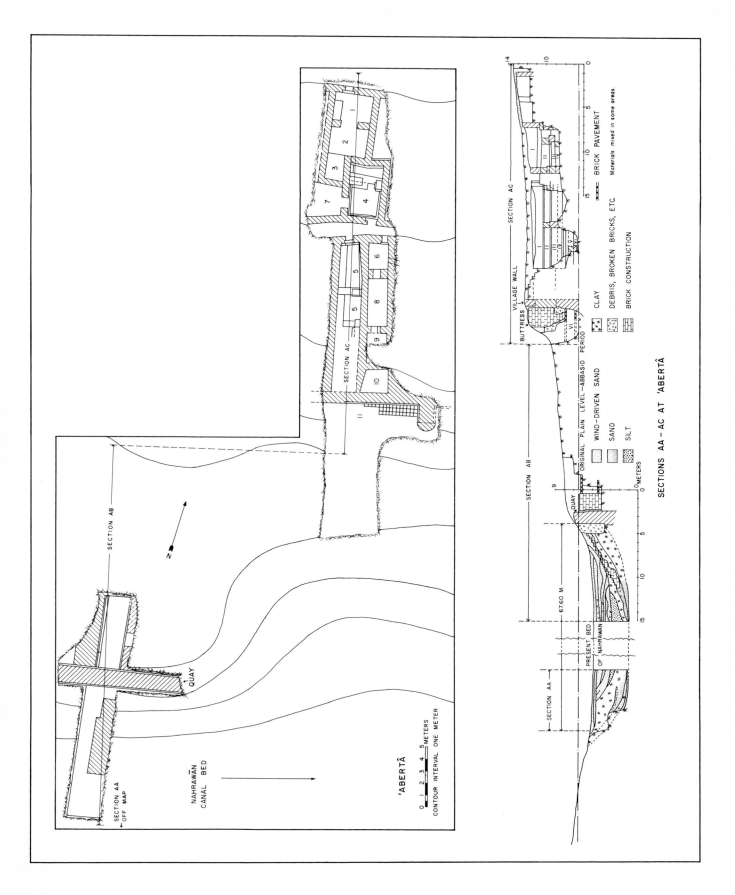

SECTIONS AA – AC AT 'ABERTÂ

FIGURE 17

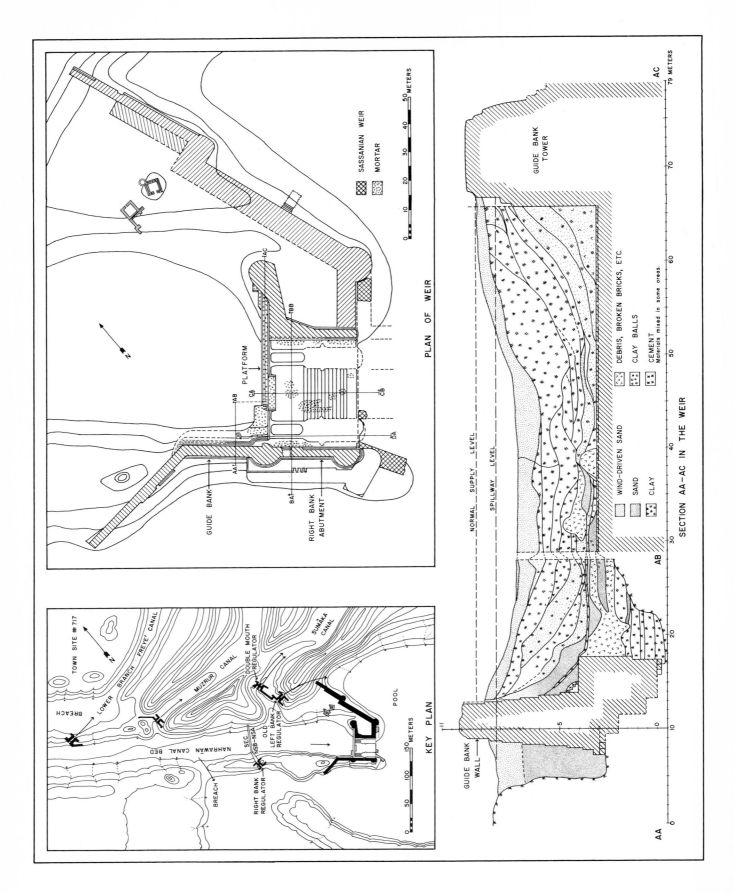

PLAN OF WEIR

SASSANIAN WEIR
MORTAR

0 10 20 30 40 50 METERS

GUIDE BANK

RIGHT BANK
ABUTMENT

PLATFORM

KEY PLAN

TOWN SITE #717

LOWER BRANCH FREYE' CANAL

MUZRUR) CANAL

DOUBLE MOUTH REGULATOR

SUMÂKA CANAL

NAHRAWÂN CANAL BED

BREACH

RIGHT BANK REGULATOR

SEC. NSB-NSA

OLD LEFT BANK REGULATOR

POOL

0 50 100 150 METERS

SECTION AA-AC IN THE WEIR

NORMAL SUPPLY LEVEL
SPILLWAY LEVEL

GUIDE BANK TOWER

WIND-DRIVEN SAND
SAND
CLAY

DEBRIS, BROKEN BRICKS, ETC.
CLAY BALLS
CEMENT
Materials mixed in some areas

GUIDE BANK WALL

AA   AB   AC
0   5   10   20   30   40   50   60   70   79 METERS

FIGURE 18

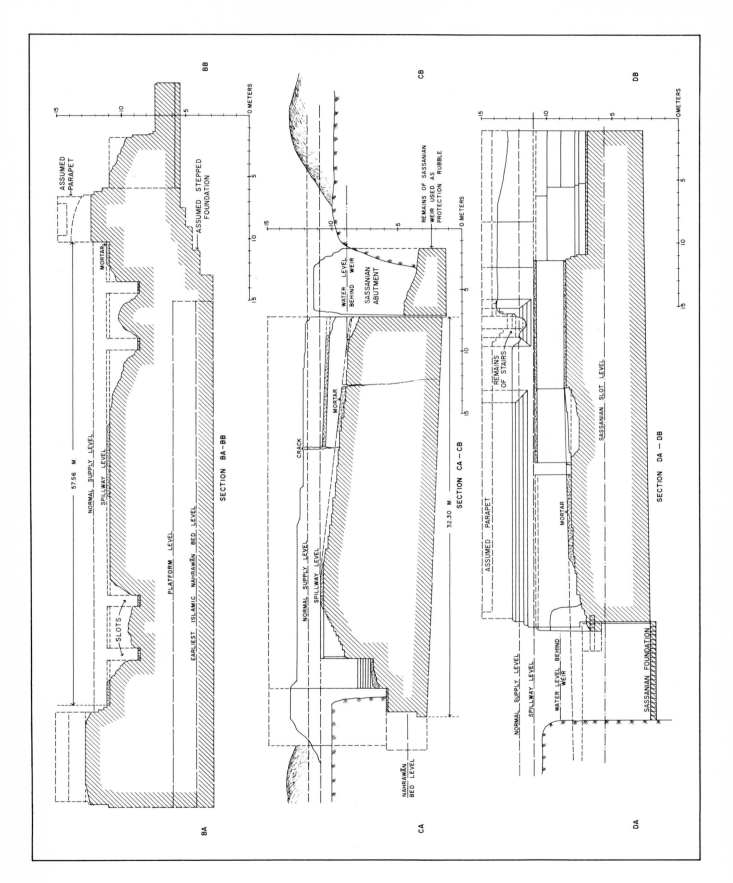

FIGURE 19

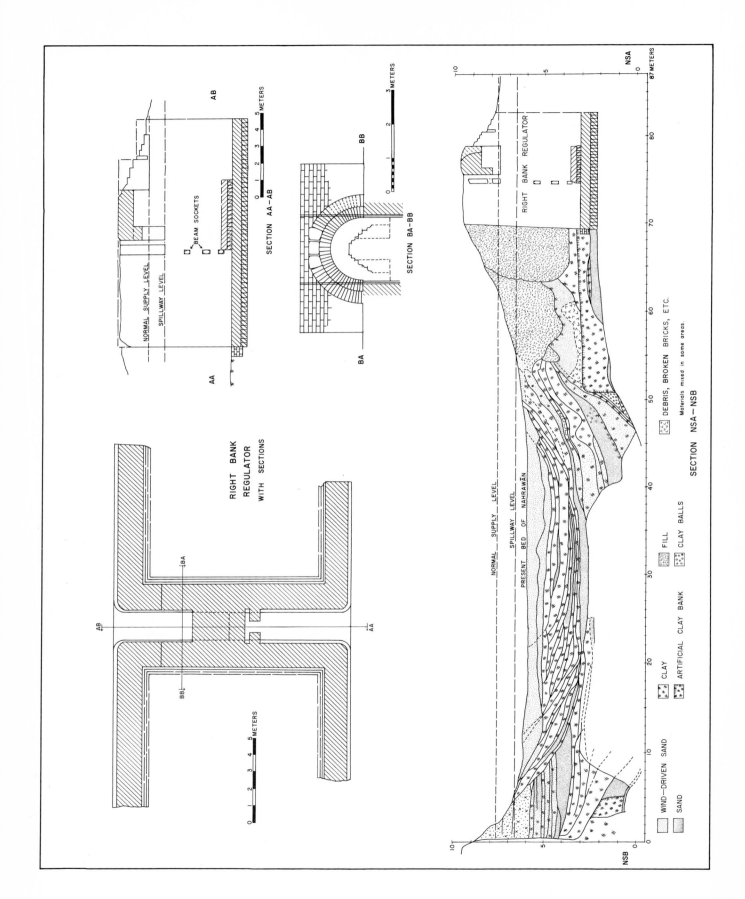

RIGHT BANK REGULATOR WITH SECTIONS

SECTION AA-AB

SECTION BA-BB

NORMAL SUPPLY LEVEL
SPILLWAY LEVEL
BEAM SOCKETS

RIGHT BANK REGULATOR

NORMAL SUPPLY LEVEL
SPILLWAY LEVEL
PRESENT BED OF NAHRAWĀN

SECTION NSA-NSB

WIND-DRIVEN SAND
SAND
CLAY
ARTIFICIAL CLAY BANK
DEBRIS, BROKEN BRICKS, ETC.
FILL
CLAY BALLS

Materials mixed in some areas.

FIGURE 20

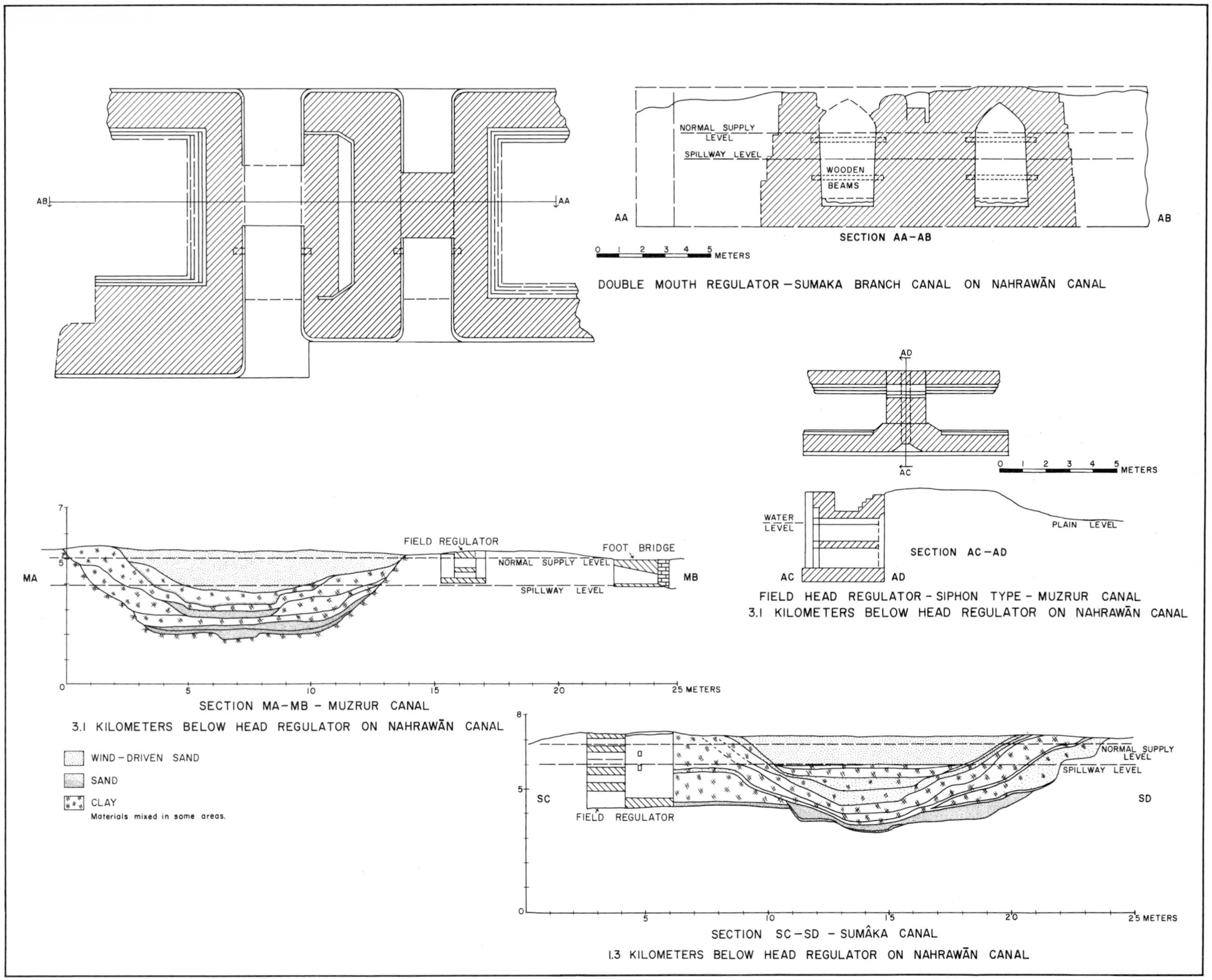

AB
AA
NORMAL SUPPLY LEVEL
SPILLWAY LEVEL
WOODEN BEAMS
AA
AB
SECTION AA–AB
0 1 2 3 4 5 METERS
DOUBLE MOUTH REGULATOR – SUMAKA BRANCH CANAL ON NAHRAWĀN CANAL
AD
AC
0 1 2 3 4 5 METERS
WATER LEVEL
PLAIN LEVEL
SECTION AC–AD
AC
AD
FIELD HEAD REGULATOR - SIPHON TYPE - MUZRUR CANAL
3.1 KILOMETERS BELOW HEAD REGULATOR ON NAHRAWĀN CANAL
MA
FIELD REGULATOR
FOOT BRIDGE
NORMAL SUPPLY LEVEL
SPILLWAY LEVEL
MB
0 5 10 15 20 25 METERS
SECTION MA–MB – MUZRUR CANAL
3.1 KILOMETERS BELOW HEAD REGULATOR ON NAHRAWĀN CANAL
WIND–DRIVEN SAND
SAND
CLAY
Materials mixed in some areas.
SC
FIELD REGULATOR
NORMAL SUPPLY LEVEL
SPILLWAY LEVEL
SD
0 5 10 15 20 25 METERS
SECTION SC–SD – SUMÂKA CANAL
1.3 KILOMETERS BELOW HEAD REGULATOR ON NAHRAWĀN CANAL

FIGURE 21

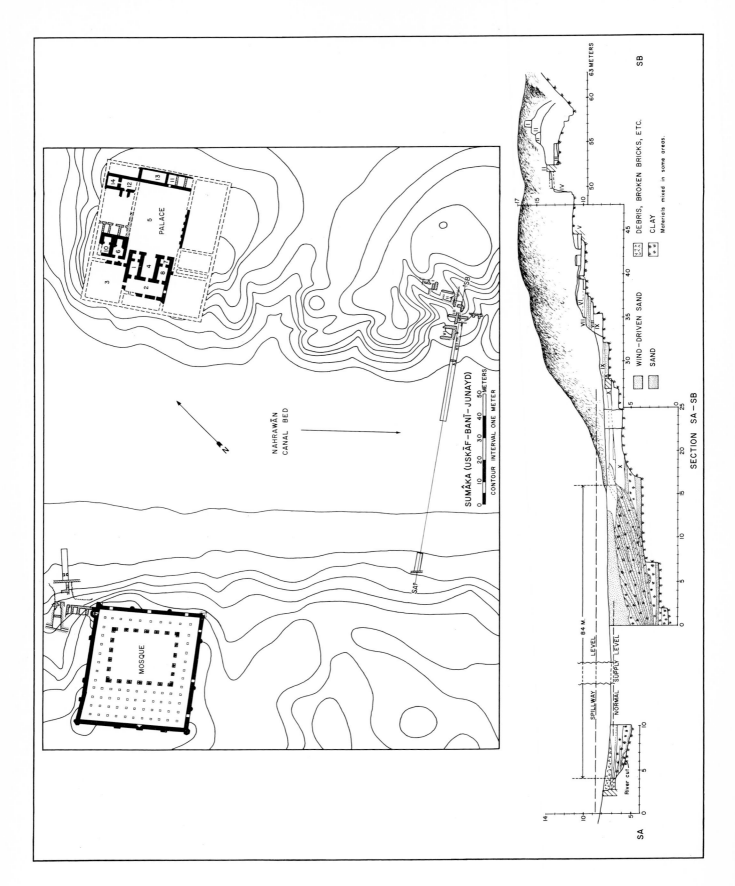

SUMÂKA (USKÂF-BANÎ-JUNAYD)

NAHRAWÂN CANAL BED

CONTOUR INTERVAL ONE METER

PALACE

MOSQUE

SECTION SA – SB

DEBRIS, BROKEN BRICKS, ETC.

CLAY

Materials mixed in some areas.

WIND-DRIVEN SAND

SAND

SPILLWAY LEVEL

84 M.

NORMAL SUPPLY LEVEL

River cut

63 METERS

FIGURE 22